SOCIAL PLURALISM AND LITERARY HISTORY

The Literature of the Italian Emigration

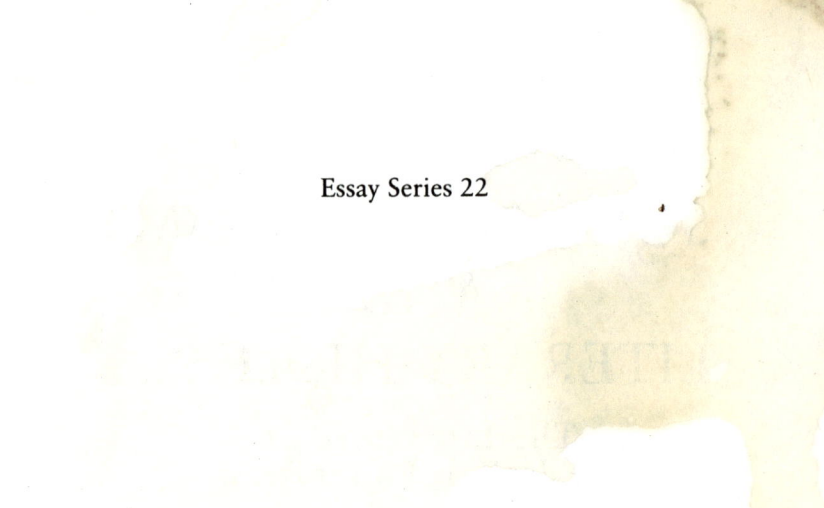

Essay Series 22

SOCIAL PLURALISM AND LITERARY HISTORY

The Literature of the Italian Emigration

Edited and with an
Introduction by Francesco Loriggio

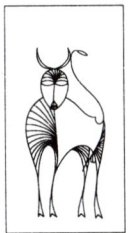

Guernica
Toronto / New York / Lancaster
1996

The Publisher would like to thank Canadian Heritage, The Canada Council,
Ontario Arts Council, and Carleton University.

Guernica Editions Inc.
P.O. Box 117, Station P, Toronto, Canada M5S 2S6
250 Sonwil Drive, Buffalo, N.Y. 14225-5516 U.S.A.
Gazelle, Falcon House, Queen Square, Lancaster LA1 1RN U.K.

Legal Deposit — Third Quarter
National Library of Canada.
Library of Congress Catalog Card Number: 95-75021

Canadian Cataloguing in Publication Data
Main entry under title:
Social pluralism and literary history: the literature
of the Italian emigration
(Essay series; 22)
Some essays translated from Italian, French or German.
Includes bibliographical references.
ISBN 1-55071-018-4
1. Italians in literature. 2. Social pluralism (Social sciences)
in literature. 3. Italian literature — History and criticism. 4. Italy — Emigration and
immigration. 5. Italians — Foreign countries
I. Loriggio, Francesco II. Series: Essay series (Toronto, Ont.); 22.
PQ4088.S63 1995   850.9'355   C95-900122-0

Table of Contents

Francesco Loriggio

Introduction

*F*or a period that has toyed with the idea of the end of history, the late twentieth century has been remarkably hospitable towards any venture proclaiming itself historical in nature. The loss of credibility of the grand narratives or of bloc politics has not given way to indifference towards the past or to the blanket disregard of chronology, genealogy and sequence. On the contrary, it has led to a series of initiatives which have explicitly the reconstruction of history or the re-evaluation of historical analysis as their objective (see, in literary criticism, the rise of the New Historicism). What is surprising, in looking back at the last two decades or so, is how inadequate all predictions have shown themselves to be. The demise of the great ideologies has not left historians a prey to micro-history, to the proliferation of the infinitely small, the circumstantial and the unconnected. Any more than the decline of bi-polar agonism (history as a duality, as a struggle between East or West, between socialism or capitalism) has consigned humanity to the everlasting return of the same, to the apothesis of *pax americana* or to the unilateral homogenizing vagaries of technology, the sign and market economy (history as world-system or as the New World Order). Indeed, if there are observations to be made, they are not quite of the either/or kind.

It seems, now, a few years after the latest forecast, besides the point to keep pitting the master narratives against the indiscriminate atomistic and self-regulating swarmings of the machinery of twentieth-century society. In retrospect, this construal of the events of the last four or five decades appears to hinge on something more akin to a conflict of *styles*, than to some ultimate social or cultural dynamic. To be sure, the developments that have transpired can be recapitulated by the now classic opposition of modernism and post-modernism. But, precisely, whether you privilege modernist structure and closure or the postmodernist play of the signifiers, you are denying or severely limiting the possibility of content, representation, subjectivity. You are still not

7

explaining the desire for identity, of which reality, instead, continues to propose always new manifestations. And this demand rubs against the entire modern/postmodern dichotomy, pulls the rug away from either structure and system or open-endedness.

The jump from the early versions of the recent cultural panorama to current thinking is probably best illustrated by the shift in vocabulary, by the way in the human sciences and in literary criticism terms such as "global," "globalization," "world," "world-system" and "local" or "locality" are slowly replacing "universal" and "particular," or, at any rate, are cutting into the semantic field once reserved exclusively for these notions.[1] The reduced abstraction, the geographical, topographical connotations of the new glossary don't only loosen the law-like features that attach to the idea of universality. They add new dimensions all around, on the various other subsidiary concepts as well. A phenomenon just isn't global by pure logical deduction. It has to spread, to achieve globality. There is a process involved, a process that pulls into its sphere all sorts of histories, histories of dominance and resistance, histories far and near, recent and less recent. Similarly, it is more difficult to conceive "global" and "local" as straightforward opposites. One feeds on the other. In pre-modern eras periods of strong political and cultural, national and international amalgamation preceded or followed periods of pluralism. The novelty of our times is that, to borrow from Mikhail Bakhtin (270-272), heterogeneity and homogeneity, decentralization and centralization occur simultaneously, their work continuing uninterrupted.

Transnational capital wants to manage cultural difference, not to abolish it (borders can be a good source of profit: they create spaces to which franchises can be exported). Yet because of this, capital must also reckon with difference, and if not promote it, at least compute it in any overall calculations, not disregard it: multinational, corporate power must let itself be affected by what it wants to control. The advent of telecommunications, the mediatization of life, the dispersal of people through migration and political exile has produced a generalized person-in-the-street previously unheard-of cosmopolitanism. Practically everyone has several additional places beyond the country of residence to grapple with, be they those that are sent into the home via the radio and the television set or the ones left behind (and now also eminently portable). In one same swoop, electronic technology and increased mobility endow individuals with a global horizon and prepare its opposite, consolidate inter-or intra-national ethnicity. Being in daily contact with a distant else-where may just as well strengthen calls for local identifications. Or it may allow threatened identifications to dissipate at a slower pace. The *Corriere della sera*, reads — in English — one of the Milanese newpapers' page-long adver-tisements, "can now be your local newspaper." Same day delivery is guaran-teed in North America.

Of course, each discipline has confronted this peculiarly late-twentieth-century unraveling of history (whereby large history is imbricated with, is recursively related to small history) in its own fashion. American philosophers have rediscovered their native pragmatist tradition thanks to their exposure to Continental texts. And those texts take on a different colouring when ap-proached after the reading of Pierce, William James, Dewey and George Her-bert Mead: they are suddenly imbued with Americana. Anthropologists have been folding their tents and returning home knowing that the Other may now be found next door, in one of their cities' neighbourhoods. And when they do travel *extra muros* once more, their awareness of — and contact with — that short range, quotidian Otherness impinges on their perception of foreign cul-tures.

In literary studies, the fall of the great ideologies and the return of history has redirected critical and curricular interests just as drastically. The most blatantly public core of the discipline, in North America during the last ten years or so, has been occupied by the debate about the second "post" — post-colonialism — and its tangencies with the first — postmodernism —, about the re-envisioning of Europe and European culture, and about questions of race, gender, and ethnicity.

Two broadly-based, contradictory yet intertwined projects have emerged from that discussion and its surrounding disputes. On the one hand, criticism has been busy defining the overlapping topographies that some of the new categories imply. Terms such as "hibridity" and "interstitial" or their cognates, coined primarily within post-colonialist studies (see Bhabha) but with analogues in other fields (gender studies for instance), have in the last few years achieved sudden and extensive saliency. The intermixing of different identities and social realities, the interaction of global and local that they stand for restores — as a by-product of adjacency and contact, hence as negotiable rather than as monolithic or totalizing — a portion of the shared public culture that had disappeared with the decay of the master narratives. On the other hand, an equally notable consequence of the many current soundings and probings on gender, ethnicity, multiculturalism and post-coloniality has been the renewed interest in cultural memory. How texts and history are used, for what purposes and by whom — not how they are structured or how they function — these also have been among the questions the *Zeitgeist* has had to ponder. Certainly, in literary studies the reconstituting of unacknowledged continuities has been to this day the major practical contribution of some of the younger branches of the field — feminist criticism, ethnic or minoritarian studies and research in gay or lesbian writing. Texts previously unread or deemed unworthy of critical recognition have surfaced, and their retrieval or their repositioning vis-à-vis the canon has impacted both on theoretical reflection and on the everyday classroom practice of teaching.

The essays collected in this volume partake of the cultural trends of the age. They would do so, to some degree, for just being what they are, essays primarily about Italian-American or Italian-Canadian or Italian-Australian literature (the one exception to the geographical and cultural parameters of the collection is an article on Italian *gastarbeiter* writers in Germany: a counter-specimen, it furnishes much needed European contrast to the other material). But the articles assembled here fit the climate because they too, like much of the criticism on or about minoritarian literature, exemplify the rumblings that traverse the two enterprises I have mentioned.

Emigration is at once one of the phenomena that have occasioned and nurtured the transnational mixedness now inhabiting Canada, the U.S.A. or Australia and a prime purveyor of identity politics. It lays bare the inner contradiction of today's cosmopolitanism. To be perhaps too blunt on an issue that calls for tact, without some work of identity maintenance — and the procedures and ideologies it involves — there would be no doubleness of any kind, no hybridity, no interstitial or borderland cultures. If cultural contact were only about metamorphosis, about merging with, trasmuting into the culture of the strongest groups, world-wide uniformity would be less inconceivable than it is today. The special qualities claimed for the new cultural spaces or the new psycho-social realities feed off first-order representations, which they require and which are therefore themselves also "new." The Little Italies or the Chinatowns of North America are forward-moving (they are not Italy or China), but they are distinct from their surroundings because they are also past-oriented, refer to an elsewhere, and because of the effort that goes into retaining, into re-presenting that past or that elsewhere.

By the same token, however, these essays respond to, rather than simply reiterate, the climate of the times. To start with, as Sneja Gunew notes in her admirable survey of the controversy over multiculturalism, which opens the volume, the "immigrant narrative" has been one of the targets of the debate on post-colonialism, ethnicity and the literature of race. And in the nineties any reconsideration which attempts to bring immigrant literature within the ken of literary studies, or which posits that the links of this literature to the cultural and literary history of Canada, the U.S.A. and Australia remain tenous, cannot but be in dialogue — directly or indirectly — with the revisionist tendencies within criticism.

During the last decade or so, emigration, as a topic of cultural or literary criticism, has found itself between the proverbial two fires. Those who lament the divisive effect of ethnic and racial studies or of multiculturalism have used the trajectories, the patterns of integration of early twentieth-century European immigrants as a benchmark for newer European and non-European immigrants. Reversing the trend of the 1960s and the 1970s — decades which celebrated the longevity, the "unmeltable" perdurance of ethnic identity — some American historians and sociologists, in particular, have reproposed variants of assimilation and the melting pot as social ideals (Gleason and Schlesinger are good examples here). What they accuse multiculturalists of — not being able to spell out their vision of the national, cultural or critical future — has just as obviously impaired their own endeavours. Adjustments notwithstanding — and some of the caveats do command respect — the view of society neo-assimilationsts promote would maintain the mechanisms of participation in the political and cultural life of the country that fueled the revival of ethnicity in the first place. It would keep intact, as an item impervious to argument, the whole legacy which underlies and underpins the history of the post-Renaissance "new worlds" and which condemns the groups that have arrived to the U.S.A. or Canada or Australia after the conquest or the early settlers to an irrevocable belatedness. You assimilate first and then speak your peace. And when you do, you can question everything but the axioms and theorems which establish assimilation as a premise or that determine the form it should assume, how it should occur. A process which occurred as it did because of specific social and cultural proddings becomes an objective, undisputable, empirical law of history.

Multiculturalist criticism has not rejected the ideology of the immigrant narrative espoused by assimilationists. It has interpreted the *dénouement* of that story — especially the ingrediencies pertaining to the *economic* integration of European immigrants — as further proof of the lack of solicitude of North American or Australian society for the fate of those who arrived to this continent in chains or who were there before the Europeans. In short, as a sign of white, European-American or European-Canadian or European-Australian obliviousness to the race factor. The racialization of recent multiculturalist rehearsals of the curriculum and the canon stems from the belief that race is (along with gender) the only outside element, the only repository of historical difference in an otherwise overwhelmingly white and Westernized, Eurocentric system.

This is not without some cost, intellectually. The notion of Anglo-conformity, a key component of the early — 1960s — ethnic studies, may have been, from this perspective, altogether too precise, based as it was on geography (even if the straw man it came attached with — the WASP — did put race up front). Dividing the population into Euro-Americans, African-Americans, Asian-Americans, Latinos and Native Indians — to cite, again, the U.S.A. — tips the balance the other way. It is not only, as Rose Romano observes in her article, that colours have many shades, or that Southern European immigrants — and therefore those of Italian origin together with others — were not upon their arrival associated with the lighter end of the spectrum. The "Europeanization" of the white ethnics blocks out a sizeable section of the history of immigration, no less unjustifiedly than the "Americanization" propounded by assimilationists does. It deprives the immigrant narrative of any plot-line (only its "now," its epilogue counts).

And it simplifies matters. The Italian immigrants who came to the U.S.A. or Canada or Australia did sustain European cultural expansionism. Toni Morrison divulges one of the great unsayable public secrets of American history when she suggests that without African-Americans to serve as the symbolic last rung of the social ladder, European ethnic groups might very well have been "at each other's throats" (1989: 68). Yet the ethical force of her admonishment derives in part also from the second hypothesis it postulates, itself unthinkable: the "bonding" race talk facilitates among Europeans (1994: 99) presupposes a backdrop of intra-European differences. Southern European immigrants aided and abetted the entrenching of Europe on North American or Australian soil from a position which, while it may not have been the bottom position, was still very much an economically and culturally subordinate position. Theirs was an "imperialism of the powerless," "of the poor" (Harney 13, 22) which had survival as it aim, not the carrying of the White Man's Burden. The idea of Europe was probably more of an abstraction to them than the idea of America. To allude to these differences and not bring them to bear on the whole picture is to take away the shadows, to de-culturalize history in order to racialize it, to substitute another symmetry to the sometimes too linear neatness of the immigrant narrative. It skirts the real difficulty, which is about how to conjugate race and emigration/immigration.

Adapted to the North American and the Australian context, post-colonialist criticism similarly glosses over distinctions. The privileging of the colonizer/colonized relation, inescapable and understandable as it is, results in the ratifying of other issues, some of which *do not* go by themselves. When Stuart Hall recalls how in setting foot in Britain the first thing he noticed was the sprouting of Wordworth's daffodils, how he felt that travelling to London from Jamaica was for him like going home (24), he undoubtedly summarizes a condition of epochal magnitude. It is the condition of those who come to the West or who encounter the West already Westernized. Hall's musings are echoed polemically by Rey Chow's critique of the Western penchant to demand from Third World intellectuals a cultural purity, an Otherness they cannot have (4), and tie in with Gayatry Spivak's and Homi Bhabha's defenses of the use of Western theory in the analysis of Third World texts (Bhabha, Spivak 1990: 67-74).

If the individual positionings of post-colonialist critics are momentarily put aside (unlike Chow or Spivak or Bhabha, some critics believe it is possible to resist the West culturally without denying Westernization)[2], it is clear where on this the dividing line is. For the sons or daughters of Italian immigrants the equivalent of Hall's gesture would be what? Going to Italy and being astonished at their residual, unexpected *italianità*? But the Italian heritage is exactly the component of their biography and their history they have had to suppress, to learn to privatize in order for them to become Americans or Canadians or Australians. More relevantly, the lingering affinities they recover would today further assign them to a cultural posture which is at best para-doxical. They would either have to accept being what they are not — North Atlantic ex-colonial Europeans — or verge near the outer edge of actuality (since in the late twentieth century vicissitudes outside of the colonizer-colo-nized relation belong to the "modern" past, a paleo-history cut off from the present) .

A racial politics which it sometimes appears too willing to collude with has made the progeny of Italian immigrants to the ex-settler colonies "paler" in ways unavailable to their forefathers. The cultural politics which have been the aftermath of colonization have, instead, limited and perhaps even pre-cluded other complicities. Commenting on globalization, Stuart Hall states: "Western technologies, the concentration of advanced labor in the Western societies, the stories and imagery of Western societies [are] the driving pow-erhouse of this global culture... It is centered in the West and it always speaks English" (28). Whether English is the language of the West, and not French or Spanish or Portuguese, as it might be in other ex-colonies, this is not an equation Italian or most European emigrants would agree with. London or Paris, the capitals of post-colonialism as they were of colonialism, are not their cultural homeland. It is slippages such as these, the resonance of these stories within the story of modern displacement, that post-colonial theory has side-stepped.

For example, the toolery of the better known (here in the West) post-co-lonialist critics is vouched for by poststructuralist philosophies whose cogita-tions owe much of their coherence to the primacy they accord to the linguistic versions of the sign. Spivak's notion of catachrestic transfer, the idea that concepts not originating in "the space of the colonizer" "decolonize them-selves," are nonetheless necessary for the portrayal of decolonized realities (1993: 13), sends back to Derrida's notion of "trace" and to his critique of the sign (which must be deconstructed but is impossible to do without). Bhabha's celebration of "hybridity" as a third space brings to mind earlier poststructu-ralist expostulations on "aporia" (the interstice is where sociocultural polari-ties transmogrify into an undecidable "both"). But in the situated, historical perimeter of the ex-colonies the same ontology of language on which these philosophies and Spivak's or Bhabha's post-colonialism rest reconfirms struc-tures of power, prerogatives that are rooted in the colonial past. In Canada or Australia or India or Quebec or the U.S.A., linguistic criteria are the thread uniting the conquest and citizenship, are what determines which activities, which programs or which groups have national, "official" status. Whereas culture levels, democratizes (it can be conceived as "multiculture"), the priority attributed to language yields at best, as in Canada, bilingualism, the founding-nations theory of the state, or the California "English only" by-laws.

Thus, just as the recent influx of non-Western immigrants in Europe or North America has permanently etched the *topoi* of post-coloniality onto the history of emigration, a detailed reappraisal of the history of emigration introduces compelling breaches within post-colonial discourse. It restricts the cultural, spatiotemporal range of the correspondences Hall adduces in his account of the Westernization of the world. Regardless of how Americanized culture in Italy has become, a present-day Italian immigrant would still have to attain by instruction, or at any rate a supplementary effort, the cultural literacy — the symbolics of Governors, Pilgrim landings, cricket metaphors, religious and literary intertextualities — that today permeates the vocabularies of the U.S.A., Canada or Australia. To word it differently, immigration insinuates within late modernity — and leaves there — the "axis of otherness," the incongruities which obtained between European nation-states up to 1945.[3] The xenophobia encountered by post-World War II Italian immigrants in Germany (see in this collection the article by Gino Chiellino), the negative stereotypes which still continue to hover over representations of the Italian-American community, the constant wrangling between Francophone and Anglophone Canadians would seem to suggest that these differences may have been diluted, may have been sublimated from the realm of the political to the realm of the cultural, but have not been altogether abolished by events. So that their removal from the current critical imaginary appears to be symptomatic more of an unexpected and unavowed desire for tidiness, than of the presumed and much-vaunted late-modern acceptance of the intrinsic messiness of history.

Reconsidering Italian-American or Italian-Canadian or Italian-Australian literature in relation to the larger critical milieu is important for a second reason. The specificities of the white immigrant narrative are being abrogated (to repeat, on different neo-assimilationist, multiculturalist and post-colonialist agendas) at a time when individuals of Italian ethnicity are gaining access to academic institutions and to the intellectual domain in general. That is, self-representation has become a possibility or an issue for intellectuals of

Italian origin at a particular phase of *their* history, at that juncture when, having begun to install themselves in the profession, they are under pressure to "discipline" themselves.

The texts collected in this volume could be seen, then, as a record of the complex push-and-pull of conflicting temporalities, institutional and individual. Not by chance, in the literature the essays focus upon, the measure of discomfort that the situation comprises takes first and foremost the form of a choice, manifests itself as the obligation — unavoidable, always impending — of saying yes or no to the profession, to the role of the intellectual as such.

What comes before, the group or the *métier*, the ethnic or the artist? The antinomy addresses head-on the many uncertainties deriving from the secularization of solidarity: it reactivates the kind of fractures wreaked upon the peasant Catholic religiousness of the early immigrants and the communitarianism it encouraged by the clash with modern urban life and its affiliational value system, its lure of advancement and upward mobility. Italian-American, Italian-Canadian and Italian-Australian immigrant fiction has often dwelled on this. As with women writers and feminist critics or other minoritarian intellectuals, the reaction of the individuals whose story that fiction has narrated has been now stark and clear-cut now more dialectically formulated. The Italian-American characters in Helen Barolini's *Umbertina* that Carol Bonomo Albright describes in her article make artistic professionalism and aesthetics their ultimate goal, almost as if it were at one with Americanization or with entering modernity. Other characters of other fiction try the opposite route: in the novel *A Piece of Earth* by Kenny Marotta that Albright also discusses, the protagonists choose a feminist ethics of care for each other which is more secularized but not far from the cooperative fellowship of the first immigrants (associations of *mutuo soccorso*, of mutual help, appear in Italian immigrant environment as soon as numbers warrant it, as a community arises).

The variation on this dichotomy, one which reduces the peremptoriness of the choices, is given directly, in this volume, by the poet and novelist Antonio D'Alfonso. His proposal — that literature and literary sensibility be detached from place and territory, be "atopic" in spirit — satisfies at once professional and ethnic demands. It frees aesthetic work from the restraining bounds of nationhood or nationalism and squares well — tactically at any rate — with pluralistic or minoritarian perspectives. Since D'Alfonso writes in Canada, with Quebec in mind, where the mood in recent years has been heavily nationalistic, Francocentric in bent, his celebration of the imagination, of the evasion from space-time, from historical contingencies is itself a political gesture.

But for criticism the dilemma that professionalism poses must be envisioned, I believe, in another manner. The value of an approach to literature that includes in its theoretical compass the proddings coming from ethnic or minority texts is by now beyond doubt. The survey of some of the major pros and cons Enoch Padolsky has undertaken in his article is more than enough to highlight the benefits that have accrued to literary theory and criticism. Which have to do not only with the issue of entitlement, with the revising of the canon, or with some of its other collateral and just as public and political offshoots (why is it that if Italian-Canadian authors write about Italian-Canadian men and women they are limiting themselves, they are ghettoizing the imagination, and if Margaret Atwood or Robertson Davies write about English-Canadians they are not?). The aspects Padolsky lists in his article often impact on the most routine and fundamental operations of reading. Diverted to the study of fiction, the politics of identity refocuses the gist of such touchstone notions as that of character or point of view or representation.

This is at present the crossroads where the literature of the Italian emigration touches base with minority literatures in general, all of which have fostered a criticism that has had to reconfigure its views of, its dependency and impact on the canon and to reassess the demands of the identitarian project on professionalism. What *specifically*, though, do Italian emigration and its fiction, poetry or theatre inspire in terms of criticism? As an object of study, are they interesting because they supply the critic with an excuse to exercise his or her professionality, to show his or her mastery of the critical apparatus currently deemed most appropriate? Or do they generate critical concerns of their own, concerns which can then be refracted back on the conversations of the day? Does the criticism dealing with Italian-American or Italian-Canadian or Italian-Australian texts, with the corpus of the Italian emigration, self-legitimate at some level, or can it find legitimation only elsewhere, only outside itself?

To ask as much is to suggest that the overall question is not whether there is an Italian-American or an Italian-Canadian or an Italian-Australian novel or poetry or theatre, relevant and central as that matter may be. Texts are aplenty, and growing in number. The question is, rather, whether there has been or there is a criticism that has read these texts not merely to "apply" but also to engage the various theories of the age. It is, in short, the question of how the case of the literature of Italian emigration/immigration can — or should — be articulated.

In a much-anthologized piece, Henry Louis Gates Jr. tells of a lecture he once gave during which he thought he had properly "schematized, formalized, analyzed" in "[his] Sunday-best structuralism" (97) a story by Frederick Douglass. The story was about slavery and the analysis was conducted in front of an African American audience. The detail Gates remembers most in thinking back is the reproach of a young man after he had finished speaking: "Yeah, brother, all we want to know was Brooker T. a Tom or not?". In a typical move (his own text is a little *Bildungsroman*, a story of education and redemption), Gates ends his essay with another autobiographical anecdote, meant to further support his main contention: that African American critics should acquire a voice of their own and can do so by recovering and reappropriating the "eloquence" inherent to their communal tradition. Intellectuals of Italian origin in North-America or Australia have still not reached that point. They have yet to fully meditate on their — and their works' — relation to the Italian community and to the community at large, or how that relation might impinge on their critical practice.

The arrival of multiculturalist and post-colonialist criticism has therefore merely laid bare their crisis. The "difficulty" of being Italian in North America or Australia is felt in every cultural context, and it is triggered any time the issues of citizenship and entitlement come up (Rose Romano chronicles one such moment in her account of the publishing mores of the U.S. lesbian community). Perhaps, along with feminist criticism, multiculturalist and post-colonialist criticism has demonstrated better than other contemporary critical movements that in our age critical diligence, professional acculturation may not be all there is to the game. A critical discourse also may also have to forge a specific identity for itself in order to be recognized or to have the corpus of texts it deploys recognized.

And this, it goes without saying, is a rule that holds for all the other relations contemplated by immigrant literature or criticism. The lack of sympathy of Canadian departments of Italian towards Italian-Canadian writers that Joseph Pivato so lucidly documents in this volume is emblematic of an alienation, an institutional unhousedness that historiographers of modern Italy need to record no less than the historiographers of modern Canada. As Pivato portrays it, the refusal of Italianists to create suitable slots for Italian-Canadian texts in their graduate or undergraduate programs bespeaks of their suspicion towards any tampering with the accepted, normative notions of canon or of literary and cultural value, and of their unwillingness to draw any curricular consequences from the shifting interplay between language, culture, territory and literature in the globalized context of the late-twentieth century. In such cities as Toronto, where the Italian-Canadian population borders on the half-million mark and where departments of Italian can boast of large enrolments of students of Italian origin, courses in Italian language, literature and culture have a double function: to impart knowledge about a certain subject (the culture of Italy) and — directly or indirectly, wittingly or unwittingly — to provide cultural maintenance. University resistances, therefore, can also be imputed to the lack of incisiveness, of persuasiveness on the part of the critics who would support the inclusion of Italian-Canadian texts in the curriculum.

This volume does not have any sure recipes on how to resolve the crisis. Clearly, the establishment of "voice" in the sense someone such as Henry Louis Gates would intend it is a greater problem than might at first be expected: there is no Italian immigrant "eloquence" to fall back on critically. The silence of the critic's immigrant parents or grandparents is complete; it never becomes language, let alone a style to be assumed or simulated. The greatest attempt to translate or re-encode the idiom of Italian immigrants into English — Pietro Di Donato's *Christ in Concrete* — is a magnificent literary accomplishment, but its very literariness, its very originality disqualifies the speech it is written in as a linguistic model: Di Donato's Italianate vocabulary, his Italianate syntactical rhythms clash too stridently with English for the language of his novel to be anywhere close to an historically viable and socially acceptable American vernacular.

What the essays collected here do is to offer, each with its own different slant, inklings about how the crisis might be faced in its many ramifications. By setting emigration as the initial, preliminary stop of Italian-Canadian or Italian-American or Italian-Australian criticism, by insisting that "ethnics" were first emigrants, that the starting point is the recanvassing of the *history* of ethnicity, the volume points to some alternatives to look to when weighing critical pros and cons.

The first of these has been continuously resonating through these pages but receives more precise and focused attention in William Boelhower's and Robert Viscusi's articles. The processes emigration sparks off are fundamental for the charting, the proper updating of the setting within which literature and the representations it vehicles situate themselves in the contemporary world. In settling the new landscape, immigrants, remarks Boelhower, infuse it with names, with "ethno-archaeographic signs" of other locations; the scene wherein the characters act out their stories becomes amenable to "site-analysis."

Overlappings arise. For in deterritorializing Italian culture, in being themselves its prime overseas carriers, Italian emigrants make Italy both greater — or, rather, transnational — and, to echo Viscusi's happy formula, more little. The Italian communities that dot Canada or the U.S.A. or Australia are a sociocultural entity dissimilar to but as historically real as the former British Commowealth or the *Francophonie*. They are the bridge between the nation and globalization, between colonialism and the countries unmarked or (like Italy) marginally marked by the colonial experience.

And so emigration gathers together a number of objects of inquiry, in a number of disciplinary or interdisciplinary venues. In so far as the various Little Italies are composed of ex-Italian nationals and their offspring, they can be deemed to be a cultural addendum to the territorialized, geographical, political Italy, and can be studied in relation to and starting from Italian history, as its propagations/disseminations. But immigrant communities are cultural, non-political external fragments that drift away from the origins. In their new locales, minority spaces don't benefit of the mechanisms of reproduction that state-cultures enjoy; they graft new languages, new customs, new allegiances on the ones they came with. As entities equally bound to and autonomous from the origin, they can refract their own transformations on to it. The dispersed, pluralized, diasporic *little* Italies can, as Viscusi maintains, reinterpret Italian history, even remould it in their own image (it is one of the signs of the progressive, emancipatory features of their trajectory).

For that very same reason, Little Italies can be studied as instances of the *precarious pluridimensionality* of the nation in the twentieth century. If they move beyond the origin, immigrant enclaves also resist the location, the structure hosting them, the nation of nations of which they are a part. With respect to one or with respect to the other, as a non-territorial extension or as an internal component, they are always somehow centrifugal, never quite coincide with the political units (or unities) which purport to enclose them or to define them. Canadian or American or Australian history reverberates back within Italian history because Italian history is built into the history of Canada or the U.S.A. or Australia. For this duality, which is geographical *and* something else, there is yet no name.

In still another swerve, Italian emigration can be studied as the memorization of a *particular* space and its culture, as a phenomenon which introduces a specific intra-European past within the post-colonial "new worlds," within world history (the culture Italian immigrants re-present has a lineage that dates back to the long classical and pre-Renaissance preamble to modern Europe, and is non-metropolitan in temper).

As relevantly, site-analysis of this sort meshes with the instigations that emanate from the work of Ernesto De Martino, a figure elicited briefly in this volume by Cesare Pitto. In such texts as *Il mondo magico* [*The World of Magic*] or *Morte e pianto rituale* [*Death and Ritual Mourning*], *La fine del mondo* [*The End of the World*], among the seminal titles of twentieth-century Italian anthropology, the crisis which befalls the individual or the group whose continuities with a previous life-world are disrupted is of ontological magnitude. The image that in these works best conveys the implicit psychical and societal disarray is that of the apocalypse, of the end of history. The loss of "presence" — De Martino's term for the individual's sense of control over self, intention and action — can be countered only by culture, by the (re)construction of a world-picture that accords satisfactory identifications.

For De Martino essentialism, as we would state it today, is always, by definition, strategic; it always entails some collision with or some response to historical circumstances, practices which are negotiations. Re-examining emigration or ethnicity through the filter of De Martino's writings would amount, then, to intervening on the contemporary ethos. Demartinian "presence" conjoins matters of self to matters of historical empowerment and agency. As a condition forever precarious, forever lost and forever regained, it raises the ante of the politics of recognition and identity, which turn out to be politics of survival. Most all, De Martino is entirely unknown outside of Italy[4], and his anthropology would permit a significant re-inflecting of key elements of the current glossary of criticism, which is beginning to sound pre-packaged. It would add an historal, more sequential, more plot-like (not just temporal) purview to the current concern with setting and space.

No less enabling — critically — and no less compatible with site-analysis is the theme explored by Pasquale Verdicchio in his paper. With some exceptions (Frank Lentricchia, above all, would have to be mentioned), the work of Gramsci has been strangely ignored by intellectuals of Italian background who have spoken about themselves here in North America or in Australia. Verdicchio's revisitation of the concept of subalternity corrects the oversight, thereby paving the way for all kinds of interesting traffic. You wonder how other Gramscian notions, particularly those that have to do with the role of intellectuals in the organization of culture, would illuminate the discussion about the relation of immigrant or ethnic writers and academics to their group and to the community at large, or the discussion about the social and cultural relevance of literature and literary representation in polyethnic nations. Conversely, you have to wonder whether approaching Gramsci through emigration might not inspire revisions to his thought, which might in their turn then interact with other revisions launched by other critical ventures (Stuart Hall, the Subaltern Studies Group) or with the other topics the Gramscian frame of reference services.

But the constellation of proposals that I have outlined is one of the yet-to-be-contemplated theoretical alternatives that the volume lets discern. On a more immediate and concrete basis, the essays collected here contribute to criticism by putting the question of Italian ethnicity or of its articulation from different locations. If the premises of minoritarian studies require nuancing, so does the study of the internal goings-on of Italian emigration and its history: it also needs to be pluralized, to be more readily available to inquiries of a comparative type.

Here too some of the issues of greatest cogency are broached in the essay by Sneja Gunew, with which the volume begins. Although the various Italian immigrant communities dispersed throughout the world have a common mnemonic and cultural referent in Italy, they obviously presuppose different contingencies, different situations of contact. Even the ex-settler colonies that this volume has privileged form an uneasy set. There are as many discrepancies between the U.S.A., Canada and Australia (many would cringe at seeing the U.S.A. in such company, so patently coterminous with post-coloniality), as there are between them and South-American countries, which also have large Italian communities, or between these and Germany, the other country represented in the volume.

In her essay Gunew stresses that in any gauging of the progress of multiculturalism within the U.S.A. or Canada and Australia the level of actual implementation should be a key criterion. The two latter countries have had some sort of legal commitment (an "agenda" in Australia, a policy in Canada) in place for over twenty years. But this — and Gunew's careful, cautious rehearsal of the complexities of the topic confirms it — is an ambiguous difference: it is both much deeper than it seems and more fragile.

As far as immigration goes, the existence of Canadian or Australian legislation on multiculturalism attests to crucial historical disjunctures. Numerically speaking, Italian, and generally non-French and non-British, immigration to Canada and Australia became relevant after World War II. The new arrivals were still unskilled labourers but had better educational records than their nineteenth-century or early twentieth-century U.S.A. predecessors. They entered a changed societal environment (a market in expansion, already geared towards tertiary, service industries, which had greater opportunities for white collar work and which, hence, rewarded that part of the labour force with college credentials). Politically, they found Canadian and Australian nationalism at an earlier level of growth, much more unformed and undefined than the American (the two countries were British dominions until the 1930s; the U.S.A. had long before moved from being a land of colonized colonizers to a post-colonial nation, and was, after World War II, quickly transmuting into a neo-imperialist superpower). This made it possible for the sons and daughters of immigrants who embarked on an academic or an intellectual career, most of whom had themselves been born in the old country, to embrace openly the utopian aspirations that motivated and animated their parents' voyage. Or, to rephrase this, it was possible for the children to believe that full participation in society, which the economic circumstances of Italy had denied to the older generation, would not be refused to them in the new land they were helping to populate.

As an ideology-cum-policy, multiculturalism in Canada and in Australia held the promise of full parity. Civic and cultural, no less than economic or social. It meant you were assured the right to shape the future of the country on the same rules and regulations by which majority groups operate, without having to give anything up. That the policy could be subject to manipulation (there is no "ethnic" I know who isn't aware that multiculturalism is also a strategy by which to contain minoritarian difference), was only a secondary drawback: legislations can be monitored, governments can be petitioned to implement and properly abide by their own laws. Moreover, late twentieth-century technology — the advent of satellite communication, Internet, facsimile publication of newspapers, transportation systems conducive to quicker, greater mobility — has enhanced the chances for identity maintenance, rendering the contact with the culture of origin easier, faster, accessible to all and more direct. So that a truly new form of togetherness could be envisaged, one which redeemed displacement and, in accordance with the electronic, globalized reality of the times, accepted cultural doubleness, acknowledged that the modern "here" is necessarily permeated by a "there," lightened the incapacitating (economic) weight of history but did not request as trade-off the erasure of historical continuities.

In the U.S.A. of the second half of the century, utopian prospects of this variety are less imaginable, or are imaginable in a highly modified version. The bulk of Italian emigration occurred under the aegis of melting-pot ideologies which it was not equipped to question or to resist. The benefits technology and societal developments afford cannot be politicized in the way they could be in Canada and in Australia, since the Italian-American parents or grandparents have already gone through the process of assimilation. The chronology of ethnicity that literary historiographers have worked with, and that Anthony Tamburri comments upon in his paper, may or may not be overly schematic, but the problematic that pervades it seem, from outside the U.S.A., peculiarly American. The transition from hyphenation to de-hyphenation, to above-the-fray mixedness (or, as another version has it, a phase in which the "Italian-American writes mature fiction harmonizing the traditions of his distinctive heritage with those... of his own nation". See Green 24) functions generationally or temporally only and only if the American models of acculturation are perfectly duplicated. How could they apply to Germany, where the guest worker remains a guest worker, and, for all intents and purposes, has no hope of receiving citizenship?

While no Italian-Canadian or Italian-Australian would think himself or herself less of a Canadian or an Australian citizen for declaring his or her cultural past in his or her self-descriptions, that past is less distant, qualititatively as well as chronologically, than it is for a third- or fourth-generation Italian-American. In Canada and Australia, there would exist the opportunity for an integration that reduces the gulf between first-, second-, third or fourth-generation Italian immigrants in favour of the first and second generations. The pattern that took five or six decades to reach its completion in the U.S.A., takes a lot less in Canada and Australia, but could also be open to a different ending, could marshal greater first-generation cultural retention. American *italianità* is now a primarily "symbolic" affair; because of the historical and ideological divergences already mentioned, the Italian communities in Canada or in Australia are still not quite there yet.

The literary and critical implications of these discrepancies are many, and they should not be underestimated. As William Boelhower reports in his article, the depictions of Italians or Italian immigrants, and their "dark alien countenance" in works by such authors as Hawthorne, Melville, James precedes by far the depictions Italian-Americans have given of themselves. In Canada and Australia, the gap is much less wide: the beginning of out-group representation and the beginning of self-representation are practically concurrent. Intellectuals of Italian background have a different relation with their community, whose cultural identity is yet to be fully delineated and to the begetting of which they might contribute with their portrayals. In the overviews Gaetano Rando's and Giovanni Andreoni's essays sketch of Italian-Australian literature, a significant number of writers still write in Italian. So much so that a *questione della lingua* has arisen in that country about what constitutes literary Italian outside of Italy or about the literary merits of the Australian Italian vernacular (see Andreoni and Bettoni). In Canada the works of writers such as Pier Giorgio Di Cicco give voice *at the same time* to the thematics of all the social stages and most of the corresponding literary features Tamburri expounds upon in his article.

Making these caveats is necessary not just to avoid the mistake of saddling Italian immigrant culture with a homogeneity that simply isn't there but also to unpack the specific, historical contents usually ascribed to that homogeneity. In a world in which globalization is more and more synonymous with Americanization, the distinctions on which I have been insisting reflect different situations of power, along with different situations of contact. Recently, Gay Talese has contrasted the poor success rate (and output) of Italian-American writers with the acclaim — critical and public — bestowed on Italian-American cinema. Although the various Coppola, Scorsese and Cimino have a sophisticated filmography and their vision shouldn't be confused with that of run-of-the-mill commercial cinema, it is true that the Little Italy they narrate, is caught, by intertextual co-optation if nothing else, in the politics and the ideology of the Hollywood dream factory. Mainly through the gangster film, Italian-Americana has been woven into the modern urban epic of American mass-culture. And it is that distanced, stylized Little Italy that often gets superimposed on the Italian immigrant communities outside the United States.

The risk in overlooking distinctions is marginalization, permitting Italian-Americana to become, out of sheer cultural and mediatic might, the metaphor for the rest of all Italian emigration, for the other varieties of international, outside-of-Italy *italianità*. This would penalize initiatives that deserve a place in the contemporary cultural arena. The Italian-Canadian or Italian-Australian or Italian-German communities have no great captivating epic, no myth to correct or to piggy-back on. They have only history at their disposal. And while some of the literary works that they have produced may appear to be quaintly anachronistic, to be the replication (in Canada or Australia) of the documentaristic first-encounter tales of the early Italian-American immigrants, this is a feature which interlocks, today, with some of the crucial literary developments of this age. They corroborate and themselves embody the poetics and problematics of emergence that the return of autobiography in other areas (feminism, the literature of race and ethnicity in general) have thrust into the limelight. Expressions of the yearning to be recognized, they stand for the disappointment that falls upon the feeling that emergence may be nothing but a desire, or for its effect, the wish to make emergence the constant, permanent condition of all literature.

So the final lesson — historical, critical, and literary — that this book bears is a banal but sobering one, for all concerned. As always, intellectuals

must work on several fronts. To engage the challenges of multiculturalist thought, critics whose field is Italian-Canadian, Italian-American, Italian-Australian, or Italian-German literature must also learn to talk to each other. And if they are of Italian origin they must do this, regardless of whether they feel (or are told) that they are arriving at this conclusion after the fact, as they are learning to speak to the non-Italian citizenry of the countries of which they are a part, and as the tide is turning against identitarian auscultation and self-reflexivity. For, if listening to others teaches them much about themselves, only in being able to speak about themselves will they really learn to speak to others.

Notes

1. On globalization and its effects see Featherstone and King.
2. I take this — how resistance to Westernization or to Western culture is accented, as possible or not, as describable or not — to be the main difference between the work of Bhabha, Spivak and Said or Hamad.
3. I am picking up here — and transposing — an argument Fredric Jameson makes in his 1990 essay. The phrase "axis of otherness" is his. Jameson speaks of the European imperialist powers and their history up to about 1945. I think this works with Europe in general, whether imperialist or not, and that, in ways perhaps different than the pre-World War II period, it still applies, as the debate on the kind of union Europeans should embark on demonstrates.
4. The only sustained text on De Martino here in North America that I know of is the one by Saunders. It deals with "critical ethnocentrism," another central concept of De Martino, and one which, again, could illuminate the current debate about the self and identity. On this see also Loriggio.

References

Andreoni, Giovanni. *La lingua degli Italiani d'Australia e alcuni racconti*. Roma: Il Veltro Editrice, 1978.

Bakhtin, Mikhail. *The Dialogic Imagination*. Ed. Michael Holquist. Trans. Caryl Emerson and Michael Holquist. Austin: The University of Texas Press, 1981.

Bhabha, Homi. *The Location of Culture*. London and New York: Routledge, 1994.

Bettoni, Camilla. *Tra lingua dialetto e inglese*. Leichhardt, NSW:FILEF Italo-Australian Publications, n.d.

Chow, Rey. *Writing Diaspora*. Bloomington: Indiana University Press, 1992.

Featherstone, Mike, ed. *Global Culture*. London: Sage Publications, 1990.

Gates, Henry Louis, Jr. "The Master's Pieces: On Canon Formation the African-American Tradition." In *The Politics of Liberal Education*. Ed. Darryl J. Gless and Barbara Herrnstein Smith. Durham and London: Duke University Press, 1992.

Gleason, Philip. *Speaking of Diversity*. Baltimore and London: Johns Hopkins University Press, 1992.

Green, Basile Rose. *The Italian-American Novel*. Rutherford: Fairleigh Dickinson University Press, 1974.

Hall, Stuart. "The Local and the Global: Globalization and Ethnicity." In King, 19-39.

Hamad, Aijaz. *In Theory*. London: Verso, 1992.

Harney, Robert, F. "Italian Immigration and the Frontiers of Western Civilization." In *The Italian Immigrant Experience*. Eds. J. Potesto and A. Pucci. Thunder Bay, Ontario: The Canadian Italian Historical Association, 1988, 1-28.

Jameson, Fredric. "Modernism and Imperialism." In Terry Eagleton, Fredric Jameson and Edward Said. *Nationalism, Colonialism and Literature*. Minneapolis: University of Minnesota Press, 1990.

King, Anthony D., ed. *Culture, Globalization and the World-System*.Binghamton: Department of Art and Art History, State University of New York at Binghamton, 1991.

Loriggio, Francesco. "Introduction." *Refractions: Literary Criticism, Philosophy, and the Human Sciences in Contemporary Italy*. Eds. Francesco Loriggio and Peter Carravetta (forthcoming).

Morrison, Toni. "The Pain of Being Black." *Time*, May 22, 1989, 68-70.

——————. "On the Backs of Blacks." In *Arguing Immigration*. Ed.Nicolaus Mills. New York: Touchstone Books, 1994, 97-100.

Said, Edward. *Culture and Imperialism*. New York: Knopf, 1993.

Saunders, George. " 'Critical Ethnocentrism' and the Ethnology of Ernesto De Martino." *American Anthropologist 95*, 4, 1993, 875-893.

Schlesinger, Arthur M., Jr. *The Disuniting of America*. New York: Norton, 1992.

Spivak, Gayatri Chakravorty. *The Post-Colonial Critic*. Ed. Sarah Harasym. New York and London: 1990.

——————. *Outside in the Teaching Machine*. New York and London: Routledge, 1993.

Talese, Gay. "Where Are The Italian-American Novelists?" In *The Columbus People*. Eds. Lydio Tomasi, Pietro Gastaldo and Thomas Row. New York: Centre for Migration Studies, 1994, 465-474.

Sneja Gunew

Multicultural Multiplicities

Canada, U.S.A. and Australia

1. Setting the Debate

*M*ulticulturalism is being discussed everywhere, it seems, but is inflected very differently across a number of national sites. In the U.S.A. it is currently at the centre of the P.C. (politically correct) debates and it seems almost impossible to rehabilitate the concept in terms of radical theory since it translates most often into cultural pluralism and the return of the unified authentic subject via unproblematically conceived minority texts. In Canada ethnic minority writers are generating a certain amount of interest but once again the reception of their texts as well as those by indigenous writers are often contextualized in terms of their communal authenticity rather than their textuality or writing. Their positioning in terms of the French-English axis as well as the terrain of "visible minorities" (questions of race) are other factors. In the light of such variations this paper attempts to position the Australian debates around multicultural critical theory and asks whether there is any way that this can continue to be a politically challenging discourse? The density of this paper is due to the fact that it attempts to present a schematic overview of a vastly complex debate. The opening quotation is a way of situating a point of departure:

> I'm in favor of a multicultural curriculum that emphasizes what Matthew Arnold called the best that has been thought and said. Non-Western cultures have produced great works that are worthy of study, and I think that young people should know something about the rise of Islamic fundamentalism. To do so it is helpful to be exposed to the Koran. Young people should know something about the rise of Japanese capitalism. Is there a Confucian ethic behind the success of

Asian entrepreneurship in the same way that we hear about Max Weber, the Protestant ethic, and the spirit of capitalism? These are legitimate questions. (D'Souza and McNeil 31)

These words come from one of the leading participants in what have been designated the P.C. (politically correct) debates in the U.S.A. What are the major assumptions in this passage and how do they differ from those we are used to hearing when multicultural issues are aired in Australia? The reference to Arnold is a standard rhetorical ploy for those who invoke cultural excellence and some may recall that Arnold is a rather ambiguous ally since he was raising the bastions of culture against the anarchic forces of what would now probably be called cultural democracy (Bérubé 134). So the quotation gestures towards a certain elitism, implicitly at least. The setting up of multiculturalism as being centrally concerned with an assault on the West is probably not so familiar as a general framework. We note too that the speaker's arguments for studying the non-West are not simply presented in terms of the West in general but of its American capitalist incarnation in particular where "the West" translates into the American capitalist system.[1] In this construction, students should be exposed to other cultures insofar as these are structured by sympathetic capitalist resonances, for example, "Is there a Confucian ethic...?" Similarly there is the stereotypic move of invoking Islam in terms defined by and confined to the spectre of fundamentalism, as though this were exclusively a non-Western or Islamic characteristic. In Australia the term multiculturalism usually refers to a homogenized version of those groups defined oppositionally as non-Anglo rather than non-West and indeed the separation of the postwar European communities from more recent non-Europeans does not usually occur unless it be in the context of curtailing Asian (another homogenizing term) immigration while in the same breath referring to the "Asian market" as the hope which will lift Australia out of its current recession. Given these culture-specific connotations, this quoted passage represents, in its way, a defence of multiculturalism. The piece continues in the following manner:

But they are not the questions routinely pursued in most multicultural courses, which instead have degenerated into a kind of ethnic cheerleading, a primitive romanticism about the Third World, combined with the systematic denunciation of the West (Berman 1992a: 31).

Can this once again be translated into the Australian context? Apart from the reference to the West, this probably accords with many people's perception of what happens in the name of multicultural pedagogy, or, possibly an amalgamation of multiculturalism and post-colonialism since the latter does not really resonate to the same extent in the U.S.A. as it does in Australia and Canada.[2] So the quotation would be more appropriate to the Australian context if we merge issues relating to multiculturalism as well as to post-colonialism. One notes in passing that the relationship between those two in Australia is worth thinking about and the paper will return to this issue. At this point it is appropriate to reveal the curious fact that the quotation defending multiculturalism comes from Dinesh D'Souza who is of course cited as one of the chief architects of the "anti-P.C." debates in the U.S.A., a controversy which some have described as involving a covert attack on all the reforms which have happened in the name of cultural democracy in the post 1960s era in the U.S.A. (Berman 1992: 19). Others have termed these debates as a "call ... for the politicization of academic knowledge by the Right, in the name of 'the mainstream' or of 'Western civilization' " (Chicago Cultural Studies Group 552).

How we stage our culture is not entirely governed by institutional fiat either in state or academic arenas. In other words, while policies designed to manage demographic diversity come and go and the institutions set up to be conduits for state edicts are comparably ephemeral, this does not guarantee that the problems or, more neutrally, the issues which produce the necessity for "management" are going to disappear with equal ease. Nor does the closing down of the multicultural program, for example, in one of this State's newest universities which services a largely "ethnic" constituency,[3] mean that there is no longer any need to think about the nature of our cultural diversity and the impact this is and should be having in terms of our pedagogical visionary planning. Australia has, and in some respects has always had, a population characterized by the variety of their linguistic and cultural reference points but until relatively recently this obvious fact has not been fundamentally addressed as a key element which should be registering on every aspect of its national institutions and, indeed, its certified national imaginaries, the arts and culture industries. In other words, the ways in which Australia defines itself both internally and externally should be thoroughly infused with this perception at a conscious level. Unconsciously it is registered quite clearly in a number of symptomatic irruptions testifying to the ways that this knowledge is repressed, to the extent that one can envisage a future research industry dealing with this element, just as, increasingly and analogously, Australians are attempting to deal with the suppression of the histories, cultures and lives of Australia's indigenous peoples.

Whether Australians acknowledge it or not, the challenge represented by its demographic mixture links it to comparable debates around the world. Because this simple fact is not generally being explored in intellectually rigorous ways, there is a tendency to create some lazy slippages, for example, bundling questions dealing with cultural difference and nationalism under the general umbrella of postcolonialism where academic courses so labelled deal belatedly with Australia's legacy of oppression toward its indigenous peoples. In effect this absolves all non-Aboriginal Australians from having to analyse Australia's neo-colonialism or its internal colonisations or the many other ways in which power relations operate unequally in this country. Consideration of one kind of history produces an even more total amnesia regarding other histories, notably in this instance, postwar migration histories. Australians are still caught up by the desire to create national unities, coherent narratives of the nation and it is particularly difficult for those who fought initially from the position of outsider to insert their own differences as women, or Irish-Australians, or the old Left, to in turn recognize competing claims by other excluded groups. In short, if Australians consign the need for a continued analysis of multiculturalism to the sidelines they run the risk of losing the momentum which for a while allowed Australia to be a pioneer with regard to acknowledging its hybrid population and all this entails. Furthermore, far from averting divisiveness (as the opponents of multiculturalism constantly argue) they would be compounding it. The necessary theoretical work on this subject is hardly encouraged within Australia.

In North America the analysis of ethnic/racial difference, sometimes under the heading of multiculturalism, has outstripped Australia's initiatives in this area, since Australians are still embroiled in arguments based on first principles: whether to treat the linguistic and cultural diversity of its population as anything other than a set of sociological problems. In the current socio-political climate this diversity merely registers as the supply of convenient scapegoats and functions as imperative to close the traditional ranks.

Consequently, this paper is about what perspectives Australian-based analysts might offer on this topic both in relation to their own situation and in interpretations of this phenomenon in Canada and the U.S.A. To some extent it is unnecessary to become too engrossed in determining the correct terminology for anchoring these debates because this deferral has long operated as a way of excusing a refusal to deal with substantive socio-political issues. Certainly under the banner of multiculturalism different elements are aligned in Canada and the U.S.A. from those familiar to Australians. To some extent one might say that the difference can be measured in terms of a movement between ethnicity and race. For example, many have pondered the etymology of ethnicity as a way of teasing out some of its coded or hidden meanings, that is, that, on the one hand, it means those like ourselves and, on the other, it refers to the pagans and barbarians.[4] It differs from race in that it may incorporate the dimension of the self-chosen. Those defined in terms of race are in a sense defined by racism in that they often have no choice as to whether they are designated "other." One cannot choose to stop being black or possessing other external characteristics, that "mark of difference" as Joan Scott calls it (1992: 216) which indicate a visible minority which in turn precipitates a host of prejudices amounting to the paralysing process of stereotyping (Bhabha).

2. How does multiculturalism circulate in the U.S.A.?

As indicated in the opening remarks, in the U.S.A. multiculturalism is to some degree subsumed in the notorious P.C. debates, whose history is conveniently detailed in two recent publications (Aufderheide 1992; Berman 1992). In these volumes are arrayed the major statements, individuals, organizations revealing that what was initially perceived as a binary structure is now a more complicated spectrum of positions in which the Left can sometimes sound like the Right and vice versa, as the paper tried to demonstrate with the D'Souza quotation. For an example of the Left sounding like the Right one could refer to Miles Harvey's article which argues that P.C. actually contributes to sexism, racism, etc (Harvey 142). There is also the realization that far from being a recent phenomenon these controversies, one way and another, are at least a decade old (Berman 1992: 4). In the P.C. context the multicultural factor comprises an array of assaults on cultural norms as defined within a national context. Joan Scott contends that: "If 'political correctness' is the label attached to critical attitudes and behaviour, 'multiculturalism' is the program it is said to be attempting to enact' (Scott 1992a: 13). The Chicago Cultural Studies Group defines multiculturalism as, "a desire to rethink canons in the humanities — to rethink both their boundaries and their function... to find the cultural and political norms appropriate to more heterogeneous societies within and across nations, including norms for the production and transmission of knowledges' (CCSG 531). While the terrain and terminology are much-contested in the context of the P.C. debates (Berman 1992a: 6), multiculturalism includes: ethnics (including Hispanics and Asians), Blacks (pertaining to the African-Americans who are united by their common history of slavery which has in turn functioned as an excuse for occluding their contribution to the construction of the nation), indigenous peoples, feminists, gays and lesbians, ecologists, deconstructionists (by which is usually meant anything poststructuralist or postmodernist) (Bérubé 143) and a generalized Left. Clearly, these discussions are not characterized by a nuanced attention to detail or accuracy. These motley groups are apparently united by their opposition to the West or Western values, also defined as Eurocentrism, and by a framework in which universal propositions or truths are intoned from positions which remain immune from being defined as positions. Given this restrictively coded and to some degree metaphoric meaning for the "West," we have the absurd situation, for example, that Hispanics are at times arrayed against the West and outside Eurocentrism (Fernández 1992). To comprehend this we need to realize that the defining element in such formulations is oppositionality and the substantive nature of the opposition remains valid whereas the terms used are often misleadingly ambiguous, or, at the very least, function metaphorically.

Critics of multiculturalism operate from a number of positions. Those from the Right see it as an undermining of Western/American values including those of individual liberty and free speech. Even a cursory analysis reveals that the degree of dissidence supposedly represented by P.C. advocates has been much exaggerated and is scarcely impinging on "business as usual" across American campuses (Bartlett; Ehrenreich; Mowatt). For an analysis of the contradictions in the free speech argument, Stanley Fish (1992) helpfully points out the anomalies inherent in trying to dissociate speech from its performance and content so that free speech is only appropriate if speech is seen as contentless or as mere noise. In a related vein Richard Perry and Patricia Williams ponder the implications and effects of permitting "freedom of hate speech." The Right sees multiculturalism in those caricatured terms intrinsic to the binary approach which translates any questioning of power or positionality into rule by the other, that is, not the redefining of power structures but their inversion (Grosz). Those who represent the dissident groups, critique multiculturalism differently. One of the most powerful oppositions emanates from the African-American lobby and theorists situated in Black or, as they are sometimes called, Afrocentric studies who see it as a deflection from dealing with racism (Asante 303; Carby; Wallace). For example, in her recent study *Playing in the Dark*, Toni Morrison asserts:

> ... the imaginative and historical terrain upon which early American writers journeyed is in large measure shaped by the presence of the racial other... Explicit or implicit, the Africanist presence informs in compelling and inescapable ways the texture of American literature (46).

Critics in Black studies perceive multiculturalism amongst other things as focusing on the older ethnic groups who have by this stage been thoroughly assimilated, for example, Italians and Jews and various Northern Europeans. In such a framework hegemonic America is constructed as a movement from Anglocentrism to Eurocentrism (Spivak 1992: 10) which effectively leaves out the visible minorities such as African, Indigenous, Hispanic and Asian Americans. In other words, embraced in this version of multiculturalism is the a-political smorgasbord of cultures where everyone is free to either offer tit-bits or taste them (Gitlin 188). Versions of this operate in Australia also of course in the contention that "we're all ethnics," which has long functioned to foreclose on analyses in the name of any specific ethnicity (Docker; Dessaix).

Little attention in this pluralist approach is paid to unequal power relations because the focus on culture supposedly guarantees a neutral and a-political space. One is reminded of Henry Louis Gates's 1990 statement that culture often functions as a Trojan horse for ideologies of race (Gates) and of Hazel Carby's thesis that: "Black cultural texts have become fictional substitutes for the lack of any sustained social or political relationships with Black people in a society which has rigidly maintained many of its historical practices of apartheid in housing and in schooling" (Carby). On the other hand, references to race in the context of combating racism are also fraught with the dangers of reinstating traditional essentialist constructions of race, as explored in another paper (Gunew) , and as Paul Berman (1992a) suggests when he notes that there is sometimes the hint of the fascist doctrines of recent history when race is unproblematically invoked in these debates.

3. Canadian Multiculturalism

Like Australia Canada, in much the same historical time-frame dating from the early 1970s, has progressively installed a public commitment to multicultural-ism, though arguably its has given this greater political and other kinds of institutional emphasis (Fleras and Elliott). There is a Department of Multicul-turalism and Citizenship and not merely an understaffed and underfunded Office of Multicultural Affairs and there is a Multicultural Act rather than an Agenda.[5] In other words, Australia is proceeding rather more cautiously which also means that it is easier to use issues relating to multiculturalism as a politi-cal football and policies are never in place long enough to allow for real action and implementation (Blonski).

As in the case of Australia a firm distinction exists in Canada between multiculturalism as a set of government policies designed to manage cultural diversity and multiculturalism as an attempt by various groups and individuals to achieve full participatory cultural democracy. In ways similar to Australia (though to a greater and more nuanced extent) Canadian critics have revealed official multicultural policies to produce often restrictive notions of ethnicity which are still fuelled by assimilationist and to some extent racist principles (Blodgett; Kamboureli; Mukherjee).

There is also the differing factor that the Canadian indigenous peoples are generally included in the multicultural terrain, which is perceived as deal-ing with cultural difference rather than being overly defined by migration issues. In addition Canadian nationalism is effectively split between two founding powers: England and France. Thus from the outset, while the Anglo element has been a dominant feature of the hegemonic group, it has never been as complacent in character as in Australia because of the historically divided cultural reference points functioning in the country. What has on the other hand served without doubt as a unifying force has been the American cross-border threat in relation to anxieties concerning cultural and other take-overs.

Within Canada, multicultural literature or ethnic minority literatures[6] have to a greater degree than in Australia been defined, at least initially, as comprising the work of those born overseas (Miska). There was also an initial emphasis on other languages, although now there has been a shift to questions of ethnicity in literature rather than simply ethnic literatures, so that, for example, works in English by minority writers are also examined as part of this general field. In some ways this corresponds to what in Australia are referred to as second and even third-generation ethnic writers. Canadian discussions are also increasingly affected by the cross-border P.C. debates which code multiculturalism in terms of racism, that is, signalling an emphasis on so-called visible minorities (Corelli; Smith). Increasingly there have been charges comparable to the ones operating in the U.S. debates that multiculturalism circulating as liberal pluralism focuses too much on the older ethnic groups who have long managed to secure a footing at the expense of newer groups who are perceived as being more difficult to "assimilate." Thus multiculturalism in terms of official policy (in ways which remind us of critiques in Australia) is seen as a covert form of assimilationism (Brand; Onufrijchuk). As one critic and writer put it:

> Multiculturalism to me is a way of managing seepage of persistent subjectivity of people that come from other parts of the world, people that are seen as undesirable because they have once been colonized, now neo-colonized. So we are not talking about Germans or Finns and Swedes or the French... We are talking about the undesirables. It is southern Europeans, sometimes, and Third World People who have to be ethnic. (Bannerji 146-7)

There appears to be as much racism and occlusion of these groups in Francophone as in Anglophone Canada (see the Summer 1992 issue of *Tessera*).[7]

Interestingly, in ways related closely to Australia, there has also been the critique that multiculturalism is too often structured by appeals to notions of community evoked in often unproblematic ways. In Australian government policy circles, for example, attempts to implement access and equity decrees relating to multiculturalism glibly solve existing inequities by promising piously to communicate and "outreach" with "the ethnic communities." There is never any attempt to understand that these communities themselves are fragmented by many kinds of differences within which individuals have comparably complex affiliations. In more abstract terms one thinks of the formulations used by the Chicago Cultural Studies Group when they ask in relation to notions of local community: "Does the authenticity of the local become a trope to escape the problem of mediation and alienation?" (CCSG 539). Furthermore ethnic cultures are supposedly continuous with these communities and are constructed as simply constituting the perpetuation of the past, in petrified form, the spectacle of the exotic artefact useful for establishing cultural tourism (Onufrijchuk).

Insofar as we focus on specific discussions of multicultural literatures there has of course been much more activity in some respects than in Australia and certainly more official activity, for example, the Secretary of State's commissioned bibliographies on specific language/cultural groups. There has also been a national project organized by the Comparative Literature Department at the University of Alberta titled "History of the Literary Institution in Canada" (HOLIC).[8] This project has used the Polysystem theory, based on the work of Itamar Even-Zohar in Israel, as a way of approaching literature as a set of institutional relations: "The polysystem theory understands literature as a dynamic, functional, semiotic system which is perceived in the form of an institution" (Dimic and Garstin 178; Dimic 4). The work has so far resulted in the publication of five volumes (Blodgett and Purdy 1988; MacLaren and Potvin 1989; Blodgett and Purdy 1990; Pivato; MacLaren and Potvin 1991) offering a sustained examination of the literary institution in many of its complexities in Canada. Those who find points of critique with respect to systemic approaches of this kind would find an echo in the statement by the Canadian critic Francesco Loriggio (1990: 44) who suggests, mildly, that it does not sufficiently take into account the impact of "creative disorder." Whatever one's reservations it is an admirably ambitious commitment to researching the workings of literature as an institution and suggests possible useful Australian parallels.

More so than in Australia, and possibly under the impact or influence of pressures from indigenous Canadian writers, there has been an anti-postmodernist strain in relation to the interpretation of minority literatures in Canada.

Poststructuralist or postmodernist approaches have been condemned by a number of critics as being inappropriate for looking at such texts. Instead their major contribution has been identified by such critics as that of bearing witness (Dimic 18; Loriggio 25; Blodgett 19), of linking history to fiction (Padolsky 26) particularly insofar as this concerns the history of a community or the fictional expression of a community (Onufrijchuk).

These debates have also been associated with the "appropriation of voice" controversies, where the rights of mainstream writers to create minority characters from another minority culture or race have been challenged (Maracle; *Books in Canada*; Stasiulis).

4. Australian Differences

There are a number of similarities to and differences from the Australian situation.

One of the recurrent points made in the P.C. debates is that its proponents are supposedly "politicizing" cultural and academic life (Ehrenreich). This is viewed both negatively, as in Roger Kimball's case, and positively as is emphasized, for example, in Joan Scott's (1992) much quoted essay or Kate Stimpson's notorious 1990 address to the MLA. In Australia, possibly because there is less of a division between the academic and public sphere, there have not been the same doubts or at least revelatory dimensions attached to the contention that culture and the study of culture are intimately linked to the political. As well, the fact that interdisciplinarity and cultural studies have more of a purchase in the Australian academy means that anxieties over the erasure of disciplinary borders do not appear to have the same emotional impact as they do in the U.S.A.

Questions to do with race are also differently figured because Australia's migration patterns have a different history and constituent membership. Thus racism is constructed as much in terms of those who are non-Anglo as referring to those who are non-white. One needs to recall here that Italians were designated "blacks" around World War II and that Arab-Australians are described so now and one hears Australian-Greeks speak of themselves as "black." In other words, echoing earlier discussions concerning the meaning of "West," such terminology registers opposition to a dominant group over perceived adherence to a notional race.

Indigenous politics are also configured differently in that the indigenous peoples here have distanced themselves from multiculturalism which they say is defined in terms of cultures of migration. As a result there have been some unfortunate alliances at times between right-wing spokespeople fulminating against Asian immigration, those who speak of sustainable population, and some Aboriginal spokespeople. On the other hand, there have also been understandable and substantiated fears expressed by Aboriginal activists that discussion of multiculturalism can sometimes function as a distraction from land right campaigns. In Canada on the other hand there appear to have been more frequent alliances in the past among indigenous and ethnic groups, particularly insofar as both sectors have been united by being the targets of racism, that is, by virtue of their status as "visible minorities."

Discussions around ethnic or minority literatures have also been differently positioned in institutional terms and appear to find their haven in Comparative Literature rather than in Language departments, as often happens in Australia.[9] One could probably add that multicultural or ethnic literatures as such have barely figured in Australia at all in comparison to Canada when one measures this, for example, in terms of publishing and reviewing activities.

But to what extent can discussions in Australia benefit from these debates and what do Australian critics have to offer from their own perspectives?

5. Shared Problems

The discussions in all the three nations share a concern with identity politics and whether a renewed emphasis in this area comprises a retrograde step or whether, after poststructuralism and postmodernism, one should reconsider what identity politics entails. Generally speaking, identity politics have returned to confound those who felt espoused to notions of decentred subjects and the demise of universalist principles mainly in relation to minority struggles for legitimation and agency. Thus, indigenous peoples in the three countries all have versions of what appear to be appeals to unproblematic identity trailing guarantees of authenticity in their wake. Their speaking positions are indeed legitimated through speaking itself (appeals to oral traditions); to speaking on behalf of particular groups; to ownership of traditional stories (Maracle).[10] Other versions of renewed identity politics, for example, in relation to gay and lesbian rights have produced speculations on whether this amounts once again to a convenient sidestepping of questions of access to power, since legitimation is once again predicated on an individual basis with the authority of experience or appeals to hierarchies of victimage (Boyte 178; Scott 1992: 219). In such a context one can understand the contention by Elizabeth Fox-Genovese that multiculturalism is "primarily the quest for an acceptable autobiography" (231). In a recent critique of the work of even such sophisticated poststructuralist theorists as Spivak and Trinh, Sara Suleri accuses the latter in particular of finally resting her own discussions of difference on appeals to insufficiently theorized conjunctions of identity and experience.[11] On the other hand, one also recalls Spivak's references to cultural productions where identity becomes a commodity made for exchange (1992a: 798) which need to be distinguished from the notion of identity analysed as a process of struggle and fracture (Spivak 1992: 2). In other words, identity politics constitute a differentiated field where there are no immediate certainties which can simply be dismissed, as they were for a time, as appeals to essentialism that placed one in a pre-structuralist era (Scott 1992a). One could also argue that identity in relation to agency refracted through poststructuralism may be usefully formulated as being both provisional and strategic (Gunew).

6. Future Challenges

In all three countries surveyed questions raised by cultural/racial difference under the banner of multiculturalism have proved to be a way into the prevailing impetus to challenge the traditional production of knowledge either in relation to universalist propositions and truth-claims or in surveying the implications of institutional boundaries. Common to all has been the cautionary injunction that if these debates around cultural difference are not linked to power inequalities, consisting of access to resources and structures of legitimation, then we are lost in the maze of liberal pluralism described by Todd Gitlin (188) as "the shopping center of identity politics" or by Gayatri Spivak (1992: 6) as "contrite universal humanism in the place of the same, and us being studied as examples of otherness." One kind of answer to this danger is provided by the Black Faculty Caucus (Gordon and Lubiano 249) when they suggest the empowering of minorities within institutional structures. Although this may seem an over-simplification, in certain quarters, for example institutions regulating Australia's culture and heritage, these policies repeatedly prove to be the most difficult to implement. Actively seeking a range of people to "represent" diverse aspects of the demographic constitutency, although admittedly in some respects an essentializing gesture, is at least a step in undermining and challenging the at least equally essentialized composition of most of Australia's institutional representative bodies.

Within Australia's own academic terrain, one notes Spivak's suggestion that the teacher within what she describes as the "emergent dominant" (those dissident groups brought together under P.C.) needs to be committed to the spread of transcultural literacy. One registers as well, Edward Said's (1992) examination of identity within new nations as a necessary but necessarily transient phase which consolidates national forces in the service of decolonization but cannot remain there, for they are implicitly continuous with an epistemology of imperialism. Ultimately, he suggests, one centrism should not be replaced by another and intellectual efforts should entail the restoration of texts from their status as "informative ethnographic specimens" to their place as literatures in and of the world.[12] This too is a version of transcultural literacy.

In the rush for cross-cultural training programs we note as well the warnings offered by the Chicago Cultural Studies Group of the flattening effects of certain kinds of corporate multiculturalism predicated on an ideology of interchangeability and the possibility for commensurate translation. The grotesqueness of related intercultural performances or "ventriloquisms" are analysed in detail by Spivak (1992a) in a recent edition of *Critical Inquiry*, though examples of both corporate multiculturalism and intercultural performances in all three countries would not be hard to find.

Amongst the ways of preventing such transgressions there is the need to reconfigure the status and function of the so-called ethnic community in relation to diasporic histories and to differences within such notional groups linking them, for example, to other traditional categories of difference such as gender and even region (Minni 101). Literature itself could profitably be conceived of as a set of relations (Dimic 9) rather than simply a list of texts, canonized or not. Ethnicity here becomes not just the conveniently marginalised study of ethnic literatures but of ethnicity in literature (Padolsky 26ff).

Both approaches unsettle the cultural and linguistic reference points of traditional literary studies (Blodgett; Loriggio 1990a). The simplistically oppositional strategy of casting the "West" or "Eurocentrism" or English Literature or American culture as entities under siege in the P.C. context is usefully reinterpreted by reminding us of their own histories of hybridity as Reed Way Dasenbrock and Cornel West (1992: 327-8) both point out. West's analysis represents one of the few examples in the P.C. debates which attempts to analyse multiculturalism outside the parameters of the U.S.A. alone.

We return to the dialogue, or non-dialogue, between multiculturalism and post-colonialism, bearing in mind that the division is possibly more appropriate to Canada and Australia than the U.S. Post-colonialism is often a way of dealing with off-shore differences, the old Commonwealth (Spivak 1992: 16), or concentrating on one kind of difference, for example Australian Aborigines, where guilt is safely located in the past and does not deal with neo-colonialism or with other kinds of differences in the present. Thus, settlers confront indigenous society, and the "migrants" are a passing phase eventually assimilated and subsumed in the first group. But multiculturalism is not a passing phase to be contained by questions of migration or "foreign" languages and should no longer be constructed in terms of a set of problems or the homogenizing of differences into pluralism. Just as Australia cannot simply be redefined as a post-colonial society because it is attempting to cut its ties with mother England (this usefully eclipses its neo-colonialism), so the differing relations of its many groups to the indigenous peoples as well as to the first settler groups need to be reinterpreted and linked to wider debates around such questions. The statement by Shawn Wong (159) — that "students know they will be unable to compete in twenty-first century America with a monocultural, monolingual education" — could usefully be reiterated within the Australian context.

Finally, to return to the question which opened this paper: is there any way that debates around multiculturalism can continue to be a challenging discourse? To echo a Canadian commentator: "Because multiculturalism uses the rhetoric of inclusion it cannot properly address the politics of exclusion" (Creighton-Kelly 4). This is largely the case in Australia also, particularly if discussions remain dominated by discourses of multiculturalism as public policy. Finding the right terminology will not guarantee that this fundamental paradox is solved. The P.C. debates have shown us at the very least that the right words are no guarantee of correct politics. It is crucial, however, that Australia does take issue with the complexities these discussions have engendered in a global context so that its own engagements with cultural difference and/or multiculturalism move beyond the repetitive and predictable stage they are locked into at present.

Notes

1. One notes the election rhetoric where George Bush claimed credit for the demise of Soviet Communism in the name of U.S. capitalism rather than democracy. See also Spivak 1992:10.
2. This seems to occur because the U.S.A. does not see itself as ever having been either a colonised nation or a colonial one. The latter is probably a necessary blindspot.
3. The Victoria University of Technology, Melbourne, Australia.
4. On the etymology of ethnicity see also Spivak 1992:14.
5. The Australian Agenda for a Multicultural Australia foreshadows a possible future Act.
6. The term is favoured because it signals that there is something complementary called ethnic majority literatures thus indicating that ethnicity is a factor which might usefully be explored in all literatures.
7. My thanks to Barbara Godard at the University of York for her very helpful information on this topic.
8. My thanks to Joseph Pivato at the University of Athabasca for information on this project and many other aspects of the multicultural debate in Canada. Thanks as well to Steven Tötösy de Zepetnek, University of Alberta, for his help in researching this area.
9. Deakin University is an exception in this regard.
10. See the appropriation of voice debates in Canada (Maracle 1990; Books in Canada 1991; Stasiulis 1993).
11. My thanks to Suvendrini Perera for bringing Suleri's article to my attention.
12. This point is discussed at much greater length in Said 1993.

References

Asante, M.K. "Multiculturalism: An Exchange." In Berman 1992, 299-311.

Aufderheide, P. ed. Beyond P.C.: Toward a Politics of Understanding. Minnesota: Graywolf Press, 1992.

Bannerji, H. Interview. Other Solitudes: Canadian Multicultural Fictions. Ed. L. Hutcheon and M. Richmond. Toronto: Oxford University Press, 1990, 145-152.

Bartlett, K. T. "Surplus Visibility." Beyond P.C.: Toward a Politics of Understanding. Ed. P. Aufderheide. Minnesota: Graywolf Press, 1992, 122-125.

Berman, P. ed. *Debating P.C.: The Controversy Over Political Correctness on College Campuses.* N.Y.: Laurel, 1992.

Berman, P. "Introduction: The Debate an Its Origins." *Debating P.C.: The Controversy Over Political Correctness on College Campuses.* Ed. Paul Berman. N.Y.: Laurel, 1992a, 1-26.

Bérubé, M. "Public Image Limited: Political Correctness and the Media's Big Lie." In Berman 1992, 124-149.

Bhabha, H. "The Other Question — the Stereotype and Colonial Discourse." *Screen*, 24. 6. (1983), 18-36.

Blodgett, E.D. and Purdy, A.G. eds. *Problems of Literary Reception.* Research Institute for Comparative Studies. University of Alberta, Edmonton, 1988.

Blodgett, E.D. & Purdy, A.G. eds. *Prefaces and Literary Manifestoes.* Edmonton: Research Institute for Comparative Studies, University of Alberta, 1990.

Blodgett, E.D. "Ethnic Writing in Canadian Literature as Paratext." *Signature*, 3 (Summer, 1990), 13-26.

Blonski, A. *Arts for a Multicultural Australia 1973-1991. An Account of Australia Council Policies.* Sydney: Australia Council, 1992.

Books in Canada. "Whose Voice Is It, Anyway?" (Feb., 1991), 11-17.

Boyte, H.C. "The Politics of Innocence" In Aufderheide 1992, 177-179.

Brand, D. Interview. In *Other Solitudes: Canadian Multicultural Fictions.* Ed. L. Hutcheon and M. Richmond. Toronto: Oxford University Press, 1990, 271-277.

Carby, H. Unpublished Talk given at the Humanities Institute. N.Y.: SUNY Stony Brook, 1992.

Chicago Cultural Studies Group, "Critical Multiculturalism." *Critical Inquiry*, 18 (Spring, 1992), 530-555.

Corelli, R. "The Silencers: 'Politically Correct' Crusaders Are Stifling Expression and Behavior." *Maclean's* (May 27,1991), 40-50.

Creighton-Kelly, C. "Report on Racial Equality in the Arts at the Canada Council." Ottawa: Canada Council, 1991.

Dasenbrock, R.W. "The Multicultural West." In Aufderheide 1992, 201-211.

Dessaix, R. "Nice Work If You Can Get It." *Australian Book Review,* (Feb/March, 1991), 22-28.

Dimic, M. "Preface" and "Canadian Literatures of Lesser Diffusion: Observations from a Systemic Standpoint." In Pivato 1990, 1-20.

Dimic, M. and Garstin, M. K. "Polysystem Theory." *Problems of Literary Reception.* Ed. E.D. Blodgett and A.G. Purdy. Edmonton: Research Institute for Comparative Studies, University of Alberta, 1988, 177-184.

Docker, J. "The Temperament of Editors and a New Multicultural Orthodoxy." *Island* 48 (Spring, 1991), 50-55.

D'Souza, D. and Macneil, Robert. "The Big Chill? Interview with Dinesh D'Souza." In Berman 1992, 29-39.

Ehrenreich, R. "What Campus Radicals?" In Aufderheide 1992, 133-141.

Fernández E. "P.C. Rider." In Berman 1992, 322-325.

Fish, S. "There's No Such Thing as Free Speech and It's a Good Thing, Too." In Berman 1992, 231-245.

Fleras, A. and J.L. Elliott. *Multiculturalism in Canada: The Challenge of Diversity*. Scarborough: Nelson Canada, 1992.

Fox-Genovese, E. Untitled Statement. In Aufderheide 1992, 231.

Gates Jr. , Henry Louis. "Critical Remarks." *Anatomy of Race*. Ed. D.T. Goldberg. Minneapolis: University of Minnesota Press, 1990, 319-32.

Gitlin, T. "On the Virtues of a Loose Canon." In Aufderheide 1992, 185-190.

Gordon, T. and Lubiano, W. "The Statement of the Black Faculty Caucus." In Berman 1992, 249-257.

Grosz, E. "Idle Speculations on Political Correctness." Unpublished talk, 1991.

Gunew, S. 'Feminism and the Politics of Irreducile Differences: Multiculturalism / Ethnicity / Race.' In *Feminism and The Politics of Difference*. Ed. S. Gunew and A. Yeatman. Sydney: Allen & Unwin and Halifax: Fernwood, 1993, 1-19.

Harvey, M. "Politically Correct is Politically Suspect." In Aufderheide 1992, 142-147.

Kamboureli, S. "The Technology of Ethnicity: Law and Discourse." Unpublished paper, 1992.

Kimball, R. "The Periphery v. the Center: The MLA in Chicago." In Berman 1992, 61-84.

Loriggio, Francesco. "History, Literary History, and Ethnic Literature." In Pivato 1990, 21-45.

————."Italian-Canadian Literature: Basic Critical Issues." *Writers in Transition*. Eds. C.D. Minni and A.F. Ciampolino. Montreal: Guernica, 1990a, 73-96.

MacLaren, I.S. and C. Potvin, eds. *Questions of Funding, Publishing and Distribution*. Edmonton: Research Institute for Comparative Studies, University of Alberta, 1989.

MacLaren, I.S. and Potvin, C. eds. *Literary Genres,* Research Institute for Comparative Studies. University of Alberta, Edmonton, 1991.

Maracle, L. "Just Get in Front of a Typewriter and Bleed." *Telling It: Women and Language Across Cultures*. Ed. Sky Lee, Lee Maracle, Daphne Marlatt, Betsy Warland. Vancouver: Press Gang Publishers, 1990, 37-42.

Minni, C.D. Interview. *Voices of Change*. Ed. J. Hesse. Vancouver: Pulp Press, 1990, 95-103.

Miska, J. *Ethnic and Native Canadian Literature:A Bibliography*, Toronto: University of Toronto Press, 1990.

Morrison, T. *Playing in the Dark: Whiteness and the Literary Imagination*. Massachusetts: Harvard University Press, Cambridge, 1992.

Mowatt, R.V. "What Revolution at Stanford?" In Aufderheide 1992, 129-132.

Mukherjee, A. *Towards an Aesthetics of Opposition: Essays on Literature, Criticism and Cultural Imperialism*. Ontario: Williams-Wallace, 1988.

Onufrijchuk, Roman. "Post-modern or Perednovok: Deconstructing Ethnicity." *Ethnicity in a Technological Age*. Ed. Ian Angus. Edmonton: Canadian Institute of Ukrainian Studies, University of Alberta, 1988, 3-16.

Padolsky, E. "Establishing the Two-Way Street: Literary Criticism and Ethnic Studies." *Canadian Ethnic Studies*, 22, (1990), 22-37.

Perry, R. and P. Williams. "Freedom of Hate Speech." In Berman 1992, 225-230.

Pivato, J., ed. *Literatures of Lesser Diffusion*. Edmonton: Research Institute for Comparative Studies, University of Alberta, 1990.

Said, E. "The Politics of Knowledge." In Berman 1992, 172-189.

Said, E. *Culture and Imperialism*. N.Y.: Knopf, 1993.

Scott, J. "Campus Communities Beyond Consensus." In Aufderheide 1992, 212-224.

Scott, J. "Multiculturalism and the Politics of Identity." *October* 61 (Summer, 1992a), 12-19.

Smith, D. "The New MacCarthyism." *Canadian Dimension* (September, 1991), 8-13.

Spivak, G.C. "Teaching for the Times." *MMLA* Journal for the Mid-West Modern Language Association, 25. 1 (Spring, 1992), 3-22.

Spivak, G.C. "Acting Bits/Identity Talk." *Critical Inquiry*, 18 (Summer, 1992a), 770-803.

Stasiulis, D. "'Authentic Voice': Anti-Racist Politics in Canadian Feminist Publishing and Literary Production." *Feminism and the Politics of Difference*. Ed. S. Gunew and A. Yeatman. Sydney: Allen & Unwin and Halifax: Fernwood, 1993, 35-60.

Stimpson, C. "On Differences: Modern Language Association Presidential Address 1990." In Berman 1992, 40-60.

Suleri, S. "Woman Skin Deep: Feminism and the Postcolonial Condition." *Critical Inquiry*, 18 (Summer, 1992), 756-769.

Tessera. "Other Looks: Representation, Race and Gender." 12 (Summer, 1992).

Wallace, M. Untitled statement. In Aufderheide 1992, 232.

West, C. "Diverse New World." In Berman 1992, 326-332.

Wong, S. "Stereotypes and Sensibilities." In Aufderheide 1992, 158-160.

2

Antonio D'Alfonso

Atopia

The stubbornness of ethnicity is as strong as human psychology and culture, for it is woven of these.

Richard Gambino, *Blood of My Blood*

I end up feeling like I have to pay for the rape of Canada. But I didn't have nothin' to do with it.

Keith Richards, *The Biography*

The respect of human life and the protection of the freedom of individuals and minority groups are concerns which we, intellectuals, must defend. There is no other choice. We must become active thinkers, by which I mean that men and women have to give themselves the duty of questioning any idea that is lifted before the world as, what Maurice Allais (Nobel Prize for Economics in 1988) calls, "established truths" (14).

> Universal consent, or the consent of the majority, cannot be considered a criterion for truth. The only valid way of measuring truth is by agreeing on factual experience... In every field the continuous calling into question of "established truths, no matter what these truths might be, is the principal criterion to the progress of knowledge (111-112).[1]

Our century began in a most terrible way, with an assassination in Sarajevo and, by the looks of things, it may very well end where it began — in a sea of nationalist blood. Almost one hundred years of social contract have been far from being happy ones for democratic countries. These one hundred years show us repeatedly how a number of politicians and, near them, artists of every kind — many of whom chose to adopt the role of token artists — have bowed before the rise of ideologies which a majority of citizens blindly embraced. In every part of the world we have seen men and women defend political concepts that in their eyes appeared to be incontrovertible truths and, in doing so, ostracize other men and women who refused to side with the majority. When one thinks one has the key to happiness, what is there to do? The spirit closes on itself like a clam and is impermeable to the outside world. Alain Finkielkraut is right when he asks: "What is a conversation? It is the act whereby a person who does not know the truth beforehand can see his point of view shaken by another person's point of view " (1).

From narrow-mindedness to taking up arms it is but a short step. In a world where we witness the crumbling of walls and borders, what we call the majority of the citizenry of every territory is about to take that fatal step because it feels that the neighbor's vice is slowly closing in. We are about to notice not so much holy wars — how can any war be holy? — but stern nationalistic wars.

Obsessed by the quest for purity of blood and the fear of racial cross-breeding, by the inevitable demographic drop within one's ethnic group or by the uncontrollability of migratory processes, or by how men and women can easily change political or religious point of view, people in nations everywhere know that they have to unite if they want to stop the destruction of their boundaries. They will need to resort to the creation of arbitrary laws that will keep at bay the massive influx of immigrants. To find a solution for the breakdown of *the* nation governments remind us that it is necessary to institute measures of control to restrict entry in the country, decrees which will protect their language, their culture, their religion, and the traditional and already established way of conceiving the state and the territory of the nation. Speaking of Quebec, Pierre Vallières writes:

> The present linguistic conflict is, in reality, a struggle for power, not only between francophones and anglophones, but also, and more and more, between the old immigrant stock and the recent one. This struggle for power, which began with the genocide of the native people carried out by white Europeans (our dead intolerant and conquering ancestors), will not end before the day when all

citizens decide in an honest way to cohabitate in justice and solidarity, regardless of their ethnic origins (4).[2]

In Western culture, we have yet to discover the reasons why people don't procreate anymore. Nor have we been able to prove why, exactly, Arab, Indian, and Asian immigrants represent a threat to the Western world. That governments all over the globe should suddenly feel the need to invent countless laws to curtail the proliferation of languages on their territory appears suspicious to the extreme. Politicians still rely on the family to play its role in guaranteeing the sacrosanct connection between national territory and blood: "What is needed," they scream, "are children so that we can safeguard our cultural identity. Not more immigrants. Why should we search abroad for a remedy that will help in the survival of our nation? Mothers of every nation make babies for the good of our people!"

One day we will have to congratulate those women who were able to see through these racist politics of manipulation which never had anything to do with the well-being of women. Unfortunately, there are thousands of women and men who hide in their homes or offices who are ready to follow these absurd orders sent down from government headquarters in order to wage war against the "wogs and barbarians" that have come to spoil their earthly paradise. And in the name of Truth (with a capital T), these women and men act quickly to send to the chambers of death any person who will not comply with their laws and convert.

It is useless to sink into an historical analysis of nationalism. There exist plenty of excellent books which defend every possible aspect of this very volatile issue. What is needed, however, during these terrible times of growing patriotism is a vision that goes beyond such troublesome reaffirmations of the nation-state. Technology in our global villages has shrunk the earth's surface. Everything is smaller and closer to home. If it is true that we can go around the world in less than eighty days, it is also true that we would be completely foolish to think that after such a trip we would still remain simple tourists. To close ourselves within is absurd. The arrival of immigrants on any territory is a phenomenon that spares no one. Even those men and women who have never moved from their little piece of land must ultimately accept the fact that they will never be able to live "as a single family" again. We may look back to our native land as much as we wants. But it will soon become apparent that whatever this native land is, it was not, nor will it ever again be ours alone.

The claim to rights over territory has been definitively shaken at its roots, here in Canada, by recent Amerindian protests. If there is much debating going on about territory these days, be it in America or abroad, it is because people have rapidly realized that there was always someone here before they moved in. We can never apply the concept of virginity to identity. The earth is too weightless and fragile to rest our identity upon it. Julia Kristeva explains:

> The foreigner can be defined primarily by two legal systems: *jus solis* and *jus sanguinis*; the first being rights derived through land and the second rights derived through blood. One would have to consider as belonging to the same group of people born on the same land, or children born of indigenous parents (here, the rights of belonging are established, depending on the civilization, according to paternal or maternal lineage) (140).[3]

More for sentimental than political reasons — so closely studied by Alain Finkielkraut in his brilliant long essay entitled *La défaite de la pensée* — we have brazenly tried to root the individual's identity to his or her native land, and it is the sum of individuals literally entrenched in one same piece of land that have constitutes the nation. Miraculously, there have always been, throughout history, nomadic peoples who have defied the validity of such a proposition. These nomads preferred living in a society that was the association of individuals bound together by an elective contract or singleness of religion or commonness of language (often different peoples scattered across a territory shared a common language or practiced similar religious rites).

The specificity common to two or more persons should therefore not be mistaken for nationhood. Confusing the common denominator of "territoriality" among individuals with whatever other sort of link individuals might entertain in a specific nation or geographic entity would, in fact, be an invitation to the gas chambers of the nation-state. Nevertheless, let's be cautious: people that adapt themselves to a chosen religion or choose to express themselves in a certain language do not necessarily belong to a common culture. An Irish Catholic speaking and an Italian Catholic do not belong to one culture even when they speak English to one another. To confound communication with belonging will lead to complications.

Defining the nation can be hazardous. I totally agree with Nathan Glazer when he writes that the concept of the nation, when applied to Europe, refers to an ethnic group, but that this reference should not be mistaken for the state, since the state irremediably suggests a political entity binding individuals to their citizenship (140). In the U.S.A., explains the American sociologist, the nation does not refer back to a specified ethnic group. It is an entity defining all individuals who choose to become Americans. Hence, it would be unthinkable, in the U.S.A., to anchor an ethnic group to any sort of territory or to associate it with any one language. For these reasons the U.S.A. cannot, by any stretch of the imagination, be considered a nation-state, such as the concept is used in Europe.

"Ethnicity," says Richard Gambino, "is an identity of person with himself and his experience" (360). In the wake of nineteenth-century nationalism, most ethnic communities in Europe, endowed with distinct cultures and languages, formed, through a variety of processes, singular and indivisible structures and social systems. When an ethnic minority arrived in these clearly-defined territories, it was obliged to assimilate or leave. European countries came to be identitied with a particular space, a particular people, a particular culture, and a particular language. They gradually turned themselves into the nation-states that they have come to be known today:

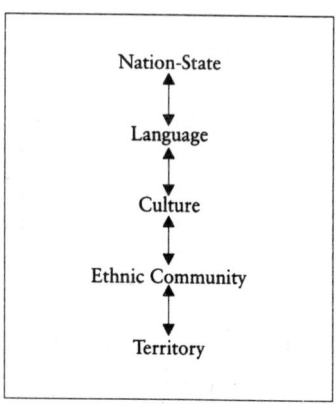

At the other end of the spectrum is the U.S.A., where the one nation became identified with "many people without territorial concentration..." (Glazer 248). Despite what has often been written about the melting pot, the U.S.A. is very much a pluriethnic society where the English language has managed to gain a more or less official national status. To quote Edgar Morin, English is only "the principle language of communication" (200). It is a common denominator and nothing else.

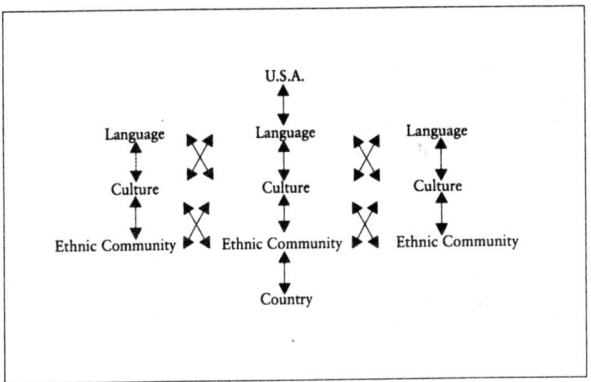

European ethnic nationalism presupposes a system of parallel countries, each of which requires its own allegiance and laws. These allegiances and laws are vertical-like and thus never cross over the allegiances and laws of a neighboring country. If ever these were to overlap, the outcome would be what Edgar Morin calls the creation of a *meta-nation*.[4] In the U.S.A., where there is the total absence of the fatal equation "territory = ethnic community," ethnic communities are free to interweave one into another and, thus, to form a complex and organized network of interrelated societies. This omnipresent and circular mosaic unites different ethnic communities under common laws and civil rights. It allows for the creation of "interest-defined groups" and assures, as much as possible, equal representation of each ethnic group without ever questioning the individual's allegiance to the country as a whole.

Not a day goes by without when European intellectuals from every nation asking themselves, and often quite dramatically, if people will ever abandon their "monstrous superstitions" (Allais 11) concerning national sovereignty and embrace the dream of an economic, political and culture unity of all European states. Yet, after reading a multitude of studies published in France, England and the U.S.A., I must confess that I have become quite pessimistic about ever seeing a single European confederation.[5] Individual nations are sinking, it seems, deeper and deeper into the mire of forced redefinitions of nationality and do not want to realize that the more we attach ourselves to territory the closer we approach renewed versions of irredentism.[6]

In his book, *L'Europe face à son avenir: que faire?*, Allais lists a number of conditions necessary for the realization that the destiny of each state is ultimately one to sink in. On of the conditions is the creation of the *Grande Communauté Fédérale* (the Great Federal Community). A laudable goal no doubt, but, again, the method is not truly as democratic as it should be. To paraphrase George Orwell: we might be heading for a state where some will be more equal than others!

European unification can occur if and only if cultural identity is not associated to territory, nation and ethnicity. If the present European nation-states were to unite, what would happen, for instance, to the growing minorities that have refused to assimilate into territorialized ethnic communities? Governments may continue stuffing such ideas as assimilation and integration down peoples' throats. However they will have to face the fact that such concepts will only diminish the spread of individual freedom.

Some may defend the custom of granting more rights to certain ethnic groups because they are wealthier and more numerous, or because they might even be considered more "native," more "indigenous" than others. But they shall soon learn that collective rights must be given to all or to none for these rights to be valid. Others repeat that the individual must never be forced to confine his or her identity to an ethnic group. Isn't it also true — at least one hopes it is — that each person born within a community will find that the community will protect his or her rights? As the saying goes, strength comes with solidarity. There is nothing more reassuring for a citizen than to know that his or her vote will indeed help the interests of his or her community in general. The primary concern in the ethnic debate is and continues to be the search for a synthesis between individual rights and freedom and collective rights and freedom.

With such preoccupations in mind, one must conclude that it is therefore best to do away with the connection that binds the individual to a territory and nation.

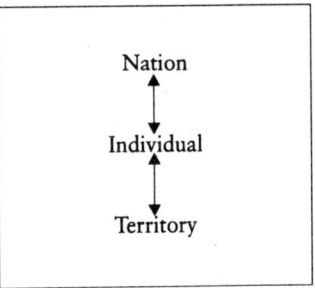

In order to reduce the chances of having a perilous rise of racial wars again, it is important that we uproot the individual from the land where he or she was born and to displace this person, if not physically — one may not want to move — then surely mentally, by temporarily putting the person in a state of exile, minus the rifts so commonly associated to the experience of exile. It is clearly *in exile* that the individual will discover his true identity, and not by consuming the salts of the earth. An individual who knows how to fly lives closer to his identity, than one who crawls in the wet soil of nationhood. Here is the identity that is shared by many and everywhere across the world. Autonomous individuals who find their "aterritorial" identity will then be free to constitute their own collectivity which may end up being distinct from other collectivities that have risen in the meantime. These organized, independent and borderless collectivites will agglomerate into economic, cultural, and educational centers which may very well become the new bases for a new enlarged country. I know that all of this sounds like Utopia, but isn't one of the tasks of the artist to destroy hell and create a better world? Or are the intellectuals and artists deluding themselves when they think that they knows what is best?

Since we need to replace what has been destroyed by something else, wouldn't one solution be to substitute the obsolete triad — nation, individual, territory — by a different type of triad? At one end, there is identity and, at the other end, the country; and, in between and at the center, the collectivity:

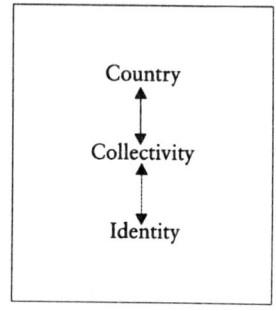

Belonging would thus be viewed as the awareness of one's identity, a redis-covered identity, a *conscious identity*. This way a person would have the pleas-ure of knowing that he or she is not alone in his or her individuality but that he or she can, if she or he desires, participate in the livelihood of a group of persons instead of sinking deeper and deeper into the quagmire of territorial-ity and nationhood. But this collectivity must not become a cult; what we have are collectivities bound together by a common allegiance to something higher — civil welfare. The country could be envisaged as a confederation of interre-lated collectivities and individuals, rather than a centralized representation of nationhood. To quote a past Prime Minister of Canada, Pierre Elliott Trudeau: "We must separate the concepts of State and Nation, and make Canada a truly pluralist and polyethnic society" (187).

A literature that reflects such a pluralist and polyethnic vision of a coun-try is called, to quote Anthony J. Tamburri and Fred Gardaphé, a *literature from the margin*. A literature from the margin should not be lumped in with the avant-garde. The problematics of the latter is the natural outcome of a nation-state that has fallen into the mirror of irony and cynicism. A literature from the margin is not, however, traditionalist, since no nation can claim to have been its exclusive producer. Culture is pluralist *a priori*, therefore anti-nationalist. A literature from the margin (and I include cinema and all the arts in this definition) exists parallel to mainstream culture, that is, the official and centripetal culture of any one nation. Being at the margin means that one's work is centrifugal, baroque and collective in spirit. Texts from the margin can be written in any language or in a language that is not the language spoken in a specific nation. But we must beware of associating too closely any literature to the language in which it is produced, for, paradoxically, literature can never be imprisoned by any language.

All of literature gambles its existence whenever it is pushed to silence. To enclose literature, be it one from the margin or another, in a single language would imply that in the long run we wish it to die totally. Because mainstream literature today is in the hands of nationalists, literature from the margin has become the kite for exiles, the *mongolfier* for stateless persons. The men and women who create a literature from the margin are nationless baroque writers[7]: working in the context of borderless collectivities theirs is a literature constantly banished because it will not feed into the myth of the nation-state.

The main issue for writers at the margin is to be able to protect their integrity vis-à-vis political change. Avoiding to compromise with the fashions that briefly monopolizes a country is paramount for artists wishing to maintain their dignity. Every artist should learn from the tree which bends in the storm but never breaks.

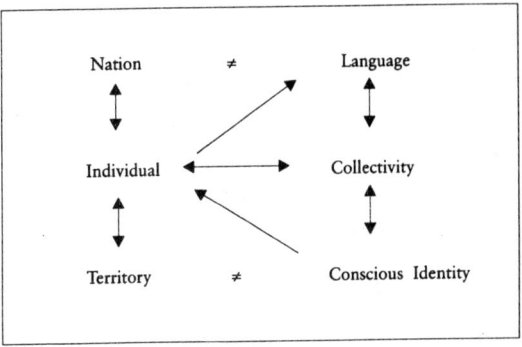

Nations everywhere are presently in such turmoil that intellectuals can no longer afford to remain silent. The intellectual must defend justice when it succumbs to humiliation and constriction. The main issue is to find ways for the intellectual to speak and respect his or her inspiration without having to resort to facile reasoning and shrewd hypocrisy. Countertruths have become a common occurence. Day after day newspapers mention complex notions which are only superficially analyzed. Politicians, journalists, and many writers deceitfully support on radio and TV fundamental concepts about our social contract without ever examining them in detail or their implications. Readers and listeners can never get the complete range of possible scenarios that could help our society in crisis. If it is true that in every nation there is a social class that is the sad prisoner of prejudice, as a nation's cultural elite so quickly reminds us, are we to accept, as educated men and women, the fact that the industry of ethics for an entire population is circumscribed by passing trends and smug racism?

Notes

1. Unless otherwise noted, all translations are mine.
2. *La Criée*, in which Vallières's article was published, is a Montreal downtown journal.
3. Suddenly I also recall the brilliant explanation Julia Kristeva gives of the Hebrew word *guer*, which means the stranger that converts to the (Jewish) religion-nation. See Kristeva (100).
4. See Morin (199): "Ainsi, la nouvelle situation nécessite beaucoup plus qu'acceptation et adaptation; elle oblige à deux conversions, apparemment contradictoires, en fait complémentaires: l'une qui nous fait dépasser la Nation, l'autre qui nous réduit à la Province. Il est nécessaire de lier en un seul, l'acte de se ressourcer en Europe-Province et l'acte d'assumer le destin planétaire, c'est-à-dire de réassumer, de façon nouvelle et concrète, cet Universel dont notre culture a établi le concept. *L'Europe doit se métamorphoser à la fois en Province et en Méta-Nation.*"
5. There is a number of books which, though they may offer sound analyses, kindle the flame of discord because of the "regionalistic" attitudes. Examples are the collection edited by Olender and the volume by Voisard and Ducastelle. But the authors of these books are not the only ones who, after an eloquent elaboration of the meaning of pluriculturalism, end up with the most curious and dubious results: Alain Finkielkraut, Maurice Allais and Nathan Glazer all arrive at the solution of assimilation and by praising the virtues of meritocracy. I believe that a pluriethnic and aterritorial society will alter, once and for all, our traditional (*Volkgeist*) or postmodern (transcultural) vision of what a country is. The biggest gamble that the future offers is for us to find an alternative to the way a country based on the idea of a territorialized ethnicity or one of "confined communities" as explained by Jacques Voisard and Christiane Ducastelle. What must be invented is a country composed of an "association of autonomous individuals" (Finkielkraut) who would also have collective rights that would not hinder with their individual rights. The risk is great but its outcome profitable if properly achieved.

6. "Irrédentisme: Doctrine et mouvement politique des nationalistes italiens qui, après la formation de l'unité, ont réclamé l'annexion des territoires de langue ou de population italiennes non encore libérés de la domination étrangère (*Italia irredenta*)... Tout mouvement national s'inspirant des mêmes principes" (Robert 84-85). "There is no easy way to make ethnic boundaries and state boundaries coincide... When political bounds and ethnic bounds fail to coincide, problems have risen. Thus, the history of Europe in one respect has been, until recently, a history of efforts to make ethnic and political boundaries coincide... Ethnically defined states were created, after the cataclysm of World War I from the debris of the Austro-Hungarian and Russian Empires; and that was considered sound and good. Boundaries were moved to arrange that Italians live under the political rule of an Italian state, unfortunately causing a good number of Austrians and Slavs to become 'irredentist' in their turn" (Glazer: 245, 298).
7. This notion of the New Baroque, of which I wrote back in 1984 (see *The Other Shore*, 1986, or its translation, *L'Autre rivage*, 1987), is more successfully developed by Guy Scarpetta and by Omar Calabrese.

References

Allais, Maurice. *L'Europe face à son avenir: Que faire?* Paris: Robert Laffont/Clement Juglar, 1991.

Bockris, Victor. *Keith Richards: The Biography*. Poseidon/Simon & Schuster, 1992, 1993.

Calabrese, Omar. *Neo-Baroque: A Sign of the Times*. Trans. Charles Lambert. Princeton, N.J.: Princeton University Press, 1992.

D'Alfonso, Antonio. "Il Nuovo Barocco," in *The Other Shore*. Montreal: Guernica, 1986, 145-158.

Finkielkraut, Alain. *La Défaite de la pensée*. Paris: Gallimard, 1987.

——————. "Interview with Martin Turenne," *Le Devoir*, 28 september 1992, Cahier Société, 1.

Gambino, Richard. *Blood of My Blood*. Toronto/New York: Guernica, 1996 (first ed. 1975).

Gardaphé, Fred, Giordano, Paolo, Tamburri, Anthony, eds. *From the Margin: Writings in Italian Americana*. West Lafayette, Indiana: Purdue University Press, 1991.

Glazer, Nathan. *Ethnic Dilemmas: 1964-1982*. Cambridge, Mass.: Harvard University Press, 1983.

Kristeva, Julia. *Étrangers à nous-mêmes*. Paris: Fayard, 1988.

Morin, Edgar. *Penser l'Europe*. Paris: Gallimard, 1987.

Olender, Maurice, ed. *Émigrer Immigrer*. *Le Genre humain*, 1989.

Richards, Keith. See Bockris, Victor.

Robert, Paul. *Dictionnaire alphabétique et analogique de la langue français*. Tome quatrième. Paris: Les Dictionnaires Le Robert, 1963.

Scarpetta, Guy. *L'Impureté*. Paris: Grasset, 1985.

Trudeau, Pierre Elliott. *Le Fédéralisme et la société canadienne-française*. Montréal: Éditions HMH, 1967.

Vallières, Pierre. "Nous sommes toutes et tous des immigrant(e)s," *La Criée*, 20 February 1989, 4.

Voisard, Jacques et Christiane Ducastelle. *La question immigrée dans la France d'aujourd'hui*. Paris: Calmann-Lévy/Éditions du Seuil, 1990.

4

Robert Viscusi

Making Italy Little

Fare l'America.[1] Make America. Do America. This phrase, according to the novelist Garibaldi La Polla, names the enterprise of many an emigrant from Italy. *Fare l'America* means not only *to go and to do elsewhere than in Italy.* That is its most general sense, easy to understand. But it also has two meanings more precise, more specific to the the migratory universe of Italian Harlem, La Polla's theme in his masterpiece *The Grand Gennaro* (1935). First, it means *to make a new Italy* in America: La Polla's characters recreate the social world of their youth in Southern Italy. Second, it means *to make oneself* in the process. It means "that a nobody, a mere clodhopper, a good-for-nothing on the other side, had contrived by hook or crook in this new strange country, with its queer ways and its lack of distinctions, to amass enough money to strut about and proclaim himself the equal of those who had been his superiors in the old country" (3-4). It means to stand up against the figure of the *barone* or the *padrone*. That is the Italian half of it: in America the *cafone* remakes himself *padrone*. But the American half of this is, or will be, quite different. For *fare l'America* also means to endow oneself with status that only comes from making oneself through this particular route, which passes through America. To make America means to construct oneself. First to make Italy and then to make oneself: the self constructed by this historical ritual is the subject of Italian American literary history.

1. Making Little Italy

This story begins in the Risorgimento, a vast Hegelian epic energetically composed by many an articulate Italian, from Leopardi through Cavour and Mazzini — right down to the moment of triumph, when Massimo d'Azeglio announced, "We have made Italy, now we must make Italians."[2] The Risorgimento had constructed Italy on a specifically Hegelian plan as a unitary Subject, a State that could speak with a single voice. The makers of Italy expected this Subject to create for itself, as it were retroactively, the numerous subjects whose collective it had forestalled by coming into existence thus prematurely — precisely on the promise that it would, as soon as possible, bring these creatures into existence.

If the project sounds elaborate, then perhaps it is worth reflecting that the enterprise in question is as intricately *theoretical* as it is bottomlessly *Italian*. Political discourse in Italy persistently — one might say, systematically — displays a weakness for theoretical speculation. Even the most practical Italian enterprises frequently foreground the subtleties of abstraction that give them shape. The ritual recurrence of circular buildings and square piazzas, of curlicues and pyramids, remind one that Italy is the country of Pythagoras, Fibonacci, Leonardo, and Galileo. In Italy, a plan of the nature of things, even something as bleakly abstract as the mathematical physics of perspective, has often served to adorn the rituals of daily life. Much Italian culture displays a real relish for imaginary projects. The tower of Pisa that was built atilt, the concrete monolith dome of the Pantheon, the diminishing stairway in the lobby of the Laurenziana — any one of these exhibitions of *constructed* reality can serve as a signifier for *Italian* reality. The New World itself, with its roots sunk equally deep in Renaissance astronomy and Renaissance banking, bore many of the telltale signs belonging to a theoretical project of the Florentines: Florentines mapped out many of its presuppositions during the Quattrocento and Florentines supported it before the King of Spain, seeing in it, no doubt, an undertaking certain to require vast lucrative syndicates of lending. Of all such Italian schemes, the Risorgimento shows the deepest measures of self-conscious deliberation and articulate ambition, beginning with a theory and concluding, after the better part of a century, with a practical result. In this case the result was an entirely new Italy.

This newly constructed country features in European chronicles as the very archetype of an historical achievement. In its moment of glorious fulfillment, Unified Italy appeared more splendid than anyone had quite dared to imagine. Victorian journalism never had a more perfect newpaper hero to celebrate than Giuseppe Garibaldi, whose glistening brow adorned the front pages as if he were some preternatural survivor of Troy at last arriving home.

The orgies of confetti and parades that accompanied Garibaldi's entrance into capital after capital provided programmatic liberals in the two worlds with the most unabashed military victory they would, perhaps, ever come to taste. On the morning after the consummation, however, the new arrangement of Italy turned out to have requirements rather more severe than most people had calculated in advance.

The first requirement was that Italians remake themselves according to the same theoretical model which had produced the new country. To this end, a unit modality became the practical philosophy of culture in Italy. Railroads, factories, armed services, national anthems, pompous monuments, articulated ministries in labyrinthine marble palaces, national coinage, national banks, national language: all such projects flowed out from and back into the project of making Italians.

Italians as subjects must tend to a unit modality — in order, so it seemed, to justify the unitary character of the Hegelian State, which turned out to be not only something unprecedented in Italy but also something whose demands were unremitting. Before the Risorgimento's success, *Italian* had named, above all other things, a *divided* subject. Italy had not known Italy. Italy had disagreed with Itself. Such themes, indeed, frequently sounded in the laments of the early Risorgimento, echoing the famous German definition of *Italy* as a geographical expression. But after the victory of the movement, *Italy* became the name of a new Subject, whose unitary character moved itself by means of high industrial machines concealed inside its shapely stone torso. *Italian* now became the label on a whole series of styles that were marketed as national — styles in music, clothing, food, seduction, war, finance, dance. What had thrived for centuries as a diverse collection of provinces, each with its ancient history still aglow on some altar in the heart of town, now stepped onto the high street of the world as a carriage-trade emporium — not only a world-class pasta factory, but purveyor of equestrian statuary to heads of state both far and near, warehouse of mustachioed headwaiters, and, in sum, a cornucopia *di lusso.* Resurrected Italy, a hundred thirty years later, looks to have been the first Argentina in Europe — not just a nation, but a nation representing itself globally as variations upon an ideological theme, a tango palace of Platonic ideas and ambitious capitalists, where sopranos and violinists danced by the light of the moon.[3] The spectacle of this new Italy representing Itself to Itself *as* Itself has left behind some astonishing deposits on an almost geological scale. From the Museo Napoleonico (commemorating the beginning of the process), one looks out across the Ponte Umberto I at the turn-of-the-century Palazzo di Giustizia, one billion tons of vermiculated marble standing on the river bank. Goethe had been able to look down the via del Corso from the Piazza del Popolo and to make out, down there in the vanishing point, the ghosts of umbrella pines and cypresses above the Roman Forum. The triumphant Risorgimento erected there its wall across the prospect, the Victor Emmanuel monument that rises implacable and Northern and white against the smoky travertine and roseate stucco of Piazza Venezia. In these pompous exaggerations, the meaning of *Italian* announces itself insistent and unitary. Think of the trumpets in *Aida*. Think of the parade of elephants. This concentrated motive, this brazen shower of noise, sounded out the message of United Italy. In the echo of that brass choir, one began to hear the voice of Little Italy.

The second requirement of Italia Unita was the creation of Little Italy. Italy needed an Other. At the theoretical level, this need flowed from the nature of the first requirement. Little Italy collected everything Italian that unified Italy could not unify. As a consequence, the Kingdom of Italy produced Little Italy by a reflexive subjectivity steadily projecting into the world the firm image of its own blind spot. In that place arises the subject of Italian American literary history.

The process began in practical difficulties. The Hegelians would say that Little Italy as a subject began with an absolute, irremediable rift in the unitary state. Simply put, there was not enough to go around. New Italy was an expensive innovation, requiring steady investment in industry, in roads and railroads, and in national organization. There remained neither money nor space nor life-chances enough to accommodate the vast populations who now possessed the right to carry an Italian passport. The ancient peoples of the peninsula had lived for centuries in the territories of the old kingdoms and principalities that Italy had now superseded. After unification, these peoples became too numerous, too poor, too insistent, too troublesome for the new nation to deal with successfully.

Out of what Italy could not manage, it fashioned the rough matter of its emigration. Out of their systematic expulsion, Italy fashioned the program of Little Italy: in the United States, *Little Italy* meant a captive market of eternal exiles, who could neither enter the order of English America nor return to

Italy.[4] The Little Italian identity fed upon a narrow and insistent diet of ideological themes including flags, songs, royal images, processions, statues of Columbus, and, above all, the notion of Italian literary history as the guarantor of Italian identity.[5]

All such items, of course, drastically changed their meaning when they entered the ambient of Anglo-American language and literary history. These Italian themes did not become nonsense precisely, because their genealogy was too long and the unitary drive of the Italian state by then too effectively triumphant, but they did acquire a new and astonishingly self-diminishing identity. *Little Italy was not only little by definition, but it was always getting smaller.* It recited its patriotic poems, it recited its Dante, it published its Italian language journals,[6] all to a sense of wide and growing incomprehension in its posterity. In literary history, Little Italy has had two favorite themes: its own nostalgia, and its own death. These themes have been sounded from a lofty Italian perch by such commentators as Mario Soldati and Giuseppe Prezzolini, and they have more recently inspired the gloomy Italian American sociology of assimilation[7] as well as the straightforward elegies of poets like Lawrence Ferlinghetti:

The Old Italians Dying

For years the old Italians have been dying
all over America
For years the old Italians in faded felt hats
have been sunning themselves and dying
You have seen them on the benches
in the park in Washington Square
the old Italians in their black high button shoes
the old men in their old felt fedoras
                with stained hatbands
have been dying and dying
                day by day
You have seen them
every day in Washington Square San Francisco
the slow bell
tolls in the morning

in the Church of Peter & Paul
in the marzipan church on the plaza
toward ten in the morning the slow bell tolls
in the towers of Peter & Paul
and the old men who are still alive
sit sunning themselves in a row
on the wood benches in the park
and watch the processions in and out
funerals in the morning
weddings in the afternoon
slow bell in the morning Fast bell at noon
In one door out the other
the old men sit there in their hats
and watch the coming & going
You have seen them
the ones who feed the pigeons
                cutting the stale bread
                with their thumbs & penknives
the ones with old pocketwatches
the old ones with gnarled hands
                                and wild eyebrows
the ones with the baggy pants
                        with both belt & suspenders
the grappa drinkers with teeth like corn
the Piemontesi the Genovesi the Siciliani
                        smelling of garlic and pepperonis
the ones who loved Mussolini
the old fascists
the ones who loved Garibaldi
the old anarchists reading *L'Umanità Nova*
the ones who loved Sacco and Vanzetti
They are almost all gone now
They are sitting and waiting their turn
and sunning themselves in front of the church
over the doors of which is inscribed
a phrase which would seem to be unfinished

66

from Dante's *Paradiso*
about the glory of the One
                    who moves everything...
The old men are waiting
for it to be finished
for their glorious sentence on earth
                    to be finished
the slow bell tolls & tolls
. . . .
The old Italians with lapstrake faces
are hauled out of hearses
by the paid pallbearers
in mafioso mourning coats & dark glasses
The old dead men are hauled out
in their black coffins like small skiffs
They enter the true church
for the first time in many years
            in these carved black boats
                    ready to be ferried over
The priests scurry about
            as if to cast off the lines
The other old men
                    still alive on the benches
watch it all with their hats on
You have seen them sitting there
waiting for the bocci ball to stop rolling
waiting for the bell
                    to stop tolling & tolling

for the slow bell
                    to be finished tolling
telling the unfinished *Paradiso* story
as seen in an unfinished phrase
                    on the face of a church
as seen in a fisherman's face
in a black boat without sails

67

making his final haul (147-150).

The unfinished phrase on the church, concerning the glory of the One who moves everything, opens the first terzina of the *Paradiso*:

> La gloria di colui che tutto move
> per l'universo penetra, e risplende
> in una parte più e meno altrove (1975: 3).

> The glory of the one who moves everything
> penetrates the universe, and shines
> in one part more and less elsewhere.

Ferlinghetti's old men who loved Garibaldi, Sacco and Vanzetti, even Mussolini, sit on their benches sunning themselves. They need sunlight, because they live in that part of the universe where the glory of the one who moves everything *shines less brightly*. By proverbial courtesy, *La gloria di colui che tutto move* shines its face upon the hills of sunny Italy rather than those of San Francisco. Captains of ideology would insist upon this distinction. Only Italian sun had this spiritual authority. Italian wine had a divine genealogy not available in California (until recently). Indeed, Arturo Toscanini once called California *Italy without the soul*,[8] a phrase that precisely renders the economy of light which Ferlinghetti maps in his poem. Little Italy loses its soul to nostalgia and to the fear of its own diminution and desolation. The geography of relative darkness, carefully laid down by Dante Alighieri, became the world geography of that same theoretical Italy whose foundations he had established.

Here we encounter, in purest form, the rule-observing character of a theoretical culture. Post-Risorgimento Italians venturing into any Little Italy around the world have carried with them canons of entitlement elaborated and re-elaborated continuously in Rome almost since the dawn of writing. In this archive, all roads lead away from the Eternal City. The well-trained Italian literary historian, arriving in the provinces for a long political exile, would unfurl his scrolls of relative prestige and begin to survey the landscape of his desolation. Giuseppe Prezzolini played this part for many a long year at the Paterno Library of Columbia University's Casa Italiana, built with the contributions of Italian Americans. Prezzolini did not hesitate to scorn the immigrant poets for their presumption in loving Dante, as well as for the impoverished voice that they gave to this love.

"In his baggage, the immigrant had brought along some Literature," Prezzolini once wrote. His sentence, in Italian, lands firmly on the word *letteratura*, a complex notion that in such critical usage signifies not primary texts alone but the whole society that sustains the copying and reading of books. *Letteratura* means *the world of letters* — a large institutional complex reproducing itself in the written form of its own history. Its history is its *myth*. The Myth of Italian Literature has always had deep power in Italy, never more so than during the Risorgimento, a revolution made by poets more than by guerrillas or diplomats — though both of these have claimed the glory in England and America, where the heroism of poets tends to sell at a heavy discount.

Letteratura, then, like all myths recapitulates a social liturgy, whose rituals include both texts and the adepts of texts. In Italian, these rituals celebrate Priesthood and Exclusion. They do not particularly care to dramatize the shoemaker who writes odes or the carpenter who composes verse tragedies. Immigrants carrying *letteratura* to some degree appear Objects of Suspicion to members of that Priesthood. For Priests of *Letteratura*, these book-brandishing immigrants resemble dismissed servants seen carrying elegant lamps.

"The immigrant had brought some Literature," Prezzolini wrote, let us say, with superb condescension. Why *condescension*? The passage continues as follows: "When the poor fellow tried to express things he may have been feeling, but certainly did not know how to express, then he could but repeat things he had been reading." Prezzolini here summarily convicts the Little Italian of the capital crime of living in a colony. Everything in a colony is secondary. Everything is susceptible to the penetrating scorn of the city slicker Futurist. "Incredible!," the Futurist exclaims, "when one actually *looks* at the poetry — the versification, rather — produced by the migration, incredible how little one finds of reality, of freshness, even of sincere expression." At this point in his paragraph, Prezzolini appears to pause and look around the shelves of the splendid library. For then he adds: "There are tens and tens of these slim volumes, every one of them 'Privately Printed for the Author.' The literary tragedy stings nearly more than the social one."[9]

Prezzolini was a sublime example of the type, but in fact the literary history of Little Italy sparkles with his sort of radioactive diamond from the high streets of capital Italy. One thinks of Count Luigi Palma di Cesnola, who filled the Metropolitan Museum of Art with pricey *antichità*. Or, a century later, with a similar panache, Luigi Ballerini conducted at New York University a fifteen-year vaudeville starring featured players from the art gallery circuit of the Pianura Padana.[10] In the metropolitan centers of the Americas, such fragments of imported light have always promised, and sometimes delivered, to Little Italians a steady bleach of reflected sunshine, a memory of what the real thing might be. Even as Little Italians spiral down the darkening whirlpool of terminal nostalgia, they continue to batten on CDs of Luciano Pavarotti singing *Fenesta vascia* and on twenty-five-dollar dishes of *penne alla vodka* at make-believe-Milano-ristoranti in the upper sixties. Their reminiscences of Imaginary Italy fall into the same shadow of lesser glory where we find Ferlinghetti's old Italians, still reading *L'Umanità Nova* and still in love with Garibaldi.

In a similar moment of darkness, the history of the State Italy first opens its eyes, in the first lines of Giacomo Leopardi's allegorical poem *All'Italia*:

> O patria mia, vedo le mura e gli archi
> e le colonne e i simulacri e l'erme
> torri degli avi nostri,
> ma la gloria non lo vedo, non vedo il lauro e il ferro
> ond'eran carchi
> i nostri padri antichi (3).

> O my country, I see the walls and the arches
> and the columns and statues and the solitary
> towers of our ancestors,
> but I do not see the glory, I do not see the laurel
> and the iron with which our ancient fathers were laden.

The reminiscence of a splendor that is no more — a frequent theme in English Romantic poetry, where it often figures as a sunlit childhood — in Italy expressed itself as this more precisely outlined object of political desire: *la gloria*. *La gloria* resembles a transcendental imaginary in its effect, but the poet means by it rather the *prior incarnation* of such an imaginary. The sometimes-subtle difference between these two generates that powerful simulacrity which characterizes the best Italian art, its sense of conforming-with-a-difference to some ideal notion of itself.[11] A similar echo characterizes both the artifact Italy of the Hegelians and the artifact Little Italy of the Little Italians.

The Leopardian and the Dantesque darkness of Italian California sun — this is where Ferlinghetti lays down a line that follows how Italy has constructed the subject of Italian American literary history, which is expected to remain indefinitely in the dim dungeon of a paralyzed imaginary. If Little Italy were a state and if it had a seal, one might write on it the line — *I love but I do not see, Amo ma non vedo.*

Dana Gioia's poems specifically place this scarcity of light in the landscape of Italy itself as the Little Italian sees it. In a garden in the campagna, he says, "The sundial stands perpetually in shade." In a poem that follows the journey and the arrival of an Italian American woman in Italy, Gioia concludes with a dream:

> ... you are also in another room
> finishing a letter in a language
> you don't understand, your dark hair pulled
> back loosely in a bun, and the crucifix
> you bring everywhere set upon the desk
> like a photograph from home.
>   Long ago,
> had someone told you this would happen,
> you would have thought then only of escape
> of returning to yourself. Instead you feel calm,
> relaxing in this dying body
> like a swimmer on a sunlit beach, and death,
> the light you cannot look directly into, seems
> as illuminating and warm.
>   Now the hand, your hand,
> is sealing up the envelope, and you turn to face
> an old man in a dark-red uniform.
> He nods. You speak affectionately.
> And word by word the language too becomes
> familiar. But still you wonder,
> who is he? Husband? Servant? Ancient friend?

Too late. He takes the envelope and leaves.

The door has closed and from outside you hear
his footsteps fade into the murmuring
of swallows in the eaves.
                            Where do they come from?
Why can't you see them from the window?
No use to look. There's only this blue patch
of sky and endlessly empty afternoon,
where the light is fading.
                         Close your eyes. Accept
that some things must remain invisible.
Somewhere in the valley a grey fox
is moving through the underbrush. Old men
are harvesting the grapes. And the dark swallows
you cannot see are circling in the sunlight
slowly gliding downward in the valley
as if the light would last forever (249-250).

This poem sharply satirizess the Little Italian dream of Tourist Italia — the *Belpaese* itself complete with living relatives — as the prison of a constricted vision. In this vision, the Little Italian woman revisits Italy in the spirit of a box of candy returning to the factory. The door has closed. She cannot see the birds. The letter speaks a language she cannot understand. The envelope is sealed. Gioia has written: "If Italian-American poetry can be said to exist as a meaningful part of American literature, it is only as a transitional category." That is, he supposes that only the original immigrant connection to Italianità is a real one:

> ... each new generation of Italian-Americans finds its cultural links with the old country more tenuous. As Little Italys disappear and families move to the suburbs, mainstream America gradually transforms their original ethnic identity. If a third-generation Italian-American speaks Italian, he or she usually learned it not in the kitchen but in college.[12]

Gioia's argument proceeds with consistency from this ontology of nostalgia: the only living approach to Italy, for him, passes through the gate of Little Italy — receding ever further into the disappearing distance.

Such a position flows irresistibly out of the process of reflection that produced Little Italy to begin with. In the traditional narrative of Italian diffusion, Rome stands at the center, *fons et origo*, of all authority, *mater et caput ecclesiarum*, and diffuses its essence first upon itself and afterwards upon the terrestrial globe, *urbi et orbi*. So long as Little Italy constructs itself in conformity with this ancient tax-gatherers' map, it will see nothing in the prospect but its own diminution.

2. *Making Italy Little*

Rome, however, no longer so firmly can teach the world's Italians how to live or what to think. Now Rome must listen as well as speak. Its Little Italians, planted in five continents, have planted generations of their own, generations that have achieved substantial new lives unimagined in the days when their independent histories began.

Surprises occur when a world diffusion matures. For one thing, its original arrangement of centers and peripheries may no longer hold. The most notorious example of such a transformation comes from the history of Rome itself. The Emperor Constantine, born at York in the island of Great Britain, moved the capital of empire from Italy to Byzantium in Turkey, facing the mainland of Asia across the Straits of the Bosphorus. A very cosmopolitan story: to such a man as Constantine, the world chart looked very different than it could have done to a contemporary of Julius Caesar. Even Caesar himself can hardly be imagined to have anticipated such a displacement of "Roman" authority. Or, to choose a more recent case, one may reasonably doubt that George III or his minister Lord North expected the political center of the English-speaking world ever to remove itself to the banks of the Potomac River. Little more than a century later, however, Yeats was observing that "the centre cannot hold" (211-212),[13] as the world entered that large-scale rearrangement of powers which has proven to be the heaviest burden of the European and North American twentieth centuries. The center of Italian culture in the contemporary world has not so much moved itself as it has entered a new period of global diffusion.

Networks of telegraph cable, rail, steam, automobile, and air communication in the century after the Risorgimento have successfully placed Italian centers of population at wide intervals throughout the entire Europeanized world. While Rome may still serve as an emotional capital for these centers, its desires and images no longer command the slavish reflection that once they did. Indeed, Italian images find it hard to capture even the attention, much less the obedience, of the Italian Americans.[14] At any given point in contemporary time, Italian Americans will most of them be unable to name either the head of state or the head of government in Italy. Very few will know the name or the tune — we can forget about the words — of the Italian national anthem. Umbertine Little Italy is dead. Even the Made in Italy Little Italy of the 1960s and 1970s is dead. Now Little Italy has changed its mode of existence.

The Italian global network has begun to carry not only transmissions from Rome but also the truths of its reflected realities back from the otherworld of the Americas and onto the high streets of towns that were old when Brutus was young.

Little Italy has become a world condition, and one may watch *The Godfather* with a sense of local urgency in Hong Kong almost as readily as in New York or Istanbul. But nowhere has Little Italy begun to leave its mark so visibly on everything as in Italy itself. Every aspect of Little Italy reproduces. It is a gloss on the houses in Cosenza and a triumph on the faces of successful *impiegati dello stato* (government workers) in Taranto. Gloss, glitter, inflation, the spread of restaurants, and the plague of cars: all these explosions of *benessere* (consumer confidence) blot the Italian landscape like scatter bombs out of a dirigible bearing the legend F. W. Woolworth painted on the sides in letters fifty feet high and picked out in little blinking red lights. In Italy, the taste for American luxury is so great that the uncrowned King of Italy Gianni Agnelli maintains a huge apartment on Park Avenue where his wife, the Principessa Caracciolo, spends much of her time and does much of her shopping. In Italy, too, the word *America* more often than not suggests murky and enviable cousins somewhere near Schenectady or Pittsburg, California. We may compare the subtle presence of Little Italy in Italy with such other well-known American phenomena as the appearance of Pepsi Cola in Minsk, of blue jeans in Beijing, and of Disneyland in Paris. But Little Italy by now is far more than an export entity. Rather, it is deeply established in the production of reality in Italy.

In Italy one meets Italian American dancers like Heather Parisi on television and Italian American writers Nat Scamacca on the island of Sicily. More than that, however, one comes to recognize the very nature of Little Italy itself as a sign. Little Italy has outlived its history as a reflected image. *In the new age, Little Italy can be anywhere.*

The narrator of *Astoria* (Viscusi 1995) indeed sees Little Italy as the central, the persistent, Italian reality. For him Astoria, a Little Italy in North Queens, turns out to be brighter than sunshine and older than Rome. An Italian American looking for his historical center, he seeks the real Italy as if he were following the trail of a great secret. He follows the clues it leaves, and this becomes a long *percorso*, an imaginary journey through European history, starting with the tomb of Napoleon and tumbling backwards in time, ending in the Foro Romano. What is he looking for? He seeks everywhere the secret of Italian identity.

In the end, he discovers that the world capital of Italy *for him* is not Rome or Milan or even the caves in Campania but Astoria, which he finds reflected in Paris and in Rome. This American Little Italy has for him become the capital of every possible Italy. It has a magic, an originality, that he tries to explain by saying that it is where his mother grew up. His mother's parents were among those who had made Astoria into a complete Little Italy. And in Rome, reflecting upon these immigrant grandparents, he writes, "They travelled tighter than they knew":

They brought all the ghosts with them to New York. Their graves — go see them in Long Island, in Westchester — are rippling like oiled muscles. They have stabbed themselves into the lawn like daggers the size of the silver Chrysler Building with the hook-beaked eagles at the corners. And they give off their polluted light, you can't escape it, you go blind with it on the Tappan Zee Bridge. No, they didn't mean to do this. They meant to fade into the fescue like fodder, just as the gospel advises, but they didn't know how, they had no acid, America had no acid, powerful enough for that. For they had become everything Italy was supposed to be, but without the choking rubble and godawful mess that in Italy always reminds you how long a ruler you need to measure a lie, they became the subterranean Italy of the etymological dictionary with its toes in India and its cock laid out across Greece like a slender marble salami, with a pair of eyes blinking away the sunrise water of New York Harbor as they looked about at the raw new fury, dignified as they were by all they had either almost been or never been, it didn't matter which, and sanctified by having had to leave it behind, and, further, endowed with the prestige of martyrdom by having lost America, first discovered by them, before arriving in it, so that they were from the start great gods and filthy crucified beggars all at once, and was it any wonder that when they died America suddenly became for me what Italy had been for them, impossibly full of preposession? — and that Rome, after I had wandered in it half a year, revealed itself to me as plain as a glass of water in Springfield, Illinois? There was no Italy here any more. Not that great Italy of the double-dealing pope and the suicidal opera house. They had taken it away and made it better and planted it like a dogwood tree in Valhalla. Compared with that glistening mystery I knew as a boy and put in the ground with my mother, this, this Rome, this old welfare-distribution-center, smelled of oaktag and binder's glue. If this is Italy, I thought, I must be an Italian (294-295).

He comes to this conclusion, as it were, independent of consular realities. He does not get a new passport. He is already Italian. He ends his narrative by proposing to commemorate Astoria with a huge monument on the Gianicolo.

Why does it deserve a monument? His grandparents and their coevals had reproduced in their immigrant world the entire system of *italianità* with a completeness rarely if ever met with in Italy itself. And his discovery goes beyond any personal attempt to make sense of a personal inheritance. Indeed, it implies a globalization of the regional principles upon which Italian literary history has always been constructed, according to Carlo Dionisotti.[15] Italian literature has many tributary centers, Agrigento to San Zenone, and many tributaries of language, Albania to Zurigo. In the modern world, Italian literary history has deployed an endless variety of languages, most of them related to Latin at some distance. Even English has a filial tie to the language of the Romans (Viscusi 1988). Italian literature has also been written in every continent of the world. Consequently, when Italian Americans write about Little Italy in English, what they produce will find deep and intricate formal parallels throughout the formidable archive of Italian literary history.

In saying as much, one refers not only to the past, as Dionisotti outlines it, but in a very material way to the present and the forseeable future. The rapidity of change during the present century, the fluidity of travel and of juxtaposition that grow in influence with each passing season — such developments have changed by now not only the world of Italian emigrants but the world of Italy itself.

There are deep material changes. The global marketing scheme that the migration once supported and institutionalized has now found multicultural markets and has entered the general stream of simulacra, so that Italia Unita, which used to stand at the center of its own imaginary empire, now struggles to hold up its head at the conference tables of the European Community. Such a change implies also great alterations in the equations of relative value between itself and places that used to derive most of their authority by presenting themselves as its faithful reflections. Italy has diminished in pretense. Little Italy has come over it like a possessing spirit. Italy has had to face sharp limitations upon its imaginary projections. Questions of national debt and of rampant inflation have begun to leave more effect upon national prestige than any medieval roll-call of illustrious ancestors or any Alitalia sigla on the tail fin of the Papal Boeing. Completely to understand the transformation, one must reflect that the spread of near-instantaneous electronic communications has made tables of organization flatter for *every* world system, whether this system belongs to a large multinational corporation or to a large Mediterranean peninsula that has maintained a positive balance in the world labor exchange for most of the past hundred and twenty years.

In this new arrangement, Italy no longer pretends to offer itself as the origin of light. Indeed, Italians in the contemporary cosmpolis tend, if anything, to exaggerate the unimportance of their own metropolitan centers. And, like many another empire in receivership these days, the successor governments to Mussolini's have left the marketing of light to the victorious Americans.

Thus, without serious hindrance, Little Italy projects itself into the world on an American light, as if it were a celluloid of Martin Scorsese's. Though American light sometimes actually employs a machine, it more frequently employs an articulate point of view because it does not originate in a technology, nor even in so grand a material object as a nation. Rather, American light flows from that older American device, the transcendental Self. This absolute luminescence does not only make movie stars (De Niro, Stallone, Shire), but it also continues, as always before in America, to make poetry. It radiates throughout the work of Diane Di Prima:

every man/every woman carries a firmament inside
& the stars in it are not the stars in the sky

w/out imagination there is no memory
w/out imagination there is no sensation
w/out imagination there is no will, desire

history is a living weapon in yr hand
& you have imagined it, it is thus that you
"find out for yourself"
history is the dream of what can be, it is
the relation between things in a continuum

of imagination...
(...)
the war that matters is the war against the imagination
all others are subsumed in it

the ultimate famine is the starvation
of the imagination

it is death to be sure, but the undead
seek to inhabit someone else's world

THE ONLY WAR THAT MATTERS IS
            THE WAR AGAINST THE IMAGINATION
THE ONLY WAR THAT MATTERS IS
            THE WAR AGAINST THE IMAGINATION
THE ONLY WAR THAT MATTERS IS
            THE WAR AGAINST THE IMAGINATION

ALL OTHER WARS ARE SUBSUMED IN IT
(...)

intellectus means "light of the mind"

it is not discourse it is not even language
the inner sun

the *polis* is constructed around the sun
the fire is central (154-155).

This sun shines with an equal briilliance everywhere. Di Prima evokes the interior firmament — *fare l'America* with a vengeance. Such making of America summons the image of Vespucci naming someone else's old world his new one, and it summons the Emersonian desperation of self-construction. It invokes primal light, the dawn of a new eye. If such an invocation is possible, then the old economy of nostalgia no longer prevails, and it becomes possible to construct new maps, maps whose centers have distributed themselves almost indifferently across the landscape.[16]

In such a world, Little Italy may appear anywhere. It may shine as reflection in Italy, as when Madonna Ciccone comes on tour wearing brass underwear, infuriating the priests enough to turn their Sunday sermons into unpaid advertisements for "Blonde Ambition." Or Little Italy may construct itself as a shattered mirror — the name of a set of hopeless contradictions. Here is Rose Romano, a poem called "Mutt Bitch." She opens describing the desperation of an imaginary subject constructed inside an alien rhetoric:

It's not easy being an angry poet
when you come from a culture
whose most profound statement of anger
is silence.
No one knows

what you're talking about.
No what knows
what your problem is.
No one believes you.
A poem needs a lot of explaining
but refuses to do it itself.
It expects the culture
to back it up.

If I have no culture
I can say nothing;
therefore, if I say nothing
I have no culture.

Then she explains the construction of her enclosure, a long string of noncommunicating internal differences:

I'm Neapolitan
on my father's side,
Sicilian on my
mother's side.
After my mother died,
when I was eight years
old, my mother's people
slowly faded away.
I grew up
in a Neapolitan family,
always silently
defending Sicilians.
(Sicilians were
my sainted mother.)
If I misbehaved
or did something
stupid, it was because
I'm Sicilian.
I don't remember
ever doing anything
that got me called
Italian. I grew up
thinking Naples
is in Northern Italy.

Sicilians don't want
me, either.
The few words

of Italian I know
are all Neapolitan.
I'm not serious
enough. I'm not
oppressed enough. I
haven't been conquered
enough. I'm not Olive
 enough. I may as well be
Italian. Don't say
Neapolitan — say
Italian. Remember
the Renaissance. Remember
how Italy saved Europe
by inventing art
and science. (Don't say
Florence.) But my guts —
what do I do with my guts?

Non-Italians don't know
what I'm talking about.
They think I'm weird.
They think the only
difference, if
there is any, between
Italians and Sicilians
is that, unlike Italians
(who aren't too bright,
either), Sicilians make pizza
the way morons make
wheels.

So much for that problem.
Now, maybe I've had
some inconveniences
as an Italian,
but if I changed

my name, dropped
the vowel, the barriers
would fall with it.
I'd have nothing
to lose.
If I ever felt
lonely, I could
go to the supermarket
and fill my cart
with cans of
spaghetti and meatballs
and no one would
suspect a thing.
Maybe it's time to take inventory.
I'm a woman.
I'm a contessa
on my father's side,
a contadina on my
mother's side.
I've got a high school equivalency diploma
and an associate's degree
in liberal arts.
I'm a skilled blue collar worker.
I'm a published poet.
I've got a Brooklyn accent
with Italian gestures.
I'm a dyke.
I'm a single working mother.
All this stuff doesn't add up to
just
one
person.

Fuck it (37-39).

Geografia e storia della letteratura italiana: Romano uses her inheritance of Italian regional divisions just as Italian poets, d'Arezzo to Zanzotto, have always done. Romano makes her decentered force-field the constructive principle of an identity that must remain divided against itself: the childhood war between her Sicilian and Neapolitan families predicts and reflects the difficulties she faces as a woman. Exiled into the lesbian community, she finds that Italians do not get there the moral credit that belongs to the oppressed. An accomplished poet, she finds herself stigmatized for having an associate's degree and a G. E. D. "All this stuff doesn't add up to just one person."

Romano takes what might have been her membership in Little Italy and renders it as a displaced sense of self. No unitary subject now survives, except in advertising or in dreams, not even the diminutive refraction of the lucidly little. Instead, Romano paints her position as the inevitable slippage between one blank icon and another. This passage has become the place of the Italian American subject, always in motion, always refusing to add up — and always exporting itself, like so many other American cultural products, wherever it goes.

We are likely to see the creation of some Little Italy, some intricacy of passages, everywhere the Little Italian takes this scene of slippage. The opera gives way to the movies. Allegorical subjects of Verdian will — the very voice of the collective Risorgimento shouting and gesturing its way onto the stage of European history — have fallen silent, or have subsided into the Limbo of advertising. The automobile rolls along in the California hills. The heavy parade of Hegelian elephants yields to a single quiet voice, perhaps, trying to strike a single inner balance. Mario Pietralunga, an Italian poet teaching film in Sacramento, concocts a set of equivalences that leave behind forever the problematic of operatic and unitary subjects, and of their reflections, losing the very notion of reflection, which disappears into the alternative sense of starting all over again:

Autostrade

Luce californiana
che mi sorprende qui
vicino a Sarzana
in uno slargo grande

83

ferito dall'autostrada
come là nella valle
di Davis e poi Fairfield
prima della salita
che va verso la baia,
e in certe mattine
a una simile ora
la luce d'allora
veniva da piane emiliane
con dei pioppi, gaggiai
e sensazioni improvvise
in cui s'annullava
la geografia dell'esilio
e che mi dava
un'altrettanta
perfezione di ora
sia pur nella fugace
fissità di momenti.

Highways

The California light
that seizes me here
near Sarzana
in a wide sweep
slashed by the highway
just as there in the valley
of Davis and Fairfield
before the ascent
that turns toward the bay.
and in certain mornings
at a similar hour
the light of then
came from the plains
of Emilia, my land

with poplars, acacias
and sudden sensations
of vast breathings,
of spatial perfection
in which vanished
the geography of exile
leaving an equivalent
perfection of the hour
even in the fleeting
fixity of moments (108-109).

While the equivalence claims nothing more than its "fleeting fixity of moments," the claim remains large. Like Rose Romano's demotic ramble, this reflective murmur insists upon constructing something that, whatever its mildnesses and its deficiencies, nonetheless can lay a claim to originality, to centrality, of a highly qualified and self-contradictory variety. Little Italy: a California light that is not empty, not darkening, not exactly first but not exactly second either, a light in which, he says, the geography of exile vanishes.

What replaces it? A geography of new makings. Little Italy ends by replacing Italy. Little Italy — transportable, reversible, and perhaps only accidentally Italian — so differs from any familiar vision of the New World that the best way to think of it is as a perpetually varying reflection, an economy of shadows — what Marina La Palma calls, in the title of a poem, a "Permanent Analogy":

The tides, full of the pull of
our own forces, sometimes coincide.
Each interior as a monologue
opening up into wide mesas above steep
cliffs, each adjective clinging firmly
to the proverbial noun.
Amid and despite "the tenderness and enthusiasm
of the human race," where would all your friends
align themselves, the web that you think
sustains you, if a blow to the head
should render you a vegetable?

But this is not what I wanted to talk about
(Between the authoritative totality
of French culture and the
boisterous polyvalences of Italian culture
I'm always in a sort of Swiss proximity.)
I meant to discuss Ragged Dick, child hero,
the eponymous orphan inside each of us.

What can we learn if we "take
the annual homicide figures in a given society
as the most comprehensive index of the degree
to which the State holds
the monopoly of violence there"?
How our fortunes open and close
like fans

in the cities of our making, our fate?

Tell me, have you ever been alone,
really alone, or lonely, hungry,
afraid somewhere... Pick a continent,
any one will do for this purpose: Admitting
"the permanent analogy of things."

But don't let me get maudlin, all right?
I was just asking. Because it matters (121-122).

Little Italy as a world message: "Pick a continent, any one will do." Little Italy as a secondary culture (not French, not Italian, but sort of "in a Swiss proximity") has achieved in this moment — and for this moment only, no doubt — the peculiar glory of seeming to offer a universal gloss, a "permanent analogy of things." Making this universal gloss means Making Italy Little. The Little Italian accomplishes this feat in the obsessive contemplation of inner dividedness, or, more clearly, by collapsing the distance from a center that, once the divided character arrives in it, no longer even pretends to remember what it used to pretend to do for some so-called peripheral condition. Even in Rome, the world has grown larger, has begun to speak with a more evenly distributed voice, to live on a wider network of messages than before (Viscusi 1993). This network does not sleep. In taking over the world, it has laid down its iron rule: since attention is now global, since there is not much time for any one theme, all messages must grow short, and all possible Italies grow little.

"I meant to discuss Ragged Dick, child hero/eponymous orphan inside each one of us." We can close the meditation on the littleness of Italy with this superbly taut remark. It signifies the end of a certain pretense which used to insist with violence upon the sexual in the national. Ragged Dick resembles mutilated Mussolini. He speaks for a will to pleasure that has failed in its career as a will to power. After the collapse of these pretensions — after, let us say, 1950 or so, when the full grimness of destiny has overtaken the leaders of republican Italy — the history of that country grows absent-minded and vague. Its politicians never seem to make any sense when they talk. Its merchants and artists no longer seem to remember, or to care, where Europe begins or where America leaves off. A universal orphan moves to center stage in all the Italies, little or large, old or new, in Rome or under California sun.

Notes

1. I wish to thank Francesco Loriggio and the students and faculty of the School of Comparative Literary Studies, Carleton University, Ottawa, and the Doctoral Program in English, City University of New York, who heard and usefully discussed parts of this paper during Fall term 1991.
2. This tag frequently arises in discussions of Italian regionalism. See, for example, Frederick Spotts and Theodor Wieser (222).
3. Nicholas Shumway outlines how a national culture constructed on ideological lines has served to obscure and to perpetuate long-standing contradictions in the life of a people.
4. While a great deal has been written about the Italians who *did* return to Italy, no one doubts that they were a distinct minority. The reader should note that the arguments in this paper refer specifically to Italian who migrated to the United States. Italians who migrated to latin America and to Canada in the early twentieth century had a distinct history, in its way equally indebted to the ideological program of Italia Unità, but different enough to require separate treatment.

5. See Kathleen Neils Conzen, David A. Gerber, Ewa Morawska, George E. Pozzetta, Rudolph J. Vecoli (37-62) for a survey of the large field of historical investigations of how the new identity of Italians in America were confected.

6. Pietro Russo of the University of Florence has found more than 3000 titles of Italian-language periodicals published in the United States. His work awaits publication.

7. Mario Soldati, Giuseppe Prezzolini, both observe, as if from a great distance, the powerful energies released in the rituals of nostalgia in Little Italy. Richard D. Alba is constructed upon a cognitive dissonance: even as he evokes the great success of the Italian Immigrants in constrcting a world for their posterity, Alba evokes an elegiac imagery of twilight and disappearance. The disparity between these two narratives, one full of triumph and the other gloomy and guilt-ridden, suggests the persistence of the same cultural complex which gave us such eternal guilt rhapsodies as "Torna a Surriento": "questa terra dell'amore/hai la forza di lasciar?"

8. For the captain of ideology, see Joseph Horowitz. For the remark on California, I have as yet only the hearsay of a colleague, but I am still looking. It certainly *sounds* like Toscanini.

9. "Nel suo bagaglio l'emigrante portava della letteratura: e quando ha tentato di dire quel che forse provava, ma non sapeva dire, non ha fatto che ripeter quel che aveva letto. È incredibile, quando si esamina la poesia, o meglio la versificazione che è nata dall'emigrazione e si è trapiantata in America, sopravvivendo come una ciste, quanta poca realtà, quanta poca novtà e sincerità di espressione si trova. Ci sono decine e decine di questi volumetti, stampate a spese degli autori, che sono una tragedia letteraria quasi più dolente di quella sociale." The reader with little Italian must try to read the translation with rather a heavier sarcasm than I have been able to convey across the language barrier. Indeed, I have gone so far, elsewhere and in Italian, to make a play upon this author's name, using the Italian word for *contempt*, disprezzo. See Viscusi (1991).

10. Highlights of this regime include the unveiling of *pensiero debole* in the conference *The Unperfect Actor*, avant-garde Italian poetry in *The Favorite Malice*, and Italian poetry revisited in *The Disappearing Pheasant* (1991), a conference whose title announced Ballerini's departure from New York, symbolized on the poster by the image of a golden apple full of worms.

11. For a different approach to this phenomenon, see Mario Perniola.

12. Dana Gioia (1991: 3). Gioia's use of the hyphen in the expression "ItalianAmerican" rides across the problematization of this usage that serious critics of this literature, from Lino Papparella to Anthony Tamburri, have been making for the past dozen years. See especially Tamburri.

13. Yeats' "The Second Coming" makes an excellent companion piece to the Treaty of Versailles: "Things fall apart; the centre cannot hold;/Mere anarchy is loosed upon the world,/The blood-dimmed tide is loosed, and everywhere/ the ceremony of innocence is drowned..."

14. This change has led to any number of "important" surveys, such as "L'italiano negli Stati Uniti," a conference at Fordham University in June of 1984 (proceedings in *Il Veltro*, XXX, 1-2, 1986), "Lingua e cultura italiana negli Stati Uniti: la presenza e l'immagine," a conference of the Ministero degli Affari Esteri held in Rome in March/April of 1987 (proceedings in *Il Veltro*, XXXIII, 5-6, 1989). See my analysis of such events in 1991.

15. This is the thesis of Dionisotti, an epochal essay which, for the first time, gives to Italian literary history a structural principle that can be developed in such wise as *to adequate* the actual diversity of the languages and literatures subsumed under the encyclopedid heading *Italian*.

16. When thinking about the relations between historical entities, the concept of rhizome, a plant whose any point can be connected to any other, replaces old images of rooted trees and imperial centers in the cultural theory of Gilles Deleuze and Felix Guattari, enunciated in (1987). In this theory, "America is a special case. Of course it is not immune from domination by trees or the search for roots. This is evident even in the literature, in the quest of a national identity and even for a European ancestry or genealogy (Kerouac going off in search of his ancestors). Nevertheless, everything important that has happened or is happening takes the route of the American rhizome: the beatniks, the underground, bands and gangs, successive lateral offshoots in immediate connection with an outside. American books are different from European books, even when the American sets off in pursuit of trees. The conception of the book is different. *Leaves of Grass*. And directions in America are different: the search for arborscemce and the return to the Old World occur in the East. But there is the rhizomatic West, with its Indians without ancestry, its ever-receding limit, its shifting and displaced frontiers. There is a whole American 'map' in the West, where even the trees form rhizomes. Americ areversed the directions: it put the Orient in the West, as it were precisely in America that the earth came full circle: its West is the edge of the East "(19). This is one account of how the European networks came eventually to overlap so intricately in the "New World" that lines of force started following new and unpredictable paths.

References

Alba, Richard D. *Italian Americans: Into the Twilight of Ethnicity*. Englewood Cliffs, N.J.: Prentice Hall, 1985.

Alighieri, Dante. *Paradiso*. Ed. Charles Singleton. Princeton: Princeton University Press, 1975.

Conzen Neils, Kathleen; Gerber, David A.; Morawska, Ewa; Pozzetta, George, E; Vecoli, Rudolph J. "The Invention of Ethnicity: A Perspective from the U.S.A.' *Altreitalie* (Aprile 1991), 37-62.

Deleuze, Gilles; Guattari, Felix. *A Thousand Plateaus: Capitalism and Schizophrenia*. Trans. Brian Massumi. Minneapolis: University of Minnesota Press.

Dionisotti, Carlo. *Geografia e storia della letteratura italiana*. Torino: Einaudi Editore, 1967.

Di Prima, Diane. "The Only War That Matters Is The War Against The Imagination." In Gardaphé, Giordano, Tamburri, 154-155.

Ferlinghetti, Lawrence. "The Old Italians Dying." In Gardaphé, Giordano, Tamburri, 147-150.

Gardaphé, F.; Giordano, P.; Tamburri, A., eds. *From the Margin: Writings in Italian Americana.* West Lafayette, Indiana: Purdue University Press, 1991.

Gioia, Dana. "The Journey, the Arrival, and the Dream." In Gardaphé, Giordano, Tamburri, 248-250.

——————. "What Is Italian-American Poetry?" *Poetry Pilot,* December 1991.

Horowitz, Joseph. *Understanding Toscanini: How He Became an American Culture-God and Helped Create a New Audience for Old Music.* New York: Alfred A. Knopf, 1987.

La Palma, Marina. "Permanent Analogy." *VIA: Voices In Italian Americana,* I, 1 (1990), 121-122.

La Polla, Garibaldi, M. *The Grand Gennaro.* New York: Vanguard Press, 1935.

Leopardi, Giacomo. *Opere.* Tome 1. Ed. Sergio Solmi. Milano-Napoli: Riccardo Ricciardi, n.d., 3-7.

Perniola, Mario. *La società dei simulacri.* Bologna: Cappelli, 1983.

Pietralunga, Mario. "Autostrade." Trans. Janice Bona Livingstone. *VIA: Voices in Italian Americana,* I, 2 (1990), 108-109.

Prezzolini, Giuseppe. *I trapiantati.* Milano: Longanesi, 1963.

Romano, Rose. "Mutt Bitch." *Vendetta.* San Francisco: malafemmina press, 1990. 37-39.

Shumway, Nicholas. *The Invention of Argentina.* Berkeley: University of California Press, 1991.

Soldati, Mario. *America primo amore.* Milano: Arnoldo Mondadori, 1959 (First edition 1935).

Spotts, Frederick, and Wieser, Theodor. "Regional Devolution and the Problems of the South." *Italy: A Difficult Democracy.* (Cambridge: Cambridge University Press, 1986.

Tamburri, Anthony J. *To Hyphenate or Not to Hyphenate. The Italian/American Writer: An Other American.* Montreal: Guernica, 1991.

Yeats, William Butler. "The Second Coming." *Collected Poems of W. B. Yeats.* London: Macmillan & Co., 1963, pp. 211-212.

Viscusi, Robert. "Coining." *Differentia: Review of Italian Thought,* 2 (Spring 1988), 7-42.

——————. "La letteratura dell'emigrazione italiana negli Stati Uniti." In *La letteratura dell'emigrazione: gli scrittori di lingua italiana nel mondo.* Ed. Jean-Jacques Marchand. Torino: Edizioni della Fondazione Agnelli, 1991, 125-137.

——————. "The Italian Commonwealth." *The Columbus People: 500 Years of Italian Migration to the Americas.* New York: Center for Migration Studies, 1994, 483-490.

——————. *Astoria.* Toronto: Guernica, 1995.

4

Francesco Loriggio

Going South

Notes for a Cultural Portrait of the Immigrant (As a Middle-Aged Academic)[1]

*T*he Africans (Somalians? Eritreans? Senegalese?) at the Termini station stay in bunches in front of the coffeeshops, talking and as if forever waiting for absentee friends to join in. Looking at them in the crepuscular light they reminded me of the first Italian immigrants in Vancouver, back in the 1950s, or the ones I run into on Booth Street here in Ottawa.

Looking at them: they appeared distant, as in a snapshot. Or perhaps it was, again, the embarrassment. My Roman colleague was surprised when I told him I wasn't really that interested in visiting the burgeoning North African quarter around the station. You don't get used to the idea that the "ethnics" may be other people, and not you and some other people. Kept seeing myself with Baedeker and Michelin guide in hand, and still couldn't quite handle it.

This is the first thing that changes once you notice the presence of immigrants in Italy — the usual play of roles. For years and years, tourists *were* our alter egoes. Until up to about the end of the 1970s in Italy there were, ultimately, only them, the Italians, and us, the periodical returnees. A relationship that remained steadily triangular, although the ambivalences it concealed do deserve some recognition in the history of the mores of the century.

Returning gave you the well-earned right — you felt — to observe with some pleasure the linguistic and cultural uneasiness of individuals who elsewhere would probably listen ironically or patronizingly to your father's or your mother's English, or perhaps your own. On the other hand, even for those of us born and raised in Italy the contact with our ex-compatriots was never altogether perfect. You could tell something is amiss by the way hotel representatives in the station always somehow managed to pick you out, among the throng just off the train, as the ones to whom to offer lodging in English, or by the swift, almost imperceptible second or third takes, the slightly delayed looks of appraisal with which taxi drivers or side-walk sellers greeted you. Not to mention the hesitation of friends of friends when confronted by the inflections of your Italian — an Italian too bookish, too grammatically correct, too glaringly deprived of any proximity to everyday street language, an Italian spoken with an accent too delocalized, too revealingly anonymous in a country with over three dozen major dialects and countless minor ones.

The slippage often encouraged a kind of solidarity of the road, identification with those who were, after all, travellers, regardless of the different circumstances. It is there, in Italy, where everybody's vulnerabilities could properly surface, that many of us finally encountered our overseas friends or neighbours.

The triangle, in short, set the parameters of our difference: what we were seeking in Italy was the very loneliness that comes with being neither a total foreigner nor simply a visitor. As a returnee who will continue to be an emigrant, to live abroad, you don't attempt to start the old life anew, so to say, to reinsert yourself into the everyday Italian reality. Labourers or academics, for you Italy is where you temporarily suspend the calendar, where you can experience the past without its encumbrances, as a holiday.

It is a process that simultaneously consents to and resists the lures of the age. Yes, postmodernly, you transfer to the origins attitudes reserved for more paradigmatic, more prestigious or more exotic topographies. No, the climate of the return is festive *and* uncommodifiable. Italy offers you the opportunity to meditate on what you might have been and are not, to ponder on the constant, repressed "if" of your private history, on the hypothetical, subjunctive mood forever pervading your life. Call it narcissistic tourism. But it is also a tourism beyond the Rome-Florence-Venice circuit, the Italy of the Renaissance, of the Western imaginary, of the crowds. Italian emigrants don't come from any of these cities, and if you visit them upon your return, you do it in homage to myths that no matter how much you may want to uphold are still not you, the private you the trip is all about.

After the first two or three trips back, what has attracted me most about Italian society has been the banalities — neighbourhoods that I knew and whose transformations (or mutations) I feel compelled to keep track of, the trattorie, the sea, small hotels, dilapidated villages with no plaques on their buildings, provincial landscapes which have no cachet for travel agencies, those junctures of place and time outside official history where chance might have deposited me and that allow me to be — in some measure, at any rate — actor and spectator, without restrictions or obligations or perhaps even commitments of any kind, take it or leave it...

The African immigrants bring the suitcase back into the picture, put you face to face with the fragility of your holiday. I look at them, and I am thrust into a different, external time, as if the spatial and temporal gap the return fashioned for me, into which I venture ghost-like in each occasion, were suddenly itself absorbed into the great juggernaut of things.

The embarrassment at Termini and later: it stems, I realize now, from a sense of unpreparedness, history catching you off guard, asking you a question and you being unable to answer, at least in a satisfactory manner (satisfactory to yourself, even before history).

How to start? The only way we know is by comparing stories. The immigrants in Italy are now writing about their arrival. The Italians are likewise now acknowledging them as permanent presences in the peninsula. Our own narratives — *our* first step in the now larger panorama — will take some major rearranging: mere updating won't quite serve. Going down the Italian South, on the train, the landscape is a big sprawling, many-layered hallway, a chronotope with time warps and space fluctuations, the terminal to end all terminals. If destiny is destination, if where you are, where you're coming from and where you're heading to is what you are (where your head is), in the 1990s the emigrant-tourist-Narcissus returns to a pond which has grown larger and larger, deeper and deeper, and which will grow enormous as he or she once again departs from it.

In the tales my grandparents used to tell me as a child — legends of raids up the coast, of Norman counts building the castle on top of the hill, of fiesty bishops in battle against everyone else, of chivalrous and very learned emirs — Africans were *i Saraceni*. I interpret the emphasis on religion as a dividing line to indicate that the South is a place where colour is less relevant, where you're dealing, not with opposites, but with subtle gradations of skin. Every time I go down to the town in which I was born the associations pile up: anecdotes about the inhabitants of villages where they still speak demotic Greek; descriptions of the dressing habits of people in the Albanian enclaves near by; the high-pitched wailing sounds of Southern women singing or the decisive incidence of percussion instruments in Southern Italian folk music; the Phoenician colonies before and after the Punic Wars (Hannibal crossed the Alps with over fifty thousand men, who eluded the Romans for many years, long enough to intermarry); the pre-historic migrations from the Caucasian regions towards the coastal countries; Southern, Mediterrenean Italy as *limen*, as the land of passage, of transition, from the Greco-Roman era to the Middle Ages to now, Western Europe jutting towards Africa and Asia.

It's what makes the quasi-North America that you encounter even in typically Italian surroundings, and that sometimes is in the air like the smell of McDonald fries, nothing more than a recent version of European *trompe l'oeil*. Rather than New York's Central Station, the closest parallel to Termini is the Roman forum, a few miles down Via Nazionale, with its reminiscences of Augustan or Christian mixture. And it sediments — this Mediterranean space-time — onto the other now wider and more complex network of relationships. The African immigrants are our link to Italy and to the post-colonial world, as we are theirs to Italy. They who are now where we could not stay, in those places which are receding from the immediacy of our everyday life, who here have other things to worry about than us. We who are now only beginning, in North America, to grasp the implications of the switch from the adjective "Black" to the double adjective "African American."

Going down South, for the umpteenth visit to the town where I was born, I keep wondering if we figure at all in the African immigrants' stories, or how we might figure in them (are we the allusions they appeal to in their conversations with the Italians, as they point out that Italy was until the 1970s a land who sent its people out in the world?). I keep thinking at how in North America for a long time Italian immigrants didn't notice African Americans or Canadians of African descent, just shaded them into the background (they were American citizens or British subjects, spoke English, had been there longer than we had). I argue mentally with the vague resentment I sometimes detect in Italians when I tell them that I haven't given up on the Europe I carry within me but that what for them is a ball and chain, a negative possibility, is a biographical necessity for us. (They state: "We must not lose our last chance to become part of this continent because of the South," and mean: "What will the Germans or the French say?")

Early North American urban planners assigned the university to a specific locality, far from the madding crowd, quite aside from the hustle and bustle of the city. They endowed it with an ecology verging on the picturesque or the pastoral (trees, lawns, surroundings more or less "natural"). In this, urbanists were merely acting upon on solicitations that were entrenched in Western culture.

All things considered, the best analogue for the university is still the one insinuated by its monastic topography, the one with the Church. The two spaces host activities whose focus of attention pertains to "other" worlds, to worlds that reveal themselves textually and can be envisioned only through interpretation or analysis. Moreover, their histories have continuously interlocked: monks were the intellectuals of the Middle Ages; up to the eigthteenth century it was not uncommon for intellectuals to be ordained into the ministry.

What is interesting perhaps about the analogy in the late twentieth century is the intricacy of the tangencies it evokes. It's not solely the fundamentalists within America, or conservative scholars, who have pushed for the separateness of knowledge and history. Careers of various and/or contrasting disciplinary propensity intermingle.

In literature, for example, the split you expect when you try to grant secularization its due purchase isn't so complete as it might seem at first. For a Dante and Boccaccio theology and the theological defined the height of art, the poetical sublime. The writer who in the mid-nineteenth century sits at the edge of modernism — and is thus also utmostly serious about his vocation — may no longer suffer from the pangs from Christian faith, may have to contend with *ennui* — a capital sin for the likes of Dante — but has a soul which constantly beckons to be taken "out of this world" (Baudelaire 1961a: 303). Similarly beyond the pale, beyond the quotidian, untractable here and now, was the classical Parnassus or, even more, its successor, the Republic of Letters that so often kindled the pre-modern and pre-modernistic secular mind. Fiction too, like the numinous immensities of religion, needs its sanctuaries, earthly, professionalized enclosures that expound on it, communicate with it.

Nor is literature — poetry, fiction, theatre — a special case. In the era of immanence, when the relation with religion changes from one of co-operation to one tension, the intellighentsia as a group does little more than translate the older glossary, the older categories and adapt them to secularized realities. Among the pivotal mythogemes of the times, the *éxperience des limites* so influentially parlayed by a Nietzsche or a Bataille and so fervently pursued by avant-garde movements is designed as a *via negativa*, an upside down theology. The gotha of the humanities teems with philosophers, theorists and critics who either had training in theology (Hegel, Kierkegaard, Heidegger) or were ex-ministers (Northrop Frye) or converts (Gabriel Marcel, Marshal McLuhan) or sympathizers of religion (George Steiner). And their striving or penchant for other-worldliness is surprisingly compatible with that of their estranged cousins, the scientist who, as the title of Thomas Nagel's book on the philosophy of science and scientific method would have it, aims for "a view from nowhere," outside latitude and longitude.

The current debate about the university here in North America is in some fundamental way about this inheritance. For some (serious critics, as well as mass culture and popular journalism) the university no longer has any autonomy. Campus life is going downhill because the teachers have lost sight of their original purpose, because they have politicized themselves, have turned to advocacy, abandoning their arms-length stance towards the larger space, the public sphere. For others (serious critics, as well as mass culture and popular journalism), the coin-operated machine for the professionalization of thinking that the university is produces primarily trained incapacities. Academics are too sheltered from the "out there" and, hence, are unlearned about it, are unable to deal with practical issues in general (the professor is always absent-minded). Or, when they are experienced, they don't know how to talk about the world in language comprehensible to their next door neighbour or to the ordinary person in the street (the professor is always a jargon-laden specialist).

In this controversy over space and the deployment of the metaphors it encourages, "ethnic" academics have their own role to play. Like all intellectuals, they have to grapple with their specific corporate dilemma: how to defend the campus as the site of knowledge, as an egalitarian domain, without detaching it from other sites, without making it unworldly; how to conduct unhindered inquiry well aware that ivory tower distance condemns you to irrelevance and obsolescence, and indeed distorts your intention or your mandate. But as individuals who have also a stake in a particular, minoritarian piece of the national, collective "out there," "ethnic" academics perhaps better than anyone else can remind the various interested parties that *all* the components of the identi-kit of the university are agreed-upon illusions, that, however necessary, the suspension of historical situatedness, the positing of a place from which understanding occurs or where knowledge resides is a trick of the trade.

Whether or not the university is a state apparatus in the Gramscian and Althusserian formulation (let's not forget that the flow of knowledge has its sources, that academia has its capitals, and these — be they Paris or Berlin or London or Berkeley or Oxford or Harvard or MIT — add an international dimension to the geographical contours, which further compromises the relations between campus and society), it *is* permeable to the state and its parameters. At every level. Contrary to some of its secular antecedents — the academies of earlier centuries — the university can't compel faculty members or students to assume pseudonyms, can't impose ciphered anonymity. Contrary to its religious counterparts, it can't stop temporal powers at its doors. In places such as the U.S.A. or Canada, even the usage of English or French as the language of knowledge, the very item which announces the secularized nature of the university, betrays the campus' long-standing connivance with history. On the separation between knowledge and state or knowledge and the public sphere the Middle Ages were much more coherent than we have been. As the language of liturgy and the language of scholars, Latin was sufficiently dissevered from any of the European vernaculars, could act as the non-contingent vehicular language of the age. The search for a non-historical, universal vocabulary has been a mainstay of European culture (on this see Eco), and it testifies both to the symmetries, the affinities between the university and the Church, and to the ancientness of the concern over the political bias of everyday speech.

Thus from an "ethnic" perspective both camps in the debate about the location of culture seek a perfection which is impossible, and therefore is inevitably ideological, partisan. At some stage or other, calls for a strong autonomy of the campus vis-à-vis society dovetail into a heads-I-win-tails-you-lose kind of strategy. The most rigid of barriers would still be permeable to language, which comes with a certain, specific past behind it — the past of majority groups — and hence preserves some privilege. As for the proponents of a university more responsibly attentive to societal developments, how many of them would support laws declaring the U.S.A. officially a multilingual or a multicultural country? For that matter, how many of them would support faculty boards that did away with the label "foreign" in referring to the language departments (usually departments of German or Italian or Spanish or Hebrew or Japanese, etcetera) and with the distinction between those departments and departments of English (or, here in Canada, departments of English and French)?

In this sense, "ethnic" academics are the purveyors of imperfection. Total, irrevocable imperfection. The faces in Giovanni's Snack Bar, all riveted on the transmission from the San Siro Stadium in Milan when I went to pick up the Italian newspapers this morning, what are they to me? I know most of those people, with some I play soccer Sunday mornings, but what are they to me intellectually, now that I am in my office? The knowledge of the historical character of knowledge — *our* knowledge — is, here where we are, unanchored knowledge, perhaps even abstract knowledge. Having to constantly remind others about history leaves scarce room for positive, participatory intervention. Italian-Canadians emerge into a plot-line that is already well advanced when they come into the picture. Both within or outside the university, attempts to re-orient the future of that narrative through the politics of identity appear more and more quixotic, more and more utopian. In the inhibiting atmosphere of the 1990s, even to suggest that Institutes of Canadian Studies might do well to reflect the demographic multiplicity of the country, rather than the two-nation view of Canada, and ask for input from departments of German or Italian or Spanish or Japanese, besides departments of English and departments of French, is to indulge in Divisiveness, the Culture of Complaint or the Discourse of Victimization.

And so, as tales by and about bearers of bad news, "ethnic" accounts of the debate about the university must become private before they can become public again. Those who do sign these accounts must be prudent enough to declare that their intention is silence, that they speak from a desire for silence. In traditional iconography Hell was very strictly sectioned and Heaven without regions. If your job is to explain that culture has often prescribed and marketed varieties of that Heaven for fear that it might otherwise actually duplicate the "hellish" plurality of everyday life, or that abolishing the borders between the university and society will still leave residues, spaces for which the borders will still obtain, you have, in our day and times, gone beyond words. Everything you say will be strident or petulant, or both. But for this reason, too, silence itself is really not an "ethnic" option. While it would safeguard the connections "ethnic" intellectuals enjoy with the campus, while it would keep at their disposal the profession's most cherished assets (objectivity, irony), it would demand of them that they let others — from Paris, Oxford, Harvard, the English or French departments — speak for them. And that would not only perpetuate the schizophrenia. It would deprive "ethnic" intellectuals of their last and most secret counter-hope. For although Purgatory, like Heaven and Hell, would also not be a good metaphor for the twentieth century (no salvation will await you at the end of pluralism, there is no end), in telling your story, convoluted and self-reflexive as it may be, you automatically consign to it some sort of purgative function.

Types of critical temperament. Gayatry Chakravorty Spivak:

> Within the historical frame of exploration, colonization, and decolonization — what is being effectively reclaimed is a series of regulative political concepts, the *supposedly* authoritative narrative of whose production was written elsewhere, in the social formations of Western Europe. They are thus being reclaimed, indeed claimed, as concept metaphors for which no historically adequate referent may be advanced from post-colonial space... A concept metaphor without an adequate referent may be called a catachresis by the definitions of classical rhetoric. These claims to catachreses as foundations also make post-coloniality a deconstructive case... Claiming catachreses from a space that one cannot not want to inhabit and yet must criticize is... the deconstructive predicament of the post-colonial (60, 64).

Catachresis and deconstruction as the grin-and-bear-it, the stiff-upper-lip approach to criticism. You stipulate the unavoidability of certain concept metaphors and you critique their use. But how are we to understand the "cannot" in Spivak's passage? If you must "criticize" the space you inhabit you cannot fully want to inhabit it. And if an element of necessity is also present, in what fashion is catachresizing a less ideological exercise than the "pathetic" dramatizations of victimage or the assertions of identity Spivak rejects in her work (63)? How much less emotion does it entail, given that it is a "predicament"? And in any event, if vigilance is the premium deconstruction accords post-colonial criticism (58), why is *it* permitted to escape examination? Could worrying about showing too much pathos not itself be a cultural tic?

With Italian-Americana, the ambivalence towards ethnicity and identity registers somewhat less obliquely. Here is the Frank Lentricchia of the early 1980s:

> [W]hen I write, I'm aware, at some level — not always, but intermittently — that I'm writing from a position as a critic who is not in a typical position in the American academy. That fact sometimes weighs heavily upon me. I can't say that it's shaped all of my work: if you read some of my early stuff you'll see no relationship with my Italian-American working-class background. But these days, I have to say that one of the things I'm aware of is that I'm not a gentleman scholar. And, especially in my last two books, this has made me wary of theories of literature that avoid the kinds of differences you can't avoid.

> I think it's very easy to become sentimental about what I'm talking about, and that's one of the reasons why I don't talk about it very much. I feel impelled to write an autobiographical essay once in a while about this stuff, and I've always held back, because I fear this goddamm sentimentality about it. There are many negative things I could tell you about my background, about being an Italian-American. It's not wonderful, in many ways; but it's real to me, it's how I came into the world; and I can't help but see these differences in people, in writers. What I'm working on right now depends very heavily on making such differences count, not in the so-called background of a writer — as if the text had some sort of identity which we could accept as an autonomous thing — but in the foreground. If that means not talking about literature as literature, well, for me that's just fine (182-183).

The best rejoinder to both Spivak and Lentricchia is a line from a poem by the Italian-Canadian poet Pier Giorgio Di Cicco:

> Life is one foolishness or another. Sentimentality is

choosing (1986: 14).

Di Cicco clearly benefits from a licence that the century has not made available to essayists and critics. Can pathos be assumed? In a context in which coolness and stoicism have been and continue to be the most valued directives, effusiveness (be it historicized, of the Italian-American sort, or not) may very well offer a writer opportunities for tonal and other deviations. But Di Cicco's lines are instructive on other grounds too. Modernity is not just liberation from the passions. Heidegger: "Dasein is always disclosed moodwise" (173). Being-there manifests itself as fear, dread: it is that which you are within and you cannot detach yourself, take your distance from. Or see Bakhtin:

> An event can be described only participately... Everything that I have to do with is given to me in an emotional-volitional tone, for everything is given to me as a constituent moment of the event in which I am participating (1993: 32-33).

You become emotional about whatever it is that affects you, that you invest in, identify with, or on whose instigations you act (anything: even irony and science, even deconstruction!).

Within twentieth-century criticism, sentimentality wasn't an explicitly viable alternative before the last decade or so. The second implied clause of Di Cicco's syllogism — not only that choosing is sentimental but that you can choose to be sentimental — recapitulates *ante-litteram* the ethical resonance of the current performative penchant of critical writing. In particular, the frequent recourse to narrative forms of presentation or, still more evidently, the addition of autobiographical markers to the usual cogitativeness have personalized the scholarly essay. And perhaps the entire phenomenon has to be seen in line with the considerations Richard Rorty has been voicing recently — that criticism works best when, like some literature, it attends less to foundations and/or irony and more to the "sentimental education" of its readers. When it recognizes its many spaces and "participates." When its writers write as specialists *and* as citizens.

The voyage is our myth, the myth from which, as immigrants or descendants of immigrants, we have to start. It's not easy. Allusions to exile, migrancy (not emigration, interestingly enough), and nomadism have become too frequent and prominent in recent critical vocabulary, and too burdened with symbolic valences: when they come up in an argument, the sheer sequentiality of the syntax seems to install you always but a step away from some "transgression" or "postmodernity" or "poststructuralism," which refer to adjacent but different concerns.

We need to distinguish between the various types of travel, between adventure, exploration, tourism, emigration, wandering, and their significance for literature or for our idea of what the century is or has been. We need to take a second look at the phenomenology of voyaging (by moving in space, objects and persons are no longer sensorially there) and at the many variables of voyaging: distance (is the journey inter- or intra-cultural?); direction (are you leaving or returning; does the voyage contemplate a return?); site of departure (it is one thing to go from Paris to Algiers and another to go from Algiers to Paris); duration (is the voyaging terminable or interminable, a one-time affair or repetitive and obsessive?); role and motive of the voyager (are all the other features of voyaging decided upon by the person doing the journey? Does the perception that the voyager has of the voyage remain constant throughout, or does it change?). Finally — of paramount urgency for criticism — we need to discriminate between the various discursive usages of the voyage, between those allusions in which the voyage is a metaphor and those allusions which are more strictly referential.

Both the meaning of a voyage and its historical or critical attractiveness depend on the way these and other variables combine. Recent glorifications of nomadism in intellectual circles, for instance, expand on the anti-domesticity inherent to that form of travel, the unrestrained, a-directional, on-the-road freedom it promises. Nomadic drifting updates in neo-Romantic garb, by intertextual linkage with the hitherto primarily "exotic" environments (the desert and the steppe are the core spaces this voyage celebrates), the prestige of adventure, of ad-ventura: the individual it posits is a bit knight errand, a bit *picaro*, a bit wandering Jew.

At the same time, quite apart from the new post-colonialist (and perhaps neo-Orientalist?) background, the major promoters and philosophical sponsors of nomadism, Gilles Deleuze and Félix Guattari, endow the usual genealogy of adventure with one crucial twist. What counts, they say (588, 619), is not actually being nomadic, but *devenir* nomadic, becoming it (or minoritarian or ethnic or gay or female). So that, technically speaking, once nomadism is transformed into an attitude, a state of mind (in this particular case, a refusal of bordered statalism, of linear thinking), you don't even have to budge from your living room or your study (602).

This is something more complex than the nautical metaphors ancient or medieval literature employed to describe itself, and by which a lyric poem was a short navigation for which a small boat would suffice, while the epic, a genre of the high seas, required greater tonnage and heavier sails. Here, within the European literary and cultural tradition, the antecedents of the nomads of Deleuze's and Guattari's *Milles plateaux* are Blake's mental travellers (who can conjure up "such dreadful things/As cold earth wanderers never knew," 475) and, more directly, Baudelaire's "vrai voyageurs," who leave shore "sans vapeur et sans voile" and plunge "au fond de l'Inconnu... pour trouver du nouveau" (1961a: 155 ff.). That is, the adepti of the imagination — writers, artists. Much as, in the very period Blake and Baudelaire lived, producers of fictions had supplanted priests as the supreme cognizers and confidants of the spiritual realm, of the Word, they also replace the soldiers, explorers and departees, the category which traditionally spawns a culture's heroes. By incorporating secular adventure into the notion of literature, by redefining travel, Blake and Baudelaire contribute to the story of the artist its most patently epic chapter. In the shrinking world that humanity has inherited, only the literary or artistic work, "Le Voyage" painstakingly cautions, can cure the ennui non-fictional travelling now arouses, can furnish the sensations physical voyage once provided.

That Deleuze and Guattari enlarge Baudelaire's and Blake's move does not exempt them from its limitations. In the late twentieth century, anyone capable of properly interiorizing can enjoy the advantages of the sedentary profession, can "become" nomadic. And this acknowledges the social impact of the rise of writers and artists as public figures, as a professional group, and the cultural prerogatives of the texts or the entities (the worlds, the characters) they produce. High, canonic modernity historicizes ancient and medieval nautical metaphors. A master trope of literature, the mental journey occurs in an abstract dimension but is as real as any actual journey since it defines the activity of an extremely influential professional group, whose creations shape the everyday world.

Is it enough to offset the aristocratic, elitistic —however epochal — discomfort that underlies "Le Voyage," the malaise which is at one with — and probably derives from —Baudelaire's traumatic and equally epochal encounter with mass society, his realization that the crowd fills the streets of modernity? In Deleuze and Guattari, too, an exaggerated overestimation of the powers of art rebounds quickly off an exaggerated underestimation of the value of experience. On what basis are Deleuze and Guattari authorized to believe that armchair nomadism will yield anything but home truths? That staying in the metropolis will put them in touch with "l'Inconnu," and not with the metropolis' processed, pre-cooked version of it? And what about the millions in Baudelaire's time and in Deleuze's and Guattari's time who never get to the armchair, never *become* but *are* nomads or minoritarians, and are thereby constrained to first order travel and experience? Who will tell their story? And how is it to be told?

The mental meanderings of intellectuals often end in self-validation, with a profession confronting Otherness only to assimilate it and replicate it in its own guise, to whitewash it out of the way.

And this doesn't hold merely for the postmodernist phase of modernity, for nomadism. The most common type of travel of modernist intellectuals is directional, albeit ambiguously so. You go from New England or the Mid-West to the more "cultured," less parochial Britain, France and Italy, or from some metropolitan environment to places embodying the archaic, or, as often, to both refinement and innocence (Italy for some British travellers encompassed Ariel and Caliban, the Renaissance and Mediterranean primitiveness). A departure which is a return, a return which is a departure. Whereas nomadic zig-zagging operates on a hidden forward-looking agenda (the one whim Deleuze's and Guattari's or Baudelaire's immobile voyagers cannot satisfy is the retracing of steps — going back, memory), modernist travellers leave home so that they may recover, in one single gesture, the cultural past and the historical present. By going to Paris or to Florence or Venice the American Lost Generation rediscovered Villon or Dante or the *Quattrocento* but — as important literarily — it re-envisaged and re-learned the America it had left behind. American everyday speech was never as perfectly rendered as in the pages of Gertrude Stein and Hemingway, American history relives furiously in Pound's poetry.

The ambiguity of Baudelaire's voyaging is that — strangely, for someone who balked at physical travel — its concealed, future-oriented, and to some extent emancipatory, motion, its boot-straps approach to cultural production relies on pre-Copernican notions of geography: in the mind, you reach the Columns of Hercules and you dive "dans le gouffre," you're off the known world. The flatness of Deleuze's and Guattari's world is deliberate, judging by the metaphorical pre-eminence they confer on the desert and the steppes, yet no less troublesome. The planet the two philosophers depict is too solid, too unbendable. When it gets to the liquid portion of the world, their panegyric of the "espace lisse," of smooth space, disregards altogether the quality of greatest historical salience. From the Renaissance on, the seas and the oceans have been, cosmographically, the domain by which and through which to uncover and map the earth's volume, its sphericity, its circularity.

Modernist ambivalence, thus, might have been better ministered to than it has been. The aim of a Yeats, or a T.S. Eliot, or a Pound is not revelation — the "nouveau" as absolute, ahistorical, non-terrestrial "Inconnu" — but relative novelty. And that goal can be achieved mundanely, by rummaging within this world. In modernist writing newness is to oldness as difference is to same. You don't have to invent *ex nihilo*, seer-like. All you have to do is to establish your perspective by incongruity, in the phrase of Kenneth Burke, to cross some border or recollect some past, and let the distance or the culture of the elsewhere or of the period you are eliciting or are in contact with impinge on your private here and now. In the Europe of the teens or the twenties, Japanese etches, African masks, twelfth-century troubadour poetry, Giotto, any non-Western or Western archaicness, are "new" or can provoke newness. And so are American or British mores reconstructed by the expatriate who has travelled to another land in order to be able to return home mentally.

It is the lesson twentieth-century hermeneutics has been trying to teach. There is novelty anytime the continuity of a tradition is interrupted, and re-trieval, interpretation or re-interpretation become necessary. The answer to Baudelaire's image of the writer is the verse which, not long after Baudelaire,

Rimbaud has his drunken, nomadic boat pronounce, "je regrette l'Europe aux anciens parapets" (69). During modernism, T.S. Eliot's critical dictum — that what we know is Homer or Dante or Shakespeare (1953: 21) — or the first line of "East Coker" — "In my beginning is my end" (1974: 196) — proclaim with still unsurpassed trenchancy the inevitability of the *nostos* (which is also the only aspect, probably, today that atones for the otherwise too emphatic Eurocentricism of his notion of literature, or of the "we" that runs through his argument about the relation of tradition and individual talent).

Geographically and, if you accept that sort of metaphorizing, culturally or personally, you proceed as the geographers would recommend: you set out, and if you continue with the appropriate stubborness you'll reach the place from which you started. Internal and external, mnemonic and actual, the space modernists quest for or endeavour to recover is ambiguous in that it can be uncanny. Where you have already been to, when you return to it, will be unfamiliar, *unheimlich*, Freud intimated in his famous essay (368 ff.), and Freud, we know, was a connaisseur of geography: the psyche has borders, rules of passage, a protagonist — psychic energy — that sallies forth, is pushed back, escapes by detour, surreptitiously. Novelty in the developmental history psychoanalysis and turn-of-the-century anthropology devised is a consequence of space-time, of the anachronism of any return. The gigantic Hellenistic statues that the paintings of the Greek-born Italian artist Giorgio De Chirico put next to draftmen's tools and other twentieth-century paraphernalia are pensive and fragile, or, like the muses that the same painter alludes to in some of his titles, *inquiete*.

Emigrant travel can contain but not fully embrace modernist or postmodernist aspirations. In the Southern Italy of the postwar decades, I remember, you went first of all to *l'America*, if you could (Australia, also a major geographical destination, had no mythical allure: it was a second pick). Within America, you went either to Buenos Aires or to New York (or, better, *Nuova* York), which covered, respectively, everything from Mexico down and everything from Mexico up. However much you ambled in the two continents or whatever else your destination may have been, those were the two fixed lights, the shorthand metonymic labels. And immigrant nostalgia, too, obviously, is unrequited, although not necessarily uncanny. But the travel of emigrants differs from other types of travel already in its form. It has a trajectory and it culminates in re-settlement.

Emigrants erect the distance between present and past, the disynchrony which dooms their return to failure. The long pause which follows their departure, which precedes any return, temporary or permanent, has a finality that expatriates or exiles or explorers or pilgrims or tourists or other voyagers don't know. The question of dwelling haunts emigrants from start to finish. They leave one land to escape the burden of living conditions, and when they get there, living, fitting in — in its many facets: psychological, sociological, anthropological, existential — is still the concern that epitomizes their story. Emigrants experience the modern crisis of *habitare* head on and at an accelerated pace. In a few short years, they have to learn how to in-habit the new land, how to co-habit with people of another culture, how to collage together an habitation, a new habitus for themselves, how to cope with the even faster mutating habits of their children. Always dwelling and building, dwelling and building. They travel — basically — to construction sites, to places which have space for new houses (the protagonists of some of the early classical Italian-American novels, works such as *Wait Until Spring, Bandini* or *Christ in Concrete*, are bricklayers). Whereas, curiously, nomads or well-travelled cosmopolitans, who are constantly on the road, plod on undaunted and unaffected, manage to salvage their selves, and can be said to move about in order to protect that inner "I," to be everywhere as if they were at home, the migratory journey would not be complete without the struggle with metamorphosis. The reluctance to change usually chided to Little Italies or Chinatowns is itself a symptom of change; it is a supplement of reflexivity unneeded in Italy or in China.

This is why, you surmise, emigration has never actually made it as a trope, as a metaphor for the century's cultural aspirations. Emigrants are the clichés of the century. Not abducted like slaves, nor banned out of a territory like refugees, nor condemned to a land, like the convicts who founded some of the British colonies, they hover between choice and non-choice. They depart of their own free will, but only apparently. Necessity (the other side of circumstance, which locates emigrants in an underdeveloped, unacceptable environment to start with) is as much a "cause" as desire (America and its surrogates, the last historical, worldly paragon of social equity). As well, the voyage and the process of re-inhabitation take place on a collective scale: immigrant settling — and the voyage leading to it — is done, by the wagonload, the trainload or the shipload, in massive numbers and for the group. Who goes with the dandy or the writer as he or she sets forth towards the unknown? Reduced transiency, reduced freedom, lack of sublimity (even the democratic sublimity that the imploded metaphorical space of Deleuze and Guattari encourages, the sublimity whereby all and sundry can "become" nomads) — the difficulty with emigration is thus that it can't partake of the romance of the Book which literary, professionalized travel has helped compile, that it is travel whose epilogue is not the Book. "Silence, exile, and cunning," Stephen Daedalus' program (Joyce 247), the experience of total absence, is the nightmare emigrants would like to wake up from.

From here in Canada the Italian South is recapitulated for me, these days, by bits of two poems, one written by Pier Paolo Pasolini, the other by Franco Costabile.

In strophes shaped in the form of a cross, Pasolini's text tells the story of Ali Blue Eyes and the thousands of "tiny-bodied men/with eyes of wretched dogs" who sail with him from Algiers and land on the Calabrian coast, "clad in Asian/rags and American shirts." They are greeted by their Calabrian counterparts, who will join them and then move with them up the peninsula and throughout the world "carrying the seed of Ancient History." The last lines of the poem read as follows:

> e prima di giungere a Parigi
> per insegnare la gioia di vivere,
> prima di giungere a Londra
> per insegnare ad essere liberi,
> prima di giungere a New York,
> per insegnare come si è fratelli
> — distruggeranno Roma
> e sulle rovine
> deporranno il germe
> della Storia Antica.

Poi col Papa e ogni sacramento
andranno su come zingari
verso nord-ovest
con le bandiere rosse
di Trotsky al vento... (1965: 493).

...and before arriving in Paris
to teach the joy of living,
before arriving in London
to teach how to be free,
before arriving in New York,
to teach how to be brothers
— they will destroy Rome
and upon its ruins
they will sow the seed
of Ancient History.
Then with the Pope and all the sacraments
they will hasten like gypsies
to the north-west
with the red banners
of Trotsky in the wind... (1991: 99).

The lines by Costabile are from a poem entitled "Canto dei nuovi emigranti" ("Song of the new emigrants"):

Cancellateci dall'esattoria
Dai municipi
dai registri
dai calamai
della nascita

Levateci

Scioglieteci
dai lemoni
dai salti

del pescespada.
Allontanateci da Palmi e da Gioia.

Noi
vivi
Noi
morti (19).

Erase us from the books of the collector's office
From city halls
from the registers
from the inkwells
that record our birth

Remove us

Untie us
from the lemon trees
from the leaps
of the swordfish.
Take us away from Palmi and from Gioia.

We
the living
we
the dead. (My translation)

Pasolini published his vision of Mediterrenean post-colonialism, in the early 1960s, at a time when Western intellectuals still believed in the revolutionary potential of the Third World and in the emancipatory prospects of Third-Worldism as a position (the poem is entitled "Prophecy"). For us, Pasolini's posterity, the vision is only half-right, and it touches us with all its flaws, as poignantly as predictions for which we might have wished a better future sometimes can, but it does properly forecast an aspect of postmodern society often overlooked or minimized: that the plurality and/or mixture of cultures is also a plurality and/or mixture of temporalities. For Pasolini the advent of

Post-History presupposes the resurgence of Ancient History, that which the West had placed before or outside historical time. Costabile's poem points to the internal dynamics of one of these temporalities. Why are emigrants here "living" and "dead"? And how does their death-in-life relate to the "birth" of the earlier lines or to the references to erasure and to writing and its institutional sites?

The immigrant narrative of loss and recovery here summons correspondences that are not just "literary" or "poetic" in the usual meaning of these terms. In Costabile's text the words "living" and "dead" hark back to a culture which has maintained a profoundly ritualized approach to death and funeral practices. With the women in black of traditional iconography, go professional grievers, the unusual importance of cemeteries in the topographical economy. It is an experience of death and dying which history has, in its own fashion, corroborated, or even enhanced. As the novelist Corrado Alvaro, used to put it, Southern cities have been perennially "in fuga" ("in flight," quoted in Teti 14). Their citizens have been accustomed to — have made a custom of — departure and absence. In Southern Italian folklore (see De Martino 78), to go to another world is to go to *the* other world. By leaving you dis-appear, you no longer appear to those who stay behind, just as they dis-appear to you. A vanishing act.

In Costabile's poem, like in Southern culture as such, what offsets the effect of dying is the artifact. Down South it was still quite common, in the 1960s, to see photos of migrated relatives next to the photos of dead relatives. The request of the collective voice in Costabile's poem is therefore an extreme one: erasure from writing is final, irrevocable erasure, and by invoking it you express the full extent of your desperation.

The ancientness, the folkloric reminiscences are, it goes without saying, only falsely inactual. Italian anthropologists (especially Ernesto De Martino) have been quick to establish parallels between the role Costabile's poem attributes to writing and traditional or contemporary Western thought. As conveyor of death and life, of absence and of memory, as a reminder of that which has passed away and that which ought not to be forgotten, culture constitutes for emigration the working through of the fear of disappearance that all travellers must overcome. Like mourning, it de-erases by re-enacting the erasure. Heideggerrian *angst* meets with the Viconian intuition that culture is always monumental, both a necrologism and a celebration, both elegy and eulogy.

Without re-settlement — and the process of cultural memorization, of cultural inscription that accompanies it —emigrant travel would remain apocalyptical, protracted, unsalvageable non-being, the equivalent (personal and collective) of the end of history. In an age which has often been too euphoric about travel, which has plastified and sanitized dislocation, Southern emigration reinstates the moment of risk. However you look at it, as an earlier form of travel to be recuperated historically or as a particular form of contemporary travel, it stands for the view that if you are at home everywhere you go, you haven't gone anywhere, that to journey you must walk the wire, submit to the delicate interplay of resistance and metamorphosis, which may jam and drag you down anytime.

Inscription and invention: both, rather than either/or. To inscribe you must create; when you invent you are inscribing. This is the gloss I would append to the historiography or the literary criticism or the anthropology which thinks that it has sidestepped the problems that ethnicity or race or gender pose by insisting on their constructed nature (see Hobsbawm, Sollors). When it comes to identity or literature, invention doesn't free you from constraints. No mind is a *tabula rasa*, and Vico's exhortation to consider "memory... the same as the imagination" (313) could be readapted to read "the imagination is the same as memory." Particularly when you have insufficient written, official history.

The advantage of the notion of inscription is that it puts more emphasis on the "why," on the pragmatics, of cultural memory than on the "how," on the form. Any text that circulates can inscribe, naive or sophisticated, bestseller or avantgarde, fictional or non-fictional, in any genre and in any style (literary criticism is one of the most efficient modes of inscription: it renders a text public). The conclusion of Vico's passage on memory states:

> Memory thus has three different aspects: memory when it remembers things, imagination when it alters or imitates them, and invention when it gives them a new turn or puts them into proper arrangement and relationship, For these reasons the theological poets called Memory the mother of the Muses (313-314).

Inscription is language at its mediatic degree zero, performing its most minimal function: language that fixes on paper, records and transmits both spatially and temporally, a memorandum from (a past, another person, another place) and a memorandum for (future or other-oriented memory). Vico, again: "The poets must therefore have been the first historians of the nations" (314). Except that poets don't simply come before historiographers. Literature works better as history than history books because it cannot be corrected, because it inscribes as fiction. The Father's impatient, emotional explanation of his and his family's desire to be dramatized to the Director in Pirandello's *Sei personaggi in cerca d'autore* (a play about inscription, if ever there was one!) is precisely that characters in plays do not change, that "anyone fortunate enough to be born a character can laugh at death." When all is said and done, texts inscribe a "what" — characters, events, stories. Already postmodern experiments in self-reflection and the autonomy of the signifier are going the way of the many "portraits of the artist" of earlier decades, present themselves as a theme, a content, as part of the history of the condition of literature or of the writer in the twentieth century.

The need to inscribe is the need to emerge. Or to re-emerge. And it arises as a response to some break — or some feeling of impending break — in the historical continuity from which important ingredients of selfhood derive. This is, as far as I can see, the function of the many Italian-American or Italian-Canadian texts which deal with the passing away of relatives or parents or ancestor figures, of the genealogical *topos* in Italian-American or Italian-Canadian literature.

Lawrence Ferlinghetti's poem, "The Old Italians Are Dying," sets the tone for a good number of the contributions in the most recent anthology of Italian-American literature (*From the Margin*, edited by Fred Gardaphé, Paul Giordano and Anthony Tamburri). Images of Italians-Americans wandering aimlessly and balefully, like last survivors, in neighbourhoods they can no longer (or no longer know how to) inhabit, commemorations of youthful friends, or fathers and mothers, or grandfathers and grandmothers, intimations of mortality in middle-aged speakers or their children recur over and over again in the other fiction and poetry of this collection (see the contributions of Tony Canzoneri or Diane Di Prima, Felix Stefanile, Maria Mazziotti Gillian, Joseph Tusiani). Scenes of funeral wakes have an important structural function in such classics of Italian-Americana as Pietro Di Donato's *Christ in*

Concrete and John Fante's *Dago Red* or in such classics-to-be as *Mac* and *A Bronx Tale*, the 1992 and 1993 films by, respectively, John Turturro and Robert De Niro. One of Coppola's more remarkable strokes of genius in *Godfather I* is his decision to begin the film with a sequence between a mortician and Vito Corleone (Bonasera's close-up right in the first frame of the film, not to mention his name — Mr. Good Evening, in English —, projects heavy dosages of dramatic irony on the narrative but also serves to put in relief the old-country sensibility of the older don: vice versa, one of the signs of Michael's cultural alienation is his inability to grieve — until, perhaps, the latter half of *Godfather III*).

In Italian-Canadian writing, the elegy/eulogy continuum is, if anything, more palpable. Antonino Mazza's reassurance, in the poem entitled "Canadese," that...

> in time we'll belong;
> we'll acquire own sense of this land;
> we'll record the life and death of our million births;
> we'll have families above and below the earth

> (in Di Cicco 1978: 39).

is almost nutshell Vico. As are Frank Paci's comments about his own novels: "I had in the back of my mind to celebrate my parents and others like them" (in Minni 6). Or as is Antonio D'Alfonso's summarizing aphorism about literature: "[T]o write is to remember the voices of your people, the voices of those who came before you" (107). And since the majority of Italian immigrants arrived in Canada after World War II, and several of the major writers have first-hand, personal experience of Italy, the process also now invests the Italian landscape and culture: you bury and mourn/celebrate Italy or your childhood memories along with your relatives.

Inscription is not always voluntary or explicit. An Italian-American novelist may not write much about Italian-Americana but his or her texts may be perceived as examples of the Italian-American perspective on the particular issues he or she writes about. The mechanics and politics of inscription act together with the mechanics and the politics of recognition, which have many and specific prerequisites. Ethnic texts aren't exempted from the obligation of being successful, in accordance with the concerns of the literary system. Self-recognition may be a major undeclared *intention* of inscription, but it is for nought if in the long run it is not reinforced by the confirmation of others. While the question of authorial signature is not, in a multicultural setting, and in modernity as such, a critical anachronism, it is adjunctive to and a qualifier of the other questions that animate the cultural climate of a given period (and which may foreground this or that style, this or that genre).

The give-and-take between inscription and recognition is therefore also where literature, identity and ethnicity shade off into ethics. The literariness a text must abide by in order to be noticed by others, or for inscription to occur, lends strength to the argument against views that cast identity as rigid, as homogeneous and impermeable to external contact. Since identity is acquired, maintained or lost socially, through exchange, it is always dialogical, traversed by the presence of others. If I am speaking to a lawyer, it is probably the client-lawyer relation that will prevail during the encounter.

To look at dialogue this way, however, is to limit and impoverish the concept. And no-one knew it better than Bakhtin, whose writings are often cited to vouch for the intrinsic double-voicedness of subjectivity. Dialogue unfolds on a temporal plane, no less than a spatial one. It also implies turn-taking. And if I am the Other to my interlocutor, as he or she is to me, what do I offer to him or her in our encounter? In such works as *Art and Answerability* or *The Philosophy of the Act* or *Speech Genres and Other Essays*, I consummate, I complete the person I am talking to. Of that person I can see traits which will always escape him or her. I can know or bear witness to parts of his or her story better than he or she ever will (I can be there at his or her birth or his or her death). And that happens, Bakhtin reiterates over and over, because of our extra-locality, in so far as neither of us occupies the Other's place:

> *Creative understanding* does not renounce itself, its own place in time, its own culture; and it forgets nothing. In order to understand, it is immensely important for the person who understands to be *located outside* the object of his or her creative understanding. For one cannot even really see one's own exterior and comprehend it as a whole, and no mirrors or photographs can help; our real

exterior can be seen and understood only by other people, because they are located outside us in space, and because they are *others*... In the realm of culture outsidedness is a most powerful factor in understanding. It is only in the eyes of *another* that foreign culture reveals itself fully and profoundly... We raise new questions for a foreign culture, ones that it did not raise itself; we seek answers for our own questions in it. Without *one's own* questions one cannot creatively understand anything other or foreign... Such a dialogic encounter of two cultures does not result in merging or in mixing. Each retains its own unity and *open* totality, but they are mutually enriched (1986: 7).

What in an encounter can be a source of danger (the "unknown" in the other person, the "no" he or she may respond with) can also be the source of greatest benefit. I can be *useful* to you to the extent that I am not you. Culturally, some position, some measure of identity — negotiable and modifiable though it be — must be available for true dialogue to occur. And what is available at the moment of the encounter is what I have inherited or established, and in which I believe.

In this blood-tainted fin-de-siècle, it may very well be that stressing the commonalities upon which to ground conversation is of greater urgency than insisting on the possibilities conversation may offer. Yet in the long run the two gestures must go together. Ideologically, in places such as the U.S.A., Canada and Australia, the appeal to unity ends up being a plea for things as they are, on behalf of the traditions that have served as the vehicular languages, the vocabularies of communication. And even when the appeals are sincere, the objection still remains: were empathy more than a preamble, an invitation to dialogue, there would actually be no need to talk to each other. As semioticians might express it, communication would yield no exchange of information (which requires the staking out of some individual position on the part of each of the persons communicating, the breaking down of the initial homogeneity). We should encourage, then, our cultural interlocutors to inscribe themselves in the collective archive, to develop some sort of identity, some sort of counter locality. If for no other reason, for the sake of efficiency, because it increases our opportunities for self-recognition, because in cultural relations altruism can be egoistic and egoism altruistic.

116

Going at it from another angle, or further caveats on the spirit of the times:

1. Interconnectedness is the alpha and the omega of history. But when we are with others what we start with is a disposition, a readiness for communication, as when we speak the same language. Being able to communicate doesn't mean a dialogue will occur, even when words are exchanged. Often talking to someone is just an indication of benign indifference, a show of phatic linkage, like the polite phrases we dispense in elevators. The interconnectedness at the end of dialogue is, instead, the outcome of an effort, whether it results in agreement, disagreement or argument. You've participated somehow, you've revealed yourself (and have had the opportunity to cognize, or recognize your interlocutor).

2. The interstitialities, overlappings, hibridities, global affiliations which everyone and sundry shares in, is caught up in — to a degree or other — are either special phenomena (in which case we ought to identify the non-hybrid, the non-interstitial etc. and think about what to do with it, how to bring it into the picture) or they are the norm (in which case they are not special, they are the new homogeneity).

3. When we speak of mixture in the singular we are referring to a *form* of the social (how socialness is lived). If we stop here, we are simplifying. Our approach verges on formalism (which *combination* of properties makes up a self, an identity?). But mixture (or globality) occurs in the plural: there are different ways of being mixed (of being global). To distinguish we need to discuss the *content* of mixture (what exactly are our cultural allegiances?).

4. There are strong and weak globalities (colonialism has produced a strong variety, in so far as its legacies are officially and publicly inscribed in the social or political fabric of the ex-colonies; migration a weak variety, in so far as its legacies are non-official, do not commit the state to anything, are left to private individuals to acknowledge or not). Relations of power replicate themselves within hybridity or interstitiality (which are not mixtures or adjacencies of equals, of symmetrical entities or values).

5. Whether singular or plural, mixture (or globality) would soon disappear without the work of cultural upkeep that ensures that all the ruins, all the fragments of identity are preserved. Were the Hispanic presence in the U.S.A. to lose its vitality, the particular "borderland" Latinos or Chicanos inhabit

would unravel with it. You learn your hybridity. As you construct it, you must allow for building maintenance.

6. Mixture doesn't supersede plurality, which is, instead, its dialectical counterpart. New difference is always being created, since no-one can embody *all* possible hybridities. Socially or historically, at a certain point the excedences must be included into the tally. Other features (class, profession, gender) being equal, it is his or her Italian background that an Italian-Canadian brings to the encounter with a Ukranian-Canadian or a Japanese-Canadian.

Nautical metaphors: the hazard of the trade, devices of boat people. Like some of today's illegal immigrants, the majority of Italian immigrants to North America had to cross the sea. The ships they sailed on — the *Saturnia*, the *Vulcania* — had names that at times appear shamelessly overdetermined, but such are coincidences (further compounding the allegorical neatness of the correspondences — by adding some irony this time — is the fact that it was tourist-class travel).

In the imaginary, literary ships I have been tracking down in order to situate Italian emigration as an historical or cultural phenomenon, emigrants, or their metaphorical stand-ins, are only implied presences. With minor exceptions, literature has been about the burden of command — the officers, the navigator-explorers and similar roles. Modernism and postmodernism in particular have been obsessively re-enacting or rewriting the Siren episode from Book XII of the *Odyssey*. Always Ulysses tied at the mast, listening to the song upon which ordinary beings flounder, Ulysses the all-round man, father, husband, lover, warrior, wise councillor, trickster and aesthete nonpareil, while the crew keeps rowing, the ears stuffed with wax in order not to hear.

Even the most sharp twentieth-century critique of the Sirens episode jars flagrantly with the practice, the literary preferences of its authors. In Horkheimer's and Adorno's *Dialectik der Auklarung*, the pages on Ulysses turn out to be a parable about the oarsmen. The alienation of labour: no time for beauty, must keep the machine running, must take care of the routine of survival so that the writer — in this case a male — can properly test himself, can seek out that which cannot be heard under ordinary physical or psychological strain. Yet Adorno was one of the great promoters of avant-garde writing, which he considered the sole worthwhile kind of writing, the bulwark against the devastations of pop or mass culture. Literarily he had other tastes, found more palatable the kind of literature for which the Ulysses of the Siren episode is to this day the inescapable metonym, and in which the rowers' story has no place. A very visible if unacknowledged thread joins the evasion of the "real," historical voyages on the part of high modernist literature to the idea of literature as "deviation," "estrangement," "defamiliarization," "distanciation," to the process by which criticism can introduce spatial (if not nautical) metaphors into definitions that purport to describe literature *juxta sua propria principia*, that give the professional's version of literariness.

Postmodernist criticism is less direct on the subject, but the ease with which self-fashioning occurs in its descriptions of late twentieth-century cosmopolitanism, the interweavings of that process with the subtle revisions of emigration that it has undertaken, put it not far from its predecessors (in all the talk of globalism, diaspora and the new ethos, it is difficult to say whether it is the old type of the *emigré* that is being downgraded into an immigrant or whether it is the immigrant that is being upgraded into an *emigré* figure: the immigrants that seem to emerge from some of the portrayals have known English from birth, skied regularly at St. Moritz, hold a university degree and have considerable funds in Hong Kong or in Swiss bank accounts).

Most of all, what is missing from modernist or postmodernist variations on the Sirens episode are the children of the rowers. In a re-writing of Homer that would feature Italian emigrants — or immigrants as such — they would be indispensible figures.

I don't know if the return to the *before*, to the scene of the parents that is often re-enacted in current Italian-Canadian or Italian-American or Italian-Australian literature signals some generational dissatisfaction with the present, if it should be taken as proof that the parents' fearful, suicidal but optimistic and active restlessness has left only a pessimism without fear. I would want neither to disavow the "success" of Italian immigration, which would mean diminishing the project — the labour — of earlier generations, nor to accept at face value the interpretations of it and — all the more so — the social, political agendas it is frequently attached to ("look at the Italians, they assimilated or are assimilating without complaining, why can't you?").

There's no doubt that these writers are key players in their parents' deferral of desire, the ruse that made displacement, the tough self-denials of survival somehow bearable. In this, too, Italian emigration was a family enterprise. But in the immigrant household roles were never one-dimensional: as translators with the outside world, as cultural mediators, the children wielded enormous power over adults, who often were dependent on them for much of the the everyday business of living. And I would like to believe that those who write about previous generations do so not just because they were the stowaways of the mind in the ships their parents or their grandparents sailed on, the planned offspring groomed to tell the tale for elders who had lost their wisdom, who didn't have the words. When I read the works of the grown-up pre-ordained scribes or the works of their children, the stories they narrate articulate for me unique solidarities. I think of them as texts written by writers who realize full well that they are part and parcel of the events they narrate. I think of them, among other things, as *charitable* autobiographical writings, literature in which you inscribe yourself only by inscribing others, that can be about itself only by being about something other than itself.

Notes

1. The word "notes" in the title should be taken literally. The reflections that follow are part of an intellectual journal I keep from time to time. They were written between 1989 and 1993.

References

Bakhtin, Mikhail. "Response to a Question from the *Novy Mir* Editorial Staff." In *Speech Genres and Other Late Essays*. Trans. Vern W. McGee. Austin: University of Texas Press, 1986, 1-9.

―――. *Toward a Philosophy of the Act*. Trans. Vadim Liapunov. Austin: University of Texas Press, 1993.

Baudelaire, Charles. "Le Voyage." In *Les Fleurs du mal*. Paris: Garnier Frères, 1961a, 155-160.

―――. "Any Where Out of the World. N'importe où hors du monde." In *Oeuvres complètes*. Paris: Gallimard, 1961b, 302-303.

Blake, William. "The Mental Travelers." In *The Poetry and Prose of William Blake*. Ed. David V. Erdman. N.Y. Doubleday, 1965, 475-477.

Costabile, Franco. "Il canto dei nuovi emigranti." In *Il canto dei nuovi emigranti*. A cura di Goffredo Plastino. Milano-Vibo Valentia: Qualecultura/Jaca Book, 1989, 15-20.

Going South

D'Alfonso, Antonio. *The Other Shore*. Montreal: Guernica Editions, 1986.

Deleuze, Gilles and Guattari, Félix. *Milles plateaux*. Paris: Editions de Minuit, 1980.

De Martino, Ernesto. *Morte e pianto rituale*. Torino: Boringhieri: 1975.

Di Cicco, Pier Giorgio. "For My Italian Canadian Friends." In *Virgin Science*. Toronto: McClelland and Stewart, 1986, 14-15.

Di Cicco, Pier Giorgio, ed. *Roman Candles*. Toronto: Hounslow Press, 1978.

Eco, Umberto. *La ricerca della lingua perfetta*. Roma-Bari: Laterza, 1993.

Eliot, Thomas Stearns. "Tradition and the Individual Talent." In *Selected Prose*. Ed. John Hayward. Harmondsworth: Penguin Books, 1953, 21-30.

————. "East Coker." In *Collected Poems*. London: Faber and Faber, 1974, pp. 196-204.

Freud, Sigmund. "The 'Uncanny'." In *Collected Papers*. Vol. 4. Trans. supervised by Joan Rivière. N.Y.: Basic Books, 1959, 368-407.

Heidegger, Martin. *Being and Time*. Trans. John Macquarrie and Edward Robinson. New York and Evanston: Harper & Row, 1962.

Hobsbawm, Eric and Terence Ranger, eds. *The Invention of Tradition*. Cambridge: Cambridge University Press,

Horkheimer, Max and Adorno, Theodor. "Odysseus or Myth and Enlightenment." In *The Dialectic of the Enlightenement*. Trans. John Cumming. N.Y.: Herder and Herder, 1972, 43-80.

Joyce, James. *A Portrait of the Artist a Young Man*. Harmondsworth: Penguin Books, 1960.

Lentricchia, Frank. "Interview." In *Criticism in Society*. Ed Imre Saluzinsky. New York and London: Methuen, 1987, 177-206.

Mazza, Antonino. "Canadese." In Pier Giorgio Di Cicco, ed., 1978, 39.

Minni, Dino. "An Interview with Frank Paci." *Canadian Literature*, 106, Fall 1985, 5-15.

Nagel, Thomas. *The View from Nowhere*. New York: Oxford University Press, 1986.

Pasolini, Pier Paolo. "Profezia." In *Alì dagli occhi azzurri*. Milano: Garzanti, 1965, 488-493.

————. "Prophecy." In *Poetry*. Trans. Antonino Mazza. Toronto: Exile Editions, 1991, 93-98.

Pirandello, Luigi. *Sei personaggi in cerca d'autore*. Milano: Mondadori, 1959.

Rimbaud, Arthur. "Le Bateau ivre." In *Oeuvres complètes*. Paris: Gallimard, 1972, 66-69.

Rorty, Richard. "Human Rights, Rationality, and Sentimentality." *The Yale Review*, vol. 81, 4, 1993, 1-20.

Sollors, Werner, ed. *The Invention of Ethnicity*. Oxford: Oxford University Press, 1989.

Spivak, Gayatri Chakravorty. *Outside in the Teaching Machine*. London and New York: Routledge, 1993.

Teti, Vito. *Il paese e l'ombra*. Cosenza: Edizioni Periferia, 1989.

Vico, Giambattista. *The New Science*. Trans. Thomas Goddard Bergin and Max Harold Fisch. Ithaca, New York: 1984.

5

Cesare Pitto

Remembering the Voyage

On the Italian-Canadian Itinerary

*I*t is my view that the problematics we associate with emigration are directly connected in one way or another to the phenomena that underlie the original motivations for the departure. Indeed, the culture of every human group always pays most dearly at home, in the place from which the emigration begins, for the disintegrating effects of the diaspora. There are wounds that last a long time. However, from an anthropological perspective, the reasons for modern emigration are not just the ones that usually come to mind, that is, the desire to escape from hunger and misery. If those may very well be the immediate impulses that bring about migratory diasporas, one can also maintain, without too much difficulty, that the urge to leave the *paese*, to get away from the horizon and the parameteres of the peasant world, from the ancient social bonds, from the very encumbering norms of kinship relations, can also derive from the need to envisage a different future and different prospects for one's human condition.

Luigi Lombardi Satriani, in *Intervista sulla Calabria* has recalled the conflict between these two components:

> In the literature on emigration, we find already in the nineteenth century the proponents of the instrumental motivations: one emigrates because it is impossible to live in the economic conditions of Calabria or of other Southern regions. And we find the proponents of the psychological motivations: one emigrates because one wants to emigrate, because one is attracted by other ways of life, because one has enacted an anticipatory socialization with the new models (46).

This ambivalence between necessity and curiosity, that extends beyond the process by which one becomes part of the communities one arrives into and which remains active in the villages depleted by the exodus, refracts back on the premises I referred to above. Emigration (and I mean here primarily Italian, peasant and Southern emigration) has been the vital embodiment of a fascination with a dream that was to free from need. Economic determinants and cultural elements cannot be separated in the analysis of the migratory process.

One can, therefore, be in complete agreement with what Gualtiero Harrison has stated in a study of the peculiarities of the migratory exodus in Calabria:

> Among all the human phenomena that the microscope of the social sciences permits us to focus upon, emigration is precisely the one in which the *other* (power) changes the focalization, constantly displacing the readings of the observer (9).

If we move on to this level, we are obbliged to admit that this *other*, which for the moment can remain unspecified, manages to affect all the phases of the analysis of the migratory process, confronting each of these phases with the problem of an external world which conditions, constrains, sanctions, completes and finally transforms emigrants. Yet by taking this position, observers, even when they abandon their neutrality and align themselves with the emigrants, don't advance much further than simple statements of fact; to go beyond simple acknowledgement of hardship, their analysis cannot but take cover in the optimistic hypothesis of emigration as a search for a better future.

In this respect the premises that underlie emigration are not, by themselves, enough to explain the culture to which the migratory process gives rise, be it neo-ethnic culture (for example, Italian-Canadiana) or culture in the historical-local sense (for example, the modernization of the Southern Italian townships). Phrased differently, the ambivalence, the duality of the mechanisms conjoins modern migrations to the dialectic between domination and dependence as it manifests itself in modern metropolitan societies. Lombardi Satriani, again, properly underlines this point:

The motivations are of economic nature and of cultural nature: one emigrates because one is not well physically and because one is not well psychically and culturally. But the issue should be radicalized: one migrates because the model of the *elsewhere*, of all that which presents itself with the characteristics of the *different*, of the distant, operates with an intense force of suggestion and permission: for such an outlook the *city* appears more able to answer individual demands (46).

If all this is true, the analysis of emigration should be concerned less with the composition, the form of the migratory process ,than with its ethic dimension: with, that is, the degree to which it is the expression of a "cultural apocalypse." This latter phenomenon can be identified in Western societies with the demise of the notion of an invariable world, and with the very slow evolution of peasant societies. The emigration which went on uninterruptedly for over a century in Europe (but other parts of the world were undergoing similar experiences) put an end to rural societies, and, in always different fashion, reinforced a flow that went from rural areas to areas that allowed a new freedom. The compulsion to break with the older order was so strong that individuals did not hesitate to choose flight over the security of the static world, even though flight, chaotic and undertaken for different private reasons and with different conviction, inevitably brought them face to face with the panic of the unknown. In spite of this, departures never stopped. It is the drama the anarchist poet Pietro Gori captures so well in one of his verses:

> Essi vanno raminghi; e vanno, e vanno, e vanno.
> Fiumana sterminata — Dove?. . . Neppur lo sanno... (374)
>
> They set out wandering; and still they go, they go, they go. Unending stream — Where to?... not even they know...

The uncertainty that pervades the human order of the migratory process, in every period, above and beyond the variables which space and geography add to the process, culminates in the feeling that one is experiencing one's end. Hence the cultural apocalypse that each departing individual experiences. Hence the attempt of each indivdual to survive, to reproduce himself or herself in the new social order of the *new world*.

This process occurs globally, but for emigrants the known horizon is hardly greater than one's hometown, one's family and one's person. The history of emigration is made of individual histories, none of which is exhausted by any single model. Perhaps the "history of emigration" consists of the history of each of the emigrants in his or her continuing development, and of his or her slow, difficult adjustment (or lack thereof) to the new society. At that point only, the end of the known world becomes visible, as it were, becomes experience and, finally, culture.

The allusion to the Apocalypse here is necessarily linked to the phenomenological analysis of Ernesto De Martino, as he articulates it in *La fine del mondo* (*The End of the World*):

> The end of the existing worldly order of things may beconsidered a cultural theme within the framework of certain mythical configurations. For example, the motif of the periodical destruction or regeneration of the world in myths of eternal return; or the theme of the final catastrophe in views for which human history is unilinear, irreversible and eschatological. As an explicit theme, the end of the existing worldly order is an historical product of different circulation and importance. It is the task of research on cultural apocalypses to analyze concretely each of the instances of this theme, in each of the single societies and in each particular historical periods it appears (14).

The myth of the Apocalypse is thus the most forceful and concrete way by which to relate to the unknown. It stands for the continuity of the *instabilitas loci* instituted in the first place by the voyage itself. This is, I would submit, the principal feature of the process of socio-cultural change that occurs with emigration.

The voyage can be seen as both the breaking away of the single subject from his/her spatial and cultural horizon and the prelude to a new life. Of course, distinctions have to be made, since generally the voyage is not given much attention in sociological approaches to emigration. These generally highlight the moment of departure and then the moment of arrival. Discussion also has dwelt at some length on the ideological aspects of emigration, whether they involved the emigrant as "colonizer," as a representative of the power of the Italian nation-state, in the image coined by the statesman Francesco Crispi, right after the unification of Italy in the nineteenth century, or the emigrant as underprivileged subject, as part of the large mass of individuals to be directed towards the more industrialized areas of Italy or of other lands. This second alternative is how Prime Minister De Gasperi resolved the question in the postwar period, by inviting the population of the Southern regions of Italy to learn a foreign language and to buy cardboard suitcases. It was the answer of a political party that tried to translate into action, by way of ideological pressure, the indications of a reflection subordinated to its own policies and which rested heavily on appeals to patriotism and law and order.

Governmental attitudes towards voyaging, however crude, had an immense controlling effect on the masses of emigrants, especially during the years of the great exodus. To appreciate how real the concern and the interference were, one need only read some of the lines of the *Avvertenze per l'Emigrante Italiano (What the Italian Emigrant Should Know)* published by the *Commissariato Generale per l'Emigrazione* [General Commission on Emigration]. The paragraph entitled "Durante il viaggio" ("During the Voyage") contains the following advise:

> The emigrant should maintain a serious and respectful attitude towards everyone, in particular women and children.
>
> *On board*, once he has picked up the baggage required during the voyage, the emigrant should retain the slip indicating the berth assigned to him.
>
> *He should endeavor to be clean*; he should take care of personal hygiene, use soap generously, keep his hair combed, change garments; he should refrain from dirtying the pavement with peels, sigar butts or spit; he should not vandalize or damage furnishings, objects or machinery; not lie on the bunk with shoes on. He should avoid unseemingly conversations and prefer to it the reading material that the Library instituted by the General Commission on Emigration makes available to him. He should abstain from games of any sort and from smoking where it is not allowed to do so.
>
> *He should shun idleness*; if idle he must be, sleep is advised... (quoted in Cresci and Guidobaldi 64-65).

The excerpt is self-explanatory. It reveals all the contempt with which the dominant society viewed the emigrants it tried to get rid of. The voyage, in other words, is the representation of the experience of the individuals in their movement towards another world. And it constitutes the cultural motivation which founds this reality. For on a symbolic level, emigration in rural societies is a variant or a version of the passing away, of the journey of the deceased.[2]

Vis-à-vis those who stay behind, a rupture has occurred, and it renders the experience of the emigrant altogether specific and peculiar, whatever the initial premises. The voyage, therefore, is to be interpreted in terms of the individual who engages in it, not in terms of the structural reasons that make it possible. To study the voyage in the culture of the emigrant is, for the anthropologist, to re-propose in a vivid and a palpable fashion the reminiscences that attach to narrated voyages as unique and particular events. In this sense, an archive of emigrant memory becomes, not a sterile rehearsing of an improbable theory of the voyage of Italians towards their *elsewheres*, but an interpretation of the mythical ingrediency of the cultural expressiveness of emigrants.

As far as Italian-Canadians are concerned, taking such a position would entail the relinquishing of the stereotype of "feeling at home," of ethnic memory, of nostalgia in order to bring all of these elements (and others) to bear on the mechanisms whereby personal identity is formed, an identity which becomes cultural identity to the extent that it is able to communicate experience. The desire, the need to articulate experience in the vocabulary that emigration provides is not an otiose mannerism. Nor should it be linked to the stereotype of uprootedness and the concomitant loss of identity. Rather, it stems from the newly-recovered awareness of the validity of one's identity. As Gualtiero Harrison has rightly commented:

> In urban expansion the assimilation of those who have just arrived is impossible, as history demonstrates and as logic should have helped to foresee. Herein lies the oppositional value of the concept and the social politics of "integration," which is not there with the concept of "assimilation." Integration means not so much that one adapts, that one accepts the place others have already prepared for him. On the contrary, it is the project whereby one participates to the new reality that the new arrival creates with the very act of arriving. Not only of his arrival, but of arrival in itself, that is, of mobility itself (83).

In the voyage the very real fact of displacement, of moving in space and time comes to the fore: people carry with them their bodily weight, their soma, and must acknowledge the change in their sensations in accordance with the changes in the spatio-temporal horizon. If we read between the lines, some of the literary texts will quickly tell us about the specifics of this operation. Thus, it is immediately apparent that the memory of the departure is charged with special significance. The emigrants caught in the moment of leaving are fused into one, united like the chorus of classical tragedy, as in this exchange from the play *Homeground* by Caterina Edwards:

LUCIO

And that song. When I left home, in the station of Cittadella, I'll never forget.

MARIA

I know, the whole group of you were standing on the platform, waiting for the train.

LUCIO

My mother and Milvia crying, me searching for something to say.

MARIA

Gigetto Moro began to sing. Cesare has told me many times.

LUCIO

No, someone else began. Someone's brother. He was laughing, turning it into a joke. Then Gigetto joined in and his voice was so strong that he drowned him out.

MARIA

And gradually you all began to sing, the relatives, friends, the fiancées, everyone (1990:10-11).

The relation with time often annuls the geographical coordinates of the voyage. It makes movement in space coincide with death, so that the world one abandons and the world one travels to merge within a single past-present continuum. In a poem entitled "My Mother Has a Photograph," Pier Giorgio Di Cicco describes the evaporation of time, the dissolution of the voyage through the re-enactment of a joyful playfulness that reproposes, in the other world of the past, the figure of mother:

> Now it is you & I
> Taking snapshots, posing with
> happiness like a trophy, the room
> is bathed in light, the shutter clicks
> & my heart leaps
> to get out of focus (in De Iuliis 3).

The images of memory contain the past which appears far away, as in a dream. And this tends to sublimate any sign of spatical distance. The image of the origin becomes a point of reference that situates the voyage in a geography without borders. Here is how Antonino Mazza rememorizes his village in *Our House in a Cosmic Ear*:

> A village of bells crowded in the velvet street,
> no sidewalks. Sunday morning, no Monday.
> How is it? I was running home, there were cherries
> in my pocket, my mother had a nightingale
> between her lips (in Di Cicco 41).

The voyage, thus, is replaced by myth, a dimension within which it is possible to construct an imaginary space and within which actions and gestures remain always the same. Taken in its concreteness, the voyage is narrated by texts that reproduce the atemporality of myth, as if one voyage were all voyages. Which, sometimes we get the impression, is the meaning the journey assumes for the individual embarked on it. In the following passage, the Calabrian writer Saverio Strati recollects the sensations of his first voyage:

> Non avevo fame; non ebbi sonno fino a tardi. Mi feci dare il posto accanto al finestrino e guardavo la terra avvolta nella notte e a tratti mi passavano veloci davanti gruppi di luci; e vedevo altre luci in collina; mi sarebbe piaciuto di sapere chi viveva là, cosa facevano in quei paesi sparsi un pò dovunque. Poi cadde il silenzio che ad ogni fermata veniva rotto da gente che saliva e correva su e giù per cercare un posto che non trovava. Succedeva un parlare animato e poi cadeva

il silenzio che era rotto solo dal fragore del treno in corsa. In una corsa nel buio, in una corsa folle lungo una strada che lui solo conosceva; e mia madre stava raccolta in se stessa con gli occhi spersi nel vuoto (134).

I wasn't hungry; I didn't feel sleepy until late. I asked for the seat near the window and I looked at the landscape shrouded by night. At times clusters of lights passed in front of me and I saw other lights on the hills; I would have liked to know who lived there, what they were doing in those villages scattered a bit everywhere. Then there was silence, a silence that at each stop was broken by people who boarded the train and ran up and down looking for places they could not find. Animated talk ensued, then silence, broken by the clanging of the train speeding on. Speeding in the dark, in a mad race along a route only it knew; and my mother kept still and self-absorbed, her eyes lost in the void.

For Strati, the experience of emigration was to yield the awareness of the mark the voyage may may have left on other individuals before him. In particular, the description of the present led to a more sympathetic understanding of his own emigrant father:

Penso che anche mio padre abbia fatto allo stesso modo, quando arrivò alla frontiera tedesca. Ma lui non ce lo scrisse. Non tutto quello che succede viene scritto. Quante cose non si sanno perchè non vengono scritte! Pensai (134).

My father probably did things the same way, when he arrived at the German border. But he didn't write to us about it. Not all that happens is written down. How many things never become known because they're not written! I thought.

More than movement, it is the images that conquer space and reveal the specificity, the peculiarity of the voyage, that give the voyage its identity. More than the recapitulation of an itinerary, the voyage is the evocation of private, personal sensations. Within each individual consciousness, some images come to represent the gist of an entire life, the meaning (the end) of one's temporality. And it is the intensity of these images that reveals how important the voyage is for the individual emigrant. Len Gasparini's poem "Union Station, Toronto," for instance, condenses the state of mind of the emigrants at that particular juncture in which their destiny is probably most uncertain:

Under sombre umbrellas
the bewildered immigrants
huddle together
holding their heavy luggage
in front of Union Station.
It' their first night
in a big strange city
and even the rain is against them (in Di Cicco 25).

In these verses the arrival also seems eternal, a kind of continuation which, however, is static, seems to bind the person involved to the limbo of its unsure, unpredictable horizon.

Of course, any phase or feature of the voyage can be mythicized. Just as typical and and frequent as those texts that put the emphasis on the danger, on the apocalyptic element, are the texts that choose to dwell on the birth or re-birth metaphor. In emigrating one takes the first steps towards a New World. Dorina Michelutti gives voice to this positive dimension of the voyage in a poem entitled "Brother":

Sailing for Canada. You grab me as I slip overboard into the arms of the Atlantic, too young to know the ocean is pagan (46).

Thus, it is clear, constructing an archive of memory in which the real and the mythical voyage can coexist will help us to better understand the unfolding of a cultural process fundamental to our times. Recognizing the mythicalness of the voyage, for example, allows us to better address the stereotypical codifications of emigrant texts. As patterns, as themes, journeys do not belong to any ethnic group; they are at the symbolic heart of culture itself. But at the same time each voyage is specific, and each group finds ways to both diversify and de-dramatize its versions, its renditions of it. We can therefore conclude by borrowing again from Saverio Strati, whose words, on this occasion too, stand for most emigrants:

Coltivai questo sogno per anni: di partire. Quando si avverò non ci provai neanche piacere (156).

For years I had this dream: to leave. When it became a reality I didn't even feel any pleasure...

Translated by Francesco Loriggio.

Notes

1. During the crossing a brochure was distributed to emigrants which listed the norms of behaviour they should follow. They were, precisely, notes on *What the Italian Emigrant Should Know [Avvertenze per l'Emigrato Italiano]*, edited by the *Commissariato Generale per l'Emigrazione*. The front cover read: "Leaving one's country to work on foreign soil is always an important event for the individual emigrating, his family and his Fatherland. The emigrant should carefully reflect on this fact and keep in mind the practical advise that follows." The brochure was later republished in Cresci and Guidobaldi (1980: 64-65). The volume is a photographic essay.
2. On the fact that in the South emigration is lived as a form of death see Lombardi Satriani (46-47).

References

Cresci, P., and Guidobaldi, L. *Partono i bastimenti*. Milano: Mondadori, 1980.

De Iuliis, C. "Pier Giorgio Di Cicco. A Poet Amongst Us." *Quaderni canadesi*, II, 3, 1978, 3-5.

De Martino, E. *La fine del mondo*. Torino: Einaudi, 1977.

Di Cicco, P.G., ed. *Roman Candles: An Anthology of Poems by Seventeen Italo-Canadian Poets*. Toronto: Hounslow Press, 1978.

Edwards, C. *Homeground*. Montreal/Toronto: Guernica, 1990.

Gori, Pietro. "Senza patria." In *Canti dell'emigrazione*. A cura di A.V. Savona e M.L. Straniero. Milano: Garzanti, 1976, 360-389.

Harrison, G. *Viavai calabrese: L'emigrazione di ritorno rivisitata in chiave antropologica*. Roma: Quaderni del Dipartimento di Scienze dell'Educazione. Università della Calabria, 1979.

Lombardi Satriani, L.M. *Intervista sulla Calabria*. With Pasquale Falco. Cosanza: Edizioni Periferia, 1985.

Michelutti, D. *Loyalty to the Hunt*. Montreal/Toronto: Guernica, 1986.

Strati, S. *Terra di emigranti*. Firenze: Salani, 1979.

6

William Boelhower

Surviving Democracy

Italian-American Signs [1]

For Pier Giorgio Di Cicco, Antonino Mazza
and Caterina Edwards

*A*lready in the 1855 Preface to his *Leaves of Grass*, Walt Whitman observed, "Here is not merely a nation but a teeming nation of nations" (5). On board the *Pequod* in Melville's anatomy of American democracy, *Moby Dick*, Ishmael redefines the bard's "here" as "a crew... chiefly made up of mongrel renegades, and castaways, and cannibals" (162). Indeed, in Ishmael's view the establishment of the United States ushered in a new world order which in a brilliant essay the jurist Carl Schmitt further qualified as the oceanic condition. In this order, the ship, not the house, now becomes the central metaphor for interpreting the economy of dwelling, while mongrels and cast-aways serve as its representative citizens. We have all become sailors in a homeless world. In Ishmael's words, "What are the Rights of Man and the Liberties of the World but Loose-Fish?... What is the great globe itself but a Loose-Fish?" (334). "Loose-Fish," the reader will recall, are "fair game for anybody who can soonest catch it" (331). This last clarification is obligatory because it is on the distinction between "Loose-Fish" and "Fast-Fish" (those already claimed or possessed) that "the fundamentals of all human jurispru-dence" (333) are founded. As a precocious display of modern democratic textuality, *Moby Dick* has a lot to teach us when it comes to judging the difference between what is culturally "loose" and what "fast." And this com-petence inevitably introduces us to the tactics of ethnic interpretation as a way of surviving the impossible subjectivity of the sovereign democratic self.

The Sicilian Sailor: Position as Theory

I will begin, therefore, by annotating a number of ethno-archaeographic signs — mere unclaimed driftage — of Italian-Americans that can be found floating in the most unlikely pages of the nation's canonic texts, floating completely unobserved in the democratic currents of our electronic sea. That same magnanimous sea which, Ishmael tells, "will permit no records" (60). Then, towards the end of this essay, I will turn to several different kinds of Italian-American texts to see how they realign such "loose" signs in an effort to make a distinctive narrative claim from within the very flow of them. Thus, we acknowledge Ishmael's intimation throughout *Moby Dick* that the sea of oblivion is equally an uncontrollable turbulence of involuntary memory. Nothing is lost, everything is saved. Who knows what will surface next or protrude as a ripple, a fugitive cultural snag, in the ceaseless flow of information that accompanies our *Pequod*-world on its journey out. By imploding their names, by intending them as poetic *axia* (that is, of narrative value), these writers and poets momentarily illuminate an ethnic position or, if you will, launch an *ethics of positionality* into the circuit of democratic representation.

And in keeping with the Melvillean context, the use of such minimum verbal chips cannot but remind us, first, of Queequeg's decision to cocoon himself in his coffin as an extreme gesture of cultural therapy and, second, of Ishmael's riding that same wooden scroll to the surface, thus becoming the *Pequod*'s lone survivor. The point is, if he lives to recount his story it is because of the enabling presence of the coffin, the only "text" that saves. By imploding their own name, ethnic authors give a genealogical turn to their oceanic condition. This semiotropic gesture, I would add further, is radically ethical in that it traces *ethics* and *ethos* back to their common root. Taking one's name seriously — which involves one in what is perhaps the oldest form of cultural criticism, namely *interpretatio nominis* — means identifying the distinctive ethics of "character" with a specific origin. It is this philological turn that Walter Benjamin alludes to when he says, "For he who travels into his own past, name and reality are newly joined" (1980: 110).

Living in "a teeming nation of nations," on board a ship run by "mongrel renegades," means living in a semiocentric (rather than ontocentric) world and a completely semioticized culture. Modern democracy depends above all on the circulation of signs rather than their substantiation. For Charles Sanders

Peirce, who at the very beginning of the twentieth century began calling for a science of signs, a sign is "something which stands to somebody for something in some respect or quality" (quoted in Eco 33). Such a matrix of intentionality makes the jurisprudence of identifying and claiming "loose-fish" infinitely enmeshing, as sailors on the *Pequod* trying to spot Leviathan knew all too well. As we learn to expect from him, Ishmael clarifies the average sailor-democrat's new semiotic burden in his own way: "And what are you, reader, but a Loose-Fish and a Fast-Fish, too" (334)? That he is taunting us here, there is little doubt, although he is also grim enough to assert that "the world's a ship on its passage out, and not a voyage complete" (44). If, however, we are "loose-fish" on our way out, we — Ishmael included — spend a great deal of our time thinking of ourselves as "fast-fish" on our way back in. It is perhaps our great illusion or, for those who are anti-Ishmaels, belief.

This desire to return involves us in Ishmael's deadly quarrel with Captain Ahab (alias Noah, Perseus, Prometheus, St. George, Jason), who actually did set out to complete the world's voyage, strike through the pasteboard mask of appearances, get to the foundation of things, and return home to a safe harbor. Or, in terms of what has been set down above, make a "loose-fish" "fast." As a born allegorist, Ahab would have dismissed Ishmael's outlandish definition of the reader as an intolerable act of tolerance. It was clear to all who knew him that Ahab himself was a "fast-fish," that is "on his frozen brow [was] the piled entablatures of ages" (161). In short, his business was genealogy. By killing Moby Dick, he planned to "dismember my dismemberer" (147) and thus secure his own patriarchal tree. The death of the sea monster also entailed the death of the ocean as *nomos* (or world order) and, consequently, the termination of the oceanic condition. Indeed, throughout the anatomy's epic voyage, Ahab seeks to turn the world of fluctuating signs into a world of stable facts. Through a sheer act of will signs would be made to correspond, have an origin, and be locatable in space. Readers would either be "loose-fish" or "fast-fish" but not both at once.

Ahab, of course, loses the wager and Ishmael's complicated sense of the act of reading prevails. *Moby Dick* did not become a story of foundation. This is made quite clear in the aptly titled chapter "The Hat," in which Ahab loses exactly that. In itself the matter is trivial, like so many things in this text. But the implications are momentous, thanks in part to "the Sicilian seaman" (440). The scene is caused by the presence of one of those familiar Melvillean hawks that fly through the author's pages. This one has no other role than to de-throne the king or, to put it more literally, to steal Captain Ahab's hat. The theft would not have happened in the first place, "[b]ut with his gaze fixed upon the dim and distant horizon, Ahab seemed not to mark this wild bird" (440). Like a good allegorist, our "king of the sea, and... great lord of Levia-thans" (114) was horizon-conscious. He had a global mind. His job, as he saw it, was to establish the essential correspondences and leave the insignificant details to others. Thus his hoisted position in the rigging was meant to function like a panopticon.

It is Ishmael, however, who notices what is wrong here: "only now al-most the least heedful eye seemed to see some sort of cunning meaning in almost every sight" (440). At this point in the narrative we are floating in a sea of signs that makes any allegorical siting impossible. To be alert, therefore, means to attend to the most insignificant detail, to seek meaning everywhere. Ishmael, we gather, is also talking about the business of reading signs in gen-eral, that is about how to be a reader in the semiocentric sea of modern de-mocracy. Earlier, Benjamin Franklin wrote his autobiography to inculcate in his nephew — and in all those who were to come after him — the cunning necessary to "make it" in the rapidly rising new nation. Melville's Sicilian sailor demonstrates he has the properly "heedful eye" which Franklin too considered essential in a democratic nation. "'[Y]our hat, your hat, sir!' sud-denly cried the Sicilian seaman, who being posted at the mizen-mast-head, stood directly behind Ahab, though somewhat lower than his level, and with a deep gulf of air dividing them" (440).

What we have here is a common mongrel renegade "*directly behind*" the kingly captain. The first, somewhat lower, but with an eye to everything around him; the second in a superior position and with his gaze fixed only on the distant horizon. In addition, there is a gulf of air between them. As so often occurs in Melville — the pair Benito Cereno and Babo comes naturally to mind — we are led to pay particular attention to the spatial relationship between his characters, as if narrative meaning ultimately depended on positionality. By means of their respective positions, in fact, it is clear that the Sicilian sailor is Ahab's counter figure. That is, the Sicilian is narratively marked to give an alternative site of reading, a critique of Ahab's transcendent vision of things. Thus we have one of Melville's scattered ethnographic emblems for stand-point theory, for in-position thinking. By inverting the hierarchy of significance implied in the spatial positions of Ahab and the sailor, the narrator encourages us to reassess the high/low, center/margin paradigm, the Sicilian sailor's lowness and marginality with respect to Ahab now becoming a positive semiotic factor in reading the sea of signs from on board the *Pequod*.

In "The Hat" chapter the Sicilian is more than Ahab's shadow; his position of seeing and "reading" also becomes a virtual narrative perspective. By citing him — *citare* in Latin means to put in motion, to arouse — the narrator draws attention to his storytelling potential and constitutes him as an authentic narrative voice if not subject. Of course, the Sicilian sailor will remain a virtual subject from then on, but in the meantime a new narrative position has been established. And given the democratic textuality of *Moby Dick*, we are invited to speculate on the sailor's story, especially since there are now a sufficient number of Italian-American narratives available to support our inferences. Reading always implies the desire to get to the bottom of things and, as Edmond Jabès writes in *Le retour au livre*, "Le fond est toujours le commencement." The narrator, however, leaves us few clues: no face, no defining characteristics, no hint about his past. The Sicilian remains largely a blank.

But is it not precisely for this reason that he solicits comment? Arguably, all interpretation is nothing but an attempt to fill in the blank spaces between words, sentences, chapters. The sailor, then, leaves us with a generic, autobiographical sign which is all that remains of his patrimony: "Sicilian," a typological name at that. Yet this minimum qualifier is already enough to entitle a narrative — "the Sicilian sailor." To write any story at all means to encounter an unknown face, Jabès tells us on the opening page of his book *Le petit livre de la subversion hors de soupçon*. And in this case the name functions like the portrait Picasso made of Igor Stravinsky. As Stravinsky himself tells in his *Cronache della mia vita* (66), when in 1917 he presented himself at the border of Italy and Switzerland with Picasso's portrait of him, the Italian customs officials refused to let him pass because they thought he was carrying a secret military map of the territory. For Melville's Sicilian sailor as well, name, face, and country may be linked together. The ancestral theme, then, has been sounded: when taken together, character and ethos and local dwelling become matter for story. In addition, the mere fact that he is on the *Pequod* already stirs our curiosity. How did he get there? Where did he come from? The name alone suggests a series of connections as well as a trajectory. The Sicilian is a long way from home; on the other hand, even the slightest knowledge about

137

Sicily and Sicilians would suggest that he is more likely at home riding the high seas than sailors like Ishmael. But all this intellectual scratching must remain purely speculative. The Sicilian's narrative moment in American literature, the moment when he himself will weave a story around his name, must attend Jerre Mangione, but also other Italians like Rosa Cavalleri, Constantine Panunzio, Pascal D'Angelo, Pietro Di Donato, John Fante, Mari Tomasi, Jo Pagano, Marion Benasutti, Raymond De Capite, and of course, today, a swelling host of others.

To conclude my discussion of Melville's Sicilian sailor, we should remember that Ahab did not finally recover his hat after the hawk picked it off his head. This fact, in the narrator's eyes, takes on an extremely ominous significance, especially in the light of similar auspices having to do with the founding of Rome. Thus he tells, "An eagle flew round Tarquin's head, removing his cap to replace it, and thereupon Tanaquil, his wife, declared that Tarquin would be king of Rome" (441). The source for this is most likely Book 1, section 34, of Titus Livius's *Ab Urbe Condita Libri*. Just as Livy's eagle performs a symbolic deed having a prophetic import, so too does Melville's hawk in *Moby Dick*. Ahab, in other words, will not repeat the epic exploit of Virgil. His allegory is doomed to break down. The sea will remain a sea of signs, and the ocean the normative condition. If Ahab learns this only in his last breath, the Sicilian sailor shows he already knows how to live in a semiotropic world.

The Monkey-Rope and Suonatori Ambulanti

That the two figures and the two approaches to reading are part of a single narrative economy, though, goes without saying. From the vantage point of this scene in *Moby Dick*, we might add yet one more gloss. The perduring tendency to enoble the modern order of democratic representation with allegorical meaning is due directly to the inherent symbolic weakness of political democracy. This weakness is largely due to democracy's constitutional dependence on the sovereign individual self as its single axiological alternative to those other factors that have traditionally led to the creation of one people living in the same place: namely, one language, a common religion, a single race, and shared customs and traditions. Ethnicity itself becomes an essential part of the cultural economy of democratic representation to the extent that

Surviving Democracy

democracy's utopian promises of well-being, equal rights, and full representation are perennially broken, if not ultimately impossible to fulfill. In comparison to other political systems that preceded it, therefore, democracy is radically deontological. Its form of representation is semiotic and not symbolic in the substantialist sense.

In democracy, the people are the ultimate political category, but when we seek its legitimating ground, we inevitably end up with the private subject multiplied into a formless mass. And this subject, of course, is beyond political representation. Thus, while ethnic recursiveness has become the dominant way of coping with — of surviving — the failure of full democratic sovereignty, ethnic storytelling still remains part of a "loose-fish" jurisprudence. Bonding on board the *Pequod*, the attentive (or should I say "Sicilian") reader will recall, is defined by the monkey-rope (chapter 72), evidently a metaphor derived from Italian-American street musicians: "You have seen Italian organ-boys holding a dancing-ape by a long cord. Just so, from the ship's side, did I hold Queequeg down there in the sea, by what is technically called in the fishery a monkey-rope, attached to a strong strip of canvas belted round his waist" (270). Ishmael will provide us with no better definition of what at first glance seems a transcendent form of ethnic bonding. At any rate, it is his definition of himself as a "fast-fish."

It should not be surprising, therefore, if at this point in the narration a sense of nostalgia creeps into his commentary. "So strongly and metaphysically did I conceive of my situation then, that while earnestly watching his [Queequeg's] motions, I seemed distinctly to perceive that my own individuality was now merged in a joint stock company of two...," he writes (271). If there is anything that Ishmael suffers as part of an endemic condition — which, I would suggest, is the condition of the sovereign democratic self *tout court* — it is that of being an isolato "floating on the margins" (470). There is no sense of an ethnos on the *Pequod*; people get along because they all have a financial stake in the catch. Ishmael, in fact, could easily be a prototype of Paolo Valesio's ideal cosmopolitan figure as developed in his novel *L'ospedale di Manhattan*. As Queequeg puts it at the beginning of *Moby Dick*, "It's a mutual, joint stock world, in all meridians" (61). It is precisely because of this *nomos* of modern democracy that he becomes ecstatic every time he gets involved in a seemingly fraternal situation on board the *Pequod*, even if it is only the consequence of some routine job at hand. There is, in other words, no real "metaphysical" elimination of his condition of solitude. What we do have instead is a type of semiotic monkey-rope, which is even more thoroughly explicated in Hawthorne's romance *The House of the Seven Gables*. Once again, an Italian street musician becomes a *nom parlant*, an ethnic signifier.

The Barrel-Organ as Sign of a Cultural Inside

In order to arouse Clifford from his torpor, Phoebe, the heroine of Hawthorne's romance, tries to get him interested in the life of Pyncheon Street. By looking out of his arched window, the narrator tells us, Clifford could see, among other things, "an omnibus, with its populous interior, dropping here-and-there a passenger, and picking up another, and thus typifying that vast rolling vehicle, the world, the end of whose journey is everywhere and nowhere" (160). Introduced for the first time in Paris after the Restoration, the omnibus quickly became the perfect vehicle of urban transportation. As the word's etymon suggests, not only could everybody use it but it also covered all the stops. The structural effect of this means of transportation, in the narrator's opinion, is that "everywhere and nowhere" become interchangeable. As the omnibus goes, so goes the world. In effect, thanks to the omnibus the city did become one homogeneous space of circulation. Its entire surface (of production and consumption) was in everybody's reach. The narrator's tone, of course, is negative and could perhaps be paraphrased as "What's this world coming to?" Thanks in part to mass transportation, Clifford's homogeneous city was becoming a multi-ethnic metropolis. The narrator then follows with an extended gloss on the current conditions of dwelling which he puts in the form of an allegory.

Instead of the butcher's cart, the baker's cart, the fish and vegetable carts, Clifford was now exposed to new associations, thanks to the omnibus. As he looked out of his upstairs window, "one of those Italian boys (who are rather a modern feature of our streets) came along, with his barrel-organ, and stopt under the wide and cool shadows of the elm" (162). Having spotted Clifford and Phoebe watching him from behind their arched window, he "began to scatter... melodies abroad" (162). Besides the music, "there was a company of little figures, whose sphere and habitation was in the mahogany case of his organ, and whose principle of life was the music, which the Italian made it his business to grind out" (162-3). And then follows:

In all their variety of occupation — the cobbler, the blacksmith, the soldier, the lady with her fan, the toper with his bottle, the milk maid sitting by her cow — the fortunate little society might truly be said to enjoy a harmonious existence, and to make life literally a dance (163).

But all of a sudden, the narrator esteems these figures — which would fit equally well in the preindustrial world of Clifford's butcher and baker, fishmonger and vegetable vendor — to be ridiculously vivacious; even though in his somewhat enigmatic view "they bring nothing finally to pass" (163). Their "harmonious existence," we are told, is really due to their dancing to the same mechanical tune. The monkey in particular stirs the narrator's indignation as it begs greedily for offerings. Ultimately, as the scene is brought to focus on the monkey, it comes to symbolize the unappeasable greed of a capitalist economy and the uniform rhythms it imposes. A single law seems to prevail over all and the music itself, as it is ground out, is construed as part of capitalism's repetitive tune.

This is what the narrator concludes by ingesting and then transforming a passing foreign sign into an allegorical meditation on his times. Indeed, the reader cannot help take note of his sudden souring as he temperamentally forces his bitter conceit unto the innocent young Italian. What seems to stand behind this willfulness is a profound nostalgia for what the old house of the seven gables once stood for and what the contemporary street was even then cancelling. While the narrator first takes a positive shine to the "*fortunate* little society" (my emphasis) of the youth's barrel-organ, he quickly comes to associate its music with the punctual rhythms of the omnibus, that is of the modern city. The above scene, in which curiously a dark-faced foreigner is assigned to recite, actually concerns in code form the condition of nostalgia in modern American culture.

Thus, when the Italian street musician is made to appear a second time, towards the end of the romance (in "Alice's Posies"), the narrator signals that he is about to rekey his allegory by shifting the youth from under the elm (where he was placed in his first appearance) to "the door-step of the main-entrance" (293). We have here, if only by proximity, a new semiotic nod toward the house as a cultural inside. The reason for the Italian's renewed presence also becomes more nuanced. He has returned not only because of Phoebe's generosity but also because of her "pleasant face" (292). The little "wanderer" plays with a "livelier and sweeter" (293) touch because there is now something allusively sentimental about his visit. As the narrator explains, "They remember these things, because they are the *little enchantments* which, for the instant — *for the space that reflects a landscape in a soap-bubble* — *build up a home* about them" (293, my emphasis).

Since the narrator's method is that of assimilating the ethnic sign only on the outside (that is, it remains a foreign body in his narrative), the Italian street musician is handled as little more than a type, someone the narrator assigns to a taxonomically general "they." Thus it is as hermeneutic object representing the immigrant or migrant experience that the young foreigner takes his place in the narrative economy of the romance. His bit part includes no namable tunes or intimate thoughts or defining remarks. He is there, necessarily nameless and silent, simply to provide a more effective *locus argomenti* or mini-allegory about melancholy and the impossible subjectivity of modern democratic dwelling.

As we already saw in the first appearance of the Italian youth, the narrator is as nostalgic as he is bitter. His bitterness functions as a rather thin veil for covering his delusions over the possibilities of a harmonious existence which the little foreigner's barrel-organ reminded him of in the first place. Further pathos is then generated by having the young musician *remember* the "little enchantment" of seeing Phoebe and Clifford framed by the vaguely sacred arched window of the house on Pyncheon Street. And it is through still further commentary that the narrator finally exposes his own plight of homelessness — when he adjusts his syntax to reveal that the above scene reminds the little wanderer of the intimacies of home. This tactic of deflection, however, does not spare him from his own allegory, since it is so obviously his act of configuration that draws our attention. The pathos is all his.

The issue of "home" which the narrator raises not too inadvertently is far from being a secondary concern, for along with other such emblems it serves to shed light on the romance's central icon (the house of the seven gables) and its central theme (the problematic of *habitare* — of dwelling — in Jacksonian America). Earlier, when talking about Clifford's pathetic lassitude, his desire to do nothing, the narrator offers this remark: "Persons who have

142

wandered, or been expelled, out of the common track of things, even were it for a better system, *desire nothing so much as to be led back*" (140, my emphasis). Clifford, "this poor, forlorn voyager from the Islands of the Blest, in a frail bark, on a tempestuous sea, had been flung, by the last mountain-wave of his shipwreck, into a quiet harbor" (142).

The quiet harbour is the house of the seven gables, "home" for Clifford and Hepzibah and Phoebe. It is this same harbor that the little foreigner supposedly seeks in letting his memory lead him back to the Pyncheon family doorstep: "he still looked upward, trusting that his dark, alien countenance would soon be brightened by Phoebe's sunny aspect" (294). And then, "The gloomy and desolate old house, deserted of life, and with awful Death sitting sternly in its solitude, was the emblem of many a human heart... " (295). This moral instruction, one feels, applies with equal finality to Hawhorne himself, as his own favorite narrative vehicle, the romance, now proves comparably "deserted of life," its once enchanting architectonics also a "gloomy and desolate old house." Significantly, it is the little Italian street musician who witnesses the fact for us as he plays his foreign and untitled tunes with seductive but impotent insistence.

Hawthorne, in short, condenses the narrative method and concerns of his entire romance in these few paragraphs; in which the ethnic *topos* functions less as an image displayed for casual speculation than as a scene of the romance method in itself. To put it in another way, it is the very *drama* of this scene featuring the Italian musician and his barrel-organ that raises the heuristic issue of modern dwelling in terms of a cultural inside and outside, in terms of the ancestral theme versus restless circulation. And, to complete our appreciation of its *paideia*, just as this scene implies the very notion of a separating journey so does it contemplate a drama of return and reunion. If modern democratic culture is hopelessly nostalgic and reeking with pathos, it is only because the moment of return is constitutionally enigmatic. It is this impasse in the sovereign democratic self's narrative trajectory that makes monkey-rope semiosis essential for cultural survival and converts the ethnic scene into a scene of repetition.

Ethnic Semiosis as an Ethno-Archaeography

After playing his full repertoire of tunes over and over again, the little foreigner finally leaves because, as the narrator makes clear, there can be no return. Indeed, if he plays at all it is because he is "outside" the house to begin with. And he remains outside because the ancestral house is without a heart. For that matter, neither for Clifford nor for the street musician nor for the narrator can there be a cultural inside or a scene of return. Even more importantly, however, the very idea of mining this scene so compulsively and deeply constitutes what — for the purposes of appreciating Hawthorne's "Melvillean" achievement here — we might label as an exercise in ethno-archaeography, a practice that will become so familiar to American writers in the twentieth century. To sum up, the house of the seven gables is overcome by the street. To it the Italian boy will return; home for him must remain a distant ancestral memory. The source of the pity which the narrator stirs up in us lies ultimately in the scene itself: if there are tears to be shed, and how can we any longer doubt it, they are due to the narrator's skill in *de-signing* the house of the seven gables. Its desemioticization results from the fact that there can be no *nostos* in a democratically constituted world. After Hawthorne and Melville, the problem will be assigned largely to the sons of immigrants.

Based on circulation and exchange, the citizen as *perpetuum mobile* remains forever at sea. In this spirit the narrator reminds us:

> In this republican country, amid the fluctuating waves of our social life, somebody is always at the drowning-point. The tragedy is enacted with as continual a repetition as that of a popular drama on a holiday, and, nevertheless, is felt as deeply, perhaps, as when an hereditary noble sinks below his order (38).

Once again, it is Hawthorne's little *suonatore ambulante* who occasions the pathos and tears that accompany the end of the house of Pyncheon. It is also he who sets in motion the narrator's ethno-archaeographic initiative. Whether it is a question of trying to get "inside" the house (which is tributary to the major semiotic thrust of Hawthorne's romance) or trying to feel "deeply" or dive deeply (which is Ahab's monomaniacal intention in *Moby Dick*), both efforts are intrinsic to the cultural work of American democracy. The effort to restore a cultural inside has generated a number of topoi that have given ethnic semiosis a peculiarly topological designation.

Democracy's main semiotic vector is horizontal; its economy, based on circulation. Surface fluidity in all spheres is surely its most prominent visual characteristic. If, then, citizenship is dependent on conditions such as these, participants in the country's democratic life should have to learn how to walk and act with the expertise of sailors. Is this not Ishmael's main point in *Moby Dick*? And to avoid shipwreck, citizens must certainly adjust to life in a weather of signs. As Edward Everett Hale has demonstrated in his famous short story of 1863 "The Man Without a Country," it is evidently impossible to live forever at sea without being haunted by memories of land and subject to involuntary fits of nostalgia. Hale's forgotten hero, Philip Nolan, is a case in point. In reality, we may distinguish democracy's second main semiotic vector as vertical and define it as the attempt to return to a safe harbor or return in memory to what has been left behind or lost. I have chosen to call this recursive semiosis ethno-archaeographic because any such attempt to get to the foundation or origin of things requires all the skills of one carrying out a dig or a deep form of site-analysis.

As we might imagine, there are all kinds of activities that reveal this type of recursiveness. I have already mentioned the long-established practice of imploding names, which as a form of cultural criticism is more familiarly known to students of rhetoric as *interpretatio nominis*. In the context of modern democracy, this practice of interpreting or imploding names (especially one's family name) has become largely an ethnogenetic activity. Indeed, writers who invent such implosive narratives are actually making good use of the peculiar cultural work of ethno-archaeography. In contemporary intellectual history, this form of criticism has two of its most illustrious adherents in Walter Benjamin and Ernst R. Curtius. Were we to investigate the figure of the Italian street musician in Hawthorne or in Horatio Alger's novel of 1872, *Phil the Fiddler or the Story of a Young Street Musician*, according to the principles of site-analysis — that is, according to a method of topological tracing —, we would have to go back to 45 Crosby Street and the Mulberry district in New York City and from there to Val-di-Taro, Liguria, and the hilltop towns of Laurenzana and Viggiano in Basilicata (Zucchi 7ff).

Thus, by "mining" even such a generic name as "Italian street musician/*suonatore ambulante*," we are inspired to follow a random and roving *topological* trace. It should now be evident that when subjected to this type of scrutiny, even such an insignificant sign as a casually dropped name (like Rinaldo Rinaldini in *Moby Dick*) promises to reveal a rather sustained narrative of its own, depending on how far the ethno-archaeographer is willing to delve. At the beginning of this century, if one had gone browsing in the Libreria de "Abruzzo-Molise" on 22 Magne St., Rochester, New York, one could have bought a novel titled *Rinaldo Rinaldini* for $2.00 (Bianco 101). Melville's "Sicilian sailor," surely a name disengaged from its originating context — and what character on the *Pequod* is not? —, can also be narratively redeemed by tracing it topologically forward. Possibly to Telegraph Hill in San Francisco where Sicilians first came to man the city's fishing fleets; thus, to Sidney Miller's novel *Home is Here*, Valenti Angelo's children's stories *The Hill of Little Miracles* and *The Bells of Bleeker Street*, and other more famous writers and poets whose names can be drawn into the semiotic vortex of Melville's Sicilian topos. If names necessarily imply connections, it also becomes impossible to dismiss them once they are evoked.

Already in 1840 in his proto-Melvillean romp *Two Years Before the Mast*, Richard Henry Dana spoke of the Italian ship *Rosa* and its opera-singing crew which he had the chance to become acquainted with when his own ship put to shore off Santa Barbara: "We had now, out of forty or fifty, representatives from almost every nation under the sun — two Englishmen, three Yankees, two Scotchmen, two Welshmen, one Irishman, three Frenchmen..., one Dutchman, one Austrian, two or three Spaniards..., half a dozen Spanish-Americans and half-breeds, two native Indians from Chili and the Island of Chiloe, one Negro, one mulatto, about twenty Italians, from all parts of Italy, as many more Sandwich-Islanders, one Tahitian, and one Kanaka from the Marquesas Islands" (166-67). Evidently, the multi-ethnic composition of the *Pequod*'s crew was not at all exceptional. Sicilian sailors, it seems, could be found all over. And almost as if he too were evoking the ethnic monkey-rope of Melvillean democracy, Dana advises us, "A sailor knows too well that his life hangs upon a thread to wish to be often reminded of it" (359).

Karl and Giacomo: Ethnic Cocooning in Kafka's America

Ethnic semiosis and storytelling bubble up from the flux of things, as Kafka's immigrant novel, *America*, opportunely instructs. Arguably about Karl Rossmann's insomniac anxiety over losing, carrying, and keeping his box (formerly his father's old army chest) once the ship he is on lands in New York, the novel in effect presents us with a progression of scenes in which our young immigrant tyro from Prague witnesses its contents grabbed away, lost, and stolen, until the box itself disappears in the last completed chapter. By then, however, Karl learns that "no one carried any luggage" (266), even though the entire Theatre of Oklahoma troupe is about to set out on a long, cross-country train trip. At the very outset of the novel Karl expostulates, "Good Lord, I've quite forgotten my box" (15)! To which the ship's stoker replies, "Can't you do without your box?" And when Karl reasons out loud that it cannot possibly be lost, the stoker tries to wise him up with this bit of classical advice for newcomers:

> But morals change every time you come to a new port. In Hamburg your Butterbaum [the man to whom Karl confided his trunk] might maybe have looked after your box; while here it's most likely that they've both disappeared (15).

In America, Karl apparently learns to live without his box, which is to say, without his past, his family mementos and memories, and even without his "old" familiar self. Like Benjamin Franklin, whom Kafka read with great relish, Karl Rossmann finds out he has to make it on his own, without relying on his father's connections. This, it seems, is Kafka's point in having his tyro meditate, "When his father had given him the box for good he had said in jest: 'How long will you keep it?' and now that faithful box had perhaps been lost in earnest" (18). Referring to the box as "faithful" is a clever way of shifting the moral spotlight from his own role in dissipating his German patrimony to the failing grip of his father's authority. But we are not allowed here to push this view too far. After finally recovering the box and having set out down the road like a hobo — a hobo with a box on his shoulders — he ends up late one night in a hotel room with two other boys. Tired as he is, though, he finds that he is unable to sleep for fear that he will once again lose things if he but dares to close his eyes. As if to confirm his intuition, in looking around him he notes, "It was certainly strange that no sign of luggage was to be seen in the whole room…" (96). In America, we are given to understand, everyone was quite unattached: materially, socially, and morally. Horizontal semiosis is the rule.

At a certain point, after having studied the room and the situation in general, he convinces himself that he is finally alone and unobserved. It is then that he turns inward in an act of cultural cocooning. In a scene of touching intimacy, in which the reader is made to feel obtrusive like a voyeur, Karl opens his box, takes out all of its contents, and lovingly goes through them item by item. There we find pretty much what we would expect a young immigrant to bring away with him: a Bible, letter paper to write home with, photos of his parents, a cap his mother gave him to wear against the cold sea air of the ship, a good suit of clothes to start out on the right foot with, some food, and a secret pocket with a thick roll of paper money in it. All this was neatly and tightly packed with his mother's familiar touch. Now, however, the process of subtraction inexorably begins. His good suit outrageously goes to paying the hotel room, the sausage is eaten by the other two boys, and then, a short time later, his box is broken into and the photos of his parents are either carelessly scattered or stolen by one of his traveling companions. Once the photos are gone, the box has little value for Karl. As he tells his fellow travellers over and over again, he would gladly exchange it and all it contains for them.

Since he is alone and in an unknown land, the real issue now comes to the forefront. After being treated so falsely, gullible Karl decides he must become a "loose-fish" in America. As he accuses his fellow wanderers, "I know quite well what friendship is. I have had friends in Europe too and none of them can accuse me of ever behaving falsely or meanly to him" (118). Up to this point in the novel he has been betrayed by practically everybody he has met. Then, in a peculiarly Kafkian twist, after all the ups and downs of Karl's brief life in America so far, the first job he lands turns out to be as an elevator operator in the Hotel Occidental next to a busy highway. Even while standing still, he will always be moving, like a sailor assigned to watch duty in the crow's nest. In other words, it is as if Karl had not really *landed* at all or, in Melville's words, as if he were still on his passage out. Indeed, ship and hotel in *America* are functionally similar. It is in his new capacity as elevator boy that he learns what the price of making it in America is. But he also learns indirectly how to survive his plunge. Once again, the emblem of his condition appears suddenly before him in the guise of a little Italian boy, this time bearing a name.

When the Manageress ushers Karl towards one of the lifts in order to conduct him to his room, they are suddenly faced with "a small lift-boy...

leaning against the railing of a lift, fast asleep" (126). Perhaps guessing Karl's thoughts, she takes the opportunity to sketch a typical American moral:

> "A working day of from ten to twelve hours is really rather much for a boy like that," she added, while they ascended. "But America's a strange country. Take this boy, for instance; he came here only half a year ago with his parents; he's an Italian. At the moment it looks as if he simply wouldn't be able to stand the work, his face has fallen away to nothing and he goes to sleep on the job, although he's naturally a very willing lad — but let him only go on working here and he'll be able to take it all in his stride, and in another five years he'll be a strong man. I could spend hours telling you about such cases" (126).

I quote here at length because this little figure will quite suddenly reappear, with the same emaciated face, and become a kind of youthful Queegqueg for Karl in the unfinished novel's last chapter. In this first encounter it is *Giacomo* — "in the English pronunciation it was unrecognizable" (133) — who is assigned to teach Karl his job. There is, in fact, an ironic but equally representative coda to the Manageress's little parable about laissez-faire democracy in that it is on account of Karl's arrival that Giacomo loses his job.

We can easily imagine the pedagogical fuss which one of Hawthorne's carbuncular narrators would have made over this scene. But Kafka is equally successful in presenting us with yet another mini-*récit* featuring one of those uncanny figures that momentarily appear, then as suddenly disappear, and sometimes even reappear at random in the pages of American literature exactly because it has been multi-ethnic from the very beginning. More commonly than in countries having a premodern literary tradition, names in American literature almost always present themselves as somewhat exotic *objets trouvés* demanding attention in their own right. They come off as naturally strange and often trail a sense of their cultural origin even as they reek with their current condition of semantic aimlessness. It is as if each name, besides being haunted by a mysterious narrative trajectory of its own, actually bore within its etymological nucleus a unique cultural syntax which in the flux of American life has inevitably become enigmatic.

As a result, names become stories with a vengeance. All this Kafka must have understood in planning out his American novel, for Karl's fellow wanderers in "The Road to Rameses" chapter are both foreigners. Why names become enigmatic is made clear to Karl when one of the boys introduces himself: "That chap there is called Robinson, and he's an Irishman, I'm called Delamarche and I'm a Frenchman, and now please be quiet" (98). But almost all names in America sound intrinsically foreign to begin with, as if each pertained either to an ethnos of its own or to an ecumenical ethnos in which it can be indifferently pronounced in various ways. In the last chapter, "The Nature Theatre of Oklahoma," the latter hypothesis seems to find confirmation. The placards of the Theatre announcing job openings read, "Everyone is welcome," and this for Karl is its "one great attraction" (246). The announcement reads like an abbreviated code for the American Dream, which Karl rightly interprets to mean "that he too would find acceptance" (247). The theatre, he soon learns, is the biggest in the world and has "almost no limits to it" (251).

And it is lucky for Karl that even though identification papers are requested, he is still able to get a job without them. Why? Perhaps because what he can do is more important than who he is. Identity is not the big issue. After a rather absurd number of interviews in different offices, he is given a job as "technical worker" (262) not because he is Karl Rossmann, a citizen of the Austrian-Hungarian Empire from Prague, but because he says he wants to become an engineer. As for the minor matter of his name, Kafka gives us a version of what had already then become a classical scene on Ellis Island, the official port of entry for processing newly arrived immigrants. Karl senses that in America, when it comes to successfully holding down a job, it may be best to have a name that works well with others. When asked what his name is, therefore, he replies after completing the following chain of thought:

> As soon as he had a place here, no matter how small, and filled it satisfactorily, they could have his name, but not now; he had concealed it too long to give it away now. So as no other name occurred to him at the moment, he gave the nickname he had had in his last post: "Negro" (257).

This is the name announced over the loudspeaker. But the narrator is as shrewd as Karl is naive. "Negro" pertains not only to a type of narrative but also to a kind of space. If it suggests the true web of production relations Karl has been embedded in, it is only with reference to them that we can understand what the name actually means. Karl's choice also provides a nice commentary on Mr. Green's advice to him in chapter three, "A Country House Near New York": "In 'Frisco you can tackle anything you like; just begin at the bottom and trying gradually to work your way up" (92). "Negro" captures very well what it means for Karl to be at the bottom and "trying." But Karl now has two names, one for his life as a labourer and another — virtually hidden — that was given to him by his parents. The second now begins to function ethnically, within the vertical semiosis of implosion. It will become exclusively associated with the excess of meaning generated by Karl's recursive, inward turn at the close of the chapter and of the novel as we have it.

In order to appreciate the positive effects of Karl's ambiguous situation, however, we must pick up at the point in which Kafka decides to pull off a narrative coup by reintroducing Karl's little Italian friend, Giacomo. After a photo which captures his attention has been passed around at the Oklahoma Company's banquet, Karl cranes his neck to see if still others were being sent his way. Although we ourselves are not allowed to see the picture, the narrator informs us that Karl "sat gazing at it" (264), somewhat transfixed. It is at this crucial moment that he makes his overpowering discovery, as if with a magician's sleight of hand he had succeeded in making a wish come true by substituting a presence known only to him for the image on the photo: "'Giacomo!' he cried" (264).

In keeping with the improbably bittersweet, fairy-tale turn of events, the reader is almost naturally seduced into thinking, "Only in America!" The narrative timing, in fact, seems almost too good to be true: a banquet as frame, the somewhat intimate sharing of photos among the guests, and then the surprise appearance of an old friend. A willful act of narrative magic. Indeed, Kafka is brilliantly setting up what — along with Michel de Certeau — we may call an ethnic coup (81ff, 36ff). That is, he is immersing us here in the peculiar art of ethnic semiosis by postulating a "place" at the Oklahoma banquet which Karl and Giacomo can claim as their very own. In short, they are dropped into the space of an ethnic tactic. As a textual *figura*, Giacomo signals the possibility of a diversionary art of survival in Kafka's America. It is thanks to this *deus ex machina* find that the novel seems set up for a happy ending. Through his little Italian Kafka makes his most implosive appeal. Let us see how this works.

Once he has recognized him, Giacomo immediately gestures for Karl to come over and sit by him as "they had a lot to tell each other and should stick together all the time" (264-5). Here, then, in the very last chapter the novel introduces a significant, albeit momentary, reprieve from the sweeping horizontal semiosis of drifting that has characterized most of Karl's life up to then. Newly aligned by the recursive tactics typical of such scenes of reunion, names now become a way of remembering. They evoke shared experiences and map out "inward-turning histories" (de Certeau: 108). The narrator even mimics the emotion of the moment when he reports: "What memories of the past were recalled! What had happened to the Manageress? What was Therese doing? Giacomo himself had hardly changed at all in appearance... " (265). Karl once again becomes "Karl" and Giacomo hears his name pronounced correctly as the narrator proceeds with his ethno-archaeographic demonstration.

Karl and Giacomo, we infer, begin immediately to swap stories and these cross a number of places and recreate the trajectory of their names. Their storytelling is obviously a spatial practice by which a number of different places are brought and held together by the names "Karl" and "Giacomo." And this piling up, this stratification, of places becomes even more intensely committed to vertical semiosis as they talk their way back to their native city, their home, their infancy, their ancestral family. Ultimately, though, what both seek in their stories of return is their own difference and, as Pierre Nora has acutely observed: "in the spectacle of this difference the sudden explosion of a lost identity. No longer a commencement, but the deciphering of what we are in the light of what we are no longer" (Augé 29).

Having crossed two different cultures and countless places, Karl and Giacomo now begin to make positive use of their double consciousness. As Freud writes in his essay "The Antithetical Sense of Primal Words," "If everything that we can know is viewed as a transition from something else, every experience must have two sides; and either every name must have a double meaning, or else for every meaning there must be two names" (189). "In America mi chiamano *italiano*, qui in Italia mi chiamano *americano*..., " Antonio Margariti notes in his memoir *America! America!* (77). And if, in this immigrant's words, "l'America è grande ed inghiotte con facilità" (57), it does not diminish his desire to "sentirsi affratellat[o]" (83) with others from his native Ferruzzano. As Jerre Mangione informs us in *Mount Allegro*, at home he is Gerlando but outside the neighborhood, "Jerre." Tactically speaking,

Negro, alias Karl Rossmann, is now ready to see double meanings everywhere (see Tamburri).

And so, as Kafka's unfinished *America* comes to a close, Karl and Giacomo get on the train for a long transcontinental journey:

> Karl had happened to get a window-seat, with Giacomo beside him. So there they sat, the two of them, close together, rejoicing in their hearts over the journey (267).

The image of them "close together... rejoicing in their hearts" is an exemplary image of ethnic cocooning; the inference to be drawn, one of *interpretatio nominis*. "*Nisi enim nomen scieris, cognitio rerum perit*," Isidore of Seville tells us in his *Etymologiae* (I,VII,1). If you do not know the name, you remain ignorant of (the heart of) things. As Rosa Cavalleri tells in her autobiography *Rosa, the life of an Italian immigrant*, "In the old time there were more miracles than now, but I see lots of miracles — in Chicago too" (Ets Hall: 242). The Madonna who faithfully answers her pleas, of course, is the Madonna she became acquainted with during the *feste* and processions in Bugiarno, Italy.

Imploding Names, a Topological Hermeneutics

While such ethnic tactics offer the modern democratic self a degree of catharsis from the stressful conditions of his or her individual sovereignty, we should not misrepresent the function or status which ethnic subjectivity assumes in a semiocentric world. Giacomo and Karl actually inhabit a non-place. *America*'s closing gesture, it is worth recalling, suspends the two boys in a moving train: "For two days and two nights they journeyed on" (267). If they ever do arrive, Karl will begin his new life as a technician and Giacomo, not surprisingly, will pick up where he left off, as elevator operator. But we cannot be sure they will stop travelling. Consequently, the novel's ending is not really that different from the open ending of *Moby Dick* where Ishmael, the lone survivor of the shipwreck, is picked up at sea by the *Rachel*.

Nor can it be said that Karl and Giacomo are in a much different situation than Pascal D'Angelo who finally lands a job with the railroad only to end up living in a boxcar. As he recounts in his autobiography *Son of Italy*, published the year Kafka died, "But at times I would stand in front of the box car on a clear night. Around would be the confusion, whistles, flashes and grinding sounds of the never-ending movements in the yard" (148). Even Rosa Cavalleri's sense of her new country suggests what it means to be caught in a web of signs. On returning to her native Bugiarno, she is encouraged to "[t]ell about that again, Rosa. And about the streets of New York — show them how the people are always running and how they have to jump to get out of the way of the carriages and horses. And about those streetcars running right over the heads of the people" (Ets 189).

Obviously, such impressions are common enough, but what they actually allude to is a condition of dwelling that is often perceived as natural and universal. Thus, in Louis Grudin's poem "Emanuel" (Emanuel Carnevali), we are given this Italian-American poet's sense of the new cosmic dimensions of metropolitan life:

> In the chill of the dead of night,
> walked from the Bowery to Harlem
> And whispered the cosmic fault:
> "No one sees me, no one wonders at me!"
> and wrote it in his composition book
> of pages faintly ruled in blue,
> with cardboard covers that would curl and part
> like the peeling tenement walls
> burning slow, shedding their airy ash
> to be rebreathed by all who come about
> and go about and share that air (Carnevali 1980: 200).

Carnevali was another invisible man living in a democratic non-place. In his essay "I fuochi della tribù" Paolo Valesio argues that if Carnevali merits our attention today it is above all "for his fluid condition, outside of any fixed situation" (Carravetta and Valesio 277). Contrary to Kafka's Giacomo, he did not survive the cultural insult of America. As the citation in Grudin's poem accuses, Carnevali felt like a complete nobody. In words reminiscent of Ishmael, this Whitmanian overreacher says of his life in New York in the twenties, "I was like a fisherman adrift on the sea, floating helpless on a raft, kept afloat by God knows what promise or strength or hope" (1967: 116). Earlier in his autobiographical collage he describes himself as a castaway "on a raft in mid-ocean" (1967: 85).

In the city of information, in a world of signs, names are democratically cut free of the genealogical syntax that explains and gives them agency. They appear and disappear, sink and resurface without apparent origin. When young Frank Lloyd Wright arrived in Chicago in 1887 and took his first cable-car ride, he noted "names obliterating everything... They would begin to mix with absurd effect and you need take nothing to get the effect of another extravaganza" (87). Referring to his own walk among the multi-ethnic crowds in New York Central Park in 1904, Henry James called it "the mingled medium" (177). Without taking any special note of it, however, Wright too cast his topological interpretation of downtown Chicago in a similar key. Thus from the window of his cable car:

> Supersensitive ears and eyes were fixed by harsh dissonance but recovered themselves: reasoned and fought for freedom. Compelled again — until the procession... became chaos in a wilderness of Italian, German, Irish, Polack, Greek, English, Swedish, French, Chinese and Spanish names in letters that began to come off and get about, interlace and stick, climb and swing again (86-7).

Like Carnevali, Wright seems adrift and trying to stay afloat in a sea of signs. And in the United States the name-signs are from everywhere. It is especially in the metropolis that they "come off and get about" in a cultural *tourbillon* second only to the intensities of capitalist exchange. Wright correctly takes the names for Chicago's cultural a priori, noting further that they shift rapidly from "procession" to "chaos." If one travels across the country, though, one will discover that the linguistic topology of American dwelling repeats that of the big cities. This toponymic list which Pascal D'Angelo provides us with in *Son of Italy* is typical of the nomadic experience of Italian immigrants in America: "Everywhere was toil... In Hillsdale, Poughkeepsie, Spring Valley, New York, Falling Water, Virginia, Westwood, Remsey, New Jersey, Williamsport, Maryland, where the winding Potomac flows, Utica, New York, White Lake Corner, Otterlake, Tappan, Statsburg, Oneanta, Glen Falls, and many other places where we could find work, always as a pick and shovel man — that's what I was able to do, and that is what I work at even now" (74).

Furthermore, not only does every immigrant virtually represent a place of origin, she or he is also the living sign — or *topos* — of a spatial adventure and disjunction. It is in this territorial sense that *nominis stat umbra* (the shadow of the name remains). And it is also because of this involuntary attendance that ethnic semiosis and storytelling succeed in changing a predominantly temporal into a topological hermeneutics (see Vitiello). Each name, in other words, has its own horizon of significance. In order to fathom it, we must implode the name, treat it as a stratification of places. Considered as *topoi* in this sense, names are not only subjective but also spatial models of experience. Depending on whether we treat them according to a vertical or a horizontal semiotic, they will produce a different narrative axiology. Only an ethno-archaeographic form of attention is capable of explaining how a name came into being and thus of interpreting it.

Returning to the linguistic topology of the national state, we find at first sight a cultural whirlpool similar to Wright's Chicago and subject to the same accelerated trajectories of Pascal D'Angelo. But if we choose to read the national map as a heteronomous exhibition of single *topoi*, rather than a merely functional system of unheeded circulation, we will discover a discrete territory of founding deeds and first intentions. Rather than a national allegory, we will find a display of hieroglyphic sites inscribed by the local mind. To understand their stories is to gain access *ab intra* to the vicissitudes of ethnogenesis across the land. Take, for example, the story of Roseto, a small town of some 2,000 inhabitants in the northeast part of Pennsylvania.

In the early 1960s the town gained international fame for having the highest rate of longevity and immunity to heart disease in the nation. But what is more pertinent here is the fact that Roseto is said to be the "most Italian' town in the country (Bianco 16ff). As Carla Bianco's ethno-archaeographic documentation has revealed, 95% of the "Rosetani" in Pennsylvania are direct descendents of the inhabitants of Roseto Valfortore, Foggia, Italy. In the late 1880s following a process of chain immigration, so many inhabitants of Roseto, Italy, left for America that the abandoned narrow streets in the center of town were often referred to as the *vie degli americani* (Bianco 43). Likewise, the street map of Roseto, Pennsylvania, reveals that the center of town is formed by the intersection of Columbus and Garibaldi Avenues. To the east of Garibaldi Avenue and running roughly north and south is a quieter, more residential street named Roseto. With Carla Bianco's study of the town serving as base, our site-analysis — had we the time — could now begin.

To conclude, it would be a mistake to presume that we are concerned here simply with "the way it really was." As Walter Benjamin suggests in his "Theses on the Philosophy of History," recounting Roseto or Mount Allegro or Telegraph Hill as a story of foundation and a scene of origin involves us in quite a different transaction: that of our own cultural redemption (1973: 256). "History," he reminds us, "is the subject of a structure whose site is not homogeneous, empty time, but time filled by the presence of the now [*Jetztzeit*]" (263). In the story "The Return to the Source" from his short story collection *The Paesanos*, Joe Pagano provides us with an objective correlative of what Benjamin meant by "the now." The passage reads as follows:

> — fragments all of them, pieces of a childish puzzle which older fingers seek to resolve. What did that child really see? That was a real and tangible world into which he entered, that summer so many years ago; but what, what? The mind is like a series of rooms, some of them closed forever, or almost forever; one seeks to unlock these chambers, one fumbles for the key; one sits, as I sat on a certain evening in our living room after my grandfather's death, and looks at a picture, and tries to remember (195).

There is no need of comment. What the young protagonist is trying to recover may have many names, but all of them point to the site of a cultural inside. The effort to remember is characterized as a spatial practice while the mind itself becomes a labyrinth of rooms. Ultimately, through the very act of his topological seeking he presents us with an inward-turning story. Or, in the words of Carla Bianco, a "conoscersi etnicamente" (22). As Denise Nico Leto nicely puts it in her poem "What's in a Name," "She had many Names/she called them/all her own / and as her own / they called" (119). And no matter how weak this summons may be, the practice of recursiveness continues even where it can claim no place of its own. In Laura Anna Stortoni's poem "The Carob-Tree" — with its specification "(Recollections of a Sicilian Childhood)" the lyrical voice concludes, "I know I shall not find it./ And yet I must go see — /see if it's there" (124).

The Remorseless Italian's Stare

In 1904, when Henry James returned to his native land after a good twenty years' absence, he described his interest in mining terms: "The story-seeker would be present, quite intimately present, at the general effort... to gouge an interest *out* of the vacancy, gouge it with tools of price, even as copper and gold and diamonds are extracted, by elaborate processes, from earth-sections of small superficial expression" (12). Surfaces for him became all depth. And could it have been otherwise? As he returned to the sites of his childhood, he found that his birthplace in New York was torn down. After having the satisfaction of finding his father's house in Boston still intact, he went back the very next day only to find it gone. Undaunted, he continued to apply his topological gaze with even greater passion; and with the same necessity that Edith Wharton expressed when she too faced James' plight. This passage from her autobiography *A Backword Glance* is worth quoting in full:

> What I could not guess was that this little low-studded rectangular New York... this cramped horizontal gridiron of a town without towers... would fifty years later be as much a vanished city as Atlantis or the lowest layer of Schliemann's Troy... Nothing but the Atlantis-fate of old New York, the New York which had slowly but continuously developed from the early seventeenth century to my own childhood, makes that childhood worth recalling now (55).

When James went to Salem to visit the "House of the Seven Gables," somehow he got lost and had to ask a young man for directions. Once again, the reader is confronted with one of those aleatory foreign signs that we already saw at work in Melville and Hawthorne. As James recounts it, "[T]he young man... stared at me as a remorseless Italian — as remorseless, at least, as six months of Salem could leave him" (265). He then expresses his sense of disorientation at finding the American scene so changed: "On that spot, in that air, I confess, it was a particular shock to me to be once more, with my so good general intention, so 'put off'" (265). How far we have come from the little *suonatore ambulante* who stood before the "House of the Seven Gables" some fifty years earlier! One senses in James that some epic battle has been fought, as if the echoes of the little Italian's barrel-organ were ultimately responsible for bringing down the walls of his old cultural citadel. He is wrong however to suggest that his own *remorsus* (his own vexed "biting again") is not shared by the young Italian.

Indeed, it is because he is remorseful that James reveals a second thought comparable to that of Hawthorne's narrator in the scene from *The House of the Seven Gables* discussed above. "[T]hough, if my young man but glared frank ignorance of the monument I named, he left me at least with the interest of wondering how the native estimate of it as a romantic ruin might strike a taste formed for such features by the landscape of Italy" (265), he says. James is right, then, to speak of mining "earth-sections of small superficial expression," just as Melville was in citing/siting Rinaldo Rinaldini to describe the "terrible prestige of perilousness about such a whale" (176). In other words, we are not just talking about the representation of shifting cultural landscapes but above all about the topology of stratified cultural representations. Neither democracy understood as Whitman's "teeming nation of nations" nor modern democratic literature as a recombination of the West's, if not the world's, literary topoi can discount the attempt to fathom the young Italian's stare. That's what literary remorse is all about. Thus we are back to Peter Carravetta's "Guarda che da dirci c'era tanto e niente" (1991: 133), with the final cautionary reminder, "qui le parole sono pietre, e l'amore" (136).

Note

1. The core of this essay is about the uses of a topological hermeneutics and its appropriateness for modern literatures like those of the United States, Canada, and South and Central American countries. For this reason I would like to express my special debt to the work of Vincenzo Vitiello, Walter Benjamin, Georg Simmel.

References

Augé, Marc. *Nonluoghi.* Trans. Dominique Rolland. Milan: Elèuthera, 1993.

Benjamin, Walter. *Immagini di città.* Trans. Marisa Bertolini. Turin: Einaudi, 1980.

————. *Illuminations.* Ed. Hannah Arendt, Trans. Harry Zohn. London: Fontana, 1973.

Bianco, Carla. "Una ricerca antropologica." *Emigrazione.* A cura di Carla Bianco & Emanuela Angiuli. Bari: Dedalo Libri, 1980, 11-39.

Carnevali, Emanuel. *The Autobiography of Emanuel Carnevali.* Ed. Kay Boyle. New York: Horizon Press, 1967.

————.*Voglio disturbare l'America.* Ed. Gabriel Cacho Millet. Florence: Usher, 1980.

Carravetta, Peter. "Eros e Nomos." *VIA: Voices in Italian Americana.* Vol.2, No.2, Fall 1991, 133-36.

Carravetta, Peter, and Valesio, Paolo. *Poesaggio. Poeti Italiani d'America.* Quinto di Treviso: Pagus Edizioni, 1993.

Dana, Richard Henry. *Two Years Before the Mast.* New York: Random House, 1936.

D'Angelo, Pascal. *Son of Italy.* New York: MacMillan, 1924. Arno Press Reprint, 1975.

de Certeau, Michel. *The Practice of Everyday Life.* Berkeley: University of California Press: 1984.

Eco, Umberto. *Le forme del contenuto.* Milan: Bompiani, 1971.

Ets Hall, Marie, ed. *Rosa: The Life of an Italian Immigrant.* Minneapolis: University of Minnesota Press, 1970.

Freud, Sigmund. "The Antithetical Sense of Primal Words." In *Collected Papers.* Vol. 4. Trans. Joan Rivière. New York: Basic Books, 1959, 184-191.

Hawthorne, Nathaniel. *The House of the Seven Gables.* Ed. Seymour L. Gross. New York: Norton, 1967.

Isidori, Hispalensis Episcopi. *Etymologiarum sive originum.* 2 Vols. Oxford: Oxford UP, 1987.

Jabès, Edmond. *Le petit livre de la subversion hors de soupçon.* Paris: Gallimard, 1982.

————. *Le retour au livre.* Paris: Gallimard, 1965.

James, Henry. *The American Scene.* Ed. Leon Edel. Bloomington: Indiana UP, 1968.

Kafka, Franz. *America.* Trans. Willa & Edwin Muir. Harmondsworth: Penguin, 1978.

Mangione, Jerre. *Mount Allegro.* New York: Houghton Mifflin, 1943.

Margariti, Antonio. *America! America!.* Casalvelino Scalo (Salerno): Galzerano Editore, 1981.

Melville, Herman. *Moby Dick.* Eds. Harrison Hayford & Hershel Parker. New York: Norton, 1967.

Nico Leto, Denise. "What's in a Name." *VIA: Voices in Italian Americana.* Vol.2, No.2, Fall 1991, 117-119.

Pagano, Jo. *The Paesanos.* Boston: Little, Brown and Company, 1940.

Schmitt, Carl. *Terra e mare.* Trans. Angelo Bolaffi. Milan: Giuffre, 1986.

Stortoni, Laura Anna. "The Carob Tree." *VIA: Voices in Italian Americana.* Vol.2, No.2, Fall 1991, 123-24.

Stravinskij, Igor. *Cronache della mia vita.* Trans. Alberto Mantelli. Milan: Feltrinelli, 1979.

Tamburri, Anthony J. *To Hyphenate or Not to Hyphenate. The Italian/American Writer.* Montreal/Toronto: Guernica, 1991.

Valesio, Paolo. *L'ospedale di Manhattan.* Rome: Editori Riuniti, 1978.

Vitiello, Vicenzo. "Ethos e natura." *Paradoso. Quadrimestrale di Filosofia.* No. 2, 1992, 9-66.

Whitman, Walt. *Complete Poetry and Collected Prose.* Ed. Justin Kaplan. New York: The Library of America, 1982.

Wharton, Edith. *A Backward Glance.* New York: Scribner's, 1964.

Wright, Frank Lloyd. *An Autobiography.* New York: Horizon Press, 1977.

Zucchi, John. "Italian Child Street Musicians in New York in the 1870s." *Italian Americana.* Vol. X, No.1, Fall/Winter 1991, 7-30.

Rose Romano

Coming Out Olive
in the Lesbian Community

Big Sister Is Watching You

*H*aving little or no power, as lesbians, beyond their own community, lesbians with power within their community often abuse that power. Overwhelmed by straight society's determined misinterpretations of what they are, many lesbians have developed their own self definitions. In many ways, however, they've defined themselves as straight men have defined them, that is, many lesbians define themselves in relation to others. What a lesbian is depends to a great extent on where she fits in what is known as a "hierarchy of pain."

Whoever has suffered the most is most deserving of respect; whoever hasn't suffered deserves no respect. Black people, because of past slavery and present racism in this country and others, are considered to have suffered more than anyone else. As the skin colour of members of other races and ethnicities becomes lighter and lighter, those races and ethnicities are considered to have suffered less and less. Therefore, the lighter one's skin, the less respect one is entitled to.

I have been censored in the lesbian press and ostracized in the lesbian community because I call myself Olive. Politically correct lesbians have agreed with the division of people into two categories: white and "of colour."

There is no distinction made between different groups within the white community — if I am white, I am assigned WASP history and culture. In one essay, in a book meant to help its three authors and all its readers to unlearn racism and anti-Semitism, there's this question: "When women differ from us by ethnicity, by 'blood', but are white-skinned, how much does our desire to have them be like us have to do with our thinking racially in either-or categories: either you are white or you are not..." (Bulkin, Pratt, Smith 49). Although these words accurately reflect the situation in the lesbian community, they seem to be only words, and I don't think the author knows what they mean. This Presbyterian woman not only fails to overcome this problem in her own self, but, while the author seems to acknowledge her problem, she completely denies it by nearly always referring to both Protestants and Catholics as one people — Christians. A few times she mentions that she or another individual belongs to a particular Protestant denomination. Other than that, Christians do this, she says, and Christians do that. This is the experience of Christians in this country, she says, completely ignoring the fact that the experience of Catholics in this country has been more similar to the experience of Jews in this country than to that of Protestants. She mentions the Klu Klux Klan and their attitude toward and treatment of Jews, but never mentions that Klansmen are Protestant and feel and behave the same way toward Catholics. She says: "...when we [her local chapter of the National Organization for Women (NOW)] scheduled a discussion on religion, the two women who spoke were a professor of religion and a Methodist minister; no representation was requested from the women of the local Jewish congregation, since 'religion' meant denominations of Christianity" (31). My advice to this woman would be that she guess again. According to my understanding of this sentence, she and her friends at NOW consider religion to be denominations of Protestantism. As a Southern Italian/Sicilian-American pagan Catholic, I hardly consider myself to be represented by the Pope; I certainly don't consider myself to be represented by a Methodist minister.

Throughout her essay the author drops certain phrases, like Hansel and Gretel dropping bits of bread as their stepmother leads them into the forest: "Christian-raised," "Christian culture," "Christian beliefs," "Christian civilization," "Christian believers." Only twice in her essay does she make a real distinction between Catholics and Protestants: once when she talks about a civil rights demonstration organized by Protestants and once when she complains about her Catholic ex-husband and his priest who were trying to force on her their ideas about birth control. Apparently, this woman thinks that Protestants and Catholics are pretty much the same, except that Protestants do good things and Catholics do bad things. All in all, her essay not only mentions briefly the problem of the reassignment of culture according to superficial assessments of appearance, it also does a pretty good job of demonstrating the very same problem.

This reassignment seems to show up most obviously in the area of religion, as in the above, maybe because there are other ethnicities, besides Italian, who are overwhelmingly Catholic and who have always made more noise than Italian-Americans. But Italian-Americans are beginning to make noise. The problem now is that some are making American noise, probably because there is no Italian noise, at least not at a pitch Americans are capable of perceiving.

In her book, *No Pictures in My Grave* (1992), Susan Caperna Lloyd, half Sicilian-American, describes her trip to Trapani during Easter Week and her efforts to rediscover her spiritual heritage. Throughout the book, she reminds us that she's an American; the Sicilians think she's odd; people in the street recognize immediately that she doesn't belong; she doesn't know whether she'll ever be able to feel a part of things. As a photographer, Lloyd is determined to get pictures of what might be a painting of a Goddess in a cave at Levanzo. The use of the flash is not allowed because it would harm the painting. She says: "I felt irritated with this Italian penchant for obeying the rules...It never seemed to occur to them to try to get around the rules or to buy off the powers-that-be" (38). Maybe the Sicily Lloyd's family is from isn't the one on this planet. Or maybe she just forgot the Sicilians and Italians don't tell the same story to strangers that they tell to family.

Not only does she evaluate Sicilian culture according to WASP standards, she shows the same American disinclination to even recognize Sicilian behaviour if it doesn't fit into the stereotypes. She tells us about women who participate in the Easter Week procession at Trapani: her new friend, Clara, who's been helping to carry one of the saints in the procession for the three years prior to Lloyd's arrival; the old women dressed in black who walk behind the Madonna; and different groups of young girls dressed as the Madonna or as Veronica. Yet she still complains that women aren't allowed to participate. When Lloyd is invited to carry one of the saints, her participation is called "unprecedented" in the promotional material I received from the publisher with a review copy of her book. But if Clara and many other women have been participating in the procession for years before Lloyd arrived in Sicily, Lloyd's participation is obviously not "unprecedented." So the message is pretty clear — if you're Sicilian or Italian (Americans are unaware of any distinction) you either conform to the appropriate stereotypes or you're invisible.

And she tells us about the *portatori*, the men who carry the heavy statues through the streets all day and all night. I know it's important that I show respect to my people and I know it would be an honour to be asked to help carry one of the saints in this procession. But I think of the sweat and the blisters; I think of the terrible ache in the shoulders and the sharp pain shooting through the legs and I know why the job of hauling heavy loads through the village is usually reserved for donkeys. But Lloyd seems to feel that the goal of a feminist is, not to attain for women equality with men, but to be allowed to do what men do, that is, it isn't the behaviour she wants for its own satisfactions, it's the association with men. She reminds us throughout the book that men go outside and do, while women stay inside and don't and, like an American, the author considers outside and doing better than inside and not.

But I look white; therefore, I am white. And if I'm white, I belong to white culture. And, as a member of white culture, I've been told I have suffered the least and caused the most suffering to others. If there is little I can do, as an individual, to stop the suffering, I am expected to do the next best thing — feel guilty.

I have been told that by calling myself Olive I am evading my "responsibility of guilt." Because I am a light-skinned woman living in the United States, it is accepted that my grandparents, whether or not they owned slaves themselves, belonged to the group who did own slaves and were entitled to all the benefits. If they chose not to take advantage of those benefits, it's their own fault. When I tell lesbians that Southern Italians and Sicilians didn't even begin to arrive in this country until twenty years after the slave days were over I am told that this is a "wrong use of facts" and that today I am a member of an oppressor group and that I can choose to take advantage of my "white-skin privilege."

"White-skin privilege" means I don't suffer from racism. It means that whatever problems I have that might be caused by anti-Italian bigotry are of less significance than the problems of dark-skinned people because I can scrub the shine of olive oil from my forehead, pluck the hairs from my chin, change my name, and go right out and get myself a well-paying job and a luxury apartment anytime I like.

One lesbian, in a women's newspaper, writes in opposition to racism, yet uses several racist techniques to defend her position. At one point, she says, "...the more lesbians who look like the dominant culture claim that they are examples of oppressed cultures, the more invisible the members of truly oppressed cultures become." To ignore the problems of truly oppressed people is racist; to ignore the problems of merely oppressed people is not racist. Any lesbian can suggest that we fight the racist act of ignoring the problems of oppressed people with the progressive act of ignoring the problems of oppressed people and other lesbians will not notice what she's doing. If I write about the problems faced by Italian-Americans, I am taking attention away from other, more deserving, people. Therefore, if I write about the problems faced by Italian-Americans, I am a racist.

Far more important than literary merit to a lesbian editor is the extent to which a lesbian writer has suffered from oppression. While in straight literary journals contributor notes usually list a writer's publications, readings, awards, jobs, in women's literary journals contributor notes often list race, sexuality, physical handicaps, chemical dependencies, experiences of child abuse, etc. The purpose of lesbian literary journals is not so much to present worthwhile literature as it is to preserve otherwise neglected stories.

If I am Olive, if Italian-Americans have suffered oppression, my story deserves space in a lesbian literary journal. There are very few lesbian literary journals. The space in any one of them is limited, the money is tight, and the staff is an unpaid, over-worked collective that's constantly changing. It's impossible for any little magazine to print everything considered worthwhile. It's impossible for lesbian literary journals to print work representative of every different group of women. It's racist to deny dark-skinned women the opportunity to be heard, as white men have always done in mainstream publishing. It's racist for lesbian literary journals to give space to light-skinned women when they might have given space to dark-skinned women. Space given to one woman is space taken away from another; it's impractical to live up to one's ideals.

If I am white, if Italian-Americans have not suffered oppression, my story is WASP and has already been told. There is no way, and no need, to justify giving space to an unimportant variation of a too-often repeated theme that so few people can relate to, whether considered in terms of ideals or money.

If I am white, lesbians can abuse, ridicule and, by doing so, neglect my culture without being charged with racism. Mentions of Italian-Americans in women's literary journals are very rare, very brief, and always negative.

In one issue of *Common Lives/Lesbian Lives*, a story written by zana uses the name of Al Capone to remind the reader that criminals were as dangerous in the 1930s as they are today. In another issue, a character in a story by Lee Lynch claims that a firefighter's job is no more dangerous than the job of a bartender in a lesbian bar because the bartender has to put up with the Mafia. In both cases, there is the acceptance of the bigot's association of Italian-Americans with crime and a willingness to reinforce that association. A further reinforcement is accomplished by the fact that Italian names are never used to bring up positive images — or even to identify real and active characters.[1]

In *A Gathering of Spirit*, an anthology of writings by American Indian women, one of the contributors is half Italian. All the writers identify their ethnicity in their contributor notes. Although they are overwhelmingly full Native American, several mention other races. One woman describes herself as Laguna/Sioux/Lebanese, another as Blood/Chicana. One woman says her mother is French-Canadian and Native American. One contributor's name is Kateri Sardella; she identifies as Micmac.

Sardella's narrative, apparently true, includes a brief conversation between two insensitive bigots who refer to her father as a *paizan*.[2] Only Italians would use that word and only in reference to an Italian. Although she thus admits in a begrudging and negative way to being just as much Italian as she is Micmac, she never actually names herself Italian and doesn't claim that part of her heritage.

Like many Italian-Americans, Italian-American lesbians don't know which side of their pizza the sauce is on. When I told an Italian-American lesbian about this story, her immediate response was typical of those confronted by claims of oppression of Italian-Americans — she said, "So what? Everybody's got problems." She said that Sardella isn't necessarily an Italian name and that *paizan* doesn't mean Italian, it just means friend.

If Italian-American lesbians don't even know how to read about themselves, it's not surprising that they don't know how to write about themselves. One cliché in lesbian literature is the use of a massage as seduction in a lesbian love scene. Lesbians like to use different kinds of oils, choosing oils with medicinal properties or magical powers, scented or non-scented. According to work I've read as editor of *la bella figura*,[3] an Italian-American lesbian chooses olive oil every time.

In an effort to bring a better awareness of Italian-American issues to non-Italian lesbians, and to Italian-American lesbians as well, I proposed, to the editor of a lesbian literary journal, a special issue of Italian-American women's writing. This is fairly common in the lesbian literary community, in which there have been, besides the Native American issue mentioned above, special issues of various literary journals devoted to work by and about Black women, Asian-American women, and Hispanic women.

My proposal was not only accepted, I was asked to edit the issue. In preparation, I attended a meeting of this journal's collective to learn how they work together and to understand what was expected of me. When I got to the meeting, I was given, by the editor, a previous special issue of their publication on Jewish women so that I could "get some ideas about what could be written about such a small group," as though her ignorance of my culture and heritage is proof that I have none and, therefore, I needed to copy another culture and heritage to make it look as though I do have my own. The impression I had from this woman, who was Jewish and who had contributed to this issue, was that she felt, as a Jew, Jews are real and Italian-Americans are not and that if I, as an Italian-American, want to be real, too, I'd have to learn from non-Italians.

Another member of the collective said she understood my right, as an Italian-American, to have such an issue, and she was very strongly in favour of the right of all women to define themselves, although she really couldn't see how I could fill a whole magazine — this would be fewer than 150 pages — with nothing but writings by and about Italian-Americans. It reminded me of the time, when I was about ten years old, I announced to my father that I was going to write a book of short biographies of women who had accomplished great things in the arts and sciences. My father was pleased and said my ambition was commendable, but I'd never be able to find enough women to fill a whole book.

And I thought about *The Dream Book*, an anthology of about 400 pages of writings by Italian-American women. An editor of a fairly important women's literary journal, and a feminist interested in all the concerns of all women, might be expected to have heard of such a book, which, at that time, had been out for more than two years. But, when I told this editor about the book the first time, she said she'd never heard of it. Maybe it's not entirely fair to expect someone to know everything in any given area, even if it is considered her area of expertise, although one book is not everything. But when I mentioned it to her again, not too long afterward on another occasion, she said again that she had never heard of it. And when I mentioned it to her a third time, not too long afterward on another occasion, she said again that she had never heard of it. How many times does a politically correct radical lesbian feminist separatist, who's in a position in which one might expect her to know something about women's literature, have to hear about a book of writings by Italian-American women before she's heard of it... before she acknowledges that it exists... that we exist? But if it doesn't fit the stereotypes they don't see it. Italian-American women don't write; we cook.

It wasn't long before I understood what was expected of me. When I asked the editor what she thought an Italian-American women's issue would be, she said, after some hesitation, that she thought it would be an examination of the difficulties of being a lesbian in an Italian-American family and a celebration of our culture. Considered from a non-Italian point of view, these topics can be seen as descriptive of negative stereotypes — the homophobic patriarch and the harmless buffoon. Even worse, if these topics are the only ones examined, the journal would ignore more important issues (more important because they're ignored everywhere else) — the difficulties of being Italian-American in the lesbian community and how Americans and Northern Italians, including lesbians in both groups, have tried to rewrite the history of Southern Italian/Sicilian-American lesbians and straight women. What this editor wanted from me was a journal about Italian-Americans that wouldn't disturb the popular notions of ignorant people, most of whom were bigots as well. And she hoped, by asking me to do the typesetting, something not asked of other guest editors, she would be able to free herself of a good deal of the work in putting this issue together, so that she could devote that time to writing her own novel.

When I told the editor I was no longer interested in doing the issue, she gave the job to two of her friends — women who had been friends of mine until I dropped the issue. One of them told me that the editor had required them to sign a contract giving the editor full and final editorial control of the issue — something else which isn't asked of guest editors of other special women's issues since it so obviously makes impossible the whole purpose of self-definition. As a result, the official Southern Italian/Sicilian-American lesbian self-definition, as given in a fairly important women's literary journal, is a definition censored by a non-Italian who is ignorant of our culture and heritage and unwilling to learn. And there is censorship, along with a determined inability to recognize reality, working to limit the writing of Italian-American lesbians, in quantity as well as quality, in other segments of publishing as well.

There is only one Italian-American lesbian publishing novels about Italian-American lesbians. There is also Dodici Azpadu, who identifies as Sicilian-American. In her novel, *Saturday Night in the Prime of Life*, Azpadu presents a Sicilian-American lesbian whose problems, according to the lesbian press that printed the book, seem to be caused mostly by her family's Sicilian heritage. Their blurb on the book's back cover says: "Though primarily Neddie and Lindy's story, the context — the trap — is the male-dominated Sicilian culture that affects the women who exist inside and outside it." This is acceptable in lesbian literature. Lesbians consider Italian-American culture to be patriarchal; Catholicism to be a woman-hating religion; Italian-American men to be wife-beating male chauvinist pigs; and straight Italian-American women to be glued to their stoves by the starch in their pasta. These are the forms of oppression suffered by Italian-American women because of their culture; these are not the negative stereotypes of bigots. Obviously, a Sicilian-American or Italian-American lesbian has a lot to complain about.

Yet, reading this book reveals very quickly and plainly that the story revolves around Concetta, the family matriarch, to the point that "the context — the trap" that oppresses all the other characters, female and male, lesbian and straight, Sicilian and American, far from being a "male-dominated" culture, is most definitely a "Concetta-dominated" culture.

The novel is mostly concerned with Neddie and Lindy's working through their decision about what to do with Concetta, who, in her old age, is making conciliation noises at her estranged daughter, Neddie. The scenes describing how Concetta makes life difficult for everyone around her on the "straight side" of the family serve to indicate the special difficulties not found in a traditional, legal, heterosexual relationship. As Lindy points out many times,

Neddie's brothers, in spite of the real problems they have in their own situations, aren't considering leaving their wives to take care of their mother, as Neddie is considering leaving Lindy. But what's also made clear in the book is that, whether any particular character is actually afraid of Concetta or, at the other extreme, almost openly resentful of her, they are willing to rearrange at least half of their lives, if not all, to give the appearance of showing respect. Concetta's power may not be the kind that's honoured, or even acknowledged, in mainstream or lesbian culture, but it's power nonetheless — and it's a power even her sons don't want to mess with.

Goat Song, another novel by Azpadu, revolves around Brandy, a woman who was abandoned to an orphanage at birth. No one knows her ethnicity, including Brandy herself. Although Azpadu seems to make a special point of stating the ethnicity of every other character in the book, even we, as readers, are never told Brandy's ethnicity, although Catherine, one of Brandy's lovers, offers a few guesses: "Middle Eastern, Eurasian, Latin or Creole." Azpadu describes Brandy as having "swarthy skin, a large hooked nose, thick coarse black hair and brows, a trace of hair above her lip" (33). Because of her appearance, she's subjected to racism as a woman of colour. And this is why it's never stated in the novel that she's Sicilian. From conversations and correspondence with Azpadu, I know that Azpadu identifies as a woman of colour and that she knows her history well enough to produce such a brilliant metaphor — the Sicilian-American lesbian as an unclaimed orphan. While Brandy's every thought, feeling, and behaviour screams Sicilian, Azpadu understands her own culture well enough to realize that Brandy is made more thoroughly Sicilian by not being named Sicilian. Thus Azpadu succeeds in using *omertà* to break *omertà* — Azpadu would also understand that this novel would not have been published by a lesbian press if it openly named Sicilians as people of colour who suffer from racism. It simply wouldn't fit in with the politically correct lesbian's "hierarchy of pain." If lesbians make no distinction between different European groups, they certainly can't be expected to distinguish between Northern Italians, Southern Italians, and Sicilians. In fact, they seem to have no notion of how young Italy actually is or of how the peninsula and the islands became one political entity. Instead, they seem to have accepted the kinds of historical accounts generally found in the most shallow of travel guide books and believe that the name Italy is really descriptive of a single ancient civilization created by a single ancient people. If they happen to know a blue-eyed blonde who has a grandparent from Milan, there's no reason for them to upset their tidy categories by thinking that Brandy is subjected to racism because she's Sicilian.

At the other extreme is Rachel Guido deVries' novel, *Tender Warriors*. This book makes a point of labelling Italian-Americans as white and minimizing prejudice faced by Italian-Americans. One character, a Black man, obviously a token, serves no purpose in the plot other than to conclude that Sonny De Marco isn't so bad for a white guy. De Vries says: "Till Sonny, he never liked to talk to white people after that" (26). Lorraine De Marco marries a Black man: "Once [her in laws] got past an initial disappointment that Curtis was with a white girl..." (72)

Although the novel represents Italian-Americans in a positive enough way, it never goes beyond what an anti-Italian bigot could tolerate; positive enough is not positive enough. There's no really deep sense of Italian culture and heritage as there is a deep sense of Sicilian culture and heritage in Azpadu's *Goat Song*. The several small evidences of Italian ethnicity given throughout De Vries' novel could have been acquired by a non-Italian in a movie theatre. Most references are to food: lasagna, stuffed *braciole*, artichokes, meatballs, simple cue words. Other references are to "that macho Italian stuff"; to Dominic's being a patriarch and to Dominic's Cadillac.

De Vries uses three Italian words in the book. Two of them are spelled incorrectly. All three are translated on the bottom of the page on which they first appear. This is in contrast to Azpadu's use of Sicilian in *Saturday Night in the Prime of Life*. Azpadu offers no translations, just as many Hispanic feminist writers offer no translations of Spanish words, phrases, and whole paragraphs in otherwise English texts in English language publications. On the one hand, you could say it's polite to translate. On the other hand, you could say a reader might have enough respect to look up a word in a dictionary, enough awareness of an "other" people, who have contributed a great deal to this country's culture, to be familiar with a couple of simple words.

It's apparently because of this other hand that De Vries doesn't translate the Spanish word *machismo*, a popular word among speakers of English. But *capice*, (*capisce* or better, as it's used by the grandmother to address the grandson, "*capisci*") which she does translate, is also a popular word among speakers of English.

The novel describes an Italian-American family that tries to escape itself. The three children, Rose, Lorraine and Sonny, become, as Lorraine thinks of it, "a dyke, a junkie, and a weirdo." Rose has a "need to carve out her life, separate from the family, as different from the way she grew up as she could imagine" (131). After distorting Italian-American family life to fit the stereotypes, De Vries has her characters running away from that distortion as though anything's better than being Italian. Rose, Lorraine and Sonny choose non-Italians, mostly Blacks, as friends, lovers, and spouses. Even the language of the book is more similar to Black English than to Italian English. With all the non-Italian motivations of the characters and the distortion of Italian ways, DeVries could have written a very different novel exploring how an "other" culture, in an ungracious country, can become so distorted and unhealthy that its own children run from it, something that's a very real and common problem among Italian-Americans. But this is never openly pointed out in the novel; that's not what the novel is about. Instead, the author seems to have accepted this distorted and superficial view of Italian ways as simple Italian-American reality and thus seems, herself, to be running from the family.

These three are the only novels written by and about Sicilian-American and Italian-American lesbians published by the lesbian press. Each falls into one of the only three categories allowed by lesbian censorship. *Saturday Night in the Prime of Life*, according to the lesbian press that printed it, blames all problems on "the male-dominated Sicilian culture." *Goat Song* acknowledges problems of racism within the lesbian community but does not name Sicilian one of those who suffers from this racism. *Tender Warriors* names its characters Italian-American, but calls them white and middle class, and minimizes their problems.

None of these novels tells the whole story. Maybe it's not fair to think three novels should tell the whole story of a culture. Or maybe it's not fair that lesbian censorship has only allowed us these three novels.

And while lesbian censorship has made our prose difficult to write, the denial of our culture has made Italian-American lesbian poetry impossible. I've been told that poems that honour my family according to Italian-American values are "feeding into negative stereotypes"; that poems protesting against anti-Italian bigotry are racist; that offensive images, that is, Italian-American images, should be modified to be made acceptable to the "majority culture";

that benign poems are wonderful evocations of my culture but not universal or serious enough to publish.

When I didn't receive a timely response to a poem I submitted to a women's newspaper in New York, where I lived at the time, I attended an open meeting of the paper's collective to see what was happening. The collective consisted of Blonde, Hispanic, Black, and Jewish women who informed me, with politely controlled rage, that my poem was racist; therefore, it had been tossed in the trash and ignored. The poem openly discusses the lynching of Sicilian-Americans in New Orleans in 1891, even making the murder of these few Sicilians seem as horrible as the murder of so many more Blacks in other lynchings. I was told that Blacks, because they're Black, have been subjected to institutionalized racism, while Italian-Americans, because they're "white," have not. The implication was that, because Blacks cannot escape being Black, as Italian-Americans can escape being Italian-American, Blacks don't have the luxury of escaping racism as Italian-Americans have. Therefore, Blacks have a serious problem that needs to be corrected while Italian-Americans have no problem. Although it would be considered racist to suggest that a light-skinned Black woman try to pass as white in order to get ahead in a racist society, it's considered an advantage for an Italian-American to be able to abandon her culture and heritage and become something better: in this land of opportunity we can rise from lowly wops to real white middle-class Americans. Isn't that why we came here in the first place? In fact, it's not only racist, it's pointless to talk about the lynching of Sicilians and Southern Italians when I can so easily pretend it never happened, get white, and it'll never happen again.

I'll always wonder what would have happened in that room if I had mentioned that some of the people who participated in that lynching of Sicilians were Blacks and that the NAACP considers this to be the worst single incident of lynching ever to have occurred in the United States. And I wonder how many Sicilians it takes to equal one human being.

I've also been told that the internment of the Japanese during World War II was motivated purely by racism, as is the resistance to reparation today. The proof I'm given is that Italians and Germans were not interned. But Italians and Germans were interned during World War II. Imagine trying to write a poem about the internment of Italians during World War II, about the real suffering of real people. Imagine trying to make that poem sound as proud and bold and full of human dignity and energizing rage as some poems about the oppression of Black people. If history books and newspapers, such as the *San Francisco Chronicle*, continue to pretend that Italians were never interned, and lesbians, both Italian-American and non-Italian, believe the lies they read about Italian-Americans and accept the omissions, as they claim not to believe or accept about anyone else, a poem about the internment of Italians during World War II is not only impossible to publish, it's impossible to write.

There's a motto printed on the bookmarks given out at many women's bookstores across the country: "Freedom of the press belongs to she who owns the press." I used to think that meant that in order for us to define ourselves by our own standards and to preserve our stories, we would not only have to do our own writing, but our own printing and distribution as well. Apparently, I was wrong. After several years of trying to publish poetry that defines Italian-Americans by our own standards and preserves our stories and values, I've concluded that this motto means no more than it says — that the small percentage of lesbians who have access to printing, control what is printed, and by doing so, determine what every lesbian should be.

The Italian-American lesbian, if she is neither white nor "of colour," does not have a place in the lesbian's "hierarchy of pain." If every human being must be either white or "of colour," and I claim to be neither, either the lesbian's view of the world is false or I don't exist. Therefore, although there are a few individuals who are white and middle-class Americans and whose families just happen to have come from Italy, there are no Italian-Americans as a people with a heritage and a culture, in lesbian literature.

Notes

1. It should be mentioned that, when I subsequently wrote and submitted to CL/LL an essay pointing out the insults in these stories and discussing the Mafia, they accepted it for publication, including it ("The Mafia in Context") in issue 32, Fall 1989. Upon publication, I received a letter from Zana thanking me for taking the time to explain this aspect of my culture.

2. This is the way the word appears in the book — spelled incorrectly as though it's not a real word, as though it denotes nothing and nobody real. *A Gathering of Spirit*, Sinister Wisdom Books, was originally issue 22-23 of the journal *Sinister Wisdom*.
3. *la bella figura* was a little literary journal I founded in 1988 and folded in 1992. I published work by Italian-Americans, mostly women.

References

Azpadu, Dodici. *Saturday Night in the Prime of Life.* Iowa City: Aunt Lute Book Company, 1983.

———. *Goat Song.* Iowa City: Aunt Lute Book Company, 1984.

Bulkin, Elly; Pratt, Minnie Bruce; Smith, Barbara. *Yours in Struggle: Three Feminist Perspectives on Anti-Semitism and Racism.* Ithaca: Firebrand Books, 1988.

Caperna Lloyd, Susan. *No Pictures on My Grave: A Spiritual Journey Journey in Sicily.* San Francisco: Mercury House, 1992.

Guido De Vries, Rachel. *Tender Warriors.* Ithaca: Firebrand Books, 1986.

Lynch, Lee. "Hanukkah at a Bar." *Common Lives/Lesbian Lives*, 25, Winter 1988, 15-27.

zana. "Nancy Drew and the Serial Rapist." *Common Lives/Lesbian Lives*, 24, Fall 1987, 4-19.

8

Carol Bonomo Albright

From Sacred to Secular

Umbertina and *A Piece of Earth*

$\mathscr{E}$arly Italian American writers, closer in time to the immigrants, were also closer to their Italian Catholic roots. In an article applying Burton Bledstein's analysis of professionalism, Robert Viscusi points out that some early Italian American novels, such as Guido D'Agostino's *Olives on the Apple Tree*, depict a tension between the Italian Catholic communal values of virtue and loyalty to the group's well-being and the vertical vision of individualistic professionalism. According to Bledstein, middle-class individuals in America prized the ambitious professional person who "expressed his expanding expectations at ascending stages of an occupation" (Bledstein, quoted in Viscusi 42). While such an approach is enormously gratifying to the human ego, Bledstein held that it took an enormous toll on the integrity of the individual. In a society structured towards a vertical notion of career, whose aim it would be to liberate the creativity of the self, encourage the ego to explore the world, discover knowledge and revere professional expertise, responsibility to one's community can all too easily be ignored. The losses comprise a moral narrowing of perspective in which the goal of upward ascent, exercised to extremes, excludes from its pursuit any of the traditional Catholic values of fellowship, charity, loyalty, or even human decency. Bledstein tells us that starting with the Victorians this horizontal loyalty to or unity with those on the same plane as oneself is rejected, is viewed as limiting professional advancement and, therefore, self-defeating.

Whereas Viscusi analyzes how this tension between Catholic and middle-class professional values is resolved in favour of the Italian Catholic half of the equation in these novels, my consideration of two contemporary Italian American authors will shift the focus: first, away from an exclusive discussion of middle-class professionalism to the broader category of the secularization of society; and second, away from the "triumph" of Italian Catholic values over American professionalism.

I do so in part within the context of the itinerary of emigration. The agrarian Italian small towns valued a Catholic communal culture, and in that sense can be described as having a religious sensibility of the sacred. The urban America in which the immigrants primarily settled were both industrialized and secular. Devotion to one's profession was one of the marks of the secular society, for inherent in the ethos of such a society is devotion to one's profession as a means of acquiring the trappings which accrue from the materialistic rewards of the profession.

The novels analyzed by Viscusi focus on the tensions created by the differing value-systems which the characters confront. By contrast, the characters of the works I will be dealing with, Helen Barolini's *Umbertina* and Kenny Marotta's *A Piece of Earth*, have long since given up the communal value-system of the Catholicism found in Italy.[1] Written in the 1980s, these novels dismiss religious values and accept the materialism and increasing privatization which characterize the latter half of the twentieth century. In different ways, each attempts to forge a new value-system to replace the traditional values which did not root well in the New World of their characters. Both novels mirror mainstream American values.[2] *Umbertina* uses work and art as a replacement; *A Piece of Earth* employs a feminist ethic of women respecting their own needs, becoming independent, and caring for each other. The characters cannot see other alternatives to the traditional Italian values which they so clearly reject.

In analyzing certain characteristics found in these novels, I nonetheless posit a dynamic and non-monolithic aspect of ethnicity. By dynamic ethnicity, I mean that ethnicity is acted out differently in each generation, and by non-monolythic ethnicity I mean to emphasize that more than one perspective or voice exists among characters of the same generation. That such dynamic differences occur needs to be noted so that a comprehensive description of Italian American literature may develop.[3]

It is helpful to look at what Harvey Cox observes in *The Secular City* about the changes that occur in the spiritual lives of societies as they move through the tribal, town and technocratic modes, because his discussion illuminates how the concepts of the secular and the sacred manifest themselves in American society. He states that how religion manifests itself is inextricably tied to the social and economic structures of a society, and proposes three stages that cultures and religions have gone through (and which can exist simultaneously in the various groups living in the larger world): tribal, town and technopolitan cultures. The latter, his neologism, designates an urbanization that is only possible when coupled with technology and — without some new mode of being in the world — results in the secularization which typifies contemporary American urban life.

Cox maintains that, whereas in tribal societies life grows out of kinship ties and prescribes the proper relationships with any person one is likely to meet in one's lifetime, town society, with its increasing network of personal associations, gives rise to a religion which *responds* to contact with varied beliefs by forcing each group to define its divinities. Instead of ghosts and demons, incantantions and spells, shamans and sorcerers which characterize tribal life, in a town society we have prayer, gods, myths, religion and theology. The appeal of Christianity over the Greek gods lay in its dispelling of the remnants of tribalism by its affirmation of a universal God (4-13).

In Cox's portrayal of modernity, urban people manifest the sacred by evolving an I-You relationship with God, as opposed to the classic I-Thou experience. Such a relationship is marked by a working *alongside* one's fellow beings. Because the mystical experience is exceedingly rare, people meet God as a You. This mode of working alongside one's fellows will re-invent the kinship ties of the tribe. Cox's God wants people to be less interested in Him and more interested in their neighbours and their contemporaries (263-265).

Umbertina and *A Piece of Earth* incorporate elements of Cox's three stages: *Umbertina* demonstrates most nearly the third stage of secularism, found in technopolis, while *A Piece of Earth* demonstrates most clearly a gender-based combination of tribal and town mores.

These novels represent a transition in Italian American literature in the sense that they reflect problems and solutions typical of contemporary American secular values. In *Umbertina*, as both horizontal kinship and vertical authority patterns disappear, kinship ties of the technopolis will be re-established in the work place — but without the religious element (I-You) Cox attaches to his analysis. *A Piece of Earth* embraces another ethic — the feminist view of women respecting themselves, acting independently and caring for other women — which replaces the earlier religion-based altruism. Antonia, the original immigrant, practices tribal mores and Agnes, her grandughter-in-law, gender-based town mores.

Umbertina concerns itself with four generations of Italian American women. I shall confine my discussion to the first- and third-generation characters, Umbertina, the original immigrant, and Marguerite, her grandaughter. Since we are shown Umbertina in both Italy and America, we see the evolution of her thinking. It is her industry and ingenuity which is equally responsible for the rise in the family's fortunes. Marguerite, her grandaughter, is beset by the conflicts her generation experiences. She marries Alberto, an Italian, and in trying to find out who she is, she pursues photography as a career and has an affair with Massimo, a man with literary ambitions.

If a God found among one's fellow workers is Cox's mode of making the secular sacred in a technopolis, Marguerite opts for the transcendent to be found in art, the art of her photography and the art of Massimo's poetry. Photographer though she wants to be, Marguerite loses her focus. Instead of concentrating on her own work, she concentrates on helping Massimo in his literary career. Pregnant with Massimo's child, she commits suicide in a car crash. But to understand the women in this book, we must first turn to Umbertina, the original immigrant.

Umbertina views God as the highest one in a hierarchical, authoritarian order with women being passive and on the lowest level. When she dares to think about marrying the peasant whom she loves instead of the man her father has chosen, a thunder storm occurs. She takes this as a sign from God to forget the goat-herd and marry her father's choice.

For Umbertina, who posits both a patriarchal social system and a society of scarcity, God is a good provider. On the feast of Corpus Christi, Umbertina sees the traditional *coperta matrimoniale* (marriage bedspread) hanging on the lines. To her the spreads represent the luxury of having enough to eat. In a later passage she reflects again on the feast of Corpus Christie and the *coperta*, musing how even a "pittance" of money makes a difference (Barolini 1979: 44). The spiritual aspect of the feast is not portrayed, but rather its corruption. We read: "The Church was powerful and there were more ways than one for it to get revenge on those who dared think they could buy its expropriated property" (45).

Umbertina holds that the work of her and of her spouse will be their salvation. Seeing the police evict twelve people living in one room strengthened Umbertina's "resolution that they [she and her husband] had to take care of themselves and be their own salvation" (68). The hardness of life for an immigrant in America creates an intense individualism, which has no room for communal action. Hers is an absent God whose "disinterest" is seen in the parched Italian earth:

> The sound of singing that came from a patch of olive trees they approached was like a wail solacing itself in the face of God's indifference. It came from the heart of that scourged land as if from some antechamber of hell. It was a love song, but even love songs were wails of despair — the invitation to mate, to couple with one's man to produce the children who would go on perpetuating, without knowing why, the misery of lost lands, lost prospects, lost lives (52-53).

Unlike earlier immigrant characters, Umbertina only trusts God when there is a tangible basis for doing so, for example, when she sees the rich soil in upper New York state.

Her view is repeated in the next generation. Her daughters, Sara and Carla (Marguerite's mother) pray in church for the right man. They view God as the divine provider, comparable to their earthly father who is credited with providing for their economic well-being:

> [Carla] and Sara spent every Saturday afternoon going downtown shopping, and on their way always stopped for a minute at the shrine of St. Rita in St. John's Church to pray for good fortune in courtships. Good fortune was all around them; all they needed was to have it provide them the right man (135).

For Umbertina, neither God nor community is of crucial relevance; rather it is work. Thus she paves the way for the middle-class vertical movement of professionalism in her grandsons. Happiness, she says epigrammatically, is "you find your place, you work... everything grows" (139). Stressing the importance of "working hard to get ahead," she belittles "old-country people who didn't [get ahead]…"(140). She values individual effort without communal obligation and so refuses her brother Beppo's request for passage money, though she does board him in her house once he arrives. She resents him because, unlike her, he experienced no baptism of pain in America. Umbertina also resents Beppo for upsetting the economic alliance she desired in the marriage of her son with Sacca's daughter, again accentuating her materialistic view of the world.

Three of the characters of the immigrant generation are depicted musing on their lives as they near death with its pathos of self-revelation and ultimacy. Serafino, a fellow villager of both Umbertina and her husband Domenico, wonders if it was all worth it just to make money and thinks that Domenico was right: they should have all worked together as in Garibaldi's day when they all had hope. For Serafino, communal values are to be appreciated from the perspective of political action. As for Domenico, he goes even further. It is he, the person who had unsuccessfully urged his fellow villagers to political activism, who refuses to call what Umbertina has achieved success. He believes that America lacks *benessere* and that Italy is more gracious and less materialistic. He speaks of the well-being of a total person, and of a spiritual as well as a material well-being. Spiritual well-being arises from working for the commonweal, but Umbertina quickly dismisses such a formulation, similar to Cox's Protestant humanistic mode of retaining the sacred in the secular city. Umbertina reflects that being economically well-off *is* sufficient as she sees her children and grandchildren prosper. She imagines Domenico there:

> looking about skeptically and saying, "you call this success, … but in Italy there's a different *benessere* and the world is more gracious, not so materialistic. Well-being of the total person — not just money, but spirit, too. How crude is the success of money compared with real *benessere*." Ah, Domenico, she thought, this *is* well-being (145).

The price she has paid is that she cannot communicate with her grandchildren who speak no Italian, but for her the trade-off from want is worth the price. Significantly, at her death, her vision of light is not God, but the *coperta matrimoniale* which she had first seen on the feast of Corpus Christi, thus stressing once more her equation of God with material well-being:

Nearly eighty, as she lay dying, her vision dimmed so that... Carla and the others at her bedstead became dim gray shadows, and then a sudden brightening came to her eyes as in a vision of light she saw the lost *coperta* of her matrimonial bed... "Ah!" she gasped, at its beauty... Then she was gone' (146).

This religion of material success is perpetuated by Umbertina's daughter and her husband, but *their* daughter Marguerite rejects their American way of progress, epitomized by golf, country clubs, college fraternities, etc. She recognizes "for all their material well-being, a vague despair stuck to them" (153). Yet she too will experience a similar despair as she replaces their faith in material things with faith in art and self-definition to give life meaning. Her heightened self-awareness will respect the divinity within that artists revere, but it will be empty of any communal outreach to others.

Marguerite hates the "constant figuring of returns": "Family talk was always in words of commercial transaction" (154). She "felt from her mother's tone how terrifying it must be not ever to make good and be despised for it" (156). Railing against the role her father has taken on, of being economically responsible for the extended family, she wants none of the responsible life and, interestingly — though the attitude is typical of her historical time (rougly the 1950s) — says, not that she'll be a poet but rather that she'll *marry* a poet. She just wants to be herself, she continues, but again defines herself in terms of a man. Having no true spiritual model, she reacts to her husband Alberto's return to Catholicism by saying that religion is not relevant any more. She calls it a "vulgarity... an obscenity" (193). "[U]pper and outer mobility" was what she was yearning for. That and "Freedom" (195), thus baldly and unwittingly mimicking Bledstein's description of a professional person. "To be a poet is enough. What else is there?" (174), Marguerite asks Alberto. To be a good man, he responds. He chooses life and duty to family over art. But Alberto leaves unacknowledged the fact that he has not had to choose between living life and his art. For Marguerite, religion acts as just another institution to prevent her development with its stresses on women as wives and mothers without options sexually — her high school nun is remebered as saying, à propos of sex, "The woman pays the fiddler" (279).

Nonetheless, Marguerite is later able to appreciate, if not act upon, the perspective of Alberto, a generation older than she and Massimo her lover. Unlike Massimo, who represents unbridled ambition which destroys personhood as described by Bledstein, Marguerite finally admits that Alberto has become a whole, generous loving person, within the constraints of his historical time and narrow definition of womanhood.

On the other hand, Massimo, Marguerite's lover and mentor of her photography, reflects Bledstein's vertical man. He says, "The most important thing in all this business is our work."[4] Marguerite colludes with Massimo's ambition by trying to help him win the Strega prize, by introducing him to the "right" people on the jury, perhaps reflecting the upbringing of a woman of her generation and/or the means by which she hopes to cement her relationship with Massimo. She attempts to lift Massimo from his despair by telling him that once he has the Strega prize, everything will be better.

Work for ego aggrandizement and unrelated to communal benefit replaces religion, but brings with it none of the communal comfort which flows from the communal interactions of loving one's neighbor. Furthermore, the substitution of art for religion brings with it no improvement in the lives of the artists. They are depicted as composed of selfish, backbiting individuals. Little wonder that Marguerite cannot extend out to such a community.

Significantly, the Strega award ceremony occurs in the courtyard of Pope Julian III's villa. But again a negative aspect of religion is emphasized when a minor character describes Pope Julian as a *viveur*. Yet Marguerite views the invisible shadows of Julian III and his cardinals as a benevolent presence, suggesting her awareness of the limitations of an egoistically practised art and some positive aspects of religion. Despite the hedonistic pope, she admires the *ideals* of Christianity. However, Marguerite stays within her secularized world, substituting materialism with a transcendent search for self through art.

If Marguerite replaces spiritual considerations with art, Ken Marotta in *A Piece of Earth* will replace such considerations with a feminist ethic, a gender-based, quasi-tribal town stage. The narrative voice in the novel demonstrates a negative stance towards religion in its critique of a central practice of Italian American Catholics — that is, the procession — by commenting on the misguided practice of those who overlay religion with materialism. We read that on Memorial Day the crowds in the business section of town are com-

183

pared to the crowds in the streets during the religious procession and feast. But, we are told, instead of statues and crucifixes, the decorations are ties and hats for sale: "And instead of weeping in religious hysteria, the old ladies shrieked in greed as they bargained with the vendors" (11).

What can serve in lieu of this materialism? Certainly not religion or religious processions, because the narrative voice has shown them to be just another form of commerce. Another solution is needed, and that solution is not an I-You experience of God in the technopolis à la Cox, but rather feminist-based altruism. Unlike Umbertina who found material success in America, Antonia, who represents the first generation in this novel, has not. In her old age, she is totally dependent upon others for the necessities of life. God is not viewed as the good economic provider for Antonia that He became for Umbertina and Carla. A feminist perspective of the world with women caring for other women, is presented as a means of bringing meaning to life.

The story, set in the Depression, is about Agnes, who is engaged to marry Mike Bonfiglio, a character who has a manipulative mother named Madge. Agnes has defied custom in two ways: first, by choosing her own husband, and, second, by refusing to be manipulated by Madge into taking Antonia, Mike's grandmother and Madge's mother, to live with them.

Antonia is sick and maltreated by Madge, a selfish and self-absorbed woman, who works in a candy factory. Antonia says of Madge's work, "I wish God had given me such work [gossiping with her friends at the factory]. But no, He had to make me a mother instead, as He made you a devil in a mother's shape" (19). Antonia simultaneously reveres and deplores a "mother's work." She feels cursed in being assigned that role, yet she is jealous of Madge's friendships at work.

Reflecting the primarily tribal values of kinship solidarity, Antonia views Madge's work as a threat to such solidarity. She is critical and envious of her daughter's relationship with her co-workers in the factory, and feels that Madge's job and her newly-formed friendships weaken and threaten kinship ties. In this vision of the world, God ordained a woman's work to be not in a factory, among those who are not kin, but the taking care of her husband and family.

Antonia assumes this stance vis-à-vis Madge because Madge has a husband that supports her. Antonia, however, has a different attitude with regard to herself, who was the wife of a poor man and had to work for survival. In addition, now that she is old and sick, Antonia feels that Madge should stay home to take care of her. To shame Madge, Antonia, though sick, leaves Madge's home without telling her where she is going, and accepts work as a cleaning woman. At this point, Agnes comes upon Antonia and brings her to her home. Antonia, both proud and distrustful of an altruism with no strings attached, begins to earn her keep with Agnes by cooking her meals and cleaning the apartment, where Agnes has moved since breaking her engagement with Mike and cutting her ties to her family.

In one long passage — an entire chapter, actually — Antonia tells Agnes the story of her life. She confesses that when her husband periodically left home to find work she, unlike other women, did not look down the road eagerly awaiting his return — unlike Marguerite in *Umbertina*, who being of a different class from Antonia, has the economic luxury of defining herself by her husband. Rather, Antonia was looking down the road of life which ends in death. By implication, looking to a man for happiness is equated with death. And life itself, for her, as the wife of a poor man, is a road of suffering ending in death.

In the novel Agnes, her future granddaughter-in-law, takes her in not to placate her manipulative future mother-in-law, but generously, of her own free will. Representing a secular perspective of social justice, she acts lovingly and responsibly towards Antonia and cares for her. All in all, however, the novel ends with Antonia returning to live with her selfish daughter Madge, instead of with Agnes, indicating perhaps that Antonia cannot accept the self-less love Agnes offers and inevitably must collude with those who maltreat her. She never lets go of her belief that an aged mother should live with her daughter, rather than with her granddaughter-in-law.

The satire and the irony of the novel notwithstanding, the last lines underscore the dark, nihilistic tinges in Marotta's vision: "... it's right... to give thanks to the dead even if we don't know who they were, or what we have to thank them for" (251). In this sentence's conditional clause, departing from the liturgical prayer for the dead, the novel exposes the dearth of values for the characters and their offspring to live by. Neither the kin, family nor work relationships as envisaged by Cox are part of their repertoire. The only hope is that under Agnes' leadership she, Mike and their descendents (who may have nothing to thank their ancestors for) may, if necessary, be able to break with tradition to forge new values along the lines Agnes demonstrated in respecting her own needs, rejecting a prearranged marriage and acting altruistically towards Antonia.[5]

These two novels portray the *anomie* of modern America. With traditional institutions of church and family no longer capable of responding to the new demands of America, the characters adopt American solutions to their problems. In *Umbertina*, professionalism is a way to give meaning to life. Yet Marguerite's dedication to art, which in any event she upholds especially to please her lover, is devoid of the communal values of fellowship, loyalty and charity. While it is the choice of a woman who is dependent, is born too soon to benefit from the gender-based communal aspect of feminism and thus remains a victim of the double standard concerning female sexuality, it contrasts sharply with the alternative solution in *A Piece of Earth*: Agnes, who lived in the Depression and is also without today's role models, acts in a responsible manner towards Antonia. Since Marotta's novel was written in 1985, it brings to mind Puzo's dictum in *The Fortunate Pilgrim*: "Audacity had liberated them" (Puzo 1964: 9). The "them" are, of course, Italian women who emigrated to America.[6] Even when they make their life meaningful by different routes, the characters in these novels always adopt a conduct which sets their story well within the secular American tradition. Their "audacity" is one of the features which best exemplifies, today, the dynamic, multi-faceted nature of Italian American literature.

Notes

1. On folk traditions as alternatives to Catholicism see Lucia Chiavola Birnbaum (in press).
2. The relation of Italian American literature to new definitions of ethnic literature, and the one contained in Sollors in particular, is discussed in Fred Gardaphé.
3. Mary Jo Bona dwells on the desire of immigrants' descendants for self-fulfillment in. On the variety of factors that shape personality see Richard Meckel. On the generational differences in expressions of ethnicity see Carol Bonomo Ahearn (1985).
4. *Ibid.*, 261.
5. In discussing his writing, the author himself has said that his work "grows out of a desire to heal the wounds of the tremendous changes my family has gone through... I'm interested in the effects of the past on the present." See Carol Bonomo Ahearn (1986).

6. A fuller discussion of the greater freedom of action possible for Italian women in America can be found in Rose De Angelis.

References

Bonomo Ahearn, Carol. "Definitions of Womanhood: Class, Acculturation and Feminism." *The Dream Book: An Anthology of Writings by Italian American Women*. Ed. Helen Barolini. New York: Schoken, 1985, 126-139.

————. "Kenny Marotta: Exploring the Roots of a Writer." *Fra Noi*, 25 June 1986, 51.

Barolini, Helen. *Umbertina*. New York: Seaview Books, 1979.

Bona, Mary Jo. "Broken Images, Broken Lives: Carmolina's Journey in Tina De Rosa's *Paper Fish*. In *Melus*, XIV, 3-4, 1987, 87-107.

Chiavola Birnbaum, Lucia . *Dark Wheat and Read Poppies. Folklore and Socialism: Italian Popular Beliefs in a Good Society* (in press).

Cox, Harvey. *The Secular City: Secularization and Urbanization in Theological Perspective*. New York: Macmillan Company, 1966.

De Angelis, Rose. "The Italian Woman in Fiction: A Journey From Private to Public." *Italian Americana*, XIII, 1, 1995, 32-41.

Gardaphé, Fred. "Italian American Fiction: A Third Generation Renaissance." *Melus*, XIV, 3-4, 69-85.

Marotta, Kenny. *A Piece of Earth*. New York: William Morrow and Company, 1985.

Meckel, Richard. "The Not So Fundamental Sociology of Garibaldi Marto La Polla." *Melus*, XIV, 3-4, 127-140.

Puzo, Mario. *The Fortunate Pilgrim*. New York: Lancer Books, 1964.

Sollors, Werner. *Beyond Ethnicity: Consent and Descent in American Culture*. New York: Oxford University Press, 1986.

Viscusi, Robert. "Professions and faiths: Critical Choices in the Italian American Novel." *Italian Americans in the Professions*. Ed. Remigio Pane. New York: American Italian Historical Association, 1983, 41-54.

9

Anthony Julian Tamburri

Towards a (Re)Definition of Italian/American Literature[1]

And I thought, "Does this son of a bitch think he is more American than I am?" Where does he think I was brought up? Because my name is Ciardi, he decided to hyphenate the poem. Had it been a Yankee name, he would have thought, "Ah, a scholar who knows about Italy." Sure he made assumptions, but I can't grant for a minute that Lowell is any more American than I am...

John Ciardi, *Growing Up Italian*

If every picture I made was about Italian Americans, they'd say, "That's all he can do." I'm trying to stretch.

Martin Scorsese, in *Premiere* (1991)

The fortune of Italian/American literature is somewhat reflective of the United States mindset vis-à-vis ethnic studies.[2] Namely, until recently, ever since the arrival of the first immigrants of the 1880s, the major wave of western-European emigration, the United States have considered ethnic/racial difference in terms of the melting-pot attitude. The past two decades, however, have constituted a period of transition, if not change, in this attitude. Be it the end of modernism, as some have claimed, be it the onslaught of the postmodern, as others may claim, in academic and/or intellectual circles today, one no longer thinks in terms of the melting pot.[3] Instead, as is well known by most, one now talks in terms of the individual ethnic/racial culture and its relationship — and not necessarily in negative terms only — with the long-standing, mainstream cultural paradigm. It is, therefore, with the backdrop of this new attitude of rejecting the melting pot and supplanting it with the notion of Americana as a *kaleidoscopic socio/cultural mosaic*, as I have rehearsed it elsewhere (Tamburri 1991: 48), that I shall consider an attempt at (re)defining

Italian/American literature. By using the phrase "kaleidoscopic socio/cultural mosaic," I mean to underscore how the socio/cultural dynamics of the United States reveal a constant flux of changes originating in the very existence of the various differentiated ethnic/racial groups that constitute the overall population of the United States.

Ethnic studies in any form or manner — for instance, the use of ethnicity as a primary yardstick — do not necessarily constitute the major answer to filling in knowledge gaps with regard to what some may consider ethnic myopia in the United States. Nevertheless — by now a cliché — we all know that the United States of America was born and developed — at times with tragic results[4] — along lines of diversity. What is important in this regard is that we understand, or a least *try* to understand, the origins of the diversity and difference which characterize the many ethnic and racial groups which constitute the kaleidoscopic nature of this country's population. Accepting literature as, among many things, the mirror of the society in which it is conceived, created, and perceived, we come to understand that one of the many questions ethnic literature addresses is the negative stereotypes of members of ethnic/racial groups which are not part and parcel of the dominant culture. By ethnic literature, I mean that type of writing which deals, contextually, with customs and behavioral patterns that the North American mindset may consider different from what it perceives as mainstream. The difference, I might add, may also manifest itself formalistically — that is, the writer may not follow what has become accepted norms and conventions of literary creation, s/he may not produce what the dominant culture considers *good* literature. This last point notwithstanding, one of the goals of ethnic literature is, to be sure, the dislodging and debunking of negative stereotypes. In turn, through the natural dynamics of intertextual recall and inference, the reader engages in a process of analytical inquiry and comparison of the ethnic group(s) in question with other ethnic groups as well as with the dominant culture. In fact, it is precisely through a comparative process that one comes to understand how difference and diversity from one group to another may not be as great as it initially seems; indeed, that such difference and diversity can not only co-exist but may even overlap with that which is considered characteristic of the dominant group. This, I believe, is another of the goals/functions of ethnic literature: to impart knowledge of the customs, characteristics, language of the various racial and ethnic groups in this country. Finally, partial responsibility for the validity or lack thereof of *other* literatures also lies with the *critic* or *theorist*. In fact, the theorist's end goal for *other* literatures, perhaps, should not limit itself only to the invention of another mode of reading. Instead, it should become, in itself, a strategy of reading which extends beyond the limits of textual analysis; it should concomitantly, and ultimately, aim for the validation of the text(s) in question vis-à-vis those already validated by the dominant culture.

In a response to Fredric Jameson's essay on national allegory and third-world literature, Aijaz Ahmad took issue with what he considered Jameson's limited and reductive assumption that third-world literature revolves primarily around the notion of a national allegory. More relevant here, however, are not so much Ahmad's objections to Jameson, as his own notions that stand at the base of such criticisms. Therefore, bouncing off of some of Ahmad's notions immediate to post-colonial literature, of *ethnic* — or for that matter any *other* — literature we may state that, first of all, such a notion cannot be "constructed as an internally coherent object of theoretical knowledge"; that such a categorization "cannot be resolved ... without an altogether positivist reductionism" (4). Secondly, *other* "literary traditions [e.g., third world, ethnic, etc.] remain, beyond a few texts here and there, [often] unknown to the *American* literary theorist"(5). While it may be true that Ahmad's use of the adjective *American* refers to the geopolitical notion of the United States of America, I would contend that the situation of ethnic literatures within the United States is analogous to what Ahmad so adroitly describes in his article on, for lack of a better term, "third-world literature." Thus, I would suggest that we re-consider Ahmad's *American* within the confines of the geopolitical borders of the United States and, thereby, reread it as synonymous to *dominant culture*. Thirdly, "[l]iterary texts are produced in highly differentiated, usually over-determined contexts of *competing ideological and cultural clusters, so that any particular text of any complexity shall always have to be placed within the cluster that gives it its energy and form, before it is totalised into a universal category*" (23; my emphasis). Thus, it is also within this ideological framework that I shall consider further, as category, Italian/American literature.

The notion for an enterprise of this type is grounded in a slightly unorthodox mode of thought. In this poststructuralist, postmodern society in which we live, my essay therefore casts by the wayside any notion of universality or absoluteness with regard to the (re)definition of any literary category vis-à-vis national origin, ethnicity, race, or gender. Undoubtedly, one can, and should, readily equate the above-mentioned notion to some general notions associated with the postmodern. Any rejection of validity of the notion of "hierarchy," or better, universality or absoluteness, is characteristic of those who are, to paraphrase Lyotard, "incredul[ous] toward [grand or] metanarratives" (xiv). Indeed, one of the legitimized *and* legitimizing *grands récits* — metanarrative — is the discourse built around the notion of canon valorization. By implicitly constructing an otherwise non-existent category, or *sub*-genre, of American letters — that is, Italian/American literature — the notion of a centered canon of the dominant Anglo/American culture is rattled once more. Rattled *once more* precisely because there already exist, fortunately, *legitimized* — that is, considering the Academy the legitimizing institution — similar categories such as African/American or Jewish/American fiction; one need only peruse the list of graduate courses in American and English literature in the various catalogues of major American universities.[5]

In the past, Italian/American art forms — more precisely, literature and film — have been defined as those constructed mainly by second-generation writers about the experiences of the first and second generations. In a recent essay on Italian/American cinema, for example, Robert Casillo defined it as "works by Italian-American directors who treat Italian-American subjects" (374) In like fashion, Frank Lentricchia had previously defined Italian/American literature as "a report and meditation on first-generation experience, usually from the perspective of a second-generation representative" (124-5). Indeed, both constitute neat and clean definitions for works of two genres — and in a certain sense we can extend this meaning to other art media — that deal explicitly with an Italian/American ethnic quality and/or subject matter.[6] Such definitions, however, essentially halt — though unintendedly so by those who offer them — the progress and limit the impact of those writers who come from later generations, and thus may result in a monolithic notion of what was/is and was/is not Italian/American literature. Following a similar mode of thinking, Dana Gioia has more recently proposed yet another limiting definition in his brief essay, "What Is Italian-American Poetry?" There, Gioia describes "Italian-American poetry... only as a transitional category" for which the "concept of Italian-American poet is therefore most useful to describe first- and second-generation writers raised in the immigrant subculture' (3). Together with his restrictive definition of Italian/American poetry, Gioia also demonstrates a seemingly furtive sociological thought pattern in not distinguishing the difference between ethnicity passed from one generation to the next vis-à-vis a member's decision of the subsequent generation to rid him/herself of and/or deny his/her ethnicity, when he states that "[s]ome kinds of ethnic or cultural consciousness seem more or less permanent"(3).[7]

One question that arises is, what do we do about those works of art — written and/or visual — that do not *explicitly* treat Italian/American subject matter and yet seem to exude a certain ethnic Italian/American quality, even if we cannot readily define it? That is, can we speak to the Italian/American qualities of a Frank Capra film? According to Casillo's definition, we would initially have to say no. However, it is Casillo himself who tells us that Capra, indeed, "found his ethnicity troublesome throughout his long career" (374) and obviously dropped it. My question, then, is: Can we not see this *absence*, especially in light of documented secondary matter, as an Italian/American signifier *in potentia*? I would say yes. And in this regard, I would suggest an alternative perspective on reading and/or categorizing any Italian/American art form.[8] That is, I believe we should take our cue from Scorsese himself and therefore "stretch" our own reading strategy of Italian/American art forms, whether they be — due to content and/or form — *explicitly* Italian/American or not, in order to accommodate other possible, successful reading strategies. Indeed, recent (re)writings of Italian/American literary history and criticism have transcended a limited concept of Italian/American literature. New publications (literary and critical) have created a need for new definitions and new critical readings, not only of contemporary work, but of the works of the past. In addition, these new publications have originated, for the most part, from within an intellectual community of Italian Americans.[9] Therefore, I would propose that we consider Italian/American literature to be a series of on-going written enterprises which establish a repertoire of signs, at times, *sui generis*, and therefore create verbal variations (visual, in the case of film, painting, sculpture, drama) that represent different versions — dependent, of course, on one's generation, gender, socio-economic condition — of what can be perceived as the Italian/American signified.[10] That is, the Italian/American experience may indeed be manifested in any art form in a number of ways and at varying degrees, for which one may readily speak of the variegated representations of the Italian/American ethos in literature, for example, in the same fashion in which Daniel Aaron spoke of the " hyphenate writer."

Within the general discourse of American literature, Daniel Aaron seems to be one of the first to have dealt with the notion of hyphenation.[11] For him, the hyphen initially represented older North Americans' hesitation to accept the new/comer; it was their way, in Aaron's words, to "hold him at 'hyphen's length,' so to speak, from the established community" (213). It further "signifies a tentative but unmistakable withdrawal" on the user's part, so that "mere geographical proximity" denies the newly arrived "full and unqualified national membership despite... legal qualifications and... official disclaimers to the contrary" (213).

Speaking in terms of a passage from "hyphenation" to "dehyphenation" (214), Aaron sets up three stages through which a non-Anglo/American writer might pass.[12] The first-stage writer is the "pioneer spokesman for the ... unspoken-for" ethnic, racial, or cultural group — that is, the marginalized. This person writes about his/her co-others with the goal of dislodging and debunking negative stereotypes ensconced in the dominant culture's mindset. In so doing, this writer may actually create characters possessing some of the very same stereotypes, with the specific goals, however, of 1) winning over the sympathies of the suspicious members of the dominant group, and 2) humanizing the stereotyped figure and thus "dissipating prejudice." Successful or not, this writer engages in placating his/her reader by employing recognizable features the dominant culture associates with specific ethnic, racial, or cultural groups.

Aaron considers this first-stage writer abjectly conciliatory toward the dominant group. He states: "It was as if he were saying to his suspicious and opinionated audience: 'Look, we have customs and manners that may seem bizarre and uncouth, but we are respectable people nevertheless and our presence adds flavor and variety to American life. Let me convince you that our oddities — no matter how quaint and amusing you find them — do not disqualify us from membership in the national family'" (214). What this writer seems to do, however, is engage in a type of game, a bartering system of sorts which ignores the injustices set forth by the dominant group, asking, or hoping, instead, that the very same dominant group might attempt to change its ideas while accepting the writer's offerings as its final chance to enjoy the stereotype.[13]

Less willing to please, the second-stage writer, instead, abandons the use of preconceived ideas in an attempt to demystify negative stereotypes. Whereas the first-stage writer might have adopted some preconceived notions popular among members of the dominant culture, this writer, instead, presents characters who have already sunk "roots into the native soil." By no means, therefore, as conciliatory as the first-stage writer, this person readily indicates the disparity and, in some cases, may even engage in militant criticism of the perceived restrictions and oppression set forth by the dominant group. In so doing, according to Aaron, this writer runs the risk of a "double criticism": from the dominant culture offended by the "unflattering or even 'un-American' image of American life," as also from other members of his/her own marginalized group, who might feel misrepresented, having preferred a more "genteel and uncantankerous spokesman."

The third-stage writer, in turn, travels from the margin to the mainstream "viewing it no less critically, perhaps, but more knowingly." Having appropriated the dominant group's culture and tools necessary to succeed in that culture — the greater skill of manipulating, for instance, a language acceptable to the dominant group — and more strongly than his/her predecessors, this writer feels entitled to the intellectual and cultural heritage of the dominant group. As such, s/he can also, from a personal viewpoint, "speak out uninhibitedly as an American."[14] This writer, however, as Aaron reminds us, does not renounce or abandon the cultural heritage of his/her marginalized group. Instead, s/he transcends "a mere parochial allegiance" in order to transport "into the province of the [general] imagination," personal experiences which for the first-stage ("local colorist") and second-stage ("militant protestor") writer "comprised the very stuff of their literary material" (215).[15]

Pertinent to any discourse on ethnic art forms is the notion that ethnicity is not a fixed essence passed down from one generation to the next. Rather, "ethnicity is something reinvented and reinterpreted in each generation by each individual" (Fischer 195), which, in the end, is a way of "finding a voice or style that does not violate one's *several components of identity*" (my emphasis), these components constituting the specificities of each individual. Thus, ethnicity — and more specifically in this case, *italianità* — is redefined and reinterpreted on the basis of each individual's time and place, and is therefore always new and different with respect to its own historical specificities vis-à-vis the dominant culture.

An analogous discourse of one's own cultural and historical specificities may indeed be constructed around the notion of the reader. For the manner in which texts are interpreted today — the theoretical underpinnings of a reader's act of disambiguation, that is — is much more broad and, for the most part, tolerant of what may once have seemed to be *incorrect* or *inadequate* interpretations. Today the reader has as many rights as the author in the semiotic process. In some cases the reader may seem to have more rights than the writer. Lest we forget what Italo Calvino had to say about literature and the interpretation thereof, the reader relies on a form of semiosis which places him/her in an interpretive position of superiority vis-à-vis the author. In "Cybernetics and Ghosts" Calvino considers "the decisive moment of literary life [to be] reading" (15), by which "literature will continue to be a 'place' of privilege within the human consciousness, a way of exercising the potentialities within the system of signs belonging to all societies at all times. The work will continue to be born, to be judged, to be distorted or constantly renewed on contact with the eye of the reader" (16). In like manner, he states in "Whom Do We Write For" that the writer should not merely satisfy the reader; rather, he should be ready "to assume a reader who does not yet exist, or a change in the reader" (82), a reader who would be *more cultured than the writer himself*" (85; Calvino's emphasis).[16]

In making such an analogy between reader and viewer I do not ignore the validity of the writer. For while it is true that the act of semiosis relies on the the individual's time and place and is therefore always new and different with respect to its own historical specificities vis-à-vis the dominant culture — that is, the canon — it is also true that the writer may willy-nilly create for the reader greater difficulties in interpretation. Namely, if we accept the premise that language — verbal and/or visual — is an ideological medium that can become restrictive and oppressive when its sign system is arbitrarily invested with meanings by those who are empowered to do so — that is, the dominant culture/the canon-makers — so too can it become empowering for the purpose of privileging one coding correlation over another (in this case the canon), by rejecting the canonical sign system and, ultimately, denying validity to this sign system vis-à-vis the interpretive act of a noncanonical text.[17] Then, certain ideological constructs are de-privileged and subsequently awarded an unfixed status; they no longer take on a patina of *natural facts*. Rather, they figure as the *arbitrary categories* they truly are.

All this results in a pluralistic notion of artistic invention and interpretation which, by its very nature, cannot exclude the individual — artist and reader/viewer — who has found "a voice or style that does not violate [his/her] several components of identity" (Fischer), and who has thus (re)created, ideologically speaking, a different repertoire of signs. In this sense, then, the emergence and subsequent acceptance of certain *other* literatures, due in great part to the postmodern influence of the breakdown of boundaries and the mistrust in absolutes, has contributed to the construction of a more recent heteroglossic culture in which the "correct language" is deunified and decentralized. In this instance, then, all "languages" are shown to be "masks [and no language can consequently] claim to be an authentic and incontestable face." The result is a "heteroglossia consciously opposed to [the dominant] literary language," for which marginalization — and thus the silencing — of the *other* writer becomes more difficult to impose and thus less likely to occur.[18]

Turning now to a few writers, we see that their work represents to one degree or another the general notions and ideas outlined above. John Fante, Pietro Di Donato, and Joseph Tusiani — two fiction writers (Fante and Di Donato) and a poet (Tusiani) — have produced a corpus of writing heavily informed by their Italian heritage. Their works celebrate their ethnicity and cultural origin, as each weaves tales and creates verses which tell of the trials and tribulations of the Italian immigrants and their children. Fante and Di Donato confronted both the ethnic dilemma and the writer's task of communicating this dilemma in narrative form. Tusiani, on the other hand, invites his reader, through the medium of poetry, to understand better, as Giordano points out, the "cynical and somber awareness of what it means to be an immigrant," and to experience the "alienation and realization that the new world is not the 'land of hospitality' he/she believed it was" (317). So that, be it the novelist Di Donato, or the short-story writer Fante, Tusiani's "riddle of [his] day" figures indeed as the riddle of many of his generation, as it may also continue to sound a familiar chord for those of subsequent generations: "Two languages, two lands, perhaps two souls ... / Am I a man or two strange halves of one?" (7)

In a cultural/literary sense, it becomes clear that these and other writers of their generation belong to what Aaron considers stage one of the *hyphenate writer*. For this writer not only questions his/her origins, but, as mentioned above, is indeed bent on disproving the suspicions and prejudices of the dominant culture. Fante, Di Donato, and Tusiani, as also their *co/ethnics*, indeed both examined their status in the new world and, insofar as possible, presented a positive image of the Italian in America.

In turn, writers who have securely passed from the first through the second and onto the third stage of hyphenation may include the likes of Mario Puzo, Helen Barolini, and Gilbert Sorrentino. While it is true that each writer has dealt with his/her cultural heritage, each has done so both differently from each other as also from those who preceded them. No longer feeling the urge to please the dominant culture, these writers adopted the thematics of their Italian heritage insofar as it coincided with their personal development as writers.

Mario Puzo's second novel, *A Fortunate Pilgrim* (1964), recounts the trials and tribulations of a first-generation immigrant family. Ethnically centered around Lucia, the matriarch of the Corbo family, the novel examines the myth of the American dream and the real possibility of the *outsider* to succeed in realizing it. To be sure, Puzo, as he does later in the *The Godfather,* does not always paint a positive picture of the Italian American in this novel. Yet, considered from the perspective of a greater social criticism, Puzo's use of a sometimes sleazy, Italian/American character — especially those involved in the stereotypical organized crime associations — may figure as an indictment of the social dynamism of the dominant culture which refuses access to the *outsider*.[19] The novel's expansive theme of survival and the desire to better one's situation lies at the base of the variegated, kaleidoscopic view of a series of seemingly overwhelming tragedies which the family, as a whole, seems to overcome.

In considering another example, we see that Helen Barolini's *Umbertina* could not be more Italian/American. The author of a novel which spans four generations of an Italian/American family, she is, undoubtedly, acutely aware of her ethnicity and hyphenation. Her main characters are all women, and each represents a different generation. In a general sense, they reflect the development of the Italian/American mindset as it evolved and changed from one generation to the next. Yet, with this novel, it becomes increasingly clear that Barolini has gone one step further than those who preceded her, both the men and women. In *Umbertina*, Barolini now combines her historical awareness of the Italian and Italian American's plight with her own strong sense of feminism, and, ultimately, the reader becomes aware of what it meant to be not just an Italian American but indeed an Italian/American woman.[20] As John Paul Russo has demonstrated, Gilbert Sorrentino does attempt to fuse his inherited immigrant culture — which is represented by terms of nature in his poetry — with his artistic concern. Yet, explicit references to Italian/American culture seem most infrequent throughout his *opus*.[21] In his own words, Sorrentino surely "knew the reality of [his] generation that had to be written,"[22] as he too contributed to this cultural and literary chronicle. However, he took one step further than his *co/ethnics* (Italian Americans) and, so to speak, dropped the hyphen. Yet the dropping of the hyphen, according to Aaron, does not necessarily eliminate a writer's marginality. He states that the writer "… has detached himself, to be sure, from one cultural environment without becoming a completely naturalized member of the official environment. It is not so much that he retains a divided allegiance but that as a writer, if not necessarily as a private citizen, he has transcended a mere parochial allegiance and can now operate freely in the republic of the spirit." In Sorrentino's case, while he was keenly aware of the American literary tradition that preceded him, in dropping the ethnic hyphen he appropriated yet another form of marginality; with the likes of Kerouac and Ferlinghetti as immediate predecessors, Sorrentino chose the poetics of late Modernism over that of mainstream literary America.[23]

In dealing with his/her Italian/American inheritance, each writer picks up something different as s/he may perceive and interpret his/her cultural heritage filtered through personal experiences. Yet, there resounds a familiar ring, an echo that connects them all. Undoubtedly, Italian/American writers have slowly, but surely, built their niche in the body of American literature. Collectively, their work can be viewed as a written expression par excellence of Italian/American culture; individually, each writer has enabled American literature to sound a slightly different tone, thus bringing to the fore another voice of the great kaleidoscopic, socio/cultural mosaic we may call Americana — *kaleidoscopic mosaic* precisely because the socio/cultural dynamics of the United States reveal a constant flux of changes originating in the very existence of the various differentiated ethnic/racial groups that constitute the overall population of the United States. What emerges, as Fischer has stated, "is not simply that parallel processes operate across American ethnic identities, but a sense that these ethnic identities *constitute only a family of resemblances,* that ethnicity cannot be reduced to identical sociological functions, that ethnicity is a process of *inter-reference between two or more cultural traditions*" (my emphasis) and, I would add, between two or more generations of the same ethnic/racial group.

Thus, perhaps, an appropriate way to close would be to borrow from Marshall Grossman and, again, from Lyotard. For if the "power of the [hyphen, as Grossman states] lies in its openness to history [or, better still,] in the way it records and then reifies contingent events," since the "ideology of a particular hyphen may be read only by supplying a plausible history to its use" (121), the person who opts to eliminate it, to use something else in its place, or, as I have suggested elsewhere (Tamburri 1991a: 43-7), turn it on its side, does so in the search "for new presentations," to quote now from Lyotard. In this manner, then, the text the writer creates, the work s/he "produces are not in principle governed by pre-established rules [that is, canon formation], and they cannot be judged according to a determining judgement, by applying familiar categories to the text or to the work. Those rules and categories are what the work of art is looking for. The artist and the writer, then, are working without rules in order to formulate the rules of what *will have been done*" (Lyotard 81: emphasis textual).

In an analogous manner, so does the reader of these same texts work without rules, establishing, as s/he proceeds similar interpretive rules of what *will have been read.* Such is the case with the reader of *ethnic* texts, who proceeds to recodify and reinterpret the seemingly arbitrary — noncanonical (read also *ethnic*) — signs in order to reconstruct a mutual correlation of the expressive and content functions, which, in the end, do not violate his/her intertextual knowledge. Moreover, such an act of semiosis relies on the individual's time and place, and is therefore always new and different with respect to its own historical specificities vis-à-vis the dominant culture — the canon.

It is, in final analysis, a dynamics of the conglomeration and agglutination of different voices and reading strategies which, contrary to the hegemony of the dominant culture, cannot be fully integrated into any strict semblance of a monocultural voice or process of interpretation. The utterance will always be polyvalent, its combination will always be rooted in heteroglossia and dialogism,[24] and the interpretive strategies for decoding it will always depend on the specificities of the reader's intertextual reservoir. For the modernist reader, therefore, one rooted in the search for existing absolutes, an Italian/American sign system may appear *inadequate*, perhaps even contemptuous. For the postmodernist reader, instead, one who is open to, if not in search of, new coding correlations, an Italian/American sign system may appear significantly intriguing, if not, on occasion, rejuvenating, as these texts may indeed present a sign system consisting of manipulated sign functions which ultimately (re)define the sign. To be sure, then, in defense of a sustained but fluctuating Italian/American category of creative works, one may recall Lyotard's "incredulity toward metanarratives" (xiv), late twentieth-century's increasing suspicion in narrative's universal validity, for which artistic invention is no longer considered a depiction of life — or, stated in more ideological terms, artistic creation is no longer executed/performed according to established rules and regulations. Rather, it is a depiction of life as it is represented by ideology (Davis 24), since ideology presents as *inherent* in what is represented that which, in actuality, is *constructed* meaning (Hutcheon 49).[25]

Notes

1. An expanded version of this article has appeared in *Differntia* 6-7, 1994. Other versions have been read at various colloquia since 1990.
2. For more on the use of the slash instead of the hyphen, see Tamburri (1991a). With specific regard to the Italian/American writer, see especially 20-27, 33-42.
3. This is also true for the more popular press. DeWayne Wickham (1992), a national columnist for the Garnett News Service, wrote in favour of using the metaphor of "stew" rather than "melting pot" in describing the racial/ethnic composition of the United States.
4. Of numerous historical cases, I have in mind the egregious examples of Native Americans and African Americans.
5. With regard to a discussion on the general notion of canon, I leave that for a larger setting, one which allos more space for such an encompassing argument. For more on this notion see Charles Altieri and Richard Ohmann.
6. One problem with definitions of this sort is that they exclude any discourse on the analogous notion of, for example, the "hyphenate" filmmaker. I refer to Daniel Aaron essay on the "hyphenate writer."

7. One may also take issue with Gioia's revisionist history of Italian/American poetry dating back to Lorenzo Da Ponte; or his statements on Italian language that "*Toscano* [is] the standard literary dialect of written Italian" (7). Da Ponte was an Italian who, as an adult socialized in Italy, came to the United States under questionable circumstances and, as the first Italian professor in North America, became the member of a privileged class. This, I would contend, is quite different from that Italian/American literature one finds rearing its head at the beginning of the twentieth century. With regard to the *questione della lingua*, I would point out that Italian is a a national language which has evolved over the centuries, influenced heavily by its many dialects, *fiorentino* included. But there is not really any one dialect, today, that is considered the nucleus of standard Italian.

8. What is important to keep in mind is that one can perceive different degrees of ethnicity in literature, film or any other art form, as AAron already did with his "hyphenate writer."

9. Origins of recent Italian/American self-inventory can be dated back to Rose Basile Green's on the Italian/American novel. Since then, the field of Italian/American criticism has emerged sporadically in conference proceedings and, more specifically, in an acute original contribution by Robert Viscusi "*De Vulgari Eloquentia*: An Approach to the Language of Italian American Fiction" and in Helen Barolini's anthology *The Dream Book: An Anthology of Writing by Italian American Women*. The recent publication of *From the Margin: Writings in Italian Americana*, the establishment of journals such as *la bella figura* and *VIA: Voices in Italian Americana*, and the resumption of the journal *Italian Americana* further respresesent the rise of an indigenous interest in the critical study of Italian/American culture. Forthcoming, still, is a special issue of *Differentia*. In addition, the Fall 1987 (1989) issue of *MELUS* was devoted to Italian/American literature and film, and the *South Atlantic Quarterly* devoted an entire issue to the work of Don De Lillo. These are but two examples of interest in Italian/American cultural studies by non-Italian/American scholarly organizations.

10. The basic tenets of this definition came out of a collaborative brain-racking session, in the offices of City Stoop Press, with Fred Gardaphé, with the specific intent of *defining* Italian/American literature.

11. Aaron is not alone in discerning this multi-stage phenomenon in the ethnic writer. Ten years after Aaron's original version, Rose Basile Green spoke to an analogous phenomenon within the history of Italian/American narrative; then, she discussed her four stages of "the need for assimilation," "revulsion," "counterrevulsion," and "rooting" (See Basile Green, especially chapters 4-7). As I have already rehearsed elsewhere (see Tamburri 1991a), I would contend that there are cases where a grammar rule/usage may connote an inherent prejuduce, no matter how slight. Besides the hyphen, another example that comes to mind is the usage of the male pronoun for the impersonal, whereas all of its alternatives — that is, s/he, she/he, or he/she — are shunned.

12. In order to avoid repetitive textual citations, I should point out that Aaron's description of the three stages is found on page 214. I would also point out that Daniel Aaron's three stages of the hyphenate writer have their analogues in the different generations that Joseph Lopreato and Paul Campisi each describe and analyze: that is, "peasant," "first-," "second-," and "third-generation." With regard to this fourth generation — Lopreato's and Campisi's "third generation" — I would state here, briefly, that I see the writer of this generation subsequent to Aaron's "third-stage writer," who eventually returns to his/her ethnicity through the process of re(dis)covery.

13. The danger, of course, is, metaphorically speaking, of adding fuel to the fire, since there is no guarantee that such a strategy may convince the dominant culture to abandon its negative preconceptions.

14. There are undoubtedly other considerations regarding Aaron's three categories. He goes on to discuss them further, providing examples from the Jewish and Black contingents of American writers.

15. One caveat with regard to this neat, linear classification of writers should not go unnoticed. There undoubtedly exists a clear distinction between the first-stage writer and the third-stage writer. The distinction, however, between the first- and second-stage writer, and, especially, that between the second- and third-stage writer, may at times be blurred. In his rewrite, in fact, Aaron himself has recognized the blurring of boundaries, as "these stages cannot be clearly demarcates" (1984-5: 13). This becomes apparent when one discusses works such as Mario Puzo's *The Godfather* or Helen Barolini's *Umbertina*. More significant is the fact that these various stages of hyphenation may actually manifest themselves along the trajectory of one author's literary career. I believe, for instance, that a writer like Helen Barolini manifests, to date, such a phenomenon. Her second novel, *Love in the Middle Ages*, revolves around a love story involving a middle-aged couple, whereas ethnicity and cultural origin serve chiefly as a backdrop. Considering what Aaron states in his rewrite, and what seems to be of common opinion — that the respective experiences of Jews and Italians in the United States were similar in some ways (1984-5: 23-24 especially) — it should appear as no strange coincidence, then, that the ethnic backgrounds of the two main characters of Barolini's second novel are, for the woman, Italian and, for the man, Jewish.

16. That is, Calvino foresaw a reader with "epistemological, semantic, practical, and methodological requirements he [would] want to compare [as] examples of symbolic procedures and the construction of logical patters" (1986: 84-85). Caveat lector: What I have in mind here is that any reader's response in this semiotic process is, to some degree or another, content/context-sensitive.

17. See, for example, V.N. Voloshinov: "A sign does not simply exist as a part of reality — it reflects and refracts another reality. Therefore, it may distort that reality or be true to it, or may perceive it from a special point of view, and so forth. Every sign is subject to the criteria of ideological evaluation (that is, whether it is true, false, correct, fair, good). The domain of ideology coincides with the doamin of signs. They equate with one another. Wherever a sign is present ideology is present. *Everything ideological possesses semiotic value*" (10).

18. This, for Bakhtin, is dialogized heteroglossia. A work, language or culture undergoes dialogization "when it becomes relativized, deprivileged, aware of competing definitions for the same things." Only by "breaking through to its own meaning and own expression across an environment full of alien words and variously evaluating accents, harmonizing with some of the elements in this environment and striking a dissonance with others, is a [a word — or for that matter, language or culture] able, in this dialogized process, to shape its own stylistic profile and tone" (258 ff).

19. Basile Green expresses an analogous notion in her section on Puzo in *The Italian American Novel*.

20. For more on the gender/ethnic dilemma in *Umbertina*, see Tamburri 1990 and 1991b. As already mentioned, in her later novel, *Love in the Middle Ages*, the subject matter is much more universal isofar as ethnicity and cultural origin are backdrops to a love story involving a middle-aged couple.

21. I should point out that John Paul Russo deals primarily with Sorrentino's poetry. As this collection of essays goes to the printer, there is work in press that deals, in part, with the Italian/American aspect of Sorrentino's fiction. See Fred L. Gardaphé.

22. *Vort* 2 (1974: 19). I owe this quote to John Paul Russo.

23. Again, I refer the reader to John Paul Russo's essay.

24. For more on the notion of heteroglossia and dialogism, see Bakhtin: 426, 428 passim.

25. This essay is one of many steps in an attempt to explore further the notion of Italian/American literature. It could not be accomplished, without first and foremost, those works I cite throughout — especially those I have engaged in discussion. To these writers I owe a debt for affording me pieces of a puzzle to rearrange according to my own intertextual specificities. I also owe a debt to others who have often offered both encouragement and criticism along the way. They are: Peter Carravetta, Fred Gardaphé, Paul Giordano and John Kirby.

References

Aaron, Daniel. "The Hyphenate Writer and American Letters." *Smith Alumnae Quarterly* (July 1964), pp. 213-7. Revised in *Rivista di Studi Anglo-Americani* 3.4-5 (1984-5), 11-28.

Ahmad, Aijaz. "Jameson's Rhetoric of Otherness and the 'National Allegory.'"*Social Text*, 17, 1987, 3-25.

Altieri, Charles. "An Idea and Ideal of a Literary Canon." *Canons*. Ed. Robert von Hallberg. Chicago: University of Chicago Press, 1984, 41-64.

Bakhtin, Mikhail M. *The Dialogic Imagination*. Ed. Michael Holquist. Trans. Caryl Emerson and Michael Holquist. Austin: University of Texas Press, 1981.

Barolini, Helen. *Umbertina*. New York: Seabury, 1979.

———. *Love in the Middle Ages*. New York: Morrow, 1986.

Barolini, Helen. Ed. *The Dream Book: An Anthology of Writing by Italian American Women*. New York: Schocken, 1986.

Calvino, Italo. "Cybernetics and Ghosts," "Whom Do We Write For." In*The Uses of Literature*. Trans. Patrick Creagh. New York: Harcourt Brace Jovanovich, 1986, 3-27, 81-88.

Campisi, Paul. "Ethnic Family Patterns: The Italian Family in the United States." *The American Journal of Sociology*. 53.6 (May 1948).

Casillo, Robert. "Moments in Italian-American Cinema: From Little Caesar to Coppola and Scorsese." In Tamburri, Giordano and Gardaphé, 374-396.

Davis, Leonard J. *Resisting Novels: Ideology and Fiction*. London: Methuen, 1987.

Fischer, Michael M.J. "Ethnicity and the Post-Modern Arts of Memory." *Writing Culture. The Poetics and Politics of Ethnography*. Eds. James Clifford and George E. Marcus. Berkeley: University of California Press, 1986, 194-233.

Gardaphé, Fred L. *Italian Signs, American Streets: The Evolution of Italian American Narrative*. Durham: Duke University Press, 1996.

Gioia, Dana. "What Is Italian-American Poetry?" *Poetry Pilot* (December 1991), 3-10.

Giordano, Paolo A. "From Southern Italian Immigrant to Reluctant American: Joseph Tusiani's *Gente Mia and Other Poems*. In Tamburri, Giordano and Gardaphé, 316-328.

Basile Green, Rose. *The Italian-American Novel: A Document of the Interaction of Two Cultures*. Fairleigh Dickinson University Press, 1974.

Grossman, Marshall. "The Violence of the Hyphen in Judeo-Christian." *Social Text* 22, 1989, 115-122.

Hutcheon, Linda. *The Politics of Postmodernism*. New York: Routledge, 1989.

Jameson, Fredric. "Third World Literature in an Era of Multinational Capitalism." *Social Text*, 15, 1986.

Lentricchia, Frank. Review of *Delano in America & Other Early Poems*, by John J. Soldo. *Italian Americana* 1.1, 1974, 124-125.

Lopreato, Joseph. *Italian Americans*. New York: Random House, 1979.

Lyotard, Jean-François. *The Postmodern Condition: A Report on Knowledge*. Trans. Geoff Bennington and Brian Massumi with a foreword by Fredric Jameson. Minneapolis: University Minnesota Press, 1984.

Ohmann, Richard. "The Shaping of a Canon: U.S. Fiction, 1960-1975" in *Canons*. Ed. Robert von Hallberg. Chicago: University of Chicago Press, 1984, 377-402.

Puzo, Mario. *Fortunate Pilgrim*. New York: Atheneum, 1964.

————. *The Godfather*. New York: Putnam, 1969.

Russo, John Paul. "The Poetics of Gilbert Sorrentino." *Rivista di Studi Anglo-Americani* 3, 1984-5, 281-303.

Tamburri, Anthony Julian. "Helen Barolini's *Umbertina*: The Ethnic/Gender Dilemma." *Italian Americans Celebrate Life: The Arts and Popular Culture*. Eds. Paola A. Sensi-Isolani and Anthony Julian Tamburri. Staten Island, NY: The American Italian Historical Association, 1990, 29-44.

————.*To Hyphenate or Not To Hyphenate? The Italian/American Writer: An Other American*. Montreal: Guernica, 1991.

————. "*Umbertina*: The Italian/American Woman's Experience." In Tamburri, Giordano and Gardaphé, 357-373.

Tamburri, Anthony Julian, Giordano, Paolo A., Gardaphé Fred L., eds. *From the Margin: Writing in Italian Americana*. West Lafayette: Purdue University, 1991a.

Tusiani, Joseph. "Song of the Bicentennial (V)." *Gente Mia and Other Poems*. Stone Park, IL: Italian Cultural Center.

Viscusi, Robert. 1981. "*De vulgari eloquentia*: An Approach to the Language of Italian American Fiction." *Yale Italian Studies*, Vol. I, No. 3, 1978, 21-38.

Volosinov, V.N. *Marxism and the Philosophy of Language*. Trans. Ladislav Matejka and I.R. Titunik. Cambridge, MA: Harvard University Press, 1986.

Wickham, DeWayne. "U.S. Is Stew, not a Melting Pot." *Journal and Courier*. Lafayette, IN., (11 March 1992), 5.

10

Pasquale Verdicchio

Subalterns Abroad

Writing Between Nations and Cultures[1]

> Il vero divorzio è l'emigrazione.
>
> Antonio D'Alfonso
>
> If emigration could have helped the working class to emancipate itself, it would never have existed.
>
> Marco Micone[2]

*I*nvoluntary estrangement from one's place of birth is akin to existence under colonial circumstances and, in contemporary history, such a condition has come to replace colonialism as a form of control. If the result of emigration is not the altogether negation of cultural expression, often it is the deferral of cultural enunciation for the migrant or colonized person. The term "post-colonial" qualifies the specificity and critical body which manages to survive in postcolonial subjectivity, imperialist coordination of culture and its undoing. No such terminology exists for emigration. Perhaps the notion of "post-nationalism" offers a valid starting point from which may arise a critique of emigration, whether its causes be economics, politics and religious persecution. Emigration would thus function as an explicit site of engagement under the heading of post-nationalism.

Such parameters are readily applicable to the large portion of the Southern Italian population that was transplanted to the new social contexts of the U.S.A. and Canada as emigrants.[3] As history shows, these North American democracies were, and are, contrary to what might be believed, not accepting of cultural diversity.[4] Upon arriving on the shores of these "new" nations, many men and women soon found it necessary to render their culture less visible to the world outside their homes.[5]

In the following pages, I hope to establish the announced parallels between colonialism and nationalism and present e/im-migrant culture as one of the various post-colonial expressions available to Southern Italians in Italy and abroad.

Cultural expression is a difficult need to suppress, as can be attested by the abundant artistic production coming out of minority centers which also act as markets only too eager to consume these successful productions. Often such a need for expression entails a critique of the extant power structure which continues to limit diversity through its prescriptions for a national identity. In Canada, for example, while many minority writers and artists have been producing valuable works for some time, their production only began to find venues for exposure around the late 1970s and early 1980s. The first Italian-Canadian anthology, *Roman Candles,* published in 1978 by Hounslow Press, was edited by poet Pier Giorgio Di Cicco, who sought to come to terms with a background that had been partially buried and discarded. The following quotes from Di Cicco's preface are telling of a phenomenon that is common to many minorities in one way or another.

In 1974 I returned to Italy for the first time in twenty-odd years. I went, biased against a legacy that had made growing up in North America a difficult but not impossible chore (or so I thought). I went out of curiosity, and came back to Canada conscious of the fact that I'd been a man without a country for most of my life. And I became bitter at the thought that most people carry on day after day deeply aware that they do so on the land upon which they were born. It became clear to me that they had something immediately and emotionally at stake with their environment. And that phenomenon was something I had had to construct at every effort to feel relevant in an English country... In searching for contributors, I found isolated gestures by isolated poets, isolated mainly by the condition of nationalism prevalent in Canada in the last ten years. However pluralistic the landscape seemed to be to sociologists, the sheer force of Canadianism had been enough to intimidate all but the older "unofficial language" writers... [The anthology] ranges from poems that directly speak from a displaced sensibility to poems that are not conscious of any such dilemma. All the poets included have one sure thing in common — they are not emigrants. They were brought here by their families at an early age, and three were born in North America. They are in the fortunate and tragic position of having to live with two cultures, one more exterior than the other (9-10).

The sense of displacement expressed by Di Cicco is perhaps a common denominator to any writer working within the context of another culture and using a language other than his/her mother-tongue.

The problems which Italians in the U.S.A. and Canada face — perhaps most harshly in the U.S.A., where the pressures to assimilate have been at work more forcefully and for a longer period of time — are, in my opinion, the result of years of ongoing cultural repression. The colonial conditions which denied cultural expression in Southern Italy, before and after unification, never evolved into what we today have come to call *post-colonial discourse.*

The unification of the Italian peninsula in 1861 did not in fact liberate the South; it merely altered the colonial structure. Southern Italian culture had generally subsisted as a colonial culture, and much of that cultural production falls today in a category that escapes the particularity of the group of people that helped produce it and has instead been conscripted into service for the Nation. An example of this would be found in Benedetto Croce. According to Antonio Gramsci [6], Croce's great intellectual contribution to the Italian nation and its culture represents a great disservice to the South. Croce's activites, in fact, are deemed to have facilitated the absorption of Southern intellectuals into a national bourgeoisie, thereby further frustating the possibilities of a Southern revolution. [7]

The conditioning of the emigrant masses and the conditions that met them abroad were such that cultural subordination became an almost voluntary self-imposition dictated by survival. As such, the recent expressions of Italian identity in the U.S.A. and Canada must be recognized as a first instance of the expression of post-colonial discourse for Southern Italians. This defines an interesting phenomenon that alters not only the relationship of emigrated Italians to their adopted countries, but invariably must lead toward a change in the entrenched views and assumptions vis-à-vis Southern Italians, specially, and Italian emigrants, in general, in Italian culture.

The emigration of millions of Italians, two thirds of them from the southern regions of Italy, evolved from socio-politics and economic conditions. For this reason, I find it most proper to consider the question of Italian-Canadian writing through the works of a writer equally concerned with the region known in Italy as " the South and Islands."[8]

In his meditations on the "Southern Question" and the "role of intellectuals," Antonio Gramsci, the Sardinian founder of the Italian Communist Party, provides approaches and questions of the cultural determinacy that are still valid for the understanding of our contemporary context.

How can the work of Gramsci help us grasp the semantics behind the relationship linking a group of writers, such as the one formed by Italian-Canadian writers, and official culture(s)? And how will the understanding of such a relationship help us to better identify the overwhelming "official" mechanisms at work in the maintenance of an apparent system of dominance and subordination?

The makeup of a writers' group such as the Association of Italian-Canadian Writers is quite varied. It is not solely represented by Southerners, though they do form the majority of this group. Some writers were born in Italy; others were not. Most are the offspring of parents who did not have the possibility to pursue formal education. Their background is proletarian or subproletarian, and they are either of urban or rural extraction. The languages they speak also differ from each other and, needless to say, from the standardized Italian taught in schools. Their active participation in the government of their land of origin and in the structuring of that nation's official culture was at best marginal. These men and women had existed within historicall inactive or hidden groups; their potential to achieve the cohesiveness of an historical bloc through which to declare their cultural presence was further truncated by the imposition of emigration due to economic and/or sociopolitical oppression.[9]

The Association of Italian-Canadian Writers meets with some regularity and sponsors readings, talks, and the like, all of which provides a sense of community and communication for writers who had been working alone along the margins of what may be termed "official" Canadian culture (itself a problematic designation). It is fairly common to now describe this type of relationship to an "official" literature or culture as *minor*, a term borrowed from Deleuze and Guattari's long essay, *Kafka* (1986).[10] These are the elements that give minor literature and culture its definition:

1. A "deterritorialization of language" that involves an extended series of languages: dialect, standardized mother tongue, Canadian English vs American English (and the relationship of both to British English) and, of course, the relationship of Quebecois French to Parisian French;

2. The "political immediacy" of minority expression that calls for and requires the achievement of a critical stance in regards to the immigrant condition;

3. The "collective assemblage of enunciation" that relates, in this case, to the existence of the Association of Italian-Canadian Writers itself (though, so far, only in a weak and uncoordinated manner). In their self-recognition and organization as an association (in 1986), Italian-Canadian writers are potentially representative of a "historical bloc."

In a discussion on the concept of "historical bloc" in *Gramsci's Politics* (119-125), Anne Showstack Sassoon explains that the historical bloc is "specific to the national context" and suggests that while there might be an "international conjuncture," it is necessary that "a special emphasis [be] placed on the national dimension as the basic unit to be analysed" (121). It could be argued, however, that while the emergence of an historical bloc within a particular national situation may be forever stalled, it may indeed flourish within another. The self-representation of countries like Canada as multicultural mosaics provides, at least on the surface, the possibility of historical bloc formation for immigrant populations.[11]

The "international conjuncture," quoted by Sassoon, is of course the end to which Marxism aspires, but it is an insufficient vantage point for isolated, unrepresented groups whose international internal references may be overlooked. For example, the study of Italian-Canadian, Chinese-Canadian or Haitian-Canadian writing *solely as a Canadian phenomenon*, identified only with the plight of either the Canadian working or immigrant class, would be both incomplete and misleading, as would be a reading that merely reduced their relationships to a static dominant/subordinate dichotomy on the cultural level. To unpack and breathe life into this relationship, terms such as *hegemony* must be reviewed in a renewed light.

Again, I must stress the applicability of Gramsci in relation to the topic at hand and that his concepts, though communicated and applicable universally, were primarily based in a very particular Italian context. The linguistic source/reality of such concepts is of specific importance, given the relationship of Italy's South and Islands to the rest of the country. In his *Prison Notebooks* (1987), Antonio Gramsci at times makes use of the term *hegemony* to express the domination of one class or group over others; the complexity of his discussion, however, is much less definitive and simplifiable. As the *Notebooks* reveal, hegemony cannot in itself signify domination. In order for the concept of hegemony to take on a sense of domination it must be associated with a coercive political apparatus, at which time it ceases to be hegemony and becomes state. A plurality of hegemonies may coexist within what Gramsci termed an *expansive hegemony*. This designation is discussed by Chantal Mouffe in her "Hegemony and New Political Subjects: Toward a New Concept of Democracy," whose reconsideration of the influence of hegemonic theory is also part of her co-operative work with Ernesto Laclau. The association of the term with what Mouffe defines as the achievement of "plural democracy" reasserts Gramsci's use of *expansive hegemony* to express an ever active interplay of cultural entities in the creation of culture, not necessarily culminating in the emergence of a dominant group.[12]

Beginning with the assumption that subalternity and marginality are expressed through linguistic manipulations, as well as explicit thematics, I will reconsider Italian writing abroad as presenting variations not only on the level of a dominant/subordinate confrontation, as it is examplified in Italy by the North/South dichotomy or the history of emigration, but also as the relationship played out in North America between Italian-American and Italian-Canadian contexts.

The expressions of cultural identity that have emerged under the labels of Italian-American and Italian-Canadian are indicative of different assimilationist policies. With its complex double (English/French), if unbalanced, center toward which other cultural expressions must articulate themselves, Canada actually hides a stalled hegemonic interplay under its varied surface. One would think that in Quebec, if only because of the Quebecois' own struggle for cultural survival within an ineffectual dominant/subordinate system, a process of expansive hegemony might be at work. However, Quebec manifests a constant reassertive strategy in its relation to minority groups, that is, a strategy of containment by which linguistic and educational laws designate a minority's mode of expression. This failure to extend to others the rights of cultural presence that Quebecois (mostly, but not singularly, of French descendency) declare for themselves is a serious problem that maintains the system in a static tension. Such attitudes eventually meet with forceful assertions of cultural identity by other groups, and recent incidents concerning not only the Mohawk but other native groups is a result of this sort of blindness on the part of Quebecois.

The 1970s were an instance of this type of tension as experienced and acted upon by Canada's other official population; future tensions may be a direct result of a set of circumstances which perpetuate a system similar to what the Quebecois fear in their relationship to so-called English Canada. The Quebecois struggle for recognition prepared the right set of circumstances for other groups to take up similar causes. Yet Quebec's need to ensure its survival has resulted in a state coercive apparatus not dissimilar to English Canada's; systems that only barely hold on to their hegemonic principle of culture and will in time have to resort to other (violent?) means to maintain their dominance. Ironically, it would seem that the reason why Canadian society constantly fails to come together as a bipolar English/French representation is directly tied to the possibilities that the recognition of Quebec as an autonomous cultural society provides.

Here, and this could refer to Canada, the U.S.A., Germany, or to whichever place Italians may have migrated, our culture is known only in its singular, concentrated space: for example, the Italian community, or Italian culture as perceived by non-Italians. However, in Italy, maybe not surprisingly, cultural diversity is still a point of incredible conflict.[13] But, whether internal (to Milano or Torino) or external (to Germany or Canada), the disorientation these hegemonic fragments of immigrants experienced has come to stand as a mode of cultural opposition wherever they have settled.

As with all migrant or refugee groups, the distancing from their community represents a deprivation of a sense of historical continuity. Their experience is largely undocumented or disregarded in their places of origin; and in their new land they are further discontinuous, since no history precedes them.

Italian-Canadians are suspended between the English/French Canadian reality and their own cultural background, the result of which one could imagine as a center/margin relationship in which every day, every single act and thought enacts a continual switching of positions from the center to the margins, and back again. There is a play of multiple personalities and unstable subject positions where the languages of thought and expression do not necessarily match, where intellectual and social life conflict, and where the political opposition to a dominant culture often manifests itself as an internal, rather than external, experience.

Italian-Canadian writing represents a site of reterritorialization tending toward the formation of a historical bloc, even if the writers share only a partial history and their linguistic histories are dissimilar in their initial deterritorialization. Within this context, Italy is an abstraction that cannot be given dominion, just as the English language cannot. Multiculturalism proposes a mystificatory structure by which people become the creation of the cultural rather than vice versa. Multiculturalism, or institutionalized ethnicism, dictates the parameters for de/re-territorialization, and neutralizes the potentially antagonistic "political immediacy and [the] collective assemblage of enunciation" of any cultural agent.

Today, the languages of colonialism are themselves being colonized by the very elements they once sought to subdue. The writers who have taken the colonialists' language as a means of expressing their own culture are many: Nigeria's Chinua Achebe, Nuruddin Farah of Somalia, and Shiva Naipaul are among them. Nations that find themselves overwhelmed by the influx of diverse populations are hard pressed to define a national characteristic that, in turn, would represent their relationship with the rest of the world. However, it has become common that, having reached a certain point in their development, nations have had to give recognition (albeit limited) to the variety of voices that inhabit them. To quote Giovanni Arrighi:

> Whenever the political claim (and/or definition by others) is less than that of state sovereignty, we tend to call this group an "ethnic group," whatever the basis of the claim, be it common language, common religion, common skin color, or fictive common ancestry (25).

The "ethnic" is, thus, a subset of the minor condition described above, or a condition indispensable to it, thereby also representative of a threat to the dominant. In order to neutralize the expression of the ethnic, in other words, to return it to the status described by Arrighi, it has been necessary for official cultures to institutionalize the term and "circumscribe it by time" as another cultural "-ism," ethnicism.

Canada's multicultural mosaic is a euphemism for institutionalized multiculturalism, which is, in turn, *a strategy of containment* adopted out of necessity by the dominant culture in order to maintain its power identity. As it becomes obvious by what is published and what is not, whether and where it is anthologized, and whether any attention is paid to it in general, or whether it is funded by one agency or another, the strategy of containment involves a choice by which only a selected (non-representative) sample is allowed to speak for/from a particular ethnic group. The end result is one of ethnicism or culturalism, an external imposition of identity that denies past and present history in favour of abstractions such as nationhood and nationality. Among such abstractions we must include *ethnicism, multiculturalism* and the *Italian* and *Canadian* nationalities (in their singular and hyphenated forms).

All of these are ideological categories not only because they represent strategies of containment in the definition of meaning, but because they suppress alternative meanings that are a basic requirement in the interplay or challenges of hegemony.

The work read, presented, critiqued, and discovered at Association of Italian-Canadian Writers meetings is often relegated, by the official culture, to a sphere that, while inextricably connected to others such as the social, the political, the historical, is approached as if it were divorced from all these. When lip-service is given an ethnic culture, it is done as if that culture had developed *tabula rasa* and in isolation.

Immigrant, ethnic, minor, marginal cultures are products of definite socio-historical conditions that, whether originating from abroad or within a single national setting, represent a suppressed element in the hegemonic dialectic.

With the acquisition of a language of expression, with the opening provided by language as an antagonistic tool, Italian-Canadian writers have been able to turn the English language back toward those who call it their mother tongue. By stressing latinate vocabulary, by the insertion of Italian syntactical forms, and by the inclusion of linguistic elements that represent the utterances of immigrant culture, these writers have altered the semantic field of English, thereby denying expected meaning. The expression of Italian-Canadian silence becomes Anglo Canada's interpretative silence[14]; at which point begins the formation of a genealogy that provides its own subject position in opposition to a given history.

The re-instatement of a subject in history necessitates a recognition of the subject's historical situation which must take place at the level of aggregate subject.[15] As such, it would also be reflective of the forces that act upon it; becoming conscious of the conditions that outline the subject, one also discovers its oppositional potential.

I would like it to be clear that this is not a call for community. The heterogeneity of the Italian-Canadian group would negate any such attempt. Rather, it is a proposal for the exploration of an historical commonality that does not erase the group's cultural diversity but, in fact, reinforces it.

In her essay "Contemporary Italo-Canadian Literature," Susan Iannucci states that "Italo-Canadian writing is circumbscribed by time. It is the product of a moment in a writer's life, and that moment vanishes . . . Italy filters through in past tense; their present is Canadian" (225-226). Such a questionable conclusion is strongly based on the belief that ethnicity or cultural identity is something discernible in themes and subject matter, and that once explicit treatment of certain themes becomes invisible they have been surpassed or overcome. This attitude supports the formation of institutionalized multiculturalism agencies which require a specific set of themes from a writer in order to be qualified as ethnic. A failure to conform to prescribed ethnic formulas leaves some writers marginalized to an even greater degree, due to their double exclusion from both the official and ethnic categories.

What makes it possible to describe Italian-Canadian writing and, by extension, any hyphenated writing, as "the product of a moment', is buried deep in the blindness of the historical causes and effects of emigration. It is fair to say that while emigrants physically leave behind family, friends, and home they also leave behind a cultural past. What is more important is that such a cultural past may often have been deemed secondary to the official culture of their land, or have even remained unexpressed due to oppressive pressure of national compromise. Immigrants, upon arrival in their new home, are faced with another choice which, more often than not, dictates that they must once again suppress their own culture in order to embrace that of their host country.

And so, while the writing of Italian-Canadians may be "the product of a moment in a writer's life," I would oppose Iannucci's "moment" with Marshall McLuhan's "moment of change." At the moment of expression of particularity, a work defines a border with other works and comes to transform its expression into a moment of challenge rather than a short-lived instance.[16] Iannucci's view fails the very group it is analysing by regarding that moment merely as a stage resulting from the meeting of Canadian culture and perceiving it not as another culture but as a lack within one's own culture.

The supposed resolution of the crisis is achieved through a realization that leads to a finding of one's Canadian identity, as ambiguous as that may be. This approach, even while making weak overtures to heterogeneity, blatantly valorizes one culture over another, and disregards the influences at work in a phenomenon such as e/im-migration. Further, it facilitates and propagates the image of an ethnic literature as nothing more than nostalgic portrayals of the possibility or impossibility of a return to an illusionary rootedness. Often this work can be deeply reactionary, and may further alienate the subject from not only its new situation but also the distant and changing one it has left behind. Alternative reactions to displacement may come to light either as rejuvenated hegemonic representations, by which the writing subject engages the new culture in a critical dialogue that includes an awareness of his or her own historical situation, or as an attempt at full integration into, and denial of difference from, the official culture of arrival. Whatever the expression, it results from a contradictory construction of the subject and an attempt to answer that contradiction.

I believe that the most interesting expression of the Italian-Canadian as expatriate comes from the instigation of cultural dialogue and from the antagonism that it represents for the official culture. Writers such as Antonio D'Alfonso, Marco Micone and Dôre Michelut (Dorina Michelutti) seek to shake culture at its roots, an act which (in the spirit of the Viconian *verum factum*) opens the possibility of knowledge to those who undertake the challenge of making a language new to suit their expression.

In *The Other Shore*, Antonio D'Alfonso closes the book with a section entitled "Il nuovo barocco," in which he states:

I shall no longer write (in English). This notebook in which I move ahead. Alone. A step forward. A stop towards the ultimate horizon, the only path. To find myself. Ourselves. A step backwards.

The "moment of change": when one becomes another. The exact moment of transformation. The action fixed, the verb metamorphosing into a noun. The action and the verb possess a morality of their own, which rises from within; whereas the Baroque freeze frame — the artistic noun — knows nothing of morality. It exists per se and appears before our eyes naked, without pessimism or optimism, as if it were created by a mathematical force beyond our control (155-156).

D'Alfonso's "I shall no longer write (in English)" marks the instatement of silence and antagonism toward English Canada. However, rather than choose one of the other languages at his disposal (Italian or French), he continues to write in English. What begins as a contestation of English, bilingual Canada's dominant language, takes on the appearance of an act of antagonism toward Quebec and Italy as well. Indeed, the contestation retains its multidirectionality and should rather be taken as the assertion of having acquired the language of expression of Canada's "dominant" culture in order to unveil its silent dimension and, thereby, subvert its power positon. Those who believe that D'Alfonso "shall no longer write," and therefore stop reading, will not hear the emerging voice and will not notice the "moment of change" in which their language (English) "becomes another['s]."

Silence is also the currency of Dôre Michelut's poetics. In *Loyalty to the Hunt*, silence is expressed neither through Italian nor English, but through the use of Friulano. This is a silent language in many respects, first because it is an oral language and, most importantly, because it is ranked in a subordinate position (as a dialect) to Italian. The piece entitled "Ne storie" (36) reflects the paradox of orality, where reference is made to language but language is often superfluous to voice. There can be no answer to the (written) question "Dulà sêtu stade fin cumò?" ("Where have you been?"), for originally Friulano had no written language and its written form can only be a fiction. What the reader receives is a voice that, since it affords no linguistic reference, may well be overlooked. Despite this, Michelut writes in Friulano, a language the use of which brings on feelings such as "bitterness that seeps into my mouth, that shocks my teeth like icy well water" (37).

Rather than a sensation that would keep one from using the language though, Michelut's "bitterness" reveals itself to be a viable contestatory element in opposition to written language and the fixation of meaning. The memory of its orality is what enables one to "see," in other words, to hear and to understand: "And we see each other only when the Stèle floods from the mouth of the storyteller who once upon a time would go from barn to barn and say..." (37) While the author does provide English translations to her compositions, I would suggest that they represent nothing more than a silencing gesture to prevent any English reader from asserting authority over the text's inherent absence. Michelut bypasses both Italian language and an English representation of herself, and gives center stage to the emerging Friulan voice.

While the preceding examples are of a silence imposed on the English reader, in the case of Marco Micone's plays the silencing is a result of language interference, not unusual within immigrant family groups. Micone's *Voiceless People* (1984) is one example of the problems in cultural adaptation that are the results of generational difference. The attempts at acculturation that lead to conflict among family members are also the cause of internalized frustration and the cessation of communication. The playwright's more recent *Babele*[17] is extremely effective for its polyphonic structure, the white noise and silence that hinders communication, within a family whose members have adopted different languages of expression and can no longer find a common ground. In the following excerpt Pasquale, the father, proudly boasts about his son Tony's ability to speak "English like an Englishman and French better than the French." This he reports in his own dialect to a Quebecois visitor who does not understand the language; nevertheless, while boasting about his son's linguistic capabilities, he complains that Tony has forgotten Italian:

Pasquale : (*A Jacques, rapidamente dimostrando fierezza*) Ha visc'te come parle 'nglese. Pare ca 'nce vo fa'. Però . . . Parle 'nglese come nu 'Nglese e u francese meglie di Francese. I' u sacce, p' cché a isse u capische, mentre i Francese d' qua manche na parole. (*Poi, come se gli rivelasse un segreto.*) Sule u taliane, nu parle tante boune. (*Riprende il tono normale.*) Quille, doppe, u pov're uagliò, già 'nze ni té da parlà. Doppe avute a sf'rtune da capità miezz'a nuie. (*Più forte in ottimo italiano.*) Abbiamo dimenticato finanche l'italiano. (*Poi continua in dialetto.*) A ch' serv'ne i solde, i case, i mach'ne e tant'atra rrobbe, simme perze a cosa cchié bella ch' c' sta. N'n sapimme cchié bella ch' c' sta. N'n sapimme cchié parla. (*Con rabbia contenuta.*) Di vote, v' nnesse tutte e m' n' iesse... (*Dirigendosi verso gli spettatori.*) Che v'fa, a vuie, quande u figlie vuosc'tre v' parle 'nglese o francese sapenne ca vuie capite sule u mulisane o u bruzzese? (30)

Pasquale (*to Jacques, quickly showing his pride*): See how he speaks English. He doesn't let on. But... he speaks English like the English and French better than the French. I know, because I understand him, but not a word of the French in this place.(*Then, as if revealing a secret.*) Only Italian, he doesn't speak it very well. (*In the normal tone again.*) He, then, the poor boy, already has nothing to say. Then he had the misfortune to end up with us. (*Louder in excellent Italian.*) We have even forgotten Italian. (*He continues in dialect.*) What's money, houses, cars and everything else, if we've lost the most beautiful thing there is. There is nothing more beautiful. We don't know how to talk anymore. (*With contained anger.*) At times, I'd sell everything and leave . . . (*Turning toward the audience.*) How do you feel, when your children speak to you in English or French, knowing fully well that you only understand Molisian or Abrutian. (Molisian and Abrutian are dialect variations of the Abruzzi-Molise region.)

While these three examples briefly go to show the great variety of work produced within the Italian-Canadian group, their salient feature is in their position of contradiction and antagonism. This places them, through language, at the center of the mechanisms of cultural production. The work of these authors is a response to the external forces that have constructed their subjectivity as immigrants, and represents an attempt to unveil those same forces. Micone's and D'Alfonso's epigrams, quoted at the outset of this essay, demonstrate that the antagonism is not only addressed at Canada's construction of their subjectivity but also at Italy's. This declares the immigrant's autonomy from both influences and clears a ground for further cultural activity that speaks of itself and is not merely the mirror of another's image. In current debates on subaltern cultures, it has been acceptable to consider the position of subaltern groups solely within the context of their present national situation.[18] However, this designation is not universally applicable, given the fact that many such groups have definite ties to other official cultures and traditions external to that of their immediate residency. Whatever the forces of their decontextualization, be they economic, political, or other, these groups maintain a historical and cultural link with their places of provenance.

Cultural interplay is directly related to language and the undertaking of an historical critique through linguistic means. Such an exercise leads to the consciousness of the "moment of change," quoted by Antonio D'Alfonso in his discussion of the New Baroque. This designation that he would apply to expressions such as Italian-Canadian writing, and for which I am indebted to D'Alfonso, is from Marshall McLuhan's discussion of the Baroque: "Baroque art and poetry sought to unify disparate facets and experiences by directing attention to the moment of change" (17-18). The quotation's source is of added significance, given McLuhan's concept of "global village" and the cultural inter-relatedness it describes. Placed in the context of minor literature,[19] this brings us back to the moment of challenge, the point where cultures touch and mingle, where they define their positions; the moment that both unifies and distances the populations of a land.

Italian-Canadian writers must assess their value within the moments of "departure" and "arrival" that cannot but alter those who undertake the journeys, as well as their hosts and originators, thereby representing a criticism both of the place left and of the place reached. Yet these moments must find articulation in order to be of value. Such articulations are to be found in the work of D'Alfonso, Michelut, and Micone through their use of language, and in particular in their use of metaphor, the presence of silence, and deferment of meaning. They, and other Italian-Canadian writers, use the inheritance of silence against itself in their cultural self-assertion, establishing its function not only through metaphor but as a metaphor in itself. M.J. Michael Fisher, in "Ethnicity and the Post-Modern Arts of Memory," comments that "the search for a sense of ethnic identity is a (re-)invention and discovery of a vision, both ethical and future-oriented. Whereas the search for coherence is grounded in a connection to the past, the meaning abstracted from that past, an important criterion of coherence, is an ethic workable for the future" (196). Fisher further says that "ethnicity is a process of inter-references between two or more cultural traditions" (201). This assignation of ambivalence to the 'moment' finds congruency with Gramsci when he stresses the importance of relationships with all of his concepts. Fisher's conclusions, while not overvaluing either past or future, further make it clear that the processes of cultural expression and ethnic self-representation cannot be viewed as singular, unidirectional and definitive.

Italian-Canadian writers seem to be expressing a period of conscientization that achieves something that may have remained unattainable in the Italian national context.[20] Among them, we find a flourishing of "organic intellectuals" who are very specific in the expression of their immigrant position. And, as immigration also supposes emigration, the moment of challenge in these intellectuals is directed toward a critique of both Italian and Canadian national policies of culture and identity.

In order not to digress on a discussion of the "organic intellectual," let it suffice to bridge this term with the "historical bloc" designation mentioned above. Briefly, Gramsci's "organic intellectual" is to be distinguished from the 'traditional intellectual' in that s/he is the product of a particular group and upholds that group's cultural and political interests.[21] The line between the two types of intellectuals is a fine one, given that the acquired languages of communication for many, either English or French, are also the "official" languages. What differs from one group to another is the application and the mode of dissemination of that language. Of primary importance is the organic intellectual's responsibility to his/her constituency rather than to any other external institution.[22] In this context, Pier Giorgio Di Cicco's statement — that for him the question is 'not how does my viewpoint differ? but how am I differently seen in the view of the mainstream culture?' (Minni and Foschi 1990: 23) — is all important, for it declares the automatic legitimacy of a culture that the dominant is constantly attempting to de-legitimate.

Di Cicco's statement opposes the point of view of many who find it hard to conceive of ethnic or immigrant writing removed from the influence of the dominant culture, and overlook the ties with the problems associated with Italian nationhood that are part and parcel of the condition. While much of this is unintended, it is nevertheless expressed, and has often worked its magic into the writings of Italian-Canadian critics. In Joseph Pivato's essay "Nothing Left to Say: Italian Canadian Writers," the distance that has insinuated itself between many e/im-migrants and the history of immigration is apparent:

> There is no recognized tradition of ethnic writing in Canada. We have had many writers in the unofficial languages but they have remained underground, invis-

ible. For the majority culture, writers like Stephan Stephansson do not exist. There is no tradition of Italian-Canadian writing to which writers can belong or against which they can react. Without a tradition writers do not exist because they are writing in a vacuum . . . [The] dialectic with an established tradition is not yet possible for Italian-Canadian writers, unless they simply accept the still new English-language or French-language situations (Minni and Foschi 33).

Is Italian-Canadian writing or any ethnic writing the expression of a moment which may, indeed, as the title of Pivato's essay ironically suggests, leave these writers with nothing left to say? No, because it is a result of historical events through which immigrant writing persists, evolves, and makes itself felt in the society at large.

The culture of ethnic writers, while a product of the cultures of those who form the immigrant groups, cannot claim to represent the culture of their respective groups. To present the Association of Italian-Canadian Writers as the cultural representative of the Italian community in Canada would be nothing more than a variation of the rule of state and, paradoxically, reveal itself to be a need to declare and identify one's self with Canadian society's dominant dimension. Italian-Canadian writers are, indeed, partaking in the construction of a new culture, but we cannot pretend to know what that culture may be. Any agent describing hegemonic circulation must remain distant from determinative temptations, lest s/he participate in the suffocation and atrophy of its expression.

Situated thought, such as Gramsci's was to a large extent denied to express, is now being exercised by groups such as the Italian-Canadians writers. And, if for Gramsci POSSIBILITY = FREEDOM, then the production of Italian-Canadians writers has introduced a range of possibilities into the English literary tradition which is potential freedom for all users of the English language. Their work and that of other cultural groups within the Canadian context facilitates the dialectic between determinism and freedom, by which a truly multicultural society may emerge.

Notes

1. A different version of this article was published as "Bound by Distance: Italian-Canadian Writing as Decontextualized Subaltern," in *Voices in Italian Americana*, Vol. 3, No. 2, 1992.

2. "Il vero divorzio è l'emigrazione" is a quotation from graffiti in Antonio D'Alfonso's family's home town of Guglionesi, quoted in his *The Other Shore* (65). The other epigram opens Marco Micone's play *Gens du silence* (1982) and *Voiceless People* translated by Maurizia Binda. Döre Michelut's quoted work is from *Loyalty to the Hunt*, also a Guernica publication.

3. While I intend to stress that Southern Italian emigration was the result of colonial policies and activities on the part of the unifying Northern forces, I would also emphasize that the repression of cultural diversity manifested itself in areas outside of the South, especially in poorer regions such as the Friuli.

4. Interesting reading in this regard may include Arthur M. Schlesinger Jr.'s *The Disuniting of America: Reflections on a Multicultural Society* (1992).

5. Of course, a most interesting relationship is also established between each new-comer group and others struggling for status. The African-American community appears to have been the target of most immigrant groups' calumnies in the latter's struggle to assimilate. I analyze the relationships between Italian-Americans and African-Americans in Spike Lee's films in "If I was six feet tall I would have been Italian," in *Differentia: A Journal of Italian Thought*, No. 6/7, 1994.

6. "...Benedetto Croce has fulfilled an extremely important 'national' function, by having detached the radical intellectuals of the South from the peasant masses and having them partecipate in national and European culture; and through this culture, he has caused their absorption by the national bourgeoisie and hence by the agrarian bloc" (Antonio Gramsci, *The Southern Question*, translated by myself (Chicago: Bordighera, 1995).

7. Gramsci, ibid.

8. Antonio Gramsci, *La questione meridionale* (1966). and *Gli intellettuali* (1977). The latter is a collection of materials collated from Gramsci's *Quaderni del Carcere* (*Prison Notebooks*). The geographic designation of "the South and the Islands" defines the empoverished areas of Italy. This large region encompasses approximately half of the Italian landmass. The effects of the "economic boom" of the postwar era largely left it behind; industrialization has almost consistently failed, and the stereotypic imaging of Southerners as a primitive and uncultured sector of Italy still subsists in racist expressions such as "Africa begins at Naples."

9. Historical inactivity does not mean cultural inactivity; however, cultural activity itself may in fact produce historically active factors that may go un-noticed or unrecognized until a later period.

10. Gilles Deleuze and Felix Guattari, *Kafka: Toward a Minor Literature* (1986). "A minor literature doesn't come from a minor language; it is rather that which a minority constructs within a major language. But the first characteristic of minor literature in any case is that in it language is affected with a high coefficient of deterritorialization"(16). Further, "the second characteristic of minor literatures is that everything in them is political. Minor literature's... cramped space forces each individual intrigue to connect immediately to politics. The individual concern thus becomes all the more necessary, indispensable, magnified, because a whole other story is vibrating within it" (17). "The third characteristic of minor literature is that in it everything takes on a collective value" (17).

11. In Gramscian terms POSSIBILITY = FREEDOM. As such, even a superficially open environment like the Canadian multicultural mosaic provides enough of a possibility for groups to take up a struggle for self representation. See Gramsci (1987: 360).

12. Within the Gramscian differentiation of the concept of hegemony, *hegemonic principle* is that by which the official culture takes into account the demands of a certain group only to neutralize it and prevent its extention. *Expansive hegemony* is the process by which equivalences between groups are found that support the demands of equality of a number of groups.

13. A notable recent example of the vast divisions stat still hinder a full expression of Italian cultural diversity is Giorgio Bocca's *La disunità d'Italia: Per venti milioni di italiani la meocrazia è in coma e l'Europa s'allontana* (1990). See Verdicchio (1992).

14. The reference here is to English as the target language. This relationship is also evident in many Italian-Canadian writers from Quebec who write in (or also in) French. Of particular importance here are Fulvio Caccia's *Irpinia* and *Scirocco* (reprinted in his collection poems entitled *Aknos* which won the Governor General Award), and Antonio D'Alfonso's novel, *Avril ou l'anti-passion*. I also wish to point out that *The Other Shore* was also published in French as *L'autre rivage*.

15. I use aggregate because it maintains a sense of individuality within the grouping, rather than propose an individual vs group paradigm.

16. I believe that a transformation such as the one alluded to by McLuhan is also definable in terms of the metamorphosis from emigrant to immigrant. The "moment of change" is also a potential moment of challenge in which the individual or group may elect to challenge both the culture from which s/he emigrated and the one into which s/he immigrated.

17. Published in the transcultural journal *Vice Versa*, No. 26. *Vice Versa* is a multilingual publication out of Montreal, whose initial founders included Antonio D'Alfonso, Fulvio Caccia and Lamberto Tassinari.

18. Just a reminder here that Showstack-Sassoon offers a similar position in relation to hegemony. See earlier portion of this essay regarding hegemony.

19. Gillez Deleuze and Felix Guattari, *Kafka: Toward a Minor Literature* (1986). "A minor literature doesn't come from a minor language; it is rather that which a minority constructs within a major language. But the first characteristic of minor literature in any case is that in it language is affected with a high coefficient of deterritorialization" (16).

Subalterns Abroad

Further, "the second characteristic of minor literatures is that everything in them is political. Minor literature's... cramped space forces each individual intrigue to connect immediately to politics. The individual concern thus becomes all the more necessary, indispensable, magnified, because a whole other story is vibrating within it" (17). "The third characteristic of minor literature is that in it everything takes on a collective value" (17).

20. *Conscientization* is a term used by the Brazilian intellectual Paulo Freire to refer to a population's "critical self-insertion into reality," or as expressed by the editor of the English translation: "the process in which men, not as recipients, but as knowing subjects, achieve a deepening awareness both of the socio-cultural reality which shapes their lives and of their capacity to transform that reality." See Paulo Freire.

21. See also endnote (6) regarding Gramsci description of Croce.

22. Traditional intellectuals have their own "organic" group. However, the distinction is to be made between those who remain in the service of their group (organic) and those who serve the interests of the dominant or traditional (read also national) culture against those of their own.

References

Arrighi, Giovanni, Hopkings, Terence K., Wallerstein. *Antisystemic Movements*. New York: Verso, 1989.

Bocca, Giorgio. *La disunità d'Italia*. Milano: Garzanti, 1990.

Caccia, Fulvio. *Aknos*. Toronto: Guernica, 1994. *Irpinia* and *Scirocco*. First editions 1983 and 1985.

D'Alfonso, Antonio. *The Other Shore*. Montreal/Toronto: Guernica, 1986.

———. *Avril ou l'anti-passion*. Montreal: Vlb éditeur, 1990.

Deleuze, Gilles and Guattari, Felix. *Kafka: Toward a Minor Literature*. Minneapolis: University of Minnesota Press, 1986.

Fisher, Michael M.J. "Ethnicity and the Post-Modern Arts of Memory." *Writing Culture: The Poetics and Politics of Ethnogrphy*. Eds. James Clifford and George E. Marcus. Berkeley: University of California Press, 1986, 194-233.

Freire, Paulo. *Cultural Action for Freedom*. Cambridge: Harvard Educational Review, 1988.

Gramsci, Antonio. *La questione meridionale*. Roma: Editori Riuniti, 1966.

———. *Gli intellettuali*. Roma: Editori Riuniti, 1977.

———. *Prison Notebooks*. Ed. and trans. Quintin Hoare and Geoffrey N. Smith. New York: International Publishers, 1987.

———. "The Southern Question." Trans. Pasquale Verdicchio. Lafayette (IN): Bordighera Inc., 1995.

Iannucci, Susan. "Contemporary Italian-Canadian Literature." In Roberto Perin and Franc Sturino, eds. (209-227).

Laclau, Ernesto, and Mouffe, Chantal. *Hegemony and Socialist Strategy*. London: Verso, 1985.

McLuhan, Marshall. *Through the Vanishing Point: Space in Poetry and Painting.* New York: Harper and Row, 1968.

Micone, Marco. *Voiceless People.* Trans. Maurizia Binda. Montreal: Guernica, 1984.

————. "Babele." *Vice Versa*, 26, 30-32.

Mouffe, Chantal. "Hegemony and New Political Subjects: Toward a New Concept of Democracy." *Marxism and the Interpretation of Culture.* Eds. C. Nelson and L. Grossberg. Chicago: University of Illinois Press, 1988.

Showstack Sassoon, Anne. *Gramsci's Politics.* New York: St. Martin's Press, 1980.

Verdicchio, Pasquale. "If I was six feet tall I would have been Italian." *Differentia: A Journal of Italian Thought,* 6, 1993.

————. "L'Italia in Bocca." *Vice Versa*, 36, 1992.

11

Joseph Pivato

Italianistica Versus
Italian-Canadian Writing

*I*nitially this paper presented an argument for the inclusion of Italian-Canadian writing in the Italian Studies curricula of our universities, but it became a study of a larger problem in the teaching of Italian: a conservatism that resists change. It would seem logical for a natural affinity to exist between *italianistica* and Italian-Canadian writing. Instead, we find that the two areas of discourse are often in opposition to one another.

The conflict revolves around these questions: Is *italianistica* interdisciplinary or is it restricted to the study of Italian language and literature? Is Italian culture restricted to those works produced in Italy, or can it include material created by Italians outside Italy? What is the role of theory in our understanding of national cultures and hybrid cultures? In this discussion I use the example of Italian-Canadian writers but we could also use the work of Italians in Australia, U.S.A., Brazil, Argentina, Venezuela, or any other country which has a significant Italian population.

I begin with a little anecdote, un aneddoto

A few months ago a professor from another university telephoned me in Edmonton for information about an Italian-Canadian writer. He wanted verification that this writer did in fact exist and was not some imaginary figure. I was able to assure him that she did exist, that I possessed three of her novels, two in Italian and one in English, that we had corresponded up to the time of her death in December, 1987, and that her activity as a writer could be verified by other people. The writer in question was Elena Randaccio who published

227

the novels, *Canada, Mia seconda patria* in 1958 under the nom de plume, Elena Albani, and *Diario di una emigrante* in 1979 with the name, E. MacRan.

This little story captures that lack of a working relationship between Italian-Canadian writing and writers and *italianistica*. On the one side we have the obscurity of the writers, and on the other side we have the ignorance or lack of interest of academics, and, by extension, students of Italian. Elena Randaccio is not untypical of the immigrant writer in Canada. She wrote in Italian and published her work in obscurity, her use of pseudonyms being a deliberate means she employed to protect her privacy (personal correspondence).

The fact that Elena Randaccio was, however, the only Italian woman writer in Canada in the 1950s and 1960s, and that she was publishing under curious pseudonyms, should have aroused the interest of the Italian literary community in this country. Since Montreal journalist, Mario Duliani, did publish a review of *Canada, mia seconda patria* in *Il Cittadino Canadese* in 1959, the collective non acknowledgment of her work that continued throughout the remainder of her life must have been due more to lack of interest than to a true lack of awareness.

It is a sad irony of Randaccio's life that for decades the practitioners of *italianistica* had ignored her and her work, and now some of these people doubted her very existence. From the perspective of the Italian literary institution Randaccio did not exist. She was writing outside Italy and did not have any recognition either from the writers' groups or from the academy.

In practice many other Italian language writers in Canada did not exist and are not recognized. They include Libborio Lattoni, Mario Duliani, Tonino Caticchio, Gianni Bartocci, Dino Fruchi, Ermanno La Riccia, Gianni Grohovaz, Matilde Torres, Romano Perticarini, Maria Ardizzi and others. Even though all of these writers publish in Italian and often with small presses in Italy they remain unacknowledged both there and here in Canada. Not only are their books not read in Italian literature courses, but these titles are very often not found in university library collections.

Unlike Randaccio, these writers did not hide their identities. Some — Duliani and Grohovaz, for example — were recognized public figures who wrote for Italian newspapers most of their lives. Others like Perticarini and Ardizzi are prolific writers who have published a number of books and have won literary awards. Nevertheless, they remain unknown in Italian literature programs.

Since these authors publish in Italian, language cannot be a factor for their exclusion from both the Italian literary institution and academic recognition. While the nature of the language they use may be simpler than that of sophisticated urban authors from Italy, this plain style is more appropriate for the elemental qualities of the immigrant experiences explored in their works. This simpler language also has strong parallels with the style of Italian-Canadian writers working in English and French. A careful reading of these authors makes it clear that they have to be read in terms of the North American context and not in terms of Toscana or Lombardia. The Italian used in Canada or Brazil over a half century will take on characteristics of the local cultural and social environment. The work of Alfredo Luzi and Gaetano Rando explore this use of language in Australia as does Francesco Loriggio in Canada.

In many ways the Italian language and literature programs in North America are extensions of the academic establishment in Italy and depend on it. Not only do programs here follow the literary canons established there but they also share the same biases for literary value, language style, interpretation, literary history and critical methods. In this context of political conservatism and intellectual elitism, programs in Canada have allowed themselves to remain in a colonial position. In this subordinate position Italian language authors in North America can never write well enough to be included in the long tradition of Italian letters. The literary values established by academics in Rome may not be so universal as to apply to Italian writers in the New World. We can also speculate that for the cultural elite of Rome, Florence or Milan the non-existence of the immigrant writers in North America is merely part of the non-existence of the ordinary immigrant, the masses who left Italy and are now forgotten. (See Pierre Bourdieu on culture and power.)

Specializations in Italian language and literature are offered in twenty universities in Canada. They range from small programs with courses that are part of a minor for an undergradute degree to full M.A. and Ph.D. programs such as that at the University of Toronto. Of the hundreds of courses listed for these programs only three deal with Italian-Canadian material. At Carleton Univesity in Ottawa Francesco Loriggio and William Anselmi offer a course on "The Italian Heritage in North America," which examines novels, plays, poetry and film by Italian-Canadian and Italian-American artists. Filippo Salvatore teaches a similar course at Concordia University. Students at the University of Toronto can join a course entitled, "The Italo-Canadians in Toronto," described as:

> A research course on certain aspects of the Italian community involving... the gathering of data, its analysis and discussion, and the tabulation of the results. Topics to be investigated include linguistic behaviour and acculturation, and social facts related to linguistic matters.

This course has a linguistic orientation, focussed on collecting statistical information on language practice in Toronto only. There is no consideration here of Italian-Canadian writers, their works or their language choices. At the University of Waterloo Vera Golini includes Italian-Canadian writers as part of her course, "Italian Culture and Civilization." Because these courses depend in each case on the interests and teaching load of a single instructor they are not offered on a yearly basis.

   In Italian studies at the graduate level there is even less work on Italian-Canadian writers. We find an Italian M.A. on Frank Paci at the University of Alberta and an Italian Ph.D. in progress at the University of Toronto. Ironically in Italian universities there is a score of graduate theses on Italian-Canadian writers publishing in English or French. Some examples are Gladis Lucia Colangelo in Rome, Irene Davi in Messina, Carla Eusebi in Bologna, and Moreno Botti in Arezzo. These are in modern language programs rather than in Italian literature programs. Even Marina Arteni's thesis on the Italian novels of Ardizzi is with the Facoltà di lingue e letterature straniere at Udine. This phenomenon is paralleled in Canada by the graduate theses in departments of English and Comparative Literature which examine the works of Italian-Canadian writers publishing in English, French and Italian as Canadian authors. Among these we have Nathalie Cooke at the University of Toronto, Sandra Saccucci at McMaster, Marino Tuzi at York, Lisa Bonato and Debra Muchnik at the University of Alberta. Implicit in some of these theses is the view that those authors working in Italian share many elements with those working in English or French. One of these elements is the Italian culture of the immigrant.

The natural relationship between *italianistica* and Italian-Canadian writing, be it a love-hate relationship, rests on three general arguments: interdisciplinarity, Italian culture and theory.

1. Interdisciplinarity

Italian studies or *italianistica* has officially always been seen as interdisciplinary. This was the view of the people who founded the Canadian Society for Italian Studies at the first meeting at McGill University in May, 1972. It was always seen as something more than a society of language teachers. In the first issue of the society's journal, *Quaderni d'italianistica* (1980), Stefania Ciccone (then president of the society) explains this interdisciplinary philosophy:

> ...una ragione d'essere per noi esiste: anzitutto nella necessità di riunire, al di là di ogni distanza geografica, tutte le forze della cultura italiana in Canada... Per questo, pur mantenendo un interesse prioritario verso la letteratura, desideriamo che la nostra rivista si presenti e si sviluppi sempre di più in un ambito interdisciplinare.

> A reason for our existence is, above all, the need to unite across every geographic distance all the forces of Italian culture in Canada... For this, while maintaining a primary interest in literature, we desire our journal always to present itself and to develop even more in an interdisciplinary sphere.

In the sixteen years that *Quaderni d'italianistica* has been published this interdisciplinary goal has rarely been achieved. Instead the journal has been devoted to literary studies of the major Italian authors, to canonocal texts and conventional interpretations. We do not find a study of the elemental peasant poet, Rocco Scotellaro, nor of Goldoni's works in dialect, or of any other author writing in dialect. Italian-Canadian writers are mentioned only once, a 1980 review of Di Cicco's *Roman Candles* written by Francesco Loriggio.

In the classroom, *italianistica* involves primarily the study of Italian language and literature. Too often this is limited to the study of standard Italian from a textbook, and the reading of a few Italian works from the accepted canon of major writers: Dante, Boccaccio, Tasso, Carducci, Manzoni, Pirandello, Moravia and Calvino. In some programs *italianistica* may also include the study of Italian dialects, Italian film, art history, Italian history and current events. Even these areas will be limited to a few selected topics. The focus is always on the same major figures; and no attention given to peasant past, *operai*, the women of the shadows, the marginalized.

In general *italianistica* in North America is not interdisciplinary but limited to literary texts. When we look at Italian programs across the continent and at publications such as *Italica, Canadian Journal of Italian Studies, Forum Italicum, Rivista di Studi Italiani* and *Quaderni d'italianistica* we see that activity is limited to literary study and language teaching. It can be argued that there is some interdisciplinarity in this activity in so far as it looks at the relations between the disciplines of literary studies and language studies. The focus is always the written text and most often the standard literary work.

What is missing in Italian Studies programs is work on pre-literary material: folk culture, the oral tradition, Italian folksongs and stories. Two books on this topic are Mathias and Raspa, *Italian Folktales in America* and Falassi, *Folklore by the Fireside*. There is also little exploration of the history of Italian migration, *Italiani nel mondo,* and the writing of *Italiani nel mondo* whether that writing is in standard Italian, a dialect or another language.

With the writing of *Italiani nel mondo* we are dealing not only with literary works, novels, poems, plays and short stories, but also with paraliterary works, letters, diaries, memoirs, amateur biographies and histories. This kind of study, exemplified by Cesare Pitto's *Al di là dell'emigrazione*, takes us into truly interdisciplinary areas of social history, sociology and anthropology, and their relations with literature and languages. We are not just looking at obscure historical events but at a living, changing culture of Italian immigrants.

We should also note that when Italian studies limits itself to selected topics from the peninsula it is dealing with only part of the demographic picture. There is a population of approximately 57 million people in Italy and an estimated 40 million people of Italian origin living outside Italy. These people have been creating a hybrid Italian culture in their countries of residence. Some *italianisti* feel that this hybrid culture should be studied as a variation on the relatively more integrated culture of the peninsula (G. Rosoli 419).

Research into these extra territorial examples of Italian culture will require interdisciplinary approaches which may bring into play social history, comparative literature, different languages, social and political conditions, economic factors, religion, educational practices, migration patterns and many other elements. This broad approach to the study of *Italiani nel mondo* is carried on by one journal, *Altreitalie, Rassegna internazionale di studi sulle popolazioni di origine italiana nel mondo*. Published in Torino by the Fondazione Giovanni Agnelli, this journal tends to be dominated by historians and sociologists but it does give some attention to the arts and the literature of immigrant Italians. In contrast to this is *Il Veltro*, a journal devoted to *la civiltà italiana*, but always from the perspective of the editors in Rome, the cultural agenda of the powerful gate-keepers.

The Centre for Italian Canadian Studies at the University of Toronto publishes an annual journal, *Italian Canadiana,* devoted to research on culture and social aspects of the Italian community in Canada and includes articles in English, French and Italian. As an extracurricular unit of the Department of Italian Studies at the University of Toronto, the Centre has little funding and depends on the volunteer work of its supporters and editors. The one slim volume per year of *Italian Canadiana* is primarily dedicated to the papers presented at the Centre's annual symposium, but often includes articles and book reviews on Italian-Canadian writing. The journal makes no links between *italianistica* and Italian-Canadian writing, since the Toronto academics seem to regard them as two separate areas of study. This journal is a modest beginning for the Italian program at the University of Toronto, the biggest one in North America. At York University the Mariano Elia Chair in Italian-Canadian Studies has so far only published Franc Sturino's *Italian-Canadian Studies: A Selected Bibliography*.

In some Italian studies programs individual academics study various problems of language behaviour among immigrants and their children. There have been statistical studies of Italian language retention in Toronto and Montreal households, for example. There are published studies in dialectology, language interference, bilingual speech and second language teaching. Students have conducted research projects in these areas and then have written theses of their results to earn degrees in linguistics. Interesting scientific studies on these topics are often published in *The Canadian Modern Language Review*,

Studies in Applied Linguistics, *Italica*, *Il Forneri* and *Language Problems & Language Planning*.

What strikes one about many of these studies is the position of the people being studied. The Italian person being examined is kept at the level of an object. This person as object does not speak. Instead the scholar who analyzes the results speaks for and about this person, or persons. These immigrant parents and children never seem to speak for themselves, unmediated by the academic researcher. Are they ever shown the results of the studies of which they are a part? Are their comments, reactions, arguments ever recorded and included in the published studies? The appropriation of voice of these people raises questions about the treatment of human subjects in academic research. Scientific objectivity here can lead to the presentation of distorted views on these people. Another aspect of this ethical question is the image it seems to perpetuate of the Italian immigrant as uneducated, inarticulate and dependent on others for arriving at an understanding of himself or herself. We get the impression that these hyphenated Italians with their hybrid cultures are less than Italian, and possibly, less than human. These language researchers should be aware of studies such as those of Gill Bottomley on the representation of immigrants in the social sciences.

Italian immigrants and their children are not voiceless; but speak clearly to each other and to all of us. One way that these people speak is through their arts, especially their writing: novels, stories, poems, plays, essays and experimental writing in mixed genres and mixed languages. They explore who they are; they record the immigrant experience; the meaning of growing up in Canada as both an Italian and a Canadian. These people with very humble backgrounds speak for themselves unmediated by the academic, the researcher or the professional journalist. Again I emphasize that this is direct speech with all its real vitality, spontaneity and peculiar anomalies (see Rando 1985).

The writing and folk culture of these people studied along with the other topics of Italianistica and linguistic behaviour offers the opportunity to do truly interdisciplinary work. This research is intellectually valid because it looks at all aspects of Italian culture in Canada, especially that culture produced by the people here. And it is ethically sound in terms of the study of human behaviour because the people are treated as subjects and not as objects. These people are drawn into the process of the research, into all aspects of the

Italian experience in Canada. They take part in the discourse, which is really their discourse. They are empowered to determine the nature of the research, to critique the validity of the findings, to learn from the process and to teach us about who we are.

In order to achieve this all-inclusive approach to Italian culture in Canada we must also look at writing in English and French. Just as Italian-language newspapers in Canada often include articles in English or French in order to represent all points of view and speak to all readers, so too, the reading of Italian-Canadian writing in Italian studies programs must also include work in English and French. This thoroughness and openness is a recognition that these transplanted people inhabit a world that is an adaptation between two or more cultures, languages, sets of values and is constantly being translated. The academics and researchers have the opportunity to observe and share in the interdisciplinarity of the lives of these Italian-Canadians. Only in this way can we hope to "riunire... tutte le forze della cultura italiana in Canada" (Ciccone).

2. Italian Culture

When we discuss *italianistica* do we share a common idea about Italian culture? What is Italian culture? Is it only that culture which is produced in Italy, the culture of RAI? Should we restrict this even more to those activities which have institutional support in Italy: the opera of the major houses; the theatre approved by the *Associazione Generale Italiana dello Spettacolo*; the literary works accepted by the *Società Italiana degli Autori ed Editori*? Is this Italian culture the officially sanctioned work, the canonical texts, produced by the elite for the elite? The answer seems to be yes if we look at the work done by the world-wide network of *Istituti Italiani di Cultura*, Italian consulates and embassies. The answer is yes if we look at the teaching, research and publication activities in Italian studies programs in North America.

From an examination of the texts used in Italian studies programs in North America one would never realize that there are millions of people of Italian background on this continent and millions more in Latin America. Italian culture seems to begin and end on the peninsula.

Not only is this not the single Italian culture in Italy it is not even that of the majority. Statistics on the use of standard Italian indicate this disparity. In 1960 only 18% of Italians habitually spoke the standard language. By 1974 this had risen to 25% and continued to rise because of education and the mass media. In 1960 about 28% of Italians spoke only their dialect and about 15% were illiterate. By 1985 almost 80% of Italian children completed eight years of compulsory schooling.

Historically, therefore, there is another Italian culture: that of the poor, the common people, *i contadini e gli operai*. Both in Italy and in immigrant communities around the world we have the Italian folklore of peasants, the oral literature and the dialects of many regions, the music and cuisine of a very diverse Italy.

This folkloric culture rarely receives recognition in the Italy of central governments and national unity. Regional diversity in Italy is often identified with economic backwardness and is being eliminated through compulsory education in standard Italian and the spread of the national media.

Since most Italian immigrants come from these economically underdeveloped regions, this unsophisticated folkculture is the one they bring with them to the New World. And it is this regional culture that is kept alive in Italian communities in North America.

Fifty years ago the Italian government and the cultural elite were happpy to get rid of their surplus populations. The millions of emigrants who left Italy were quickly forgotten by the homeland. Now these same elite are embarassed that these unsophisticated immigrants should be identified with modern Italy. We also have the negative stereotype in the United States and in Southern Italy where these peasants have often been associated with the Mafia and other crime groups. The irony of the recent revelations in the Tangentopoli affair is that it is the political and business elites who have been accomplices of organized crime groups, and not the peasants. The political leaders in the North and the South have been discredited by the revelations of corruption. This lesson in the corrupting effects of power leads us to question the influence of the cultural elite in Italy and outside Italy, and their dominance of the cultural agenda. Do they understand, or appreciate the nature of the Italian culture which has developed outside the peninsula? Do they even care?

Examples of how this clique of cultural elite can distort the perception of culture are some editions of *Il Veltro,* a journal of Italian culture in the world which presents a central Roman view. The 1985 volume of *Il Veltro* deals with Italian culture in Canada, but it is a peculiar view of this phenomenon. Of the 568 pages in this two part volume fifty pages are reserved for official messages by government representatives: the president of Italy, the Governor General of Canada, the Italian Embassador to Canada, the Canadian Embassador to Italy, ministers of culture, and others. The remaining 500 pages examine many topics in Italian culture: the study of Dante in Canada, the Italian explorers in Canada, Italian music in Canada, Italian art in Canada, Pirandello in Canada, and the Italian language in Canada. The Italian colonial mentality is epitomized by an absurd article on Italian place names in Canada. Many other important topics are not even mentioned: immigrant women, Italian-Canadian labour organizations, the role of professionals in the immigrant communities, an aging immigrant population, the work of Italian-Canadian novelists and other artists.

For the contributors and editors of *Il Veltro* the cultural relations between Italy and Canada are based on one-way export, with Italy producing and Canada consuming. The academics who run the Italian studies programs in North America subscribe to this view.

Since the only Italian culture worth studying is that produced in Italy they have avoided dealing with the writing of the immigrant masses. For these academics the focus of their work is the canon of Italy's national literature. Along with the cultural institutes at Italian consulates, they maintain the myth that Italy has one monolithic national literature in standard Italian. These cultural gate-keepers hold the view that writing produced in Italy's other languages is a quaint anomaly, a folkloric phenomenon and that there is no Italian literature produced outside of Italy. Can the *elemento popolare* be dismissed this easily?

This view of Italian writing began to change in 1989 when Jean-Jacques Marchand organized an international conference in Lausanne on Italian immigrant literature in the world.

Professors of Italian from many countries gathered to discuss the existence of an Italian literature produced outside Italy. No less than seven academics from Canada participated in this historic event.

There are several aspects about this conference which support the arguments presented here. First, organizers tried to prejudge the language question. Marchand wanted to limit the conference to publications in Italian, but several speakers, especially Gaetano Rando from Australia and Filippo Salvatore from Canada, expanded the discussion to Italians working in English and French. Gino Chiellino examined Italians writing in German and others consider Italians writing in Portuguese and Spanish. The proceedings of this important conference were published in 1991 as *La letteratura dell'emigrazione: Gli scrittori di lingua italiana nel mondo.*

Despite Marchand's title the discourse could not be restricted to Italian language writing alone. The majority of contributors are professors of Italian who had to consider the writing of Italian immigrants and their children in Italian and in other languages, the cultural contexts of the host countries, and the nature of a new Italian writing.

Second, academics revealed their biases. When these professors return to their home universities will they begin to include these immigrant writers in their courses? Few will do so. When we read the papers in Marchand's volume we often detect a tone of condescension. Many of the professors of Italian regard this writing as outside the realm of their serious university teaching and research. Some of the Canadian contributors demonstrate this questioning and doubt towards the writing of immigrants. Professor A. Franceschetti from Toronto articulates this attitude:

> ...un campo di letture nel quale mi ero esercitato solo saltuariamente e per passatempo (con interesse, diciamo pure, più sociologico che strettamente letterario)... (139).

> ...an area of reading in which I have carried on only in passing and in spare time [with an interest that we must admit is more sociological than strictly literary]...

Third, we see institutional exclusion. This conference was held not in Italy, but in Lausanne, Switzerland; symbolizing the fact that this expatriate literature is still outside the institutions of Italian culture, learning and research.

Fourth, the conference and the proceedings presage change. Such an enormous and rich body of writing is revealed by the papers from this conference that it will inevitably cause a shift in our view of Italian literature as a whole.

One problem is that this writing is scattered in many different countries. We are aware of the geographical dispersal in Canada and Australia, but are surprised by the case of Brazil. In the region of Rio Grande do Sul a flourishing Italian community has existed since 1875, and has produced a literature in Italian, in dialect and in Portuguese. The fact that these and other Italian immigrant writers have developed literatures in host countries despite many difficulties and little support from Italy indicates the extraordinary creativity of these artists (Franzina, Hohlfeldt).

The gate-keepers of Italian culture both here and in Italy have yet to recognize that there is an Italian literature produced outside the peninsula. As Antonio D'Alfonso, the founder of the Toronto-based Guernica Editions, has been pointing out for a number of years now, a concrete example of this official exclusion is the control over the International Standard Book Number (ISBN) for Italian language books. Only Italian books published in Italy get an Italian ISBN. This national monopoly not only keeps the printing and production of books in the hands of publishing houses in Italy, but it also has wide ranging political and cultural effects on Italian authors outside Italy. Books which have no ISBN for a given language do not exist for modern libraries or bookstores which order books using the ISBN codes. We should also remember that most bookstores in Italy are owned by the large publishing houses. Since the books do not exist, the authors do not exist nor the literatures in the new countries. Only immigrant writers who are fortunate enough to get their books printed back in Italy will get the Italian ISBN. Where do these books belong and how do they get distributed back in the host country? Are these writers now part of Italy's literature or some species of expatriate author on the margins of the literary institution? Is this a better condition than the Italian language writers in Canada or Australia whose books have no ISBN and therefore do not exist in Italy? The choice seems to be between a colonial condition and oblivion.

Italian-Canadian writers who publish in English or French do get the appropriate ISBN for that language. What is the relation between the Italian language books written in Canada and those produced in English or French by writers of Italian background? What does this tell us about the nature and unity of Italian culture?

Our North American view of Italy seems orchestrated by the Italian Government Travel Office. It is an image of a national culture with a long history and a standard language invented by Dante. We can visualize the great works of art and the masterpieces of literature. We like to believe that these are accessible to all, but we know that it is not always so. The publication and distribution of books is controlled by the few who also determine other activities, such as translation. The large publishing houses and their editors set the literary agenda both in Italy and beyond. National monopolies best serve the centres of power to the disadvantage of marginal groups.

If we look beyond the tourist image of a unified Italy we find a country of regional disparity, linguistic diversity and different cultures. In language and literature alone we know that works have been written and published in *siciliano, calabrese, napoletano*, the Albanian languages of Calabria, Molise and Puglia, and in *friulano* and *bergamasco* in the North. We can add German in Alto Adige and French in Val d'Aosta. These hybrid cultures are considered Italian. If hybrid Italian literature can exist within the borders of Italy in other languages and dialects; then it can exist outside Italy in Italian and in other languages. In Canada Italian literature can exist in standard Italian, in dialects, in English and in French.

We are slowly coming to accept this diversity in post-colonial literatures. Italian-Canadian critic Francesco Loriggio has pointed out:

> The fact is that literary theory has always assumed that literature is produced in an environment self-evidently unitary. When we read about German or Italian or French or English texts, we imagine them, as we have been accustomed to do, as components of an indivisible entity in which language, culture and sometimes territory coincide. Ethnicity introduces a series of wedges, of hyphens in that homogeneity. Since an author may write in one idiom and think in another, since a culture may be represented by a multiplicity of languages, congruence between the linguistic and the cultural can no longer be taken for granted (1987: 56).

3. Theory

The discipline of Italian studies in North America is impoverished by a significant lack of theoretical discourse on its ontology and epistemology. The postcolonial literatures of the English speaking world have produced a body of theory that challenges the existing canons and the dominant ideas of Western literature and culture. In Australia, for example, literary theorists, such as Sneja Gunew and Helen Tiffin, have published criticism which questions the assumptions underlying Eurocentric notions of literature and language. Gunew's many years of work on literary and feminist theory culminated in *Framing Marginality: Multicultural Literary Studies*. In Canada Ian Adam and Tiffin edited *Past the Last Post: Theorizing Post-Colonialism and Post-Modernism*, which deals with the study of English writing in the world. There is nothing comparable which critiques the study of Italian literature.

The theoretical rethinking of English studies is captured in the important volume by Bill Ashcroft, Gareth Griffiths and Helen Tiffin, *The Empire Writes Back: Theory and Practice in Post-Colonial Literatures*, which explores the development of English literature programs in the British colonies as part of the enterprise of empire building: "...both at the level of simple utility (as propaganda for instance) and at the unconscious level where it leads to the naturalization of constructed values..."(3).

English studies is used to maintain the colonial mentality among distant subjects with regard to the centre of power and the Crown. There are no volumes in Italian studies which try to critically examine the role of the discipline in the cultural life and the ideology of Italian immigrants and their children. We are still in the colonial period where the agenda is set by academic old boys and politicians in Rome.

Italy has a national university system which has many aspects centralized in Rome from curriculum, to hiring policies. Rome sets the agenda for the national culture within Italy as well as for communities outside the country not only in terms of the literary canon but by extension to the teaching of Italian literature (see Titone 23-25).

The colonial approach that cultural elite in Italy take towards the immigrant communities in Canada, Australia and other countries is epitomized by the diplomatic discourse. These settler communities are often referred to as *colonie italiane*, Italian colonies, even though Italy never had colonies in the New World. These immigrant communities are seen as the silent and docile importers and consumers of Italian-made culture. Vice-Consuls and Institutes of Italian Culture are often established in remote "colonies" in order to direct cultural activities there. And it has been our experience in Western Canada that these Rome-appointed career diplomats are parachuted into a community without knowedge of Italians in Canada, and sometimes do more harm than good.

In Italy there seems to be no mechanism for the review of cultural policy or institutions. The belief seems to be that if an institute survived the test of time then it must have a role to play in the life of the nation. There is no critical theory here but a conservative ideology. Just as there is no mechanism of checks and balances in Italian political life that can permit movement towards true political reform and a politics of inclusion, so too in the cultural sphere there is no system, theoretical or otherwise, to open up the cultural institutions to change. We can hardly complain about this lack of support for cultural theory in immigrant communities when there is even greater lacunae in Italy itself. Recently some writers have decried the lack of involvement of intellectuals in public affairs. Luigi Monga writes:

> Gli intellettuali brillano per la loro assenza, per il loro silenzio sui problemi piu acuti della società presente. Gli intelletuali, finiti i tempi in cui mettevano la propria cultura al servizio della politica, avvertono oggi fino in fondo il peso del proprio fallimento, un fallimento che si traduce in silenzio, in assenza o, peggio ancora, nella rinuncia alla propria vocazione di coscienza critica (5).

> Intellectuals are conspicuous by their absence, by their silence on the most acute problems of our contemporary society. The times are gone when intellectuals used to put culture at the disposal of politics; today they feel the weight of their complete failure, a failure now translated into silence, absence, or even worse, the abandonment of their very role as a critical conscience.

While some Italian cultural leaders have deserted their social vocation and remain silent on crucial issues, others hide behind a wall of obscurantism.

Monga quotes Italian philosopher Massimo Cacciari, who explains that Italian thinkers have long favoured a baroque system of convoluted esoteric language addressed to other intellectuals, the few elect and not meant for ordinary people. We know that Italian discursive writing or *saggistica* is very abstract and complex, perhaps, along with some contemporary French prose, the most tortured and esoteric in the world. By means of this inaccessible code *le voci di salotto* have kept up barriers between the academy and the ordinary people. Given the problems with dialects and literacy in Italy this obscure writing is one way of maintaining the class difference and, for some institutions, of resisting change. Even when there is social criticism and debate, it is among the intellectual elite. Literary critic Leone Piccioni deplores the political-ideological debates which were predicatble and monotonous:

> Il dibattito tra gli intellettuali in Italia, anche nel passato, era abbastanza monotono, nel senso che quelli che più dibattevano erano di schieramento marxista. Ora quello schieramento non sa più dove appoggiarsi, perche le ideologie son cadute, l'apparato di partito e caduto, e quindi... siano diminuite le loro istanze (quoted in Monga 4).

> The debate among intellectuals in Italy, even in the past, was very monotonous, in the sense that those who argued the most were aligned with the Marxists. Now that alignment no longer knows where to affiliate itself, because ideologies have fallen, the party apparatus has fallen, and so their debates have diminished.

It is a sad irony that even Marxist intellectuals are not living up to the ideas of the foremost Marxist philosopher in Italy, Antonio Gramsci, who deplored the lack of an Italian popular literature that reflected the people and who required the true intellectual to always be involved with his people. While many would find this situation of separation between the cultural elite and the ordinary people disconcerting, Italian writers accept it. This separation reflects on the freedom of Italians and on their political effectiveness. It is echoed in the massive corruption scandal that is overturning the entire political system and bringing about the indictments and resignations of many of the political and business elite. These powerful people have excluded others, have resisted new ideas and social and political change in order to remain in control.

As the colonials of this culture, Italians in North America are compromised by this situation of inequality. What is the reaction of our colleagues in Italian studies programs? Silence. This silence is not an implicit approval of the corruption among Italian leaders, but a result of the lack of a tradition of theoretical discourse linked to an ongoing criticism of Italian cultural institutions. More exegeses on the Cantos of Dante are of little help in these crises. Limited by training with a Eurocentric bias, fearful of any change, and oblivious to new developments in other fields of cultural studies, Italian academics remain locked in a narrow discipline. Our Italian colleagues in North America are concerned about preserving Italian language programs, rather than revitalizing Italian studies by opening up discussion about the nature of the theory and the practice of the discipline.

If we look at the content of Italian studies programs we find them dominated by a conservative tradition. This archivist mentality resists any review of history. What little theory is read follows traditional conservative patterns. In individual courses we may find Croce and the anti-Croce pronouncements of Umberto Eco. It is an argument about family issues — the aesthetics of the literary text — and it is no substitute for real critiques about the nature of Italian studies. We may find essays by Italo Calvino, but rarely find works by Antonio Gramsci or by Franco Fortini. In a personal communication to me, Professor Gaetano Rando of the University of Wollongong in Australia recalls the strong objections he was confronted with when he tried to include the writings of the Marxist Gramsci on a course reading list in Brisbane. In other universities students may read some theory in linguistics and language teaching but little in cultural studies.

While Italian writers are silent or self-absorbed in squabbles over ideological positions, no real social criticism takes place. And there is no "empire writing back to the centre," in the words of Salman Rushdie, since there is no real exchange of writing or ideas between the Italians outside Italy and those in the peninsula.

Italian studies programs in North America, Australia and elsewhere are in a colonial position with regard to Italy. They are materially dependent on the publications from there and ideologically dependent on the conservative ideals of nostalgia for the country of origin. In this colonial space there is no room for criticism of this very position, nor for theoretical questioning of European assumptions.

Although many Italian academics are vaguely uncomfortable with this lack of discourse on important social and cultural issues, they nevertheless remain silent. Why? We are all good sons of *Italia*, and we do not criticize our mother. We see ourselves as dependent on her for everything that is important to us. We have been trained to believe that everything of value comes from there, and nothing that is Italian and of value can come from here or any other colony. As long as we hold to this view there will be no new developments in Italian studies, and quite possibly there will be deterioration.

We fail to realize that the Italians outside Italy have created Italian studies in the loyal colonial image of a conservative Italian culture. It is up to these Italian academics and their students to recreate Italian studies to include the reality of writing and Italian culture outside Italy. Many of our colleagues fear that if we were to make the post-colonial break from Italy chaos would ensue, an ironic view given the reality of political and moral crisis in the peninsula. We will then be required to determine literary value outside the institutions and canons set down by Rome. We will begin to revitalize Italian studies and culture outside Italy and may also help to do the same within that troubled country.

There is a final image in the Taviani film, *Padre padrone*, in which Gavino has become a professor of linguistics, but instead of taking a univeristy position in Rome, returns to his remote town in Sardinia to teach school to the peasant children. The future of Italy's culture lies in the diversity of its regions rather than in the centres of power. I am looking at Italian culture from one of these outposts. In this brief essay I have only begun the critical review of Italian studies, only begun the questioning of the nature of Italian culture, only begun to write back to the centre. Some of the concerns which I articulate here were captured sixteen years ago in a poem which first appeared in Pier Giorgio Di Cicco's anthology, *Roman Candles*:

> My grandfather didn't
> read Dante
> in a rocking chair me
> at his feet....

Nor did he feel the poet
in his blood an Italian leitmotif
for southern veins....
Nonno was a cabinet maker
He could draw, tell stories, intaglio a speciality
but no Dante
just a name
instead he read the draft
for war in Lybia...
He came to Canada... (29).

References

Adams, Ian, and H. Tiffin, eds. *Past the Last Post: Theorizing Post-Colonialism and Post-Modernism*. Calgary: Univerisity of Calgary Press, 1990.

Albani, Elena. *Canada, Mia seconda patria*. Bologna: Ed. Sirio, 1958.

Ardizzi, Maria. *Il sapore agro della mia terra*. Toronto: Toma Publishing, 1984.

Arteni, Marina. *L'emigrazione come metafora esistenziale nei romanzi di Maria J. Ardizzi*. Udine: Università degli Studi di Udine, 1991 (thesis).

Ashcroft, Bill, G. Griffiths, and H. Tiffin, eds. *The Empire Writes Back*. London: Routledge, 1989.

Bottomley, Gill. "Cultures, Multiculturalism and the Politics of Representation." *Journal of Intercultural Studies*, Vol. 8, No. 2, 1987, 1-10.

Bottomley, G., de Lepervanche, M., and Martin, J. eds. *Intersexions: Gender/Class/Culture/Ethnicity*. Sydney: Allen & Unwin, 1991.

Bourdieu, Pierre. *The Logic of Practice*. Cambridge: Polity Press, 1990.

Caccia, Fulvio. *Sous le signe du Phénix*. Montreal: Guernica, 1985.

Cantasano, Caro. "My Grandfather Didn't." In Di Cicco, 29. Cantasano is a pen name for F. M. Macri.

Ciccone, Stefania. "Una ragione d'essere." *Quaderni d'italianistica*, Vol. 1, No. 1, 1980, n.p.

Chiellino, Gino. "Continuità e alternativa alla letteratura nazionale italiana. Autori italiani nella Repubblica federale tedesca." In Marchand, pp. 95-106.

Colangelo, Gladis Lucia. *The Poetic World of Mary di Michele from Tree of August to Immune to Gravity*. Udine: Università degli Studi di Udine, 1991 (thesis).

Cooke, Nathalie. "Mary di Michele on the Integrity of Speech and Silence." *Canadian Poetry*, 26, 1990, 43-53.

D'Alfonso, Antonio. *Avril ou l'anti-passion*. Montreal: VLB, 1990.

Di Cicco, Pier Giorgio, ed. *Roman Candles*. Toronto: Hounslow Press, 1978.

Duliani, Mario. *Città senza donne*. Montreal: G. D'Errico, 1946.

Falassi, A. *Folklore by the Fireside*. Austin: University of Texas, 1980.

Fortini, Franco. *La poesia di Scotellaro*. Matera: Basilicata Editrice, 1974.

Franceschetti, Antonio. "Aspetti e motivi degli scrittori italiani in Canada." In Marchand, 139-156.

Franzina, Emilio. "Brasile: fra storia e romanzo." In Marchand, 213-228.

Gunew, Sneja. *Framing Marginality: Multicultural Literary Studies*. Melbourne: Melbourne University Press, 1994.

Gunew, Sneja, and K. O. Longley, eds. *Striking Chords: Multicultural Literary Interpretations*. Sydney: Allen & Unwin, 1992.

Hohlfeldt, Antonio. "La letteratura di lingua italiana in Brasile." In Marchand, 205-212.

Kuitunen, M. "Il Canada degli anni 20": Realismo e poesia in un resoconto italiano dell'epoca." *Italian Canadiana*, 4, 1988, 27-40.

Loriggio, Francesco. "The Question of the Corpus: Ethnicity and Literature." In J. Moss, ed. *Future Indicative*. Ottawa: University of Ottawa Press, 1987, 53-71.

————. "La letteratura dell'Italia fuori d'Italia: appunti per una ridefinizione dell'italianistica." *Italian Canadiana*, 7, 1991, 75-97.

————. Review of Di Cicco's *Roman Candles*. *Quaderni d'italianistica*, Vol. 1, No. 2, 1980.

Luzi, Alfredo. "Gino Nibbi: Uno Scrittore tra Emigrazione e Nomadismo." In Rando (1983), 312-320.

MacRan, E. (1979) *Diario di una emigrante*. Bologna: Tamari editore, 1979.

Marchand, Jean-Jacques, ed. *La Letteratura dell'emigrazione Gli scrittori di lingua italiana nel mondo*. Torino: Fondazione G. Agnelli, 1991.

Mathias, Elizabeth, and R. Raspa. Italian Folktales in America. Detroit: Wayne State University Press, 1985.

Minni, C.D., and Ciampolini, Anna Foschi, eds. *Writers in Transition*. Montreal: Guernica, 1990.

Monga, Luigi. "Che fine hanno fatto gli intellettuali italiani?" *Acquerello Italiano*, 4, 2, marzo-aprile, 1993, 4-6.

Pitto, Cesare. *Al di là dell'emigrazione*. Cassano: Ionica Editrice, 1988.

Rando, Gaetano, ed. *Italian Writers in Australia: Essays and Texts*. Wollongong: University of Wollongong, 1983.

————. "Dialetto, lingua e cultura nella produzione letteraria degli immigranti italiani in Australia." *Rivista Italiana di dialettologia*, Vol. IX, No. 1, 1985, 129-153.

Rosoli, Gianfausto. "La diaspora e Magna Italia." In A. Massimo Calderazzi, ed. *Almanacco, Il libro giornale sull'Italia*. Milano: Almanacco Italia, 1982, 415-423.

Salvatore, Filippo. "La quinta colonna inesistente: ovvero l'arresto e la prigionia degli 'italianesi' in *Città senza donne*." In Marchand, 517-524.

Titone, Renzo. "Dieci tesi sull'insegnamento precoce delle lingue seconde." *Il Forneri*, Vol. 5, No. 1, 1985.

Verdicchio, Pasquale. "The Failure of Memory in the Language of Re-Membering of Italian-Canadian Poets." In Minni and Ciampolini, 115-123.

Viscusi, Robert. "The Italian American Literary Subject." *Altreitalie*, 5, 1991, 76-79.

12

Enoch Padolsky

Italian-Canadian Writing and the Ethnic Minority/Majority Binary

Paci's Black Madonna *and Atwood's* Lady Oracle

*A*rguments about the binary nature of language and meaning have been central to a great many theoretical discussions in modern literary criticism. From the work of linguists, such as Saussure, Jakobson, Chomsky and Halle, to the rise (and fall?) of Bakhtinian heteroglossia and Derridean *différance*, binary categories have been at issue. In this climate, terminology of all sorts has been subjected to close examination from different points of view. Current critical discourse now seems much less content with categorical divisions, many of them binary, that formerly seemed to serve so well in organizing analytic and critical activity: universals and particulars, *langue et parole*, form and content, writer and reader, thesis and antithesis, Apollonian and Dionysian, and a host of others. The reasons for the present discontents are almost too various to list. After a while it was noticed that form *is* content (and vice versa), that writers also read and readers write, that theses and antitheses do or do not beget syntheses, that there are other Greek gods (and goddesses) who have been neglected, that the line between modernism and postmodernism is difficult to draw, that there is no pre-colonialism to balance post-colonialism, that there is more to life (and literature) than signifiers and signifieds, that the centre has become the periphery (and the reverse), in short, that if categories are binary, writers (and texts) are multiple, and language and life are too complex and open-ended to be contained in simple binary categories. Nor is all this self-reflexive awareness of underlying categories and of differences of perspective restricted to current literary criticism and theory. A great many other disciplines participate as well. As anthropologist Clifford Geertz so aptly put it, we now seem to live in an age of the "sudden explosion of polemical prefixes (neo-, post-, meta- anti-) and subversive title forms (*After Virtue, Against Method, Beyond Belief*)" (135). It is an age that constantly challenges our critical assumptions, including the categories we employ.

With all this critical suspicion about binary (or other) categories, it would be logical to assume that critics would have ceased to employ them. In fact, however, even a cursory look at the critical literature reveals that they have by no means disappeared. Perhaps these categories are necessary stages in the development of ideas, perhaps they are just too useful as analytic, conceptual, or ideological tools. No matter. They seem to persist. Perhaps the best pragmatic conclusion to be drawn, then, given the categorical deconstruction of the times, is that critics using binary categories should at least be expected to examine them overtly, and to note the ways in which these categories fail to correspond to the more complex realities they are intended to explain.

1

It is in this spirit that I wish to turn here to some of the binary categories employed in Canadian literary criticism in discussions related to social pluralism. My reference point for this discussion is Italian-Canadian writing, though the issues go beyond the literary output of this group. I do not wish to suggest that the categories I am about to investigate are unusually problematic or indeed any weaker than categories in use in other critical areas. Rather my aim is to analyze these particular categories because they are central in Canadian criticism and because it is important to understand the weaknesses and strengths of criticism's fundamental categories. The binary category I wish to examine most closely here, the one that I feel most usefully encompasses Italian-Canadian writing, is the distinction between ethnic minority and ethnic majority. But before turning to this binary, I would like to start with an older and more entrenched Canadian category — namely English versus French. How does this older binary correlate with Italian-Canadian writing and what historical process has led to the replacement of this older binary by ethnic minority and ethnic majority? How well, I might ask, do all these categories comment on the situation of Italian-Canadian writing?

In the past, the binary distinction between English and French functioned relatively smoothly in Canadian literary criticism since there was very little challenge to the historical conjunction of language and culture. Recently, however, a number of ambiguities have arisen, or to put it more accurately, have risen to critical consciousness. On the one hand, English language writing in Canada is now being written not only by those of British origin but by writers of a great many other origins as well; on the other hand, if "English-Canadian writing" is conceptualized as a geographically based culture (that is, English Canada outside of Quebec), then it is also being written in languages other than English. Similarly, the "French-Canadian" category has become more complex. As Quebec society changes and as Quebec moves towards a redefined constitutional status, the term "French-Canadian" is being understood more and more as only a historical category or as referring to writing by French-Canadians *hors Quebec*, that is, Franco-Ontarian and Acadian. If, however, the initial category is shifted to the geographical "English Canada/Quebec," then the same question arises in Quebec as in English Canada as to who is to be counted as a Quebecois (cf. the discussion in Harel: 30). Is *Québécois* to be based on language, citizenship, birthplace, culture, ethnicity, or some combination of these?

As for Italian-Canadian writing, what seems clear is that if the English-French category impacts upon this writing (including the complexities referred to above), it nevertheless does not satisfactorily encompass it, for Italian-Canadian writers not only write in English and French, inside and outside Quebec, but also in Italian or even Italian dialects. Furthermore, neither the traditional cultural context of English-Canadian writing (that is, primarily British-Canadian) nor the issues that arise in the shift from French-Canadian to Quebecois writing lend themselves to a consideration of issues (thematic or otherwise) that might be included under the label of Italian-Canadian. Minority issues such as language, immigrant experience, discrimination, acculturation, audience relations, literary and social connections that look back to Italy, in short, all those aspects that can be related to the specific world from which the works derive, all these cannot easily and satisfactorily be included within the English-French category in itself. Italian-Canadian writers thus may in some sense work within the English-Canadian literary framework, and Italo-quebecois writers within the Quebecois framework, but this does not make them, without qualification, English-Canadian or Quebecois writers (*pure laine; de souche*). To the extent that Italian-Canadian writers continue to ask questions, like those of Luigi in Marco Micone's *Déjà l'agonie* — "Dis-moi ce que je dois faire... pour devenir un *vrai* Québécois" (29) — to that extent they will never become "*vrai* Québécois" or "*real* English-Canadians." It may well be, as Simon Harel speculates (33), that we are at the point of arriving "à une époque où l'énonciation de cette altérité peut devenir parole commune, accepter le principe d'une identité québécoise qui serait acquisition, création," but we are not there yet. Danielle, in Micone's play (31), it will be remembered, has no answer to Luigi's question.

The problems, limitations, and ambiguities that have developed around the English-French category as an analytic concept in Canadian criticism, together with the growing consciousness of Canadian cultural diversity, have given rise to a number of other categories. Many of these, I might note, respond to, or derive from, the political processes associated with the Royal Commission on Bilingualism and Biculturalism, its Report in the late 1960s, (Vol. 4 is entitled "The Cultural Contribution of the Other Ethnic Groups") and the subsequent enactment of the policy of multiculturalism (within a bilingual context) in 1971. To this process is probably owed the popularization of terms such as the "third force," the use of "ethnic" to mean "other ethnic" as in "the ethnic press" or "ethnic literature," and the restriction of ethnicity to (non-English/French) immigrant groups (aboriginals were excluded from the discussion in Vol. 4). Responses to the categories used in the Bilingualism and Biculturalism Report and the "multicultural" discourse it generated have included the aboriginals' insistence on the term "First Nations" (as opposed to the "two-nation" view of Canada), other ethnic groups' opposition to the reference to French and English-Canadians as "founding nations," the "specialization" (to use the linguistic term) of the category of "multicultural" to mean "other ethnic" or "ethnic" (as in Hutcheon and Richmond's title *Canadian Multicultural Fictions* or in former Ontario Premier David Peterson's reference during the Meech Lake discussions to the "multiculturals" of Toronto), and the development of comprehensive (and sometimes resisted) sub-categories such as "visible minorities," "South Asians," and so on. Critical terms such as Hutcheon and Richmonds's "Other Solitudes," or Tom Marshall's "third solitude" (for Mordecai Richler and Montreal Jewish-Canadian experience) can thus be seen as part of the general movement in the discourse (from "biculturalism" to "multiculturalism") in that they attempt to play off the core notion of a Canadian "two-nation" duality — the "two solitudes" — made famous by Canadian novelist Hugh MacLennan — and to extend the categorical net to include the notions of "third force" and perhaps "third world" as well. In a similar way (but different positioning), Ronald Sutherland's influential concept of the "mainstream" in Canadian literature, with its contrasting (binary) category of ethnic writing, can be seen as very much a response to the discussion arising out of this period. In his case, however, it also reflects a "mainstream" perspective on ethnicity and on what categories and what issues are centrally Canadian (pardon the pun).

The contexts I have been bringing to bear here in this discussion of categories are historical, social and political. This is as it should be, at least in part. Literary categories, in my view of literature at least, cannot be separated from these other contexts. "Visible minority" writers, for example, are grouped together (by themselves or by others) for social reasons (discrimination, racism, policy responses, etc.) and if there are literary commonalities, they relate to these social realities. Bharati Mukherjee's attack on the idea of "visible minority," ("Introduction," *Darkness*), Marlene Nourbese Philip's analysis of the problems of African, Asian and Native writers in Canada in her essay ("publish + be damned"), Nazneen Sadiq's virulent response to terminology in a recent review of the Hutcheon-Richmond book — " 'Visible minorities', 'writers of color', and 'mainstream' writers are the most offensive terms to have emerged in the history of Canadian literature..."(C21) — and many minority writers rejection of the label of "ethnic" all pay tribute to the socio-political dimension of these literary categories. Indeed, it is only in this context that terms such as "third solitude," "visible minority writer," or "ethnic" writer make sense at all.

The conclusion that I would draw is that the salient context for the discussion of the critical terminology and categories used to encompass ethnicity in the Canadian literary context is that of the social assumptions and political positions that underlie the categories. In other words, the question that arises for any particular binary category is what view of Canadian ethnicity and social status is implied by it. From this perspective, then, the mainstream/ethnic binary category can be said to reflect an underlying dominant

Canadian (that is, majority) view of Canadian literature (and of the country) as divided between a dominant political-social-cultural duality, the English-French mainstream, and ethnics, that is, everybody else. (Within this binary framework, sub-groups such as aboriginals, visible minorities, South Asians, Italian-Canadians function presumably as sub-categories of ethnics.) This category thus responds to the findings of the Bilingualism and Biculturalism Commission by making Volumes 1-3 into the "mainstream" and Volume 4 into the "ethnics."

The mainstream/ethnic binary has, not surprisingly, been resisted, both by minority writers who object to it for reasons of equity and fairness, and by critics (like myself) who wish to reflect a more de-centred and pluralistic view of Canadian society and literature (See for example Padolsky). From this more multicultural orientation, the binary of choice to replace the dominating binary of "mainstream/ethnic" is "ethnic minority/ethnic majority." The latter terms avoid the normative implications of both "mainstream" (=important, central, good, serious writing) and "ethnic" (=peripheral, unimportant, bad amateurish writing). At the same time, the category retains the older English-French dichotomy (now relabelled "majority"), is more comprehensive than English-French alone (since ethnic minorities are included too), is more universal (since ethnicity now exists on both sides), and is more overtly social (since it raises explicitly the implications of minority/majority status). From within this more useful categorical distinction, then, Italian-Canadian writing, to return to the specific focus of this discussion, can be categorized as a form of Canadian ethnic minority writing in binary contrast to Canadian ethnic majority writing, that is, British-Canadian writing in English Canada (or Quebec) and French-Canadian (Quebecois) writing in Quebec (and Canada).

If this is to be the working category which provides the context for Italian-Canadian writing, however, the spirit of investigation about categories that this paper established at the outset, suggests a need to examine some of the implications and limitations of this category as well, however useful it may be. What I would like to set out briefly now are five kinds (I am sure there are others) of limitations and complexities that surround the ethnic minority/ethnic majority binary distinction in its context of semantic and social multiplicity. After this critical examination, I would then like to see how the binary might be applied in a positive sense to two specific texts — *Black Madonna* by Frank Paci and *Lady Oracle* by Margaret Atwood.

2

The first set of limitations might be called salience limits. To categorize writers on the basis of ethnicity and social status, that is, ethnic minority/ ethnic majority, is of course to put the emphasis on these two areas in their works. To the extent that there is a variation of salience in the impact of these categories on writers and works, however, the application of the categories become distortive. One difference between, for example, Mary di Michele's "Mimosa" poems and Mary Melfi's *A Dialogue With Masks*, lies in the salience of ethnicity and status (thematic, perspective, formal) in the two works. With this difference of salience in mind, the power of the category "Italian-Canadian" or "ethnic minority" clearly becomes limited. In another sense, salience limits can be interpreted in terms of the relative weighting of social categories with reference to writer, work, or reader. Thus in some cases, other kinds of social class analyses (for example, gender, race, or non-ethnicity oriented class or status issues) might be felt to be more salient than the ethnicity /social status based category. And on an even broader basis, this salience limitation can also be interpreted in the degree to which the social in any sense impacts on the literary, since, as I noted earlier, ethnicity and status questions are social-related categories. The discussion of this area of salience limitation would thus move into theoretical, methodological, and critical questions as to the relationship between literature and society generally. I am not about to launch into this kind of discussion here (though I staked out my own position earlier) but it should be apparent that responses (by writer, reader, theoretician or critic) which de-emphasize the social in literary analysis (certain structuralist or formalist approaches, for example) would likely accord far less salience to the category of ethnic minority/majority.

A second area of limitation relates to what I might call the issue of scope. To speak of "ethnic minority" or "ethnic majority" as if they were coherent generalizable categories is all very well but within these categories lies an enormous range of diversity, complexity, and multiplicity. The experiences of different Canadian ethnic minority groups, for example, vary in a great many ways — by region, by time period, by inner dynamics, by dominant society's reception, by language, class, gender, race, and so on. And the same could be said about majority group experience in Canada. To the degree to which difference (rather than similarity) becomes important in the discussion of writers such as Maria Campbell, Matt Cohen, Waclaw Iwaniuk, Marco Micone, Régine Robin, or Joy Kogawa or in the consideration of Gaston Miron, Paul Savoie, Milton Acorn and Margaret Atwood, to that degree the underlying binary category ceases to be binary and rapidly becomes multiple. The same point, I should note, could be made about the term "Italian-Canadian" as a sub-category within "ethnic minority" writing. Region, class, gender, language and other differences can be extremely important in the discussion of this category of writers too, with a similar impact on the understanding of the category. Nor can the problems of this limitation be avoided, it should be noted, by shifting attention to structural commonalities of the category (for example, Kroetsch's discussion of ethnic narrative patterns) as a means of "sidestepping," as it were, this multiplicity. All that happens in this case is a displacement of complexities into more abstract terms of reference. At some point in the discussion, unless the discourse remains totally abstract, specifics need to be addressed, and multiplicity impinges on the broader claims based on the specific case being discussed. The limitation then comes into play.

The third limitation involves what could be termed multiple perspective implications. The complications that I have in mind here arise from the fact that ethnic minority/ethnic majority writing (and sub-categories such as Italian-Canadian within the binary) are not reducible entirely to signature per se. That is, in some cases there is a conflictual relationship between the writer's status and the perspective within which a particular text is written. This conflict arises, for example, when majority writers write from minority perspectives (or vice versa), when "minority" writers self-identify or are identified by others as merely part of the dominant culture(s), or when writers write from within the cultural perspective of minority or majority situations other than their own. There are a great many examples of writers and texts of all these kinds. These cases, like the salience limits discussed earlier, challenge easy assumptions about what "belonging" to a category entails.

Thus, using the example of the last type, minority writers adopting perspectives other than their own, I might cite the case of George Ryga's *The Ecstasy of Rita Joe*. In one sense this play can be called a "Ukrainian-Canadian" work (his signature), but the fact that this play adopts the perspective of Canadian aboriginal experience complicates its category. The reason for this is not that signature no longer counts (that is, Ryga does not become an aboriginal writer), but because the work itself enters, crosses over into aboriginal discourse and at the same time in some sense it leaves (at least in part) Ukrainian-Canadian discourse. The play can be discussed as a "white," perhaps even a "Ukrainian-Canadian" version of "aboriginal" reality, but it cannot be discussed so easily as a perspective on "Ukrainian-Canadian" experience itself, except in relation to the first point. The departure factor, if I may call it that, can be seen in the difference between, to cite another example, Rudy Wiebe's shift from a Mennonite perspective on aboriginal experience in *Peace Shall Destroy Many* to his "aboriginal" perspective in *The Temptations of Big Bear*. This shift of perspective may be more or less successful, more or less sympathetic, and more or less welcome to aboriginal readers or critics. (The cultural appropriation debate about aboriginal writing may be seen as a response to this question of perspective in which aboriginal writers and critics have resisted the loss of voice and power that occurs when others repeatedly attempt to adopt their perspective and at the same time control the means of production and distribution of these writings.) Regardless of its characteristics and its reception, however, the main point is that the multiple perspective issue complicates the category in which writers and texts are grouped because signature and perspective are "at odds." Extreme cases of this situation would include "minority" writers who write exclusively from "majority" perspectives. In what sense, then, would they be ethnic minority writers?

Similar perspective complexities also arise with writers of multiple signatures, that is, writers of mixed backgrounds and cultural experiences within minority/majority categories or across them — for example, Valgardson, Edwards, Birdsell, Nelligan(!) — and in the whole area of the multiplicity of readers' perspectives. What is an "ethnic majority/minority" reading of a particular text, and what is to be done with the diversity of positions and situations (with reference to ethnicity and status) that different readers bring to the act of reading? Now it might be argued that some of these difficulties are really just definitional but to the degree that the question of perspective raises issues of cultural insider/cultural outsider, to that degree once again the efficacy of the initial binary category ethnic minority/ethnic majority begins to run into problems.

The fourth area of limitations may be termed institutional or political. Like any terminology, the terms "ethnic minority/ethnic majority" are not value-neutral or unattached to the social issues that surround the concepts. Just as the English-French category and the mainstream-ethnic category privilege the "founding" or "two-nations" view of Canadian society and polity, so the "ethnic minority/ethnic majority" distinction privileges a pluralistic, multicultural, or cultural difference perspective on Canada. By valorizing a universal application of ethnicity and by highlighting relative status within national boundaries (both "ethnicity" and "minority/majority" can only be understood as relative terms), this category distinction raises for consideration the politics of the literary institution within the national boundaries and primarily within a dominant/subordinate context. In one sense, of course, this is a welcome development. The strength of this category, it could be argued, is that it allows, indeed raises for discussion issues of distribution, publication, reception, canonization. in a social context of difference, of power, of economic, political and cultural clout, of potential and actual discrimination, racism, prestige and other attitudinal factors. Just as Arun Mukherjee raises these issues for post-colonial theory by asking in a recent paper, "Whose postmodernism, whose post-colonialism" is it, so the focus on ethnic minority/ethnic majority implies a whole series of institutional questions: why are minority literatures in Canada "literatures of lesser diffusion," why are major Italian-Canadian writers' works allowed to go out of print, why are "visible minority" works "published and then damned," what are the institutional consequences of the cultural appropriations (such as that of the voice of aboriginals), and so on. These are questions which fall easily into the discourse of the category. The distinction between ethnic minority and ethnic majority thus implies a valorization of diversity and difference, a privileging of the pluralism of cultural perspectives and its politics, and of the social issues that arise as a result of the inequalities of power and prestige.

However welcome this institutional focus, there is, nevertheless, once again a price in terms of limitations. The problem with focusing on differential power relations at the majority/minority level is that it does not provide adequately for internal instrumental differentiation within the two categories themselves. Thus British-Canadian and French-Canadian writing are both, in a national context (as long as Canada remains intact) majority cultures but their institutional situations are clearly not the same. French writers in Canada exist within a sea of English speakers and relate to Quebec and to the larger world of Francophonie in ways not always comparable to British-Canadian experience; British-Canadian writers play off Canadian, British, American, and world English literary institutions in a totally different way. Furthermore, regional, class and gender distinctions problematize the institutional situation of majority writing just as they do for minority writing. On the minority side the situation is even more complex, since minority groups in Canada have different immigration and language histories, occupy different positions in the "vertical mosaic," have different degrees of cultural development in the official languages, have different histories of acceptance and racism by the majority (and other) cultures, and different kinds of relationships to both majority cultures and, where applicable, to the homelands of the "old ethnicity." The issues that arise from these kinds of differences complicate the category, and once again, suggest a network of multiple distinctions that infuse the basic binary category.

The fifth and final set of limitations addresses the implied national context that underlies the relativity of both ethnicity and minority/majority status. The distinction between ethnic minority/majority on a national basis does not easily function to encompass what has been called the "transcultural," that is, international cross-cultural aspects of literature as an institution. This is only partly a function of language. Sam Selvon, Austin Clarke, Rohinton Mistry all write in English but their focus on non-Canadian communities, their intercultural and intertextual links to non-Canadian writing and issues, spill over the national context of the ethnic minority/majority category. Similar points could be made about writers from a great many other Canadian ethnic groups — Josef Skvorecky, George Faludy, Walter Bauer, Émile Ollivier come to mind as examples — and of course Italian-Canadian writing as well, with its strong connections to Italian culture in Italy and elsewhere, as evidenced by the contributions to this volume on Italian writers around the world, by the transcultural focus of the journal *Vice Versa*, and by the strength of the transcultural element in a great deal of Italian-Canadian writing (Edwards'*The Lion's Mouth*, Ricci's *Lives of the Saints*). Once again the attempt could be made to define or analyze "minority" writing as characterized by this transcultural aspect but in reality the category itself, working as it does within a discourse of nationhood, is not primarily designed for this dimension. The development, on a world scale, of group literatures that function outside and across national boundaries, that respond to the "nomadic" and "migrant" spirit of the age, (perhaps the best example is South Asian writing in Britain, Africa, Canada,

West Indies, India, Pakistan) is only with difficulty accounted for by a category such as this one. There is undoubtedly scope for comparative international minority/majority analysis (a different question), but the transcultural element *per se* does seem to me to point to another area of limitation of this category.

3

I could no doubt go on, since there are many other ways in which multiplicity comments on the restrictive nature of this binary category. Nevertheless, I would like to move on now to a specific application of the ethnic minority/majority binary. In spite of its limitations, I would argue, there are useful distinctions to be made on the differential basis of Canadian ethnic minority and ethnic majority experience and some useful ways of employing the binary contrast in the analysis of Canadian literary works. The works I have chosen to illustrate this point are two novels with an "Italian" focus — Frank Paci's *Black Madonna* and Margaret Atwood's *Lady Oracle*. I choose these two works not because they are "representative" of Italian-Canadian and British-Canadian writing, (nor even necessarily of Paci and Atwood), but because they contain some intriguing parallel elements, because they both comment on *italianità* from a Canadian perspective, and because they both incorporate so clearly the difference in perspective between an ethnic minority and an ethnic majority writer. Atwood's novel is (partly) set in Italy and comments on Italian and (Canadian) Italian immigrant cultures from a "majority" perspective. Paci's novel is set in Canada and comments on the "same" cultural phenomena from an Italian-Canadian "minority" perspective. What each novel does with "Italy" and with "*italianità*," is best explained, I would argue, in terms of the difference between an ethnic minority and an ethnic majority point of view.

To treat Frank Paci as an ethnic minority (Italian-Canadian) writer is neither a "kiss of death" (to use Caterina Edwards' phrase) nor a denial of his multiplicity as a writer. Paci, like all writers, addresses a broad range of issues. He writes not just about immigrants but about families (cf. Minni's interview with Paci). He addresses philosophical and theological questions of body and spirit, issues of sibling psychology, of generational conflict and continuity, and of the relationship of art and form. At the same time, his work *is* informed by the particular perspective he brings from his own and his shared ethnic minority experience. The particular language problems his literary families struggle with, the gender and generational issues, the relationship of his characters to their communities and to the larger dominant Canadian culture, these and other aspects of Paci's works must also be addresssed critically, and the ethnic minority category helps in this analysis. In all his novels, Paci's world is Catholic; it is Italian transplanted to the specific Canadian settings of Sault Ste. Marie or Toronto, and it is Canadianized, modernized, and often in sharp contrast to the Old World poor rural lifestyle that lies in the past. The situations of Paci's characters, like the two very different brothers in *The Father*, or their two different parents, reflect from the inside the dilemmas of living with, and adjusting to, two differing cultural worlds — the Italy of before and the Canada of now. This process of adaptation, of moving between two worlds, and finding a place within them, is for Paci as for many other Italian-Canadian writers, a serious issue. Some characters fail — Stephen's father, Maria's mother — and are destroyed in the process. The young, on the other hand, are often on a search for understanding, for values, for emotional relationships, for place, and are crippled or successful (or both) in the course of this search. Almost always, there is generational conflict, a battle of values and identity on the differing assumptions of Canadian and Italian worlds.

The character who best illustrates the cultural dilemmas that interest Paci and the interior (ethnic minority) perspective that he brings to bear on them is that of Maria/Marie Barone in *Black Madonna*. As a young girl, Maria sees herself as caught in an intolerable situation, part of a family and a culture which she can no longer identify with, and tied to a mother with whom she constantly battles. Her alienation leads to a severe kind of family hatred and self-hatred, in which she flees the "sickening Italian voices" (66) of her home, refuses her mother's insistent attempts (to overcome the influence of "the English and their stupid eating habits" (32) to overwhelm her with food, and in general thinks of herself "as a foreigner in her own house" (66). As part of her rejection of family and Italian background, Maria changes her name to the more "Canadian" Marie, abandons all things Italian, including the Church, leaves the cultural restrictions (in her view) of the West End Sault for the more liberating locale of urban Toronto, and, against her parents' older generation Italian working class assumptions about education for women, goes to university, and ends up marrying an English-Canadian Protestant. Her "assimilation" is so complete that at one point, an Italian-Canadian student in her class, unaware of her origins, accuses her of prejudice against Italians.

The situation that Maria represents, to put it in a post-colonial terminology, is that of internal colonization, in the sense that her entire psychology has aligned itself with the world of the "English-speaking country" and all that that entails, against the "Italian-speaking house" (69) of family, community, and cultural heritage. What the novel explores, and not just for Maria, is the reason for, the dynamics of, and the cost of this psychological state for all concerned. Paci's treatment of these issues is rich with nuance, with irony, with judgment and with affection. Maria's rejection of her mother's food, for example, can be seen as part of her rebellion against her mother, against Italy, and against the pre-set female role of "devoted Italian wife" (25). At the same time, it is anorexic, fanatically incorrect (spaghetti is also part of English-Canadian cuisine) and it correlates with dominant (patriarchal) English-Canadian cultural valuing of thinness. Ironically, when at the end of the novel, the rebelliously thin Maria fits perfectly into her mother's (Italian) dress, her long rejection of food also becomes the means to understanding, reconciliation, and new insight into Maria's own Italian identity and family past.

Paci's treatment of Maria, as in the case of her brother Joey, fleshes out (literally and metaphorically) the implications of the cultural tensions within Italian-Canadian experience as he sees it. Maria's escape into the perceived "English" world of abstract reason, mathematics and logic at the expense of her "Italian" body and emotions, become for Paci a trope for the divisions within Italian-Canadian experience on individual, family and community levels. This divisiveness, one can infer, is unhealthy and unwise for the individuals concerned, and unfortunate, even tragic, for generational understanding and relations. The untimely death of the father (true in other Paci novels as well), and the violent dismembering death of the Black Madonna mother in this novel, illustrate the impact (symbolic and real) of the cost of immigration to the older generation. Yet the promise of Maria's "return journey" to Italy, and her symbolic (if belated) reconciliation to her parents at the end of the novel do hold out hope. Maria and Joey may never fully understand their "Black Madonna" mother (or Italian father) but each seems to find a way to move on with their lives in the Canadian context while affirming some aspects of their parental and Italian past.

This brief overview of Maria and *Black Madonna* does not do justice to the complexity of the novel or of the issues. What it does illustrate, however, is how Paci's view of *italianità* proceeds from his understanding of the conflicts within ethnic minority experience. In *Black Madonna*, "Italy" carries rich cultural, social, and psychological significance but it also is at the heart of the novel's conflicts and insights. The "open" mystery of the Black Madonna, symbolized by the open hope chest, can be "solved" by entering the past, confronting the realities and values of Italian culture. Assunta's background of rural poverty in Italy helps explain her fixation on feeding her children, and her upbringing in rural Southern Italy also helps to explain her inability to adjust to the "modern" Canadian social world in the way that her children wish her to. That Assunta dies before her children come to terms with this past only points out the tragedy of her life, and at the same time, the centrality that Paci gives to her situation. In spite of the fact that the novel is written from the children's second generation perspective, it is Assunta (and *italianità*), as the title suggests, that dominates the problematics of the novel's world.

It should be noted that Paci's ethnic minority perspective is also revealed in the way he handles the dominant (British-Canadian) culture in the novel. This culture is represented in part by Maria's English-Canadian husband Richard, who, significantly, is presented only sketchily and externally. His main function thus seems to be to act as a contrast to the Italian-Canadian culture depicted in the novel and as an outside commentator on Maria's physical and psychological state. The case of Richard, then, would seem to suggest that Paci's interest in British-Canadian culture is more in its impact on Italian-Canadian experience than in itself. What he investigates (obviously not just through Richard) is the attractiveness of British-Canadian culture to the younger generations of Italian-Canadians, and the material advantages that lie in moving into dominant society. At the same time, he also shows the costs on all levels of abandoning the past and of living between the two worlds. Both Joey and Maria are psychologically scarred just like the old Italian neighbourhood of the West End. Generational "progress" into dominant culture, like urban renewal, thus may be inevitable, but it is not necessarily or entirely positive. Joey's gesture of the pyramid, like Marie's projected return to Italy, are thus important statements in the novel in that they affirm the value of what is lost in the process, and what can be retained from that past.

There is a sense in which this process of evaluation of general Canadian culture (as seen through the filter of Italian-Canadian experience) is of course also a commentary on Canadian place and Canadian values in general. As noted earlier, Paci's interests are multiple and his discussions of, for example, the material and the spiritual, or of hockey and art, clearly do provide a broader commentary of the Canadian scene. What is interesting about these cultural discussions, however, is that they too are informed by the ethnic minority perspective of the novel for in weighing the issues, Paci brings to bear the dilemmas and dichotomies which agitate his principal characters. In the end, then, Paci's commentary on dominant Canadian values and the Canadian way of life is still very much informed by his Italian-Canadian experience and of course is all the more interesting and valuable for the particular minority perspective it brings to bear on this dominant culture.

To say that Paci's perspective on Canada and on Italy in *Black Madonna* is that of an ethnic minority writer, then, is to point out that Paci's focus is internal to the problematics of Canadian ethnic minority experience, and that his analyses and his insights about that experience and about dominant Canadian culture generally are written out of that perspective. Paci is undoubtedly different from other Italian-Canadian writers but this general point could probably be made about many others: if Pier Giorgio Di Cicco is notable for his wit, his voice, his analysis of modern society and the scientific concepts that surround us, if Mary Di Michele addresses issues of gender and pop culture and love, if Caterina Edwards, Mary Melfi, Pasquale Verdicchio innovate in form and artistic creativity, if Marco Micone and Antonio D'Alfonso and others address the social, psychological, and cultural realities of modern Quebec experience, all these, and other such writers also address, to varying extents and with whatever limitations that need to be kept in mind, the experience of ethnic minority status in Canada and Quebec today. The difference between this perspective (and the value of the diversity of perspectives available in the currently diverse cultural situation of Canadian literature), becomes obvious if it is compared to the perspective brought to bear by majority Canadian writers or works that treat, however obliquely, minority cultures.

An excellent example of this, and one particularly suitable for comparison with Paci's *Black Madonna*, is Margaret Atwood's *Lady Oracle*. In this novel too, there is a principal female character, Joan, who is caught in an ongoing battle with her mother. Again the terms of the battle are cultural. Joan's mother attempts to impose on her the culturally stereotypical feminine role of "American" culture (Joan Crawford) in its Canadian (that is, British-Canadian) middle-class, upwardly mobile version of tidiness, emotional control, Brownies (cf. the analysis of Gayle Wurst). Interestingly, the mother-daughter struggle takes place on the same battleground as in *Black Madonna* — the daughter's body: "The war between myself and my mother was on in earnest; the disputed territory was my body"(69). Yet if the two novels accord on the terrain of the generational battle, they differ significantly in the tactics of rebellion of the daughters. While Maria refuses to eat in order to become thin and "English," Joan eats incessantly in order to become "fat" (Atwood's term), thereby thwarting the controlling hand of the mother and the dominant cultural image of women. Atwood then goes on, in numerous ways, to explore the consequences, social and psychological, of this cultural non-conformity, and uses the presence of the "fat woman" in the novel as a site of commentary on Canadian patriarchal culture. Among other things, what Joan finds is that her "fatness" makes her sexually invisible to her British-Canadian peers, both male and female.

What is interesting for the purposes of this essay is that the cultural parameters of this motif in the novel, like many other aspects of it, are overtly and self-consciously presented as "ethnic majority" in nature. Joan's struggle for control of her body, as well as her quest for identity and for place in Canadian culture (her relations with men, with art, with politics) are all contextualized within the novel in relation to Canadian ethnic minority characters and to non-Canadian, that is, "foreign" place. In particular, Atwood has Joan encounter immigrant characters in Toronto, takes her not only to England (and a Polish "count"), but to Italy where the present time of the novel, which both opens and closes the story, is set. These crossings of cultural boundaries are not the central action of the novel but they do serve to provide a variety of cultural alternatives and thereby a defining of the limits of the dominant culture. The main focus in the novel, however, the interior world of experience from which the novel is written, remains clearly ethnic majority, and the main characters all fall into this ethnic group. Thus Joan in England (a kind of "return journey" to the ethnic homeland), may romantically prefer the exoticism of the Polish count or at least of a "British accent," but her one true love turns out to be "unfortunately... only a Canadian, like [her]" (165). Canadian, of course, means British-Canadian.

The cultural context for this majority Canadian culture, then, the site of otherness, is non-British-Canadian culture and "foreign" space. Thus, returning to Joan's "fatness," and its concomitant sexual invisibility, one of Joan's first insights about the cultural limits of her own identity is to discover that these assumptions about female appearance are not universal, even in Toronto. Indeed, the fleshy Joan is pursued by an immigrant, who refuses to recognize the non-sexual status English-Canadian culture ascribes to "fat ladies" and who proposes marriage to her. For Joan, this experience becomes part not only of her sexual awakening but also of the formation of her ethnic identity. Note that Atwood's interest in this immigrant man, like Paci's interest in Maria's husband, is secondary and primarily external. Thus Joan's immigrant suitor is described (98) in contrast to "a lethargic, resentful Canadian" as "a sprightly, bright-eyed foreigner, either Italian or Greek, I wasn't sure which." Even his old-country name, a tell-tale sign of cultural significance, is omitted, and we are told that "in his determination to become a Canadian, he insisted that it was John" (100). Later in the novel he appears as "Zerdo," cashing in on Canadian multiculturalism with his exotic "ethnic" restaurant. Zerdo's ethnic identity (and all the issues that go with it) are thus not important to Joan or to Atwood, except by way of contrast. From the majority perspective of the novel, Canadian society seems to be peopled by two categories — Canadians and foreigners. For Joan (and for Atwood), the content of immigrant experience is irrelevant, is all the same, is unreal, is "ethnic," is merely a contrast to the presumed complex and "real" experience of the unconscious and dominant British-Canadian majority ethnicity.

Towards the end of the novel, there is a scene which reveals this perspective very clearly, and which illustrates as well, the power and subtlety of majority dominance in Canadian society. Joan, now a thin and successful writer in "mainstream" Canadian society, sits at the table in Zerdo's restaurant with the same (foreign) "Polish" count she met earlier in London, is waited upon obsequiously by John-Zerdo her former "bright-eyed" foreign (Italian or Greek) suitor, looks at his fat unnamed "ethnic" wife (whom she might have been), and comparing the assumed simplicity of the latter's life with the disturbing complexity of her own, thinks to herself: "At this moment, I envied her" (281). Now Margaret Atwood, as we all know, is a satirist and she *may* (or may not) be satirizing Joan from a pluralistic perspective in this scene. Nevertheless, satire or not, this novelistic moment of "ethnic" generosity and "envy" illustrates very clearly one form of an ethnic majority perspective in relation to minority cultures in Canada. In a Paci novel such as *Black Madonna*, it is precisely the perspective of that immigrant woman that would be at the centre, and as the earlier discussion of Paci's novel made amply evident, the life of that immigrant woman is hardly "simple" and not necessarily to be envied. Such is the difference between an ethnic minority and an ethnic majority perspective on that experience.

The Italian setting of *Lady Oracle* follows a similar pattern. For Atwood's character Joan, Italy is an escape, and is chosen by her not just because she had visited it previously with her husband Arthur but because it is far away from Canada and culturally far removed from English-Canadian culture. Atwood could presumably have had Joan escape to London, where she lived for much longer before and after she had met Arthur. But England is perceived as not far enough away, that is, too culturally accessible to Canada. Italy is not. The choice of Italy is thus again culturally significant because of its difference. Joan's aim is to hide, to lose herself in otherness, and, as her fantasies reveal, this otherness not only provides camouflage, it also offers the exotic and erotic appeal of her former "non-Canadian" liaisons:

> I could merge into Italy, marry a vegetable man: we'd live in a little stone cottage, I'd have babies and fatten up, we'd eat steamy food and cover our bodies with oil, we'd laugh at death and live in the present, I'd wear my hair in a bun and grow a moustache... (334).

This is, needless to say, totally an outsider's comic perspective on Italian culture and all it reveals is Joan's inability to enter into or to understand Italian reality, except in the most stereotypical way. In a similar fashion, Joan's contorted relations with her kind landlord and her evaluation of the women in the village (the black Madonnas) as culturally threatening, also reflect her touristic understanding of Italy. The point, of course, is not that Atwood herself sees Italy stereotypically (she is clearly satirizing Joan on this point), but that she (and her main character) only have an interest in Italy and Italian culture insofar as they provide a context for the Canadian ethnic majority culture which is the central understood cultural focus of the novel's experience. Unlike Italian-Canadian writers like Paci (or Edwards or Minni or Micone), Italy is not meaningful in itself and in its Italy-Canada history. It is mere backdrop, otherness, difference. It could, presumably, just as easily (to quote Joan on John/Zerdo again) have been Greece. The significance of Italy in the novel, then, is not that it is Italy, but that it is able to reveal something about British-Canadian culture which Joan, Atwood and Atwood's assumed British-Canadian readers would not otherwise notice or learn.

This brief discussion of Paci and Atwood illustrates the usefulness of making distinctions within Canadian literary analysis on the basis of the category being examined in this paper. Differences between ethnic minority and ethnic majority writers do count and the category, applied comparatively, can lead to insights. Needless to say, Atwood, like Paci, is multiple, and cannot and should not be reduced to this binary alone. It need hardly be stated that she is a feminist, that she comments on modern society and culture, that she is a writer of many other qualities. At the same time, as this brief analysis shows, she also is an English-Canadian ethnic majority writer and if she is multiple, she is also binary. To do Atwood justice, just as in the case of Paci and minority writers, her ethnicity and Canadian social status have to be taken into consideration. Ethnicity and status are not questions that arise only for minority writers nor are traits of multiplicity limited to majority authors. Applying a binary category such as ethnic minority/ethnic minority to multiple authors may, like other binary categories, be problematic, limited, and full of weaknesses and unwanted consequences. At the same time, the category clearly does have its uses. The role of the critic, I would conclude, is to make sure that the category is understood, that it is better and more useful than competing categorical concepts (such as "ethnic-mainstream"), and that the critic employ it overtly in the light of its limitations and with self-awareness of its own positioning in the discourse. In this way respect can be accorded to the multiplicity of the literary experience and to its synchronic and diachronic interrelationship with a society in which authors write, readers read, and texts are ideologically constructed and received.

References

Atwood, Margaret. *Lady Oracle*. Toronto: McClelland and Stewart, 1976. Seal Edition, 1977.

Di Michele, Mary. *Mimosa and Other Poems*. Oakville: Mosaic, 1981.

Edwards, Caterina. *The Lion's Mouth*. Edmonton: NeWest Press, 1982. Reprinted Montreal/Toronto: Guernica, 1993.

Geertz, Clifford. *Works and Lives: The Anthropologist As Author*. Stanford: Stanford University Press, 1988.

Harel, Simon. *Le Voleur de parcours*. Longueuil: Le Préambule, 1989.

Hutcheon, Linda, and Marion Richmond, eds. *Other Solitudes: Canadian Multicultural Fictions*. Toronto: Oxford University Press, 1990.

MacLennan, Hugh. *Two Solitudes*. Toronto: Collins, 1945.

Marshall, Tom. "Third Solitude: Canadian as Jew." *The Canadian Novel: Here and Now*. Ed. John Moss. Toronto: NC Press, 1978, 147-155.

Melfi, Mary. *A Dialogue with Masks*. Oakville: Mosaic, 1985.

Micone, Marco. *Déjà l'agonie*. Montreal: L'Hexagone, 1988.

Minni, C.D. "An Interview with Frank G. Paci." *Canadian Literature* 106, 1985, 5-15.

Mukherjee, Arun. "Whose Post-Colonialism and Whose Postmodernism?" *World Literature Written in English*, Vol. 30, No. 2, 1990, 1-9.

Mukherjee, Bharati. Introduction. *Darkness*. Markham, Ontario: Penguin, 1985, 1-4.

Paci, F.G. *Black Madonna*. Ottawa: Oberon, 1982.

———. *The Father*. Ottawa: Oberon, 1984.

Padolsky, Enoch. "Cultural Diversity and Canadian Literature: A Pluralistic Approach to Majority and Minority Writing in Canada." *International Journal of Canadian Studies*, 3, 1991, 111-128.

Pivato, Joseph, ed. *Literatures of Lesser Diffusion*. Edmonton: Research Institute for Comparative Literature, University of Alberta, 1990.

Philip, Marlene Nourbese. "Publish and Be Damned." *Fuse*, Vol. 13, No. 6, 1990, 40-42.

Report of the Royal Commission on Bilingualism and Biculturalism. Book IV. The Cultural Contibutions of the Other Ethnic Groups. Ottawa: Queen's Printer, 1969.

Ricci, Nino. *Lives of the Saints*. Dunvegan, Ontario: Cormorant, 1990.

Sadiq, Nazneen. "Immigrant angst" [rev. of *Other Solitudes*]. *Globe and Mail*, 20 Oct. 1990, C 21.

Sutherland, Ronald. *Second Image: Comparative Studies in Quebec/Canadian Literature*. Don Mills, Ontario: Newpress, 1971.

Wurst, Gayle. "Cultural Stereotypes and the Language of Identity: Margaret Atwood's *Lady Oracle*, Maxine Hong Kingston's *The Woman Warrior* and Alice Walker's *The Color Purple*." *Cross-Cultural Studies: American, Canadian and European Literatures, 1945-1985*. Ed. Mirko Jurak. Ljubljana, Yugoslavia: University of Ljubljana, 1988, 53-64.

13

Gaetano Rando

Italian-Australian Literature

A Socio-historical Survey

$\mathcal{T}$he purpose of this paper is to is to present an overview of two diverse but interconnected aspects of Italian Australian writing: (1) the correlation between the pattern of Italian migration to Australia and the production of literary texts; and (2) the way in which this experience of migration is portrayed in the creative writing of first-generation immigrants.

The history of Italian migration to Australia can be divided into three broad periods. The period 1840-1880 was characterized by the migration of small numbers of individuals — missionaries, political exiles and businessmen — who were educated, articulate and had left Italy for other than economic reasons. There were probably no more than 2000 Italians in Australia by 1881, although to this number a further 2000 immigrants from the Canton Ticino must be added. Italian labourers and *contadini* reached Australia in ever increasing numbers between 1880 and 1930, bringing the Italian population from 3800 in 1891 to about 33000 in 1930. The first group of some 200 *contadini* from the Veneto arrived in 1881 and formed the rural settlement in Northern New South Wales which became known as New Italy. Ten years later the Queensland government recruited 335 *contadini* mainly from Northern Italy to work as sugar cane cutters. They were to replace the kanaka labourers who were being deported subsequent to the formulation of the white Australia policy. This event marked the beginning of substantial Italian migration to North Queensland, and unlike their Micronesian predecessors the Italians soon became proprietors of sugar cane plantations and other farms

— an interesting and important episode in the history of Italian migration to Australia which Giovanni Andreoni has adapted as the theme for his novel in progress *Zucchero*.[1] The bulk of Italian migration occurred in the period 1947-1972 when about 350,000 Italians came to Australia — although some 28% of these were ultimately to return to Italy — making the Italian ethnic group the largest after those from the British Isles and Ireland.

The presence of large numbers of Italian immigrants in Australia has led to the formation of a complex community structure with aspects which cover not only social and sporting activities but also religion, welfare, education, language and culture. Among these activities may be noted that of giving literary and artistic articulation to the migration experience. It is an activity which is undertaken by a very small minority but nevertheless one which has its place and importance in the totality of endeavour by the community.

A total of 179 books were published over the period 1851-1990 and this includes works of both "pure" and "applied" literature (see Table below). Of these, 137 were published in the period between 1967 and 1990, while the highest proportion of books in relation to number of Italian born residents is registered over 1851-1880, when ten times as many books per capita were published with respect to the 1946-1966 period and five times as many compared to 1881-1939 and 1967-1990. Up to 1937 works published in volume form, with the exception of Raffaello Carboni's plays, were autobiography, biography and memoirs, accounts of travel in Australia and of the country's history, society and geography.

Numbers of works in volume form published by Italians in Australia
(Long and short term residents)

	1851-1880	1881-1939	1946-1966	1967-1990
Narrative: Novels & Short Stories		1	1	19
Theatre	3			4
Poetry		1	15	43
Anthologies (a)		2		18
Applied Literature (b)	5	7	7	57

(a) Includes anthologies of Italian literature (1928-38) and anthologies of Italian and Italian-Australian literature (1967-1987).

(b) Includes memoirs and chronicles, biography, history, travel, geography as well as sporadic examples of religious and philosophical treatises, studies, grammars and dictionaries, collections of correspondence and essays, translations.

From an Australian perspective, the most important publication in the first period is Raffaello Carboni's *Eureka Stockade,* a moving and passionate eye-witness account of Australia's best known attempt at rebellion against British rule. The *Eureka Stockade* is widely hailed as a document of fundamental importance for Australian social history. More than a chronicle it contains Carboni's views and attitudes towards this new land, seen as a culturally deprived, rough and tough frontier governed by the mores of crass materialism and pragmatic expediency. Some of Carboni's literary works written after his return from Australia contain references and themes related to his Australian experiences. The melodrama *La Santola* presents the theme of Australia as a fabled land of faraway riches which however does not live up to its promise. Pastorello's experiences as a digger do not meet with material success, nor, on returning to Rome, does he succeed in marrying his sweetheart Concetta, while his *Risorgimento* patriotism and anti-clerical sentiments remain unmitigated. *Gilburnia*, a ballet-pantomime in eight scenes complete with an "antarctic vocabulary," relates the story of the love of two white men for an Aboriginal girl and contains references to the Eureka Stockade episode. The protagonist of *Schiantapalmi* is Professor Nazzareno Schiantapalmi, who is forced into exile because of his participation in the Roman insurrection of 1848-49 and has lately returned to Italy from the Australian gold fields where he had managed to accumulate a modest fortune. The account of Nazzareno's Australian experiences provides one of the central themes of the play. The characters compare Italy's past glories and present plight with an idealistic Carbonian vision of Rousseau's noble savage living the simple life down under:

NAZZARENO

Nei boschi dell'Australia i selvaggi sono abituati a vedersi giorno e notte e viceversa, uomini e donne ricoperti, ossia, vestiti o dalle ombre dei gommi o dal chiaro di luna.

MARGHERITA

Narra un poco: allora non hanno alcuna religione? avete capito, nessuna Chiesa?

VITTORIO

Qui hai battuto il chiodo a posto, caro. I fondatori della Chiesa Papale in Italia furono i Raffaello, i Michelangelo e socii di pennello e scappello! Non c'è che dire!

NAZZARENO

«Eppur si muove», disse Galileo!

NAZZARENO

In the Australian bush the savages are used to seeing each other day and night and vice versa, both men and women, covered, that is clothed, either by the shadows of the gums or by the light of the moon.

MARGHERITA

Tell me: so they haven't got any religion? No Church, I mean.

VITTORIO

There you've hit the nail right on the head, my friend. The founders of the Papal Church in Italy were the Raffaellos, the Michelangelos and the rest of the brush and scalpal set! That's for sure!

NAZZARENO

But it moves nonetheless, as Galileo said! (Carboni 1867: 112).

There are no publications in volume form between 1915 and 1927. With one exception — a collection of poems and a play by Giuseppe Giliberto's *Raggi di idealismo* — books published between 1928 and 1939 were all printed in Italy. The most interesting of these in a literary sense is a collection of short

272

stories, *Il volto degli emigranti*, by Gino Nibbi which presents a wide panorama of Italians and Australians in the 1930s. Each of the nine stories and three
brief travelogues is set in a different location — eight in North Queensland.
Nibbi does not hide his dislike for certain aspects of Australian life, especially
its pragmatism, its materialism, its rough and ready attitudes, its anti-cultural
outlook, a dislike carried over in the consideration of similar aspects of the
Italian-Australian community which Nibbi observes somewhat sardonically
from on high. Although Nibbi does deal with the Italian-Australian environment, his main concern is with his observations and comments on Australia
and the Australians. Perhaps to the modern reader these stories may seem
somewhat dated in both language and content. Yet they present a rare view
from the periphery of Australia in the 1930s. What interests Nibbi are the
unusual, prurient, complicated, aspects of life "down under." In his stories
Nibbi presents a series of reflections on a society which prudishly bans the
display of nudity in art and the circulation of erotic literature, leading to the
question of what cultural values such a society can have. For Nibbi Australians
are also a race lacking in sentiment or emotion, to the point that they consider
Italians "too emotional" (31). It is a society which segregates, old people having to live separately, sick people being sent straight to hospital, landladies not
bothering to inform their lodgers' friends even when the lodger is on the point
of death, as happens to the Swiss Italian Roberti in the short story "Melbourne" (7-40).

In a second story, "Tasmania," the death of a Yugoslav miner and the
disappearance and probable death of another in the rugged mining country of
South Western Tasmania, cause no interruption in the work, which is carried
out in all types of weather and is not accompanied by song as it is in Italy and
other South European countries (67-86). In this story, tinged at times by melo-
dramatic tones but, nevertheless, effectively told, Nibbi expounds the theme
that the sad and tragic fate of the immigrant worker who has no one to mourn
him when he dies far from home is compounded by the absence of humani-
tarianism in Australians and their relentless pursuit of material gain.[2]

After World War II the production of books seems in part to be corre-
lated to the progressive urbanization of Italian immigrants. Relatively few
were published in the period of peak migration (1947-1966), partly due to the
low education levels of the bulk of immigrants, but also because in their initial
years in the new country immigrants had little time to devote to writing. The

number of books published increased substantially over 1967-1990, particularly in the later part of this period and despite a decline in the total number of the Italian born population. In the six years between 1984 and 1990 twenty-one volumes of creative writing (poetry, narrative, theatre) have been published as well as five anthologies. Until 1973 creative literature in volume form was published solely in Italian but after that date works have been published also in English. Six authors have published solely in English, twenty-four in Italian only, and three in both languages. The most significant book to date, in terms of reaching the non-Italian reader, is perhaps Rosa Cappiello's novel *Paese fortunato*, which was published in English translation in 1984 and is also the contemporary Italian-Australian literary work most favourably received by critics in Italy. In fact Rosa Cappiello is the only Italian-Australian writer to be consistently mentioned in the standard works on contemporary Australian literature.

Since 1947 twenty-seven writers have published fifty-eight volumes of poetry while many others have seen their works published in anthologies or in the Italian language newspapers, a substantial change with respect to the 1920s and 1930s, when only one volume of poetry was published although considerable numbers of poems appeared in the Italian-Australian press. Most volumes have been published at the expense of the writer, although in the last few years some writers have been able to publish with the assistance of Literature Board grants. Unlike narrative, poetry produced by Italian writers in Australia is not necessarily tied to migration-related themes. Indeed much of it is preoccupied with "universal" issues. Some poetry, however, does deal with the social realities observed and commented upon by the writer and it is perhaps this aspect which provides the distinctive characteristics of the corpus as a whole.

Most pre-World War II poetry deals with the migration experience at an external level and as a collective phenomenon. An important aspect of this poetry is the relationship between the immigrant and the host society in a climate characterised by racism and hostility. Thus in 1934, the poem "Il monito," addressed to the Italian woodcutters of Herbert River in Queensland, comments ironically on the fact that preference for Italian immigrants in the workplace has become a thing of the past despite their undeniable reputation as hard and willing workers. In "Dici lu ngrisi," Gaetano De Luca describes the "English" as boastful and vainglorious, unable to achieve anything on their own initiative, and sighs nostalgically for the sparce but simple life he left behind in Italy.

In post-1947 production the migration experience is internalized, rendered partial and subjective and subject to alteration over time. A common starting point is that of nostalgia for ones' place of origin (Sardinia in the case of Concas' *Ballata di vento*) or the feelings of isolation and exile which such thoughts provoke (Coreno 1980; Di Stefano 1978). Forced to live away from his/her native land, the poet can only find happiness in memories of a time that came before the confined isolation as an exile in Australia, something which does not represent a new life, but which is destructive, fatal, and brings melancholy. As time progresses there is a critical re-evaluation of this position. The native land is seen not only through the nostalgic eyes of the exile, but in terms of the conditions which had instigated the poet to leave it. Australia is seen as less alien, particularly because of its acceptance of the various manifestations of the Italian-Australian community (Concas, *L'altro uomo*). Other aspects explored are the dislocation in time and space caused by the journey, both material and spiritual, from Italy to Australia; the strangeness of the new land, both in a physical and in a spiritual sense; the cultural and generation gap between the immigrants and their Australian-born children, and the reaching back towards pre-migration places and experiences. In her latest volume *Se rimarrà qualcosa...* Di Stefano reaches the conclusion that, while time has tended to weaken the ties with the native land, the reality of the adopted country does not completely fulfil all the immigrants' spiritual needs, despite its positive and satisfying aspects.

The most prolific and best known poet is Luigi Strano, who between 1959 and 1990 has published fourteen volumes of poems written over a fifty-year period, thus providing some continuity between pre-war and post-war production. Initially emanating from a classical, humanistic context closely linked to his pre-emigration cultural experience, Strano's poetry experienced a significant structural and stylistic transformation in 1934 with "Giardini bui" (Rando 1983: 124-125), a metaphysical image of Sydney in the grips of the Great Depression. Acclaimed for its ring of sincerity, its anti-sentimentalism and its ability to transpose the many facets of the migrant experience in poetic terms, his poetry tells the personal "inner" story of the migrant experience universalized to embrace that of all those who have undergone the same process, from the initial nostalgia to the physical presence in the host country, to the slow and suffered acceptance of life in the new land, or to the re-evaluation of attitudes and sentiments related both to the country of origin (Italy) and the adopted country (Australia). Strano's poetry also succeeds in externalizing the migrant experience by presenting portraits and comments related to specific cases, such as the poignant lament of the grandfather from Calabria who cannot adapt to his new environment and bitterly regrets ever having left his native village ("U pappu a l'Australia," 1964: 39 — the poem is, significantly enough, written in dialect). In *Mostratemi la via di gire al monte,* Vivenzi cannot understand why he is charged with vagrancy when he does not conform to local norms (the poem is written in a spoken variety of Italian). When Fortunato La Rosa dies during a trip back to Italy, the first after many years' residence in Australia ("A Fortunato La Rosa — buonanima," in 1984: 11) his fate is seen by the poet as poignantly ironic.

Among the more recent Italian-Australian poets may be mentioned: Rosa Cappiello, whose poetry reflects the savage irony and the linguistic disruption evident in her prose works; Cristiana Maria Sebastiani who, while appreciating the social and physical aspects of the Australian scene, nevertheless accuses the host society of rejecting the cultural contribution of the non-Anglo-Celtic immigrant; Emilio Gabbrielli, who has so far concerned himself with his reaction to the cultural and the physical contrasts between the old country and the new; Walter Cerquetti with his prose poems of subjective introspection, captured not so much as a fleeting fragment but at a more discursive level; Valerio Borghese, whose poetry presents hermetic fragments of existential introspection, and Paolo Totaro, author of finely written poems — many of the most recent in a multilingual mode — with a deep sense of anguish and irony, of linguistic and cultural disruption.

Two prose writers, Gino Nibbi (*Cocktails d'Australia*) and Rosa Cappiello (*Paese fortunato*), have been distinguished by a modicum of success in Italy and also, in the case of Cappiello, by some recognition from the Anglo-Australian literary establishment. Both writers are critical, ironic and incisive but vastly different in style and technique. Nibbi is a detached observer, traditional if not slightly old-fashioned in style, whereas Cappiello's approach is highly subjective and her language charged, impetuous, aggressive.

With few exceptions, Italian-Australian fiction concerns characters and situations connected with migration and its consequences. It comments directly or implicitly on Australian society and the migrant's relation to it. Attitudes to migration range from qualified optimism to bleak pessimism. Some writers such as Bosi have de-emphasized the problems migration causes; others, like Cappiello, have given full recognition to its painful implications, the disappointments, losses, loneliness, despair. Autobiographical elements are strongly present, though Cappiello manages to go beyond her immediate personal experience to universal aspects of the human condition. Many writers comment favourably on the natural features of the new country (Sydney harbour, the beaches), but few venture in writing beyond the city limits. Even fewer attempt to theorize about a multicultural Australia. Substantially Italian-Australian narrative treats seven broad themes: the Italian-Australian community (Pino Bosi, *Australia cane*), Italy (Pietro Tedeschi, *Senza camicia*), the bush and the outback (Giovanni Andreoni, *Martin pescatore* and *La lingua degli Italiani d'Australia*, "Cuore d'Australia"),[3] personal reactions to migration (Valerio Borghese, *La moneta e altri racconti*, Enoe Di Stefano, *Avventura australiana*), the question of identity (Giuseppe Abiuso, *Diary of an Italo-Australian Schoolboy*,[4] Andreoni, *L'australitaliano come linguaggio letterario*, Charles D'Aprano, *The Swallow*), racism (Andreoni, Cappiello) and multiculturalism (Andreoni).

While in most writers there is a rejection, or at best a wary and uneasy acceptance of the human environment, there is an almost universal acceptance of the Australian natural setting. It is this aspect of Australia which perhaps best serves to define both the uniqueness of the country and, in some cases, the justification for the decision to remain there. For Cappiello, the urban costal natural environment is a compensation for loneliness and the alienating aspects of the social landscape ("Scoprii le spiagge meravigliose," Cappiello 1981: 9) but she is much less enthusiastic about the man-made environment ("Che gente era mai questa?... Nelle case asimmetriche, squadrate, asciutte e spersonalizzate come l'anima del popolo" — 1981: 7) and scathingly critical about the Italian-Australian community. Gino Nibbi (1965) appreciates the primitiveness and tranquillity of the Tasmanian bush, although he is somewhat less enamoured of the Australian tropics, due perhaps to his perception of nature from a European perspective. The bush and outback as mystique are an important feature of the writings of Abiuso and, particularly, Andreoni, who has explored some of the parallels between migrant and Aboriginal feeling for the land.

Aspects such as the migrant work ethic (recently dubbed "migrant drive"), the Australians' fondness for drink, Australians' dress habits, are common themes. There is thus a certain thematic repetitiveness in Italian-Australian narrative, although it is also true to say that each writer deals with these themes in his/her own particular way. Australia and Australian society are presented in quite divergent ways, although the condemnation of Australian drinking habits is quite uniform and is discussed by writers as varied as Nibbi and Cappiello. Surprisingly uniform is also the presentation of the migrant work ethic theme, which is found in Cappiello (*Paese fortunato*), Di Stefano (*Avventura australiana*) and, to a certain extent, Bosi (*Australia cane*) and Andreoni (*Cenere*), as well as in Nino Sanciolo's short story, "Vito Quattara" (in Rando 1983: 260-267). Nearly all writers tend to regard the work ethic as a negative characteristic of Italian immigrants, even if from the point of view of some Anglo-Australian sociologists (see, for example, Hempel)[5] it is one of the more positive aspects of Italian emigration to Australia. Among the creative writers Pino Bosi constitutes an exception, in that he closely identifies the work ethic with pride in *italianità* and the achievements of Italian immigrants. At the other extreme, Rosa Cappiello presents a vehemently grim and bitter picture of the abject existential state of the immigrant woman factory worker, who is driven by the dictates of a crassly materialistic and exploitative host society:

Questa è la donna di fabbrica, moglie del moderno coolie e coolie lei stessa, abile nel legare il figlio al letto o al tubo del lavabo pur di non perdersi la pisciatina di contentezza il venerdí, giorno di paga. Schiava del dollaro, ormai, spedisce il neonato dai parenti residenti in Egitto, in Jugoslavia, in Spagna, in Grecia. Trascorsi alcuni anni lo ritira simile a un pacco postale, via aereo o via mare. Quel bimbo, quella bimba, in alcuni casi due, allontanati nello svezzamento, garantivano il deposito per comprare casa o il visto di ritorno in patria arricchiti senza rimorsi. Particolari amari. Struttura di una società moderna. Bisogna adeguarsi. Mettersi al passo. Chi non possiede non vale. Di moderno, però, c'era soltanto la fatica in parità col maschio… (Cappiello 1981: 19).

Se per sopravvivere devo sputare sangue, io sputo sangue fino all'ultima goccia a drenaggio moderno, meccanizzato, tipo mungitura vacche, ma non obbligatemi a leccare il culo della supervisor nana, che tra i familiari conta le croste di formaggio e si vanta di tenere un televisore nel cesso che guarda sedendo sulla tazza. No, mai e poi mai. Un anno che dura, sanguinare la paga settimanale. Adesso basta. Mi ribello. Esco dal gregge. «Mi licenzio. Mi licenzio», strillo, ma più che uno strillo è un rantolo di morte. (Cappiello 1981: 110)

This is the female factory worker, wife of the modern coolie and coolie herself, who has got down to a fine art the act of tying her baby to the bed or to the downpipe of the kitchen sink so as not to forego the happy hour on Friday which is pay day. Slave of the dollar, she sends her newlyborn babe to relatives in Egypt, Yugoslavia, Spain, Greece, and after a few years back it comes like a postal package by sea or by air. That little boy, that little girl, sometimes two, deprived of their weaning, guaranteed the deposit for buying a house or a re-entry visa to the home country with riches without regrets. Bitter details. Structure of modern society. You have to adapt. Go along with it. Those who have no possessions aren't worth anything. The only thing modern about it was that women worked just as hard as men... (Cappiello 1984: 14).

If I have to sweat blood to survive I'll sweat blood right to the last drop sucked out by modern pumping machines like they use to milk cows, but don't make me suck up to the dwarf supervisor who rules the family budget with an iron hand and boasts that she has a TV set in the toilet so she can watch television while sitting on the dunny. No I won't do it, I'll never do it. It's a year now that I've been sweating blood for my weekly pay. And that's enough. I raise my voice in protest, stand out from the herd. "I'm quitting, I quit," I scream, but more than a scream it's a death-rattle (Cappiello 1984: 113)

Perhaps these are the themes which are of more immediate interest to the writer, closer to his/her "reality" and that of the intended reader (Cappiello and Nibbi excepted). Nevertheless they do have a limiting effect and very rarely does a work transcend these limits to attain more universal values. Further, although "migration" literature in Italy deals with the experience of the emigrant both in the host and in the home country, Italy does not constitute a major theme in Italian-Australian narrative.

Unlike the poetry written on this theme, the narrative seems to contain relatively little nostalgia or longing for the native country. Few writers have dealt with the theme of Italy revisited (D'Aprano) or the emigrant's return (Borghese, Sebastiani) and there is a general tendency to write about the Italy they knew before emigration.

The view of Italy presented by the immigrant (first generation) narrative writer varies greatly and ranges from the positive to the negative. Some reject entirely the country they left, some retain fond memories, yet others deal with fragmentary and highly impressionistic aspects of the country. Giovanna Guzzardi's short stories present a fairy-tale view of Italy as romantic fantasy largely divorced from the migration process and almost completely from its socioeconomic and political realities. Fernando Basili presents a minute view of the middle and working class elements of contemporary Italian society and their struggles to cope with its complex social and political realities. He is also the only writer to take a "European" view of the Italian scene. Like Basili, although with far less success, Pino Sollazzo (*Il capolavoro del secolo*) attempts to deal with some political and social aspects of contemporary Italy, an attempt which is not particularly successful because of its lack of depth and because of the popularizing elements which are found in the story.

The question of Italian-Australian individual and group identity is an overriding issue which many writers grapple with but with which few manage to come to terms. Outcomes and resolutions to the debate on identity are varied and at times contradictory. It is an important and interesting aspect of Charles D'Aprano's unpublished novel *The Swallow*, whose protagonist, after decades of indecision and oscillation between identification as an Italian or as an Australian finally arrives at the articulation of an Italian-Australian identity which is a viscerally felt reconciliation of both worlds:

> ...in some ways I have changed. I suppose there was a time when I was Italian and refused to be anything else. And then there was a period when I was the all-assimilated Australian. Now I have a much better idea of what I am. I am much more willing to accept my dual cultural heritage and my place in the world (unpublished manuscript).

For Andreoni too the resolution of Italian-Australian identity lies somewhere between the two cultures. Attempts at assimilation such as the anglicization of names (sometimes imposed by the host society) and the imposition of Anglo-

Celtic behaviour patterns are doomed to failure. The Italian-born protagonist of "La giornataccia di Montefiore" (Andreoni 1978: 50-57), Phillip Montefiore, has taken great pains to assimilate. However, despite his status in the New England rural community as the local bank manager, he is still considered a dago and outsider by the conservative and racist landed gentry. When he and his Irish-Australian wife attend a dinner party at a grazier's alcohol and nausea force him to retire rapidly to the bathroom, provoking derisive comments from the other guests: "Quest'italiani non impareranno mai a bere la birra" (57).

On the other hand, Bosi advocates the resolution of identity through a sense of belonging to the new country. Bosi's basis for an "Italian-Australian" identity is constituted by a strong sense of pride which Italian immigrants have in their achievements and a close-knit solidarity within the Italian-Australian community, a survival strategy that constitutes an implicit defence mechanism against the "outside." Abiuso's *Diary of an Italo-Australian Schoolboy* investigates what it means to be Australian for an adolescent immigrant, Mario Carlesani, thrust into the bewildering atmosphere of a state high school in a working-class inner Melbourne suburb. The topic is explored not only in ethno-cultural terms but also in terms of class. Mario's understanding of the Australian spirit is brought about through his contacts with the history teacher's discussions on Australian culture, the encouragement by another teacher and his peer group towards commitment to political issues of immediate concern, and solidarity with his peers. Through these contacts, the immigrant (Mario) is led to become an active participant in Australian society even though he may not fully accept it.

The staging of Italian opera and plays has been a feature of local cultural activities since the mid 1840s. A performance of Verdi's *Attila* was given in Sydney in 1846 and performances of other operas followed in the succeeding years. In 1875 the famous Italian actress, Adelaide Ristori, completed a highly successful three-month tour of New South Wales. During the 1930s performances were put on by amateur Italian community groups. In the early 1950s the Sydney University Italian Club performed plays for the Italian immigrants at the Bonegilla migrant camp as well as at the University and it is also during this period that church-sponsored amateur theatrical groups were also formed. Only in the last ten years or so have Italian community amateur and semi-professional groups included in their repertoires texts by local authors and most of such activity seems so far to have taken place in Melbourne. To date the only instance of a performance of a play by an Italian-Australian author by an Australian group has been that of Nino Randazzo's *Victoria Market*.

Randazzo, whose theatre has been well received by Melbourne Italian-Australian audiences, is probably the most prolific first generation writer. His plays deal with issues which are closely related to the salient aspects of Italian-Australian social and historical reality: the 1934 anti-Italian riots in Western Australia (*Le fiamme di Kalgoorlie); the problems faced by the Italian-Australian aged (Villaggio Paradiso*); the tendency on the part of the Anglo-Australian community to construct the Mafia myth within the socio-political context of the Italian community (*Mercato Victoria/Victoria Market: Genesi di un mito*); the impossibility of communicating across languages and cultures and the dilemma which this causes for the Italian emigrant who returns to visit his native land (*Il sindaco d'Australia*) ; the themes of arrival, alienation and adaptation (*Il pane e le rose*).

L'ultima flotta constitutes a break with Randazzo's tradition of social realism and takes an extremely pessimistic view of Australian multicultural futures. Set in the year 2020, its protagonists are an embattled group of ageing first generation Italians who came out to Australia in the early 1970s and now, some fifty years later, have to battle for collective cultural survival in a society which has done away with multiculturalism and has become fiercely racist and xenophobic in an attempt to achieve a rapid and total assimilation of the remaining pockets of resistance among ethnic groups.

Osvaldo Maione (also of Melbourne), on the other hand, has tended to concentrate on the more personal aspects of the migration experience. The Italian-Australian mother cult is the theme of *Il bello di mammà* , Italian-Australian social traditions that of *Il grande ballo*. How the immigrant manages to solve his economic woes by taking advantage of the opportunities provided by the Australian welfare and workers compensation systems is explored in *L'arte di arrangiarsi*. The complications which can be caused by an insufficient command of English and an imperfect understanding of the local laws are a feature of *Bitch*. The delusion of the Italian intellectual who emigrates to Australia and finds that he cannot exercise his profession but has to take on manual work in order to survive is presented in *L'attesa* . The irrelevancy of certain Italian folk traditions in the Australian context is the theme of *Il nuovo seme*. Maione's theatre comes across as somewhat shallow and simplistic in the presentation of themes, although the comedy, which contains elements of Neapolitan popular theatre, can be effective enough in performance for an Italian-Australian audience.

The generation gap exacerbated by the impossibility of cross-cultural understanding is the main theme of a play by Tony Giurissevich *Mogli e buoi dai paesi tuoi* (published in Rando 1983: 223-231). In it the hilarity of the situation does not mask the underlying "serious" message that time does not stand still and that social change occurs in Italy as well as in Australia. On the same theme is Christine Maddafferi's *A Hard Bargain,* produced in Melbourne and transmitted by SBS TV in 1985, probably one of the best one-act plays produced to date. Its liveliness and zest blend well with the underlying serious impact of the situation. Moreover the play is produced with feeling (lacking in Giurissevich): it is evident that the members of the family are fond of each other despite cultural conflicts and the generation gap. With great reluctance the parents finally agree to allow the daughter to continue her studies and not to force her into an arranged marriage with the son of *paesani.*

There are also examples of more popular forms of theatrical expression such as *Ogni casa 'na croce* (performed over 1988-89) by the Melbourne group Broccoli Productions which has been active for nearly ten years in theatre of this nature. This performance, consists of a series of short skits, some farcical, some ironic, and a few songs on common aspects of the Italian-Australian experience. Much more *impegnato* is the Sydney FILEF theatre collective, which has produced some very effective and widely attended street theatre productions. Its first, *Nuovo paese* (1984), was performed out in the open at Leichhardt High School and explored the different experience, attitudes and life styles of a group of Italian grandparents and their Australian-born grandchildren. Their second production, *Lasciateci in pace* (1986), was a bilingual presentation on the theme of world peace and nuclear disarmament, a somewhat unsuccessful attempt at imitating Dario Fo. *L'Albero delle rose* by Sonia Sedmk, FILEF's third production, was performed in Sydney in May 1987. It is a bilingual presentation of the experience of Italian immigrant women and their daughters based on a series of oral reminiscences specially collected for the production. An interesting experiment in multilingual theatre is found in *The Journey* by Tes Lyssiotis, performed by the Filiki Players of

Melbourne in 1987. The dialogue is in English, Greek and Italian and the three languages are cleverly combined to create a dynamic dialogue accessible to everyone. The play portrays the lives, experiences and outlook of immigrants who came to Australia in the early 1930s and 1950s. It depicts the conflicts of these families and their children within an often hostile environment and the interaction between the various new and old Australian cultures is depicted with bitter-sweet humour.

Doppio Teatro, an Adelaide based theatre group, is dedicated to the development and performance of original works that extend the understanding of Italian-Australian culture. Among its recent performances is a bilingual play *Ricordi,* a play about people who live in Australia but speak two or more languages and have memories and emotions rooted in another land. It is a kaleidoscope of characters and stories, some comic, some tragic, which together quintessentially present the multiple facets of the experience of Italian migrant women, not only in their external aspects but through their desires, fantasies, expectations and regrets, their quest for identity and self-determination. Doppio Teatro's 1991 production, *Tinto di rosso,* written and directed by Teresa Crea, is based on the story of Francesco Fantin, a socialist activist who was murdered by fascists at the Loveday internment camp in 1942. It presents one of the most contentious episodes of the Italian-Australian migrant experience during the World War II when several thousand Italian male immigrants of the most disparate political convictions and social classes were placed in concentration camps in the harsh and lonely environment of the Australian outback.

Over a period of 130 years some Italians who have emigrated to Australia have produced a number of literary texts. Little has been done to examine the complex personal, social and cultural experiences and contrasts which have served as background to the production of this type of writing, which to a large extent has been the result of this experience. It is a type of writing that has both its champions and its denigrators when it comes to evaluating its literary qualities, and there is no doubt that convincing arguments can be mounted for its literary "validity." However the most forceful argument for the "validity" of this type of literature and one which is almost universally accepted relies substantially on its value as the narration of the socio-historical reality of the migration experience. While some writers deal with themes not necessarily tied to the migration experience, and Cappiello transcends these aspects, it can nevertheless be said that most writers and most works present aspects of migration as a main theme. How some Italian immigrants see Australia and Australian society, how they react to it, their appreciation of the natural beauties of the new country, what they think of the land they left behind, are all salient elements of the category. They are "inside" stories told not with the detachment or the objectivity of the sociologist or historian but from a subjective personal and visceral point of view. They relate the anger, frustration, the hopes and disappointments lived by the immigrants, the traumatic experience of leaving one's native land and of having to start again in a new country with the realization that perhaps one can never really "belong" — an irreconcilable metaphysical wandering between two worlds which only the immigrant has known. These are the aspects which make these documents worthy of perusal, irrespective of their possible intrinsic literary value. Paradoxically it is these limiting aspects which make these documents unique, possibly more so when from the standpoint of a future generation there is an attempt to evaluate the phenomenon of Italian migration to Australia.

However, this corpus contains yet another important element. Together with the writings of other minority groups (including Aborigines), it leads to a redefinition of Australian literature which now cannot exclude writings by authors of non-English speaking background and texts produced in languages other than English thus providing a new dimension to the perception of national cultural identity.

Notes

1. Chapter 3 of *Zucchero* was published in Rando 1983: 13-23; Chapter 4, 85-90.
2. Although not strictly within the bounds of the defined parameters of this paper it is perhaps worthwhile mentioning the novel *No Escape* by Velia Ercole, daughter of an Italian doctor born at White Cliffs (NSW) in 1910. It is the story of the efforts made by an Italian doctor and his wife to settle in the small country community of Banton, NSW. Leo Gherardi from Campli in the province of Teramo, a socialist activist, was forced to flee Italy at the turn of the century in order to avoid arrest. He is accompanied by his wife Teresa and their small son Dino. Although Leo gains acceptance as a doctor at a superficial level in the small country community where he sets up practice, the first few years of his Australian experience are characterized by what may be described as a sort of upper middle class intellectual angst (a state somewhat reminiscent of Henry Handel Richardson's Australian "emigrants" to Europe) as Leo and Teresa live in the hope of being able one day to return to Italy. Teresa, sensitive, vibrant and impulsive, wishes to preserve her Italian identity, to return to Bologna and complete her training at the conservatorium. She does not attempt to assimilate into the community and indeed rejects the very few lukewarm overtures of friendship made by the wives of the local professional men. Alone and desperate, she finally commits suicide, an act which is judged as the ultimate price which must be paid for the failure to assimilate. By contrast Leo's gradual acceptance of the new country and its people, evidenced by his marriage some years after Teresa's death to Olwen Ferrar, the widow of a local farmer, symbol of the new land, and his participation in the Gallipoli campaign, is presented as a successful if not entirely happy conclusion thus setting the seal on the novel's substantially assimilationist message. In this the conclusion is in contrast to that presented in Eric Baum's *Burnt Sugar* where assimilation is seen in negative terms. Ercole's second novel *Dark Windows* (London: Butterworth, 1934), although in some ways complementary to *No Escape* in that it relates the story of an Australian girl's vain attempt to adapt herself to life with her relatives in Brittany, can be seen as continuing the themes enunciated in the first through the assertion of the superiority and strength of the new Australian cultural mores over the slightly decadent and restrictive customs of the "old" (Latin) country.
3. Published in G. Abiuso, M. Giglio and V. Borghese, 151-157.
4. In Abiuso, 100-160.
5. Hempel characterizes the Italian male migrant as an opportunistic person concerned with thrift, hard work and success: "a happy migrant is a migrant who has been placed in employment suitable to his level of education and skill" (47). Hempel contains the contradiction in terminology based on class differentiation of the Italian male by locating him in the culture text of equality of opportunity, the potential for upward social mobility deriving its inertia by the unifying happiness of the job.

References

Abiuso, G. L., Giglio, M., and Borghese, V., eds. *Voci nostre. Antologia italo-australiana di novelle, commedie, poesie e ricordi, scritta da emigrati italo-australiani.* Melbourne: Tusculum, 1979.

Abiuso, Joe. *The Male Model and Other Stories.* Adelaide: Dezsery Ethnic Publications, 1984.

Andreoni, Giovanni. *Martin pescatore.* Milan: Ippocampo, 1967.

————. *La lingua degli italiani d'Australia e altri racconti.* Roma: Il Veltro Editrice, 1978.

————. *L'australitaliano come linguaggio letterario Un racconto documento.* Roma: Il Veltro Editrice, 1982.

Anonymous. "Il monito." *Il Giornale Italiano.* 21 November 1932, 7.

Arrighi, Michael (ed.). *Italians in Australia: The Literary Experience.* Wollongong, NSW: The University (Department of Modern Languages), 1991.

Bisietta [pseud. of Fontanella, Giuseppe]. *Orme.* Milano: Gastaldi, 1947.

Borghese, Valerio. *La moneta e altri racconti.* Melbourne: The Author, 1984.

Bosi, Pino. *Australia cane.* Sydney: Kurunda, 1971.

————. *The Checkmate and Other Stories.* Sydney: Kurunda, 1973.

Broccoli Productions (Melbourne). *Ogni casa 'na croce.* Unpublished script. Performed 1988.

Cappiello, Rosa R. *Paese fortunato.* Milano: Feltrinelli, 1981.

————. *Oh Lucky Country.* Translated with an introduction by Gaetano Rando. St. Lucia, Qld: University of Queensland Press, 1984.

Carboni, Raffaello. *The Eureka Stockade: The Consequence of Some Pirates Wanting on Quarterdeck a Rebellion.* Melbourne: J. P. Atkinson & Co., 1855.

————. *La santola.* Torino: Derossi e Dusso, 1861.

————. *Schiantapalmi:* Napoli: Gargiulio, 1867.

————. *Gilburnia. Lo sotta o tinge,* Vol. I. Rome: The Author, 1872, 185-248.

Cerquetti, Walter, and Phillips, Glen. *Australia e Umbria dorate e verdi.* Perugia: Casa Editrice Sigla 3, 1987.

Cincotta, Vincenzo, ed. *Italo-Australian Poetry in the 80's II: A Selection of Poems from the Italo-Australian Writers Association.* Sydney-Wollongong: Italo-Australian Writers Association, 1989.

Concas, Lino. *Ballata di vento.* Rome: Gabrieli, 1977.

————. *Uomo a metà.* Rome: Gabrieli, 1981.

————. *L'altro uomo: Poesie 1981-1983.* Gorie, BG: Editrice Velar, 1988.

Coreno, Mariano. *Yellow Sun.* Sydney: Saturday Centre, 1980.

Crea, Teresa. *Tinto di rosso.* Unpublished script. Performed 1991.

D'Aprano, Charles. *Old Wine in New Bottles.* Melbourne: Winseray Pty Ltd., 1986.

————. *The Swallow.* Unpublished novel. Excerpts published in G. Abiuso, M. Giglio, V. Borghese 1979: 104-109; G. Rando 1983: 181-194; C. D'Aprano 1986: 1-27.

De Luca, Gaetano. "Dici lu ngrisi." *Il Giornale Italiano.* 2 November 1932, 6.

Di Stefano, Enoe. *Terra australis.* Sydney: Tip. Fabreschi, 1970.

————. *Voci di lontananza.* Sydney: Southern Cross Press, 1978.

————. *Avventura australiana.* Unpublished novel, 1975. Excerpts published in Rando 1983: 63-77.

————. *Mio e non mio.* Sydney: Offset Printing, 1985.

————. *Se rimarrà qualcosa...* Sydney: Southern Cross Press, 1988.

Ercole, Velia. *No Escape.* London: Butterworth, 1932.

————. *Dark Windows.* London: Butterworth, 1934.

FILEF Theatre Collective (Sydney). *Nuovo paese.* Unpublished script. Performed 1984.

————. *Lasciateci in pace.* Unpublished script. Performed 1986.

Giliberto, Giuseppe. *Raggi d'idealismo (Poesie, poemetti e dramma).* Sydney: Tip Tomalin, 1939.

Giurissevich, Tony. *Mogli e buoi dai paesi tuoi.* In Rando 1983: 223-231.

Hempel, J. "Italians in Queensland: Aspects of Assimilation." *Quadrant* III (4), Spring 1959, 54-53.

Lyssiotis, Tes. *The Journey.* Unpublished script. Performed 1987.

Maddaferri, Christine. *A Hard Bargain.* Unpublished script. Television adaptation (by SBS TV) 1985.

Maione, Osvaldo. *Bitch.* Melbourne: Tusculum, 1979.

————. *L'arte di arrangiarsi.* Unpublished script, 1982.

————. *Il grande ballo.* Unpublished script, 1983.

————. *Il bello di mammà.* Unpublished script, 1984.

Nibbi, Gino. *Il volto degli emigranti (Scene di vita in Australia).* Firenze: Parenti, 1937.

————. *Cocktails d'Australia.* Milano: Martello, 1965.

Penninger, Hans Richard. *Mary My Hun: A Novel with a Purpose.* Campsie, NSW: The Author, 1976.

Randazzo, Nino. *Il pane e le rose.* Unpublished script. Performed 1980.

————. *Il sindaco d'Australia.* Unpublished script. Performed 1981.

————. *Mercato Victoria/Victoria Market. Genesi di un mito.* Unpublished script. Performed 1982.

————. *Villaggio paradiso.* Unpublished script. Performed 1983.

————. *Le fiamme di Kalgoorlie.* Unpublished script. Performed 1987.

————. *L'ultima flotta.* Unpublished script. Performed 1989.

Rando, Gaetano, ed. *Italian Writers in Australia: Essays and Texts.* Wollongong, Department of European Languages: University of Wollongong, 1983.

————. *Italo-Australian Poetry in the 80's.* Wollongong, Department of European Languages: University of Wollongong, 1986.

————. *Italo-Australian Prose in the 80's.* Wollongong, Department of European Languages: University of Wollongong, 1988.

Sanciolo, Nino. *La Passione di Gesù Cristo: Tragedia sacra in versi su temi d'antichi motivi popolari siciliani.* Melbourne: The Author, 1983.

Sebastiani, Cristiana Maria. *L'approdo (Ashore).* Marrickville, NSW: Southwood Press, 1984.

————. *Fragilità.* Perugia: Guerra, 1984a.

Sedmk, Sonia. *L'albero delle rose.* Unpublished script. Performed 1987.

Sollazzo, Pino. *Il capolavoro del secolo. Romanzo di vita e di avventura.* Roma: Vincenzo Lo Faro Editore, 1988.

Strano, Luigi. *Acquerelli e mezzetinte.* Sydney: Tip. Ital-Print, 1959.

———. *Poesie proibite.* Sydney: Tip. Ital-Print, 1959a.

———. *Inquietudine.* Sydney: Tip. Ital-Print, 1964.

———. *Ricci di castagne.* Sydney: Tip. Ital-Print, 1968.

———. *Una forcatella di spine.* Sydney: Tip. Ital-Print, 1969.

———. *Mostratemi la via di gire al monte.* Auckland: The University, 1970.

———. *Ruinia.* Melbourne: Dudley E. King, 1972.

———. *Churinga.* Sydney: The Author, 1976.

———. *E risplende il sole.* Mt Wilson [NSW]: The Author, 1981.

———. *Di qui ci son passato anch'io.* Mt. Wilson, NSW: The Author, 1984.

———. *Fifty Years Ago.* Fairfield, NSW: W. R. Bright & Sons, 1986a.

———. *Carmi scelti.* Milano: Edizioni Pergamena s.a.s., 1986b.

———. *I fiori ch'io non colsi.* Mt. Wilson, NSW: The Author, 1988.

———. *Fiori d'altri tempi.* Mt. Wilson, NSW: The Author, 1990.

Tedeschi, Pietro. *Senza Camicia.* Milan: Editrice Nuovi Autori, 1986.

Totaro, Paolo. *Paolo poesie.* Sydney: The Author [xeroxed], 1981.

Valli, Maria. *Poesie australiane/ Australian poems.* St. Lucia, Qld: University of Queensland Press, 1972.

14

Giovanni Andreoni

Italo-Australians

Notes on Language and Literature

In 1970 *Il Veltro* of Rome commissioned the late Prof. C.A. McCormick to write what I believe to be the first article on Italian writers in Australia. The label "literature" was considered too lofty for migrants' writing, which was relegated to the low world of popular culture. Today the picture is not drastically changed, Australian intellectuals still cling to the anacronistic notion of low (popular) culture and high culture, literature belonging to the latter category. McCormick commenced his article with a premise:

> Non credo che sarebbe esatto o utile cercare di convincere il lettore italiano che l'Australia ha gran ricchezza di scrittori italiani. Un pittore che emigri, sì, può trovare nel nuovo paese immagini nuove, forme inedite, freschezza d'ispirazione. Ma per chi usa la parola come mezzo d'espressione, un paese di lingua diversa non presenta un ambiente favorevole... Lo scrittore che emigra porta con sè il suo bagaglio culturale, come porta le fotografie della mamma e dei parenti, ma è ben difficile, specialmente in Australia, che possa rinnovare quel bagaglio che rimane, appunto come le immagini fotografiche, fissato in un certo periodo. Esso diventerà nostalgia, diventerà rimpianto, in qualche caso verrà buttato via, ma è un bagaglio che non si rifà più. Ed è anche ovvio che la base linguistica di chi emigra deve essere già acquistata prima che lasci il proprio paese (299).

I do not believe it would be correct or useful to try to convince Italian readers that Australia has a wealth of Italian writers. In a new country, a painter who migrates might find new images and unknown forms which rekindle inspiration. However, people using words as a means of expression in a country where a different language is spoken, find a less favourable environment... Writers who migrate carry their cultural baggage with them just as they carry a photo of their mother and other relatives. It is very unlikely, particularly in Australia, that this baggage can be renewed. It remains, like the images in a photo, fixed at a certain point in time. It may become nostalgia, regret and in a few cases it will be rejected but it is essentially a cultural baggage which cannot be renewed. It is also clear that the linguistic base of the migrant must have been acquired before departure from the country of origin.[1]

This quotation has not dated because the mentality has not changed. Recently, in March 1991, Mr. J. Dawkins, the Federal Minister for Employment, Education and Training, stated at an international conference in Sydney:

We cannot expect our training institutions, or the nation's employers, to offer complex courses for skills upgrading, or even more simple courses to improve health and safety, in languages other than English. Therefore, this country cannot afford to be multilingual.[2]

English is the only language needed by the people of the Island Continent, and only in this language can the true nature of Australianhood be expressed. Not all share this view but the "system" favours it.

Any attempt to prove the contrary, by indicating how migrants' children born and bred in the country are actually using the language of their parents, is dismissed as nonsense by those who hold the purse strings. Statistical data are ignored; data from other multilingual countries in Europe, Asia and the Americas, are not in the public domain. When a minority group, for example the Chinese, retains the language of its forefathers, after many generations, such retention is presented neither as an achievement nor as an enrichment for the whole country.

Significant humanistic or scientific works written in languages other than English, are unknown to the greatest majority of Australians, an appalling example being the scientific work, written in Italian in 1851, by a Catholic bishop, R. Salvado. The work done by the good bishop was translated into Spanish in 1853, into French in 1854 and into English only in 1977. Even historical, sociological or literary works, written in English by NESB (Non English Speaking Background) people, are either ignored or dismissed because of the "ethnicity" of the authors.

Raffaello Carboni is a blatant case of such discrimination. In 1855 he wrote *The Eureka Stockade*, the account of the sole revolutionary attempt in White Australian history which marks, in H.V. Evatt's words: "...a turning point in Victorian and Australian affairs." But *The Oxford Companion to Australian Literature*, published in 1985, tries to diminish Carboni's contribution to the history and literature of White Australia:

> A modern edition (1942) [of *Eureka Stockade*] has an introduction by H.V.Evatt, who asserts that "it is impossible to deny him greatness as writer and historian." Although that is excessive praise, Carboni's book has been recognized, in spite of its eccentric structure and florid style, as a vivid and reliable account of the Eureka events as well as a remarkably sound analysis of the underlying causes of these events (Wilde, Hooton, Andrews 143-144).

What better example of damning with faint praise? Life in White Australia has always been dominated by one fear or another. Fear of the possibility that other languages, other literatures, other cultures, might be able to grow and prosper in this country, has always caused the most devastating reaction. In the case of the indigenous population, genocide in the past, ethnocide in the present.

Today, conditions are much easier for the Italian community, provided its members do not step outside the stereotype assigned to them by the mainstream culture. With a few exceptions, Italo-Australian intellectuals have embraced the petty bourgeois mentality of mainstream Australia. In 1971 Professor A. Comin recognized the existence of Australitalian, the *lingua mista* of the Italian migrants.

> Intanto però l'australitaliano è una realtà, ed è perciò legittimo chiederci seriamente... se è possibile l'uso di questa lingua nella letteratura... Certamente non prevedo una fioritura d'opere letterarie scritte in questa lingua mista, e non ne propugnerei l'uso indiscriminato. Non vorrei che essa sostituisse la lingua italiana nei giornali, nei programmi radiofonici, ecc. degli italiani in Australia (298).

Meanwhile, Australitalian is a reality and it is therefore legitimate to seriously consider the literary use of this language as a possibility. I cannot see a flourishing of literary works written in this mixed language nor would I advocate its indiscriminate usage. I would not like to see Italians in Australia replacing the Italian language of newspapers, radio programmes etc. with Australitalian.

The fear that the *lingua mista* of working class migrants may be used by the media and the literati, spurred Dr P. Genovesi to write in 1983:

> non mi soffermo a parlare di quella presunta lingua parlata da una presunta maggioranza e presunto filo unitario a testimonianza di una presunta omogeneità ecc. che pare vada ormai sotto il nome di "Australitaliano"... Chiaro communque il concetto base: laddove manca lo strumento "lingua" che traduca o medi l'idea o la tradizione orale manca una letteratura o quantomeno il fatto la limita. Vero il concetto, ma non sarà certo quella la panacea. Il Verga, non dimentichiamolo, è andato all'Università (304).

I shall discuss neither that so-called language spoken by an alleged majority, nor its putative common thread and supposed homogeneity etc. which seems to now go under the label of *Australitaliano*. However, the basic concept is clear: Where there is no language to act as a tool and to translate and mediate ideas or oral traditions, there is no literature. In any case this lack does put limits to literature. The concept may be true but Australitalian would not be the solution. Verga, let's not forget, went to university.

And the first generation migrant is incapable of producing literature.

> ...non si potrà parlare di una letteratura italo-australiana prima che le seconde o le terze generazioni siano venute alla ribalta. Sarà allora che l'etnico sarà superato e la reale fusione delle due o delle varie culture darà il suo frutto. Non saranno probabilmente opere in italiano, tantomeno in australitaliano, ma in lingua inglese, nella lingua nazionale di questo nostro paese (ibid.).

One cannot talk about Italo-Australian literature until second or third generations have appeared on the scene. Only when "ethnicity" has been overcome, and there is a fusion of the two or more cultures, will the fruits emerge. It is unlikely that the works will be in Italian, even less likely that they will be in Australitalian, but rather they will be in English, the national language of this country of ours.

But even Dr. Genovesi does not present adequately the extreme viewpoint. It is B. Zuliani who does:

> Most erroneously, some non-Italian speaking people have been induced to believe that Italians have produced a conventional home-made Italian English and have been using such language as an everyday form of oral expression and efficient vector of communication. There is nothing more fallacious!... Some illiterates and semi-illiterates, merely peasants from the southern regions, the mountainous districts of Central Italy and low Veneto, in a sincere endeavour to speak English are trying to achieve this by "Italianising" some English words (2).

This attitude creates nothing but problems for the migrants and their children. They are ridiculed first for their accent because extremists condemn all regional accents and all dialects. Then they are criticized because they italianize English words. Furthermore, children who are ridiculed at school, return home full of bitterness and resentment towards their parents, who taught them a "funny" language. The parents are traumatized by the reaction to their language and, in some cases, refuse to speak it with other Italians unless they are from the same village or district.

But what is the *lingua mista* I prefer to call Australitalian? Let's first examine its function and its vitality. It is not merely an interlanguage resulting from the juxtaposition of Italian and English. Nor is it Italian giving way to English by a slow process of attrition. To assume it is the result of an imperfect knowledge of both Italian (language or dialect) and English, would explain only a few aspects of the phenomenon.

Australitalian is the natural and deliberate use of Italian to meet the challenge of a new experience. In the language used in Italy, it is impossible to express ideas and emotions, or describe moments concerning solely the migrant's life in Australia. Noah Webster wrote in 1828:

Language is the expression of ideas, and if people of one country cannot preserve an identity of ideas (with the people of another country) they cannot retain an identity of language. Now, an identity of ideas depends materially upon the sameness of things or objects with which the people of the two countries are conversant. But in no two positions on the earth remote from each other, can such an identity be found. Even physical objects must be different (n. pag.).

The problem of identity is, in my opinion, the real cause of Australitalian and the reason for its continuing development and enrichment. Migrants cannot usually lose their Calabrian, Tuscan or Venetian identities. However, the physical, social, political and cultural environment is so different from their places of origin that to express ideas, to describe objects, experiences and typical Australian situations, they must find new words and expressions which differentiate their present position in Australia from the past one in Italy, their reality and hopes of today from the memories, and often bitterness, of yesterday.

The adoption of English would not solve their problem. "Fence" does not stress the difference between the small plots of holdings in Italy and the miles and miles of Cyclone fence on the immmense properties in Australia; "la fenza" does. "Fence" does not stress the difference between the poverty of the Italian soil and the fat of the Australian land, the starvation crops harvested in Italy and the riches harvested in Australia; "la fenza" does. "Bosso/u" is the opposite of the "padre padrone" who ruled with an iron fist. "Boss" does not have this connotation because it belongs to a different culture and tradition.

A few years ago in Queensland, I was talking with an elderly Marsican, in the old days a "bracciante" from the Fucino Lake. He was proudly showing me his new "carro"; it was, if I remember correctly, a Ford Falcon. We kept on talking and, naturally, we wandered back to Italy, to il Fucino and the Prince Torlonia who used to rule there. My friend was not very impressed by the Torlonias. He also mentioned the prince's "macchina," a 2.5 Alfa Romeo. I was puzzled by the use of "carro" and "macchina" and asked him why he used both. His reply was revealing: "il carro" was a symbol of his achievements, "la macchina" a symbol of Torlonia's oppression. "La farma" stresses the ownership of the land, "la marchetta" the happy feeling of spending money. Almost every Australitalian word indicates a change which has occurred in the migrant's life.

As for the Australitalian expressions, how can one forget Pino Bosi's "la faccia a punto di domanda dell'emigrante" ["A migrant's question-mark face"]? It conveys all the feelings, fears and doubts about arriving in Australia. I do not believe that an equally effective equivalent of such locutions exists in standard Italian or English. Perhaps in any standard language it is impossible to express certain emotions or describe certain moments. The standard language is often the voice of people in power who do not migrate but merely change place of residence. Australitalian idioms, metaphors, words are the fruits of many things, but not of an imperfect knowledge of any variety of Italian or English.

So, contrary to popular belief, the Italo-Australian author is faced with a variety of linguistic choices. The language chosen will serve to reveal the author's acceptance, rejection or criticism of the world of migration. In its multifaceted aspects, migration appears in the work of every Italo-Australian author.

In the following quotation, Luigi Strano laments the loss of his village with all its values:

Mmavissi 'rrumputo l'anchi
quando partia di Jani!
lu 'mmorzu d'ortu
e lu pertusu i casa l'avia
chi mi mancava u pani? (173)

Mi fossi rotto le anche
quando partii da Jani!
Un morso d'orto
e un buco di casa li avevo
che mi mancava il pane!

If only I had broken my hip
before leaving Jani!
I had a bit of land
and a roof over my head.
I was not in need of bread.

The use of the Calabrian dialect of Jani exemplifies the alienation of "pappu" (grandfather); he is unable to come to terms with Australia. "U pappu" finds shelter from the devastating experience of migration by hanging on to the reality of his language and, by using it to express his anguish, he proclaims once again his personal identity as well as the collective identity of his people. The great Sicilian poet Ignazio Buttitta stated in 1968:

> Un populu,
> diventa poviru e servu,
> quannu ci arrobbanu a lingua
> addutata di patri:
> è persu pi sempri (1984: 33).

> Un popolo,
> diventa povero e servo,
> quando gli rubano la lingua
> ereditata dai padri:
> è perso per sempre.

> A people
> becomes poor and enslaved
> when they take away from it the language
> received from the forefathers.
> It is a people lost forever.

The dialect, in other cases, becomes a declaration of pride in one's roots. Gaetano De Luca came to Australia early this century and worked in North Queensland. He wrote in 1932 in his Sicilian dialect:

> Dici lu ngrisi ch'è di razza rara
> E tutti l'autri sunnu genti rozza;
> E allura pirchì fora compra e mpara
> E nenti sapi fari ca so crozza? (346)

Dice l'inglese ch'è di razza rara
e tutti gli altri sono gente rozza;
perchè va sempre all'estero a imparare
e con la testa sua nulla sa fare?

The English say that their race is special
and that everyone else is uncouth.
Why then do they go overseas to learn
and do nothing with their own heads?

Both Strano and De Luca used standard Italian when such variety was more appropriate to the content or message of a poem. Indeed Luigi Strano wrote more in the standard language than in his dialect. An examination of any poem in Italian by these authors, reveals immediately the cause for their linguistic choice.

De Luca reproached the sugar cane cutters who came from so many regions of Italy with so many different dialects. The reproach can only be delivered in the national language:

Voi gridate a squarciagola:
Viva questo! Abbasso Quello!
— Dite un po'— tanto bordello
A che cosa servirà?
Vi diran che siete matti,
Matti tutti da legare
E la canna più a tagliare
A chi è matto non si dà! (344)

You scream out
Long live this! down with that!
— Tell me — in such a mess
What is the use?
Everyone will say that you are mad,
Mad enough to be locked up.
You don't get asked to cut cane
If you are mad!

Strano, sailing back to Italy to visit his native village, will use Italian to warn the cheeky Neapolitan boy who wishes to ridicule the way Calabrian peasants speak:

> Attenzione, ragazzo!
> Gli dico, bloccandogli
> il passo,
> è pericoloso scherzare
> con gente
> che non sorride! (1970: 349)

> Be careful, boy!
> I say to him, stopping
> him in his tracks,
> it dangerous to make fun
> of people
> who do not smile!

At the end of his life, Onofrio Tesoriero summed up his migrant's experience in his Sicilian dialect of Panarea:

> Viegnu d'unni d'esta' si vesti di pannu,
> d'unni dicembri è esta'e giugnu inviernu,
> d'unni poccu progressu fannu la genti di sennu,
> e l'ignuranti gran furtuna fannu. (349)

> Vengo da dove d'estate ci si veste di panno,
> dove dicembre è estate e giugno inverno,
> dove poco progresso fa la gente di senno,
> e gl'ignoranti gran fortuna fanno.

> I come from where people wear wool in summer
> where summer is in December and June is winter
> where wise people make little progress
> and the ignorant prosper.

Of course the poet Enoe Di Stefano will use her impeccable Italian to address the senator from Rome:

> Ma Senatore,
> le sue parole vuote
> adatte su misura
> ad un pubblico ingenuo
> e domani già scordate,
> permetta che le chieda
> a cosa servono?
> Ha mai capito
> per un breve istante
> cosa significa
> essere emigrante?
> Ed il successo
> oggi vantato
> riesce a immaginar
> quanto è costato? (63)

> But Senator
> your empty words
> tailor-made
> for a naive audience
> and forgotten tomorrow
> allow me to ask
> what are they for?
> Have you ever understood
> even for a fleeting moment
> what it means
> to be a migrant?
> And today's
> hailed success,
> can you imagine
> the cost?

She also asks Australia for forgiveness. Di Stefano is a Triestine unable to belong entirely, and Italian is perhaps the best language she knows to implore for understanding and peace:

> Io non t'appartengo interamente,
> questo è il male,
> che se potessi esser figlia vera
> tu madre saresti uguale. (65)

> I do not fully belong to you
> that is the problem,
> if I could be a true daughter
> you would be true mother.

On the other hand, if Mariano Coreno is able to say:

> Australia
> giovane terra sorridente
> dalle acque circondata
> mi ascolti?
> Ho spezzato il mio cuore
> per saperti, per conoscere
> il sangue delle tue vene,
> per attingere nuove rose
> dai giardini della tua poesia (355).

> Australia
> young smiling land
> surrounded by water
> are you listening?
> I have broken my heart
> trying to understand you,
> to know the blood in your veins,
> to pluck new roses
> from the gardens of your poetry.

It is natural and appropriate that the dialogue with the Australian mother will continue in English. Indeed Mariano Coreno writes in both languages. Unfortunately some Italo-Australian authors in search of a larger number of readers, yield to the lure of the market and force themselves to write in English on marketable themes. The result is most unsatisfactory from every point of view. Standard Italian is also used to reject any compromise with the new country. For example Gino Nibbi said that in thirty-five years he had been unable to accept anything Australian. He remains an outsider who illustrates the degeneration of Italian and European traditions in the new country. It is not surprising that he also rejects all migrants, their dialects and their *lingua mista*.

A few Italo-Australians are fully committed to giving a human and artistic dimension to the struggle against the iniquities endured by minority groups in Australia. These writers give a voice to the victims of inept administrative or political decisions that relegate them to an inferior social status with no room for redemption. These writers make use of the full linguistic spectrum available to them, from language to dialect, to Australitalian. Two of them, have received The New South Wales State Literary Award, one of the most prestigious Autralian literary prizes (Rosa Cappiello in 1985 and Giovanni Andreoni in 1990).

I wish to conclude with a passage from Rosa Cappiello's *Paese Fortunato* which needs no explanation:

> Scoprii che c'erano inferni diversi: uno per ragazze sole, uno per giovani soli, uno per donne sposate, uno per i figli. Assommandoli, formavano un unico inferno prefabbricato, quello degli emigranti. E che il vento spirava un fiato pietrificato dalle comunità etniche. Come nuovo membro, ero irremovibile. Ci sputavo sopra, in quanto non stirpe o elemento compositivo che significa razza o costume, bensì pretesa di creare piccoli universi separati e nemici tra loro. Non volevo, nè dovevo sacrificarmi (1981: 10).

> I found out there were different hells: one for single women, one for single guys, one for married women, one for children. Together they added up to a single prefabricated hell — the migrant's inferno. The atrophied breath of the ethnic communities was wafted to me on the wind. As a new member I adamantly refused to have anything to do with it. I spat on it since, rather than being a

cohesive basis for race and tradition, it served as a pretext for the creation of separate inimical little universes. I would not, must not, sacrifice my individuality (Cappiello 1984: 4).

Notes

1. Unless otherwise indicated the translations of the citations in Italian and/or dialect are mine.
2. This is an oral statement made at the Australia/OECD Conference on Education and Cultural and Linguistic Pluralism held in Sydney on March 20, 1991.

References

Buttitta, I. "Lingua e dialettu." *Le parole di legno*. Milano: Mondadori, 1984.

Cappiello, R. *Paese fortunato*. Milano: Feltrinelli, 1981.

————. *Oh Lucky Country*. Trans. and with an introduction by G. Rando. St. Lucia: Queensland University Press, 1984.

Comin, A.. "Appunti sull'Austalitaliano." *Quaderni dell'Ístituto Italiano di Cultura*. Melbourne, 1971.

Coreno, M. "Australia." *Il Veltro*, 1973, 355.

Cinotta, Vincenzo, ed. *Italo-Australian Poetry in the 80's*. Wollongong, Department of European Languages: University of Wollongong, 1989.

De Luca, G. "Dici lu ngrisi," "Il monito." In *Il Veltro*, 1973, 344, 346.

Di Stefano, E. "Discorso vuoto," "Australia." In Cinotta, 63, 65.

Genovesi, P. "Appunti sulla letteratura italo-australiana." In Rando 1983, 301-305.

McCormick, C.A. "Su alcuni scrittori italiani in Australia." *IL Veltro*, 1973, 299-308.

Strano, L. "Rimpatrio." *Mostratemi la via di gire al monte*. Auckland: The University, 1970.

————. "U pappu a l'Australia." *Il Veltro*, 1973, p. 351.

Tesoriero, O. "Stornello." *Il Veltro*, 1973, p. 349.

Webster, N. "Preface." *American Dictionary of the English Language*, 1828. London and New York: Johnson Reprint Corportauion 1970, n. pag.

Wilde, W.H., Hooton, J., Andrews, B. "Carboni Raffaello." *The Oxford Companion to Australian Literature*. Melbourne, 1985, 143-144.

Zuliani, B. "Italiese in Australia." Sydney: N.S.W. Department of Education, 1978.

15

Gino Chiellino

Italian Literature in Germany from 1964 to Today [1]

I

$\mathcal{T}$he essential information regarding literature by Italian authors in Germany can be synthesized into two fundamental observations:

a) not all of those authors who write as immigrants necessarily place emigration at the centre of their thematic attention. If Immacolata Amodeo, Carmine Abate, Franco Biondi, Giuseppe Fiorenza dill'Elba, Lisa Mazzi-Spiegelberg, Fruttuoso Piccolo and myself do so, Giuseppe Giambusso and Gaetano Martorino do not do so exclusively, and Antonio Belgiorno, Salvatore A. Sanna and Franco Sepe do so even less;

b) this literature began and is developing bilingually in a twofold manner. That is:

i) some of its authors, as, for example, Carmine Abate, Anotonio Belgiorno, Giuseppe Fiorenza dill'Elba, Giuseppe Giambusso, Maurizio Libbi and Salvatore A. Sanna, write only in Italian, whereas others, such as Immacolata Amodeo, Franco Biondi, Lisa Mazzi-Spiegelberg, Fruttuoso Piccolo and myself, starting with the third collection of poems, write only in German;

ii) of those who write only in Italian, some have been published in bilingual editions, as in the case of the poems of Giuseppe Giambusso, Salvatore A. Sanna, and Fruttuoso Piccolo, whereas others are published directly in German, as is the case with *Den Koffer und Weg!*

by Carmine Abate, and with some of the stories of Giuseppe Fiorenza dill'Elba.

Initiating the literature by Italian writers in Germany places emigration at the top of its concerns, was Gianni Bertagnoli, with the publication of his volume *Arrivederci Deutschland!*, released in German in Stuttgart in 1964 in the Franckh Reihe 20 series. [2]

A beginning of modest aesthetic dimensions but one which, when reconsidered almost thirty years after its publication, does reserve some surprises. Already the story that Bertagnoli's book narrates presents the mixture of desire and contradiction typical of newly arrived immigrants[3], and touches on themes which starting from the second half of the 1970s have become fundamental — both for the literature of Italian writers in Germany and for the so-called *Gastarbeiterliteratur* [4] in its most general aspects.

Arrivederci, Deutschland! is certainly not just a first novel, as the publisher would have us believe when, on the back of the book, he informs the reader that Gianni Bertagnoli intends to continue to write other novels; in fact, the book was to remain the only work by the author. *Arrivederci, Deutschland!* is something between a chrono-history with strongly autobiographical lines and a literary account of the world of workers — a tendency as common in the Italian literature of the 1960s as it was in the German.

In *Arrivederci, Deutschland!* the author meticulously reconstructed such events as the hiring, through the German Commission of Verona, [5] of Rino Sorresini, who is to work as a labourer for a building company in Poldorf — a small town in the south of Germany; Sorresini's voyage from Verona to Poldorf together with a contingent of peasants and artisans from the south of Italy, who, like him, are going to work in Germany; and the first 540 days of the protagonist in Poldorf, which almost at the end of the story, cause him to remark on the "[m]any days in which he had put deep roots in another country" (177).

Among the themes of *Gastarbeiterliteratur* anticipated by Gianni Bertagnoli's book one can list, for example, the impossibility of the return; emigration as a way for women to attain emancipation; and the search for a new territory viewed as a solution to the crisis of nationality. These basic themes, synthesized by metaphors refering to "cages" or "bridges," were subsequently to be enlarged upon by other foreign authors. Such a continuity was possible, not because *Arrivederci, Deutschland!* was adopted as a model, but because it described a commonality of experience found within the world of emigration which has imposed the themes already mentioned, as well as the tendency to the social realism noticeable in Italian authors working in Germany.

Arrivederci, Deutschland! should be taken for what it is: a continuous burst of euphoria for the New, for the Different, but which little by little leads to conclusions that today, many years after the fact — and precisely because we find ourselves so distant from the magic feeling of the first arrival — are surprisingly naive. Here is one passage that illustrates this emblematically:

> [L]a cosa più bella erano i cinque minuti di treno dopo il turno di notte. Incredibile quanta gente andava su e giù. Treno dopo treno pieni di gente normale che si recava al lavoro di tutti i giorni. Impiegati, lavoratori, scolari e studenti. Un viavai da capogiro. Le particelle dell'economia tedesca. Gente che andava e veniva, che studiava e lavorava. Ecco la Germania. La Germania della sette del mattino (128).

> [T]he most beautiful thing was the five minutes on the train after the night shift. Incredible how many people went up and down. Train after train full of normal people that were going to work every day. Clerks, workers, schoolchildren and students. A coming and going that made you dizzy. The particles of the German economy. People that came and went, that studied and worked. Here is Germany, the Germany of seven o'clock in the morning, the true Germany.

At the start of the 1960s, the author was definitely not in a position to offer or develop general models through which to grasp what was new in the migratory flux which by the end of the 1950s, had carried the first millions of peasants and artisans from the fields and the workshops of the South to the shipyards and the factories in the North of Europe. And it would be unjust to demand from Gianni Bertagnoli the sort of analysis and research that was to surface in the literature of authors only during the 1970s.

Nevertheless, the reflections of a socio-political nature with which the protagonist attempts to explain to himself and to the reader the causes of emigration remain unacceptable. Not because they show themselves to be at odds with the immediacy of the experience of the author/protagonist, but because they are nurtured by the same attitude of political non-commitment that pervades the rest of the narrative.

For instance, at a certain point we run into the following passage:

> Era ritornato da un paese che era molto diverso da quello che si trovava davanti. Le cose gli saltavano agli occhi come le scintille sotto il martello del fabbro. C'era qualcosa di marcio in Italia. Ma il marcio non era nei ceti dirigenti del paese, era in tutti i ceti sociali, dai più poveri ai più ricchi. per una tale situazione non c'erano altri responsabili che gli Italiani stessi, e cioè tutti (178).

> He had returned from a country that was very different from the one he found before him. Things jumped to his eyes like sparks from under the blacksmith's hammer. There was something rotten in Italy. But the decay was not in the ruling classes of the country, it was in all the classes, from the poorest to the richest. For such a situation no one was responsible but the Italians themselves — all of them.

Read against the grain, the entire story itself — as is hinted by the title *Arrivederci, Deutschland!* — can be seen as a kind of admonition against impossible hopes and desires. Paramount among these is the long-standing one: the desire to return to the country of origin after having acquired, through emigration, the financial means required to change one's own socio-economic status. As it happens, Gianni Bertagnoli's protagonist returns to his native Verona only to discover that life there no longer makes any sense to him, since the love of his life, Gabriella de Vita, who pushed him to emigrate in the first place, is now a happily married mother. In the end, the author doesn't exclude that his character might give emigration a second try. During his very bried stay in Verona, Rino Sorresini meets a friend with whom he had emigrated and had shared the first six months of emigration in Poldorf. The friend, Sergio, while an immigrant, had learned to write and to do arithmetic. Egged on by the determination to go back to Italy with money, he opened a business selling oranges — and, judging by his elegant manner of dressing, his business had gone very well.

The return, or rather the impossibility of returning, is in effect one of the most diffuse themes in the literature of emigration, and should be linked directly to the other pole of the discussion, which has to do with identity. Franco Biondi's short story *Il ritorno di Passavanti* — published for the first time in Italian in 1976, and republished in German in his first collection of short stories entitled *Passavantis Rückkehr* (*The Return of Passavanti*) — establishes such a link right away. It is with Biondi's first collection of stories that Italian literature in Germany reaches literary levels worthy of respect, not only for the intensity and completeness of analysis with which life in emigration is presented, but also for the presence of a critical realism which gives the author a very specific literary allure.

The return of Passavanti to his home town, a place somewhere in Romagna, and therefore like Verona in an area of prosperity and low unemployment, doesn't produce the effect expected by the protagonist. This is not because there have been any changes. Rather, emigrating has sharpened the protagonist's perceptions of socio-political relations, and now won't permit him to participate in those corrupt games of petty local political power simply to enjoy his right to work — although this right is solemnly guaranteed by Article One of the Italian Constitution, which still declares that "Italy is a democratic republic, founded upon work."

The decision to return to Germany is taken with the awareness that a return, whether to Germany or to Italy, can never be transformed into a lifestyle. And it is exactly the last sequences of the story which suggest this oscillation as a unique kind of option for the first generation of immigrants within Europe:

> Er verspurte einen plotzlichen Hunger und holte sich im Speisewagen ein Mortadellbrotchen und as es am Fenster. Ein Shnellzug mit deutschen Waggons bohrte sich an ihm vorbei. Er erkannte das an der grunen Lackierung (29-30).

> Suddenly he felt hungry, he took out a mortadella sandwich and ate it at the train window. An express with German cars rushed past him. He recognized it from the green colour of the coaches.

On the one hand, the return to Germany is presented with attributes typical of departure, such as hunger, bread and mortadella, and the train window, that symbol of curiosity towards the unknown; on the other hand, the return to Italy finds its expression in the pain of that "rushing by," that in the original German of the passage the verb *Bohren* associates with the German coaches traveling in the opposite direction.

A contradiction and a conflict that even now has not found any solution, neither in Franco Biondi nor in any other Italian author in Germany. The truth is that in real life the immigrants who succeed in resolving this contradiction in the span of a generation are few. It may because an enormous amount of energy psycho-cultural and social reorientation is required of the individual, or because there is the lack of clear proposals or prospects that the host society offers to encourage permanent decisions. Here, then, one remains in midstream. One avoids to chain oneself to one form or another of participation in the daily life of a given place. One is aware that it will not be possible to reconstruct in the new land the lifestyle of the origin. As for the future, what is there to say but that one will continue to travel up and down the typewriter with one's desires.

But Franco Biondi has made great strides with this theme, which is crucial to immigrant literature. He confronts the problem of the future of the younger generations in Germany with flair and resolute force. Mamo, the young protagonist of the novella *Abschied der zerschellten Jahre* (*Goodbye to the Broken Years*), is representative of a generation that, notwithstanding all of its generational difficulties and the problems of integration, did not let itself be entrapped by a static vision of its development. Nor did it let itself be blocked by the impossibility of achieving a synthesis of the values of its society of origin with the models of life in Germany today. Mamo knows very well that if Germany is not a *Heimat* (homeland) for him, it will still always be the only country where he wants to live. This conflict explodes in the most violent fashion. It is at this juncture that the author chooses to end his novel: Mamo is barricaded in his house, armed with an automatic rifle, awaiting the assault of a squadron of police who must execute the expulsion order to remove him from the Federal Republic of Germany.

But the transition from the stories that in 1985 were published in a single volume by DTV, under the title *Passavantis Rückkehr,* to the novella *Abschied der zerschellten Jahre* is of particular interest. It is a transition that shows how international the themes of Franco Biondi's work had become. Although the characters of the stories function within substantially bi-national, Italo-German, antinomic relationships (if in the story *Gastarbeiter* immigrants of other nationalities do appear it is only marginally) in the novella the concept of nationality is completely left behind. This is partly due to the author's formal refusal to define the nationality of Mamo, partly due too to the world that these nationalities represent, which is now the cross-section of a society made up to a much larger degree of non-Germans. The society described moves towards a multicultural normality, which is the normality denied to Mamo and for which he is prepared to sacrifice himself, by becoming a symbol of the impossible return to the circumstances that created his father. As Mamo waits for the police to attack, he thinks of his father for the last time. In doing so, Mamo informs the reader that his father "war halt ein braver Gastarbeiter!" ("was a good immigrant") (141). The phrase is filled with ambivalence and irony. It sounds like a condemnation of an entire generation, of those individuals who could not, or would not, go beyond mere being or having to be "good," and who therefore avoided, or were unable, to carry out the choices inherent to emigration — a passivity and an evasiveness that weighed tragically on following generations.

Another element that underlines the passage from the bi-national and antinomic relation to a multicultural vision of the world of emigration and a future society in Germany is without doubt the carefully chosen language of the author. This moves from a phase of strict social realism (the short stories) — where it attempted to document as accurately as possible a reality rejected by the receiving society but also, in a large part, by the generation that had to bear it — to a language that in the novella has as its goal the loosening of the German language from its egocentric purism. Denying the German language its own centrality, Franco Biondi breaks it down into a large number of linguistic segments which correspond to the diverse social strata and generations often so resistant to one another. It is enough to read attentively the language of Mamo, or that of the dreams of the old Costas, or that of the author, which serves to depict the situation of the youths at the beginning of the 1980s, to appreciate how literary these pieces are, to realize that they are as valid as any created by contemporary German writers.

In a first book entitled *Der Kern und die Schale* (*The Pit and the Peel*), which borrows its title from a book by H. Abraham, *L'écorce et le noyau*, Lisa Mazzi-Spiegelberg sketches out five portraits of Italian women in Germany: Aurora, the young Italian woman still in love with her German partner; Vera, the intellectual daughter who has emigrated in order not to have to perpetuate the role of her authoritative mother; Marta, who ends up being the Mediterranean mother on the North Sea coast; the feminist and homosexual Graziella; and, the actress, Rebecca, who is afraid to accept a job in Italy. Lisa Mazzi-Spiegelberg confers on emigration a different dimension by perceiving it as a potential means of emancipation for women. This concept, already present in Italian literature abroad, as in the play *Addolorata* by the Italian-Canadian writer Marco Micone, was in Germany partially anticipated by Gianni Bertagnoli, in whose work the emigration of women with respect to the of men was described as being motivated by essentially different reasons. In *Arrivederci, Deutschland!*, the only female Italian emigrant, a young Florentine woman who is saved from the clutches of the hoodlums of Poldorf by Rino Sorresini, explains her presence in Germany in the following manner:

> Ĭch hatte eine Auseindersetzung mit meinen Altern. deshalb bin ich hierhergefahren. Ich wollte auf meine Art leben (101).

> I had some fights with my parents and that's why I came here — to live as I like.

For her own part, Lisa Mazzi-Spiegelberg begins Vera's monological self-portrait with this reflection:

> Mein Elternhaus und die Kleinstadt ein Spinnegewebe der Intrige, eine standige wachsame Anwesenheit, immer da, um mich wieder aufzufangen, wenn ich meinen eigenen Schriftenfolgen wollte (23).

> The paternal home and the small town: a spider's web of intrigues, a continuous and attentive presence, always there to block me, always ready to follow me around each time I was there.

However, to avoid any misunderstandings, it must immediately be specified that neither Lisa Mazzi-Spiegelberg nor the other foreign female writers that express themselves on the same theme, such as the Turkish writers Aysel Özakin or Zera Cirak, consider Germany itself to be the place of their emancipation. Freedom, instead, comes from the anonymity in which foreigners are compelled to live. It allows the women to liberate themselves from the role gender assigns to them, since in the anomie of emigration, of the new society any form of immediate control from the society of origin collapses, or is estranged.

It is Graziella who, having come to Germany for her love of Detlef, exploits to the maximum the collapse of social control and discovers herself in a liberating position of homosexual love and social commitment as a teacher of children of immigrants.

The stories of the five Italian women in Germany stand out both for the experiences they convey and for the structures of the individual portraits. They develop along the lines of an invented narration/interview and monologue/self-portrait, like a variation on an essential motif: the will to arrive at a new identity, one already partially reached, but continually threatened by the impossibility of a synthesis between the two poles of life:

> warum darf man nicht beides mischen? Warum gelingt es mir nicht, hier un dorf zufrieden sein? Warum bleibt diese ewige Sehnsucht? (69)

> [...] why not mix the two sides, why can I not be happy here and there?

Among the reasons why such a desire cannot be fulfilled I can here only note that, until now, the problem of identity inherent in *Ausländerliteratur* (foreigner's literature) has been put forth in a static manner. That is, it has been seen as a synthesis of elements that already exist, and rarely (as in Franco Biondi) as something that might build on the experiences undergone within the new society and which, therefore, might alter, in some form, the initial point of departure. In Lisa Mazzi-Spiegelberg another mechanism intervenes to block her capacity to analyze. The story reaches intense tones of pathos and lucidity when it lingers on experiences lived in well-known surroundings; for example, the protagonist Vera reflects on her mother's state of mind, herself threatened and devastated by the fact that her daughter has a lover:

Die Tochter wird zur Geliebten. Die Keuscheit der Mutter, jahrlang bewart und verteidigt, ist verschandet. Die Geliebte wird fur sie zur Hure (25).

The daughter that becomes a lover. The virginity of the mother, watched over and protected for years, is marred. For her, a lover is a prostitute.

As forcefully described is the passage of Graziella from the failed heterosexual relationship with Detlef to the homosexual one with Dora. The analysis, however, fails and results in stereotypes when it involves the formulation of desires, expectations or prospects with which to orient oneself in the new society. A typical example is, as always, the description of the German surroundings furnished by a Graziella completely disillusioned with Detlef:

Ich stand da un hatte ein ganz anderes Bild von deutscher Wirklihkeit vor den Augen. Ein Mann, ein Fernseher, zwei Schnitten und ain Bier. Detlef braucht nichts mehr (50).

I was there with another image of the German reality in front of my eyes. A husband, a television, two pieces of bread and a beer.

Or in the softer version of Graziella's friend:

Im Schlafzimmer finde ich einen zarten Blumenstrauss. Meinen Begurstag hat er nicht vergessen. Ich gehe zufrieden ins Bett (57).

In the bedroom I find a bunch of delicate flowers. My birthday, that he hadn't forgotten.

There is recourse to stereotypes certainly not because the writer is unable to perceive the German reality in its true colour, but because of a censorship mechanism of a moralizing and social nature very widespread among foreign writers in Germany. Until now such moralizing self-censure has prevented any resolution of all those contradictions congenital to the opposition of eroticism and exoticism. A good portion of the disappointment experienced by Graziella vis-à-vis Detlef's behaviour can be brought back to this dichotomy. As can the disillusion temporarily repressed by the character who finds "a bunch of delicate flowers instead of a loving husband" in the bedroom the evening before her birthday. Graziella's friend feels rewarded for the inattention of her husband, interpreting as a private and individual gesture that which in Germany happens with the mechanical accuracy of a rite imposed by the calendar: the punctual celebration of birthdays punctually with gifts.

In its social nature this mechanism of self-censure seems to compel all foreigners to describe Germany as a state of permanent fog, even on the rare occasions that the sun shines; and it prompts them to call all Germans Kunze or Müller, even when they are named Fried or Kühnert. This taking shelter in stereotypes, when one might instead be occupying oneself with German reality is, in my opinion, to be explained only as a strange form of self-protection. It is a reaction to the fear of being affected, almost seduced, by the knowledge of a different environment, one interesting and rich with stimuli and that could pose a threat to one's own cultural and national identity. Nevertheless, the same recourse to stereotypes also hides an apprehension about the formulation of one's own desires, expectations and demands, hence the fear of being considered troublesome, too conspicuous, seen in a bad light, or of being disappointed. These misgivings stem from German society's own incapacity to resolve the basic contradiction of its politics with regard to foreigners. Non-Germans workers have been a presence on German soil for the past thirty years, yet they are still unexpected guests, as it were.

In order to emerge from this deadlock, some authors, among which are Vito d'Adamo and Giuseppe Fiorenza dill'Elba, have attempted to envision the future of Germany within a unified Europe, within a new cultural and socio-political dimension which would guarantee to immigrants social security and cultural development beyond national barriers. It is in this sense that Vito d'Adamo's *Inno allo Schwarzwald* (*Anthem to the Black Forest*) is to be understood. It ends with an invocation to the Black Forest:

mia seconda Terra
in quest'unica Patria europea (51).

my second Land

315

in this one European Homeland.

However, even for the rare authors well-disposed towards a united Europe, it is very difficult to establish concretely how a united Europe could contribute to the solution of those everyday conflicts with which the protagonists of Lisa Mazzi-Spiegelberg are grappling. Unsatisfactory, too, is the proposal of Frut-tuoso Piccolo's latest book, *Durch die Sprache ein ander(es) Ich* (Through Language Another I), subtitled *Beziehung* ("Report"), even if it provides re-markable glimpses of solidarity at different levels: as, for example, between man and woman in the section entitled "Liebe aus der Ferne" ("Distant Love"), or between the various minorities present in Germany, in the sections entitled "der Wanderung" ("Emigrant Echo") and "Tempo Gastarbeiter" ("Immigrant Speed"), or in the clear aesthetic intuition that nationalism is incapable of producing poetry.

But even this book doesn't go beyond insistence on the solidarity of subordinate groups, which — Piccolo suggests — should transfer their unity from the world of work to that of German society. This is what the poem "Uber Grenzen" ("Beyond the Boundaries") proposes:

> Zusammenleben
> Zwischen
> Auslandern und Deutschen
> Folklore
> Ohne Charme
> Auslanderfeindlichkeit
> Gegen die Burokratisierung der Gesellschaft
> Die Sonne scheint (1987: 103).

> To live together
> between
> foreigners and Germans
> Folklore
> without Charm
> Xenophobia
> against the bureaucratization of society
> The sun shines.

As indicated, the failure of Italian literature in Germany to proceed beyond simple expressions of will can be attributed to the fact that the function of the foreign communities in Germany has not yet been clarified. Must these communities atrophy in small pockets of cultural well-being scattered about strongly folkloristic outlines, or will they assert themselves as socio-cultural enclaves with a guaranteed future?

The search for a non-trivial answer to this dilemma marks the passage from the first to the second phase of Italian literature in Germany, or, for that matter, of *Ausländerliteratur* in general. In this second phase, individual works will no longer be created in reaction to an intolerable situation of stasis, but will be parts of a plan to envisage a future within emigration. That such a search will not only be a search for new contents but also a search for aesthetic forms more pertinent to life in emigration should make this literature more interesting than it has been.

II

Among those writers for whom writing in emigration is not restricted to the theme of emigration, we find Giuseppe Giambusso. He actually places himself at the point of transition between two literary phases. His volumes of poetry, *Al di là dell'orizzonte/Jenseits des Horizontes* (*Beyond the Horizon*) and *Partenze/Abfahrten* (*Departures*), published in bilingual editions, explore the most diverse aspects of emigration. In two chapters of the first collection we encounter the theme of emigration, while the other three deal with the more general themes of peace and militarism and the loss of sensitivity towards one's surroundings.

Giambusso's position can be discerned by looking at the aesthetic models he adopts in his first collection. For the immediacy of its images and message, his poetry may be associated with the politically committed Italian poetry of the 1960s, and therefore to poetry that has not given up its social role (an example is the work of Ignazio Buttitta). The difference with Italy is that the multiculturalism brought about by emigration has obliged Giuseppe Giambusso to confront the problem of the relation between cultural and aesthetic boundaries. He is aware that the act of sidestepping the limits of one's own national culture and literature — which, however democratic a nation may be, always remain tied to the roles and visions a nation has of its culture and literature — necessarily requires an enlarged perception of culture and of inherited aesthetic models. This is the "dream" his poem "L'Aurora" depicts:

Tu sei stata soltanto l'aurora
dell'amore che ora cresco
come se fosse un bimbo.

Ma i miei sogni muoiono sempre
dove il cielo si confonde con il mare
come l'aurora dove si alza (1985: 88).

You were only the dawn
of the love that now I raise
as though it were a child.

But my dreams always die
where the sky blends with the sea
like the dawn when it breaks.

In this context one should be able to determine to what extent Giambusso refrains from alluding to non-Italian poets who, through their strong ties to their respective cultural traditions, have succeeded in breaking away from a nationalistic vision of literature and have imposed themselves as authors without boundaries. Among such poets are Nazim Hikmet and Pablo Neruda, who often make their way into many of Giambusso's poems, including "L'Aurora." The "dawn" of that poem represents the continuous revival of the great "dream" of the beyond, of moving past a "horizon" built on the interests and prejudices of the social classes and protected by national borders.

Another author deserving consideration is Franco Antonio Belgiorno. Save for *Quaderno tedesco* (*German Notebook*), which appeared in Modica in 1974 and contains twenty seven poems, he has never published a book-length collection. The theme of emigration presented with immediacy in the early poems of Belgiorno returns in the unpublished notebooks, *Quaderno di Ulisse: Liriche 1977/78* (*Ulysses' Notebook: Poetry 1977-78)* and *Aspettando la no-*

tizia: Liriche 1978/79 (Waiting for News: Poetry 1978-79), but this initial tendency is nuanced, and never connected to a program of social commitment. If anything his poetry acts as a sort of filter for primarily cultural experiences, as can be noticed in the following poem:

> A volte mi credo
> e non mi credo
> e mi consumo.
> Per dirla con Pirandello
> sono talvolta uno
> più spesso centomila
> e alla fine nessuno.

> By turns I believe in myself
> and I don't believe in myself
> and I exhaust myself.
> To say it as did Pirandello
> I am at times one
> more often one hundred thousand
> and in the end no one. (Unpublished manuscript)

The emigrants' definition of themselves, the search for their identity, the re-acquisition of trust in themselves: once these have been catapulted outside the codified forms of the solidarity of collective experience — codes which for centuries held together the small mountain and coastal communities of the Mediterranean — they become transformed by Franco Antonio Belgiorno in terms of absolute existentialism. Of this aspect, the line "I consume myself," which concludes the first part of the poem quoted above, is a most deeply felt expression. The Pirandellian paradigm, whereby each person is "one, no one and one hundred thousand," could fittingly convey those dire experiences of emigration which bring "one" to surpass the being "no one" of anonymity and to become "one hundred thousand" through identification with the community of fellow emigrants. But the overturning of the paradigm of "one, no one and one hundred thousand" into the "one, one hundred thousand and no one," as proposed by Franco Antonio Belgiorno, reconfirms the existential mistrust already announced by the "I consume myself" of the first part of the poem as well as the final "no one" with which the same poem ends.

If it is easy to object that such a position doesn't help emigration, it nevertheless should not be interpreted as being purely self-destructive. Belgiorno is motivated by the desire to minutely document the high price paid by emigrants who must move from one place to another in order to ensure themselves a stable existence, no matter how minimal a foundation they may find. Approached from this standpoint, Belgiorno's work has a positive purpose.

Gaetano Martorino's poetry seems to be moving in the opposite direction. To a large extent Martorino's poetry exists only in manuscript form (only a handful have been published in journals) and it is no surprise that it revolves around the themes of silence and solitude. In this the poems are aided and abetted by emigration. Yet the poems are never quite reducible to that experience alone: Martorino expressly avoids symbols which could codify his work as immigrant poems. Emblematic of Martorino's position is the following text:

Da quando le parole
mi tacciono non ho più senso
per te e tu non mi ritrovi
più nel mio silenzio.
Sono qui.
Anche quando l'eco
non ti riporta
più parola
non sono forse io la voce
che ti parla
e tace…? Io sono quella voce.
Io sono anche il sogno
che tu vivi
anche se
è difficile capirlo. (Unpublished manuscript)

Since words
have been silencing me I make no more sense

for you and you don't find me
any more
in my silence.
I am here.
Even when the echo
doesn't bring you back
words anymore
am I not the voice
that speaks to you
and is quiet...? I am that voice.
I am also the dream
that you live
even if
it is difficult to understand.

Silence or solitude, however, are not used to express the usual extremes of our mass-media societies' incapacity to communicate. They are options intended as new forms of language that go beyond words, that nourish themselves with life lived, as is confirmed in the "I am here" of the speaker, who is silenced by words and therefore sees himself/herself isolated by another person incapable of accepting him/her in his/her silence. A silence which has already found a new voice without sound, as dreams are without sound, in "I am also the dream/that you live." The "I" replaces the voice in the answer to the question: "am I not the voice/that speaks to you/and is quiet...?"

And what poet could deny himself or herself the chance to be a voice, be it only a tiny presence in a time in which many yearn to be liberated from solitude and silence? What could be more fundamental than those elements of language and of poetry which are born in solitude and feed on silence?

The farthest confines of the literature of Italian authors in Germany are occupied by the collections of Salvatore A. Sanna entitled *Fünfzehn Jahre Augenblicke*, *Wachholderblüten*, *Löwen-Maul*, *Feste*. For three reasons:

1. the direct references of his poetry to metropolitan literature (it was Sanna who defined his poems "de-centred literature," that is, a literature created in full autonomy and far from the centre);

2. the absence of a recognizble single topic in the poems (the themes that the poems work with are many and varied);

3. the distance of the poems from the burden of immediate social commitment common to the rest of Italian writers in Germany.

If in Sanna's collections it is easy to find the presence of towns and landscapes, these images never coalesce in a central thematic gist — as might have occurred were Sanna to write *Naturlyrik* halfway between Eugenio Montale and the contemporary German author Karl Krolow. What interests the author most is not so much the experience of facing a new town or new landscape, as much as the aesthetic stimulus they carry with them. It is here that the poems of Salvatore A. Sanna originate. His is a search for the aesthetic awakening of the person in experience. Even when dealing with the most simple element, he is careful not to let the experience degenerate into outright aestheticism.

Indeed, while one immediately notices a strong impulse towards aesthetic inquiry, this is kept in balance by a parallel work on language, which is sharpened to the maximum of lexical and syntactic simplicity, so that minimal images of an explosive expressiveness may surge forth. The "houses" of Sanna's "Liscia di Vacca" have something of this power:

> Case
> sospese
> dal vento
> sulle rocce
> di granito (1984: 22).

> Houses
> suspended
> by the wind
> on rocks
> of granite.

This continuous attention to the aesthetic implications of the perception of the everyday finds its *raison d'être* in the following verse:

Anche il sublime
diventa quotidiano
e di sè allora
riacutizza il desiderio (1984: 68).

Even the sublime
becomes quotidian
and of itself then
makes desire acute again.

Sanna's technique summarizes the kernel of his aesthetic quest, which consists in a reconstruction *à rebours* of the decline of the sublime into the quotidian, or, to put it differently, in an attempt to safeguard the desire for the sublime, as the last possible escape from routine sensations. The routinization of everyday life has reached such levels, according to Sanna, that it has annulled the tension once associated with what was once located beyond the limits (sublimes) of human experience. For this reason, the attention with which Salvatore A. Sanna dwells on the aesthetic features of daily life is above all an exercise in retrieval, the salvaging of forms of sensitivity lost in a society completely immersed in the prose of everyday affairs.

In rereading the poem which begins with the lines: "Dalla sensibilità delle tue antenne/riconosci la potenza del trasmettitore" ("By the sensitivity of your antennae/you recognize the power of the transmitter") — where the quest for the aesthetic is turned into a means for apprehending the culturally foreign or diverse — one is further led to think that Sanna is attempting to utilize his aesthetic forays in ordinary life as an epistemological strategy, as a kind of probing into an unknown and foreign environment.

Finally, a totally separate position, in this brief survey, should be assigned to the documentarist Giuseppe Fiorenza dill'Elba. A strong-willed, self-taught writer, Fiorenza dill'Elba is known among the Italian writers in Germany for the perseverance with which he has been working for more than thirty years on the reconstruction of a social microscosm composed of bits of village life dating back to the time of fascism, emigration and the economic miracle, of work in factories, of life in company lodgings, of free time spent at home, of long voyages between Sicily and Germany, and of telephone calls which are always too short if compared to the need to learn about a community and to be part of it.

His collections of poems, among which one might wish to single out *La chiamerei Anna* (*I Would Call Her Anna*), his very numerous short stories, and the autobiographical novel, *Adernò, la Roma della mia infanzia* (*Adernò, the Rome of My Childhood*), are always reconstructions of moments lived at the edge of civilized society. They are, in short, representations of the world of the working class. Fiorenza dill'Erba, however, always claims for these moments the dignity and the right to be fully lived. Depictions that at the opening of each of his pieces announce themselves as anecdotes are transformed during their unfolding into microcosms of many interests, in contrast to the penchant of the author to argue and devote himself to logic and to the rationalization of the accidental. His will to explain, to clarify for himself and for others the most obvious facts, have led him to embark on an activity parallel to writing. Dill'Elba has compiled enormous collections of documented memorabilia, among which are all the electoral notices that have reached him in the most diverse places of his thirty years in emigration, letters and postcards sent to him by colleagues at work each time they traveled somewhere, photos of every political, cultural and private event in which he was able to participate, newspaper clippings, and travel tickets. Since dill'Elba's return home in pre-retirement, all of these things have become his own private emigration museum, almost as though he wished to know himself in harmony with the past. Having assembled this material with the greatest possible integrity, he is able to view it all at once, now that the end of the experience of emigration allows him to choose where he will live and how he will spend his time — a choice always contested to him during a lifetime of work.

Translated by Alison Turner

Notes

1. This essay was written during the transition to a unified Germany. In this period the murders of immigrants in Mölln and Solingen even destroyed the hopes of the sceptics, those who had envisioned the process of reunification as the way by which to attain socio-political equality for foreigners. Nevertheless, for the writers discussed in this essay, forever accustomed to examining a daily reality of veiled xenophobia, the problem is how to identify causes and not to engage in the sensationalism by exploiting images of burning houses or of the candlelight vigils, as instead did both the German and the international mass media. The events in the cities of Mölln and Solingen prove that the resistance which characterizes the works of foreign writers have encountered is not due to the inability of the writers to adapt to the "other." These events constitute, rather, a denunciation of the socio-cultural insensibility of German society with respect to the "other." That Mölln and Solingen and the reunification have had an impact on the literature of foreign writers is beyond doubt, but in order to be able to see how much of an impact we will have to wait for the publication of new works. I'm afraid that it will be a long wait, since German publishers prefer to publish what German authors write about foreigners and not what foreigners write about their situation and the general state of the German Republic.

2. As is the case with other minority literature, German literary criticism avoids speaking about Italian-German literature. This is due firstly to the fact that Italian-German literature is written by first-generation writers who for reasons of personal identity still feel very tied to their culture of origin, even if a few of them use the language of the host country. Secondly, it is due to the fact that in Germany there is no model of socio-cultural integration similar to the Canadian paradigm which allows one to speak of French-Canadians or Italian-Canadians.

3. No longer able to employ the term *Fremdarbeiter*, of obvious Nazi origin, in the 1950s one had recourse to the term *Gastarbeiter*. *Gastarbeiter* does not mean "guest worker" but "temporary worker," one initially recruited for a contract of a determined period, and subject to rotation or repatriation at the expiry of the contract.

4. The term *Gastarbeiterliteratur* was used throughout the 1980s in a provocative tone, to indicate literature written by authors who, through the content of their respective works, directly refer to the ethnic minorities who have been establishing themselves in the Germany since 1955. In recent times, the provocation having subsided, it has become common to speak more generally of *Ausländerliteratur*. In my essay I use *Gastarbeiterliteratur* or *Ausländerliteratur* in a generic sense to indicate a literature written by authors who come from different cultures and speak different languages, and among whom German has become the language of communication.

5. Following the Italian-German bilateral contract (December 1955) on the recruitment of a labour force for the German labour market, the first German Commission for the selection of foreign labour for Germany was established at Verona. During the 1960s, it was followed by Commissions at Athens/Greece, Madrid/Spain, Istanbul/Turkey, Lisbon/Portugal and Belgrade/Yugoslavia, plus the delegations of Morocco and Tunisia. This

notwithstanding, Germany did not commit itself to a general policy regarding immigration. Germany has so far limited itself to governing immigrants on the basis of a law of 1965 concerning the temporary sojourn of foreigners that has since been subject to more reforms, the last of which dates back to 1992. Nonetheless, the only way to approach something akin to equality of rights remains German citizenship. The granting of this, however, is left entirely to the discretion of German authorities, who are obliged to look after the interests of the Republic. It is not granted in accordance with determined conditions which are accessible to every foreigner that lives and works in Germany. Moreover, since German citizenship is not a *jus soli*, those who are born in Germany of foreign parents are themselves treated as foreigners in all respects. Nor has double citizenship been considered for foreigners born in Germany or for those under eighteen years of age, who at present are about two million in number.

References

Abate, Carmine. *Nel labirinto della vita (Poesie)*. Rome: 1977.

———. *Den Koffer und weg!* Kiel, 1994.

Abate, Carmine, ed. *In questa terra altrove. Testi letterari di emigrati italiani in Germania.* Cosenza, 1987.

———. *Il ballo tondo*. Genoa, 1991.

Ackermann, Irmgard/Weinrich, Harald (Hrsg.). *Eine nicht nur deutsche Literatur. Zur Standortbestimmung.* München/Zürich, 1986.

Anonymous. *Gardenie e proletari. Storia di una comune di Francoforte 1968.* Milano, 1979.

Belgiorno, Franco A. *Quaderno tedesco (Poesie)*. Modica, 1974.

———. *Quademo di Ulisse.* Liriche 1977-78. Unpublished manuscript.

———. *Aspettando la notizia.* Liriche 1978-79. Unpublished manuscript.

Bertagnoli, Gianni. *Arrivederci, Deutschland!.* Stuttgart, 1964.

Biondi, Franco. *Isolde e Fernandez. Dramma in 13 quadri.* Poggibonsi, 1978.

———. *Nicht nur Gastarbeiterdeutsch.* Klein Winterheim, 1979.

———. *Passavantis Rückkehr (Racconti).* Fischerhude, 1982.

———. *Die Tarantel (Racconti).* Fischerhude, 1982.

———. *Ein Trattoir entlang der Liebe.* (Cycle of poems from 1983-1984, not yet published).

———. *Abschied der zerschellten Jahre (Novelle).* Kiel, 1984.

———. *Kultur der Ausländer "von den Tränen zu den Bürgerrechten." Sonderdruck des Hessichen VHS-Verbandes.* Frankfurt, 1984.

———. *Passavantia Rückkehr (Racconti in un volume).* München, 1985.

———. *Ritratti oder Wortnisse von Vexierbildersn.* Poems from 1983-1987, unpublished.

———. *Die Unversöhnlichen. Im Labyrinth der Herkunft. Roman.* Tübingen, 1991.

Chiellino, Gino, ed., *Nach dem Gestern/Dopo ieri. Aus dem Alltag italienischer Emigranten.* Südwind zweisprachig. Bremen, 1983.

Chiellino, Gino, *Mein fremders Alltag (Poesie)*. Kiel, 1984.

————. *Literature und Identität in der Fremde. Zur Literature italienischer Autoren in der Bundesrepublik*. Kiel, 1985.

————. *Sehnsucht nach Sprache (Poesie)*. Kiel, 1987.

————. *Die Reise hält an. Ausländische Künstler in der Bundesrepublik*. München, 1988.

————. *Hommage a Augsburg*. With three illustrations by Gjelosh Gjokaj. Augsburg, 1991a.

————. *Equilibri estranei (Poesie)*. Bergamo, 1991b.

————. *Sich die Fremde nehmen (Poesie)*. Kiel, 1992.

————. *Fremde: A Discourse of the Foreign*. Toronto: Guernica, 1995.

d'Adamo, Vito. "Inno allo Schwarzwald." In Romberg and Wunderlich, 51.

Fiorenza dill'Elba, Giuseppe. *La chiamerei Anna (Poesie)*. Poggibonsi, 1981.

————. *Adernò: Roma della mia infanzia (Roman)*. Poggibonsi, 1984.

————. *Fast ein Leben/Quasi una vita (Poesie e racconti It.-Ted.)*. Walter Raitz (Hg.). Rüsselsheim, 1991a.

————. *Un freddo estraneo. Memorie di un emigrato in svizzera*. Cosenza, 1991b.

Frederking, Monika. *Schreiben gegen Vorurteile. Literatur türkischer Migranten in der Bundesrepublik Deutschland*. Berlin, 1985.

Friedrich, Heinz (Hrsg.). *Chamissos Enkel. Zur Literatur von Ausländer in Deutschland*. München, 1986.

Giambusso, Giuseppe, ed. *Wurzeln hier/Radici, qui. Gedichte italienischer Emigranten*. Fröndenberg, 1981 (Bremen, 1982).

Giambusso, Giuseppe, *Al di là dell'orizzonte/Jenseits des Horizontes (Poesie It.-Ted.)*. Bremen, 1985.

————. *Partenze/Ahfahrten*. Cosenza, 1991.

Hamm, Horst. *Fremdgegangen freigeschrieben. Einfürhung in die deutschsprachige Gastarbeiterliteratur*. Wurzburg, 1988.

Heinze, Hartmut. *Migrantenliteratur in der Bundesrepublik Deutschland*. Berlin, 1986.

Hyams, Barry, C./Peter, Helge Ulrike, eds. *Emigrantenbriefe/Lettere di emigrate ai compagni del Mezzogiorno d'Italia*. Marburg, 1974.

LiLi Zeitschrift für Literaturwissenschaft und Linguistik (Hrsg). Kreuzer, Helmut "Gastarbeiterliteratur," H. 56/1984, Göttingen, 1985.

Mura, Antonio. *Lingua e Dialetto (Poesie)*. Nuoro, 1971. Ger. trans.: *Und wir, die klugen Mondmeister*. München, 1981.

Mazzi-Spiegelberg, Lisa. *Der Kern und die Schale (Prosa)*.

Muttersprache (Hg.). GfdS, Bd. 99, Literatur und Sprachalltag Ausländer in Deutschland, Mainz, 1989.

Pasquale, Ciro. *Vagabondaggi in versi (Poesie)*. Poggibonsi, 1981.

Piccolo, Fruttuoso. *1970-1980 Dieci anni fra due mondi (Poesie)*. Hannover, 1980.

————. *Arlecchino "Gastarbeiter" (Poesie und Collagen)*. Hannover, 1985.

————. *Durch Die Sprache ein ander(es)*. Ich. Hanover, 1987.

Polidori, Antonio, ed. *GAST. Antologia di opere di emigrati*. Hüflingen/Baden, 1981.

Reeg, Ulrike. *Schreiben in der Fremde. Literatur nationaler Minderheiten in der Bundesrepublik Deutschland*. Essen, 1988.

Romberg, Alice and Wunderlich M., eds. *Testi di emigrazione*. Bielefeld, 1983, 51.

Sanna, Salvatore A. *Fünfzehn Jahre*. Augenblicke (Poesie It.-Ted.) Frankfurt, 1978.

——. *Wachholdersblüte* (Poesie It.-Ted.). Frankfurt, 1984.

——. *Löwen-Maul (Poesie It.-Ted.)*. Aarau/Frankfurt, 1988.

——. *Feste*. München/Mainz, 1991.

Schierloh, Heimke. *Das alles für ein Stück Brot. Migrantenliteratur als Objektivierung des "Gastarbeiterdaseins."* Frankfurt, 1984.

Sepe, Franco. *Elegiette Berlinesi (Poesie)*. Firenze, 1987.

——. *L'incontro. Commedia in tre atti* (1987) and *Berlinturcomedea. Tragedia in un atto* (1984). With an introduction by Walter Pedulla. *Sipario*, XLV, n. 501, Sept. 1990, 34-40, 41-42.

Weinrich, Harald. "Um eine deutsche Literatur von außen bitten," in: *Merkur*, H. 8/1983. Stuttgart, 1983, 911-920.

——. "Gastarbeiterliteratur in der Bundesrepublik Deutschland," in: *LiLi*, 12-22.

——. "Deutschland — ein türkisches Märchen. Zu Hause in der Fremde. Gastarbeiterliteratur," in *Hage Voker* (Hrsg.) Deutsche Literatur 1983. Ein Jahresüberblick. Stuttgart, 1984, 230-237.

Zeifschrift. "Für Kulturaustausch:... aber die Fremde ist in mir. Migrationserfahrungen und Deutschlandbild in der türkischen Literatur der Gegenwart." (Hg.) Günter W. Lorenz/Yüksel Pazarkaya, 35.Jg. H. 1/1985, Stuttgart, 1985.

Zielke, Andrea. *Standortbestimmung der "gastarbeiter-Literatur" in deutscher Sprache in der bundesdeutschen Literaturszene*. Kasseler Materialien 6 zur Ausländerpädagogik hrsg. von Haller, I./Neuner, G. Kassel, 1985.

List of Contributors

GIOVANNI ANDREONI has lived in New Zealand and Tasmania, besides Italy, where he was born. Since 1974 he has been teaching at the University of New England. His many publications include: *L'australitaliano* (essays and short stories); *Alcuni racconti* (short stories); *Cenere* (novel). In 1990, he was the recipient of the Ethnic Affairs Commission Fellowship of the New South Wales State Literary Awards. His latest novel is *Zucchero*.

WILLIAM BOELHOWER teaches American Studies at the University of Trieste, Italy. He has published numerous articles on ethnic literature and Americana which have appeared in various international journals. A translator of Lucien Goldmann and Antonio Gramsci, he is the author of *Immigrant Autobiography in the United States* (1982) and *Through a Glass Darkly: Ethnic Semiosis in American Literature* (1984). He has edited *The Future of American Modernism: Ethnic Writing Between the Wars* (1990). A collection of essays is scheduled to appear in 1995.

CAROL BONOMO ALBRIGHT is the editor of *Italian Americana*, a semi-annual international journal, published in cooperation with the University of Rhode Island/College of Continuing Education, Providence, RI and the American Italian Historical Association. Her own writing has appeared in *The Dream Book: An Anthology of Writings by Italian American Women* (ed. Helen Barolini); *Voices of the Daughters*; the *Journal of American Ethnic History* and *Melus*. It focuses on generational differences, value systems, and the dynamic aspects of ethnicity as reflected in Italian American and other ethnic literature.

GINO CHIELLINO has degrees in Modern Languages and Literatures from the university of Rome and in German language and culture from the university of Giessen. He has been living in Germany since 1970. His many publications include: *Mein fremder Alltag* (poetry, Kiel, 1984); *Sehnsucht nach Sprache* (poetry, Kiel, 1987); *Literatur und Identitat in der Fremde* (essays, Kiel, 1989); *Die Reise halt an Auslandische Kunstler in der Bundesrepublik* (essays, Munich, 1988). In 1987, he was awarded the Adalbert von Chamisso Poetry Prize by the Munich Academy of Fine Arts. A selection of essays, *Fremde: A Discourse of the Foreign*, was translated by Luise von Flotow and published by Guernica, 1995.

ANTONIO D'ALFONSO is the publisher of Guernica Editions, which he also founded. He is the author of eight books of poetry, one of which, *The Other Shore* (1986), he translated into French as *L'autre rivage* (1989), and of a novel, *Avril ou l'anti-passion* (1990), which he translated into English, *Fabrizio's Passion* (1995). His latest book is a collection of essays, *In Italics: In Defense of Ethnicity* (1996).

329

Social Pluralism and Literary History

SNEJA GUNEW taught for over twenty years at various universities in England, Australia and Canada. She has published widely on multicultural, post-colonial and feminist critical theory. She is currently Professor of English and Women's Studies at the University of British Columbia, Canada. She has recently edited (with Anna Yeatman) *Feminism and the Politics of Difference* and (with Fazal Rizvi) *Culture, Difference and the Arts*. Her most recent book is *Framing Marginality: Multicultural Literary Studies*.

FRANCESCO LORIGGIO is Associate Professor of Comparative Literature and Italian at Carleton University, Ottawa, Ontario. He has published, in a variety of journals, on literary theory, the relation between literature and the social sciences, ethnic literature and modern Italian literature. His translation of three short plays by Achille Campanile, *The Inventor of the Horse*, has appeared with Guernica Editions in 1995. He has also co-edited *Refractions: Literary Criticism, Philosophy, and the Human Sciences in Contemporary Italy* (forthcoming).

ENOCH PADOLSKY teaches Canadian literature in the Department of English at Carleton University. He has published articles on the theory and practice of Canadian ethnic minority writing in a number of Canadian and international journals and books. Co-editor of *Migration and the Transformations of Cultures* (1992) and co-author of *A Historical Source Book for the Ottawa Valley* (1981), he is currently working on a book on ethnicity, multiculturalism and Canadian literature.

JOSEPH PIVATO has degrees from York University (B.A.) and the University of Alberta (M.A. Ph.D.) in Comparative Literature. He teaches at Athabasca University in Edmonton and has lectured in Australia, Italy and the U.S.A.. He is the editor of *Contrasts: Comparative Essays on Italian-Canadian Writing* (Guernica Editions, 1985) and co-editor of *Literatures of Lesser Diffusion* (Univ. of Alberta Press, 1990). His 1994 book, *Echo: Essays on Other Literatures*, published by Guernica Editions, explores ethnic minority writing in Canada.

GAETANO RANDO is Associate Professor in Italian at the University of Wollongong. His main area of research has been Italian Australian language and literature and contemporary Italian language. His publications include: *Australia's Italians: Culture and Community in a Changing Society* (co-author, 1992); *Language and Cultural Identity* (1990), and *Dizioanrio degli anglicismi nell'italiano contemporaneo* (1987).

ROSE ROMANO is the author of two collections of poetry: *Vendetta* (1990) and *The Wop Factor* (1994). She lives in New York.

ANTHONY JULIAN TAMBURRI is Professor of Italian and Comparative Literature at Purdue University. He has published a number of books on twentieth century Italian literature and is the author of *To Hyphenate or not to Hyphenate: The Italian/American Writer or An "Other" American?* (1991), a contributing co-editor of the volume *From the Margin: Writings in Italian Americana* (1991), and co-founding editor of *Voices in Italian Americana*.

PASQUALE VERDICCHIO migrated to Canada as a young man. He now teaches Italian literature, film and cultural studies in the Department of Literature at the University of California, San Diego. He has translated into English works by Antonio Porta, Giorgio Caproni and Alda Merini. A prolific poet, he recently published *Approaches to Absence* (Guernica, 1994). Currently he is President of the Association of Italian-Canadian Writers.

ROBERT VISCUSI is the author of *Astoria*, an autobiographical fiction published by Guernica Editions in 1995. His essays on Italian American literature have appeared in major journals in the U.S. and Italy. Professor of English and Executive Officer of the Wolfe Institute for the Humanities at Brooklyn College of the City University of New York, Viscusi was elected first President of the Italian American Writers Association in 1991.

Printed in October 1996 by

in Boucherville, Quebec